British Gods

British Gods

Religion in Modern Britain

STEVE BRUCE

OXFORD
UNIVERSITY PRESS

OXFORD

UNIVERSITY PRESS

Great Clarendon Street, Oxford, OX2 6DP,
United Kingdom

Oxford University Press is a department of the University of Oxford.
It furthers the University's objective of excellence in research, scholarship,
and education by publishing worldwide. Oxford is a registered trade mark of
Oxford University Press in the UK and in certain other countries

© Steve Bruce 2020

The moral rights of the author have been asserted

First Edition published in 2020

Impression: 1

All rights reserved. No part of this publication may be reproduced, stored in
a retrieval system, or transmitted, in any form or by any means, without the
prior permission in writing of Oxford University Press, or as expressly permitted
by law, by licence or under terms agreed with the appropriate reprographics
rights organization. Enquiries concerning reproduction outside the scope of the
above should be sent to the Rights Department, Oxford University Press, at the
address above

You must not circulate this work in any other form
and you must impose this same condition on any acquirer

Published in the United States of America by Oxford University Press
198 Madison Avenue, New York, NY 10016, United States of America

British Library Cataloguing in Publication Data

Data available

Library of Congress Control Number: 2020930745

ISBN 978-0-19-885411-1

Printed and bound by
CPI Group (UK) Ltd, Croydon, CR0 4YY

Links to third party websites are provided by Oxford in good faith and
for information only. Oxford disclaims any responsibility for the materials
contained in any third party website referenced in this work.

Preface

The Problem

In 1851 a government-organized count of church attendance showed that somewhere between 40 and 60 per cent of the British population was in church on Sunday, 30 March. An unknown but doubtless large percentage of those who missed church that Sunday would have attended on many other occasions. In 1948, only 15 per cent of a sample survey said they attended church the previous Sunday. Seventy years on, data from central church organizations, from surveys of claimed attendance, from time-use diaries, and from third-party censuses that follow the 1851 method of asking clergy to count attendances, all point to a figure less than 7 per cent. Churchgoing was once normal; it is now rare. Over the twentieth century, church membership fell from about 34 per cent of the population to around 10 per cent. A 1957 survey showed nearly a quarter of respondents saying they did not belong to any religion or denomination. The corresponding 2018 figure is 53 per cent.[1]

Similarly drastic declines can be found in almost every measure of religious interest or participation. In 1851, baptism was near universal. In 1962, the Church of England baptized 55 per cent of England's infants. In 2008, the figure was 13 per cent, and very little of that decline was compensated for by baptism in other churches. In the 1960s, some 70 per cent of weddings in England were religious; in 2003, less than a third were. In 2017, there were more humanist than Christian weddings in Scotland.

The power of religion is more difficult to assess than its popularity, but there is no doubt that the churches are far less of a force in the twenty-first century than they were in the nineteenth. They opposed every change in socio-moral legislation and attitudes from the 1960s onwards. Easier divorce, the decriminalization of homosexuality, the liberalizing of licensing laws, the expansion of Sunday trading, the availability of contraception, the legalizing of abortion, gender equality, gay rights—the British churches argued against and they lost.

It is always possible that religion has not so much declined as changed its form. New expressions of religious and spiritual interest may have grown to fill the gap left by the collapse of Christianity. But there is no evidence of this. Migration has brought significant numbers of Muslims, Hindus, Buddhist, and Sikhs to Britain since the 1960s, and more recently they have been joined by West African Pentecostalists and by European Catholics, but there is no evidence that the native British are converting to these new faiths in the sort of numbers that would compensate for mainstream decline. The new religious movements of the 1970s (such as Scientology, Hare Krishna, and the Moonies) have never had more than a few thousand members, and, with less than 1 per cent of the population showing any serious interest in it, 'New Age' spirituality has similarly failed to fill the gap.

The first ten chapters of this book describe and explain the collapse of religion. The final chapter considers the likelihood of the secularization of Britain being reversed.

Qualifying as an Expert

Expert witnesses in court cases begin their testimony by presenting reasons why their claims to expertise should be accepted. In the same spirit I will briefly explain the research career that has led to this end-of-career summation study.

My first research project was an ethnographic study of a conservative Christian student society in an overwhelmingly secular university; I was fascinated by the problem of how people maintain an unpopular minority worldview when their claim to be an outgoing 'witness' to the faith prevented them from the obvious recourse of protective introversion. My doctorate extended that research first into a historical comparison of the conservative Christian Unions and the radical Student Christian Movement, and then into a wider study of the contrasting fates of conservative Protestantism (which was then apparently growing) and its declining liberal counterpart.

My move to the Queen's University of Belfast in 1978 led me to study the church and party founded by Ian Paisley, and contacts in that world led me gradually into the confidence of Ulster's loyalist terrorist organizations. That interest in the interaction of religious identity and political agendas gradually widened with studies of the Christian Right in the United States and sectarianism in Scotland. An invitation to join an ambitious international study of fundamentalism stimulated my interest in the links between religion, ethnicity, and political conflict in such other parts of the world as northern Europe,

South Africa, and the Middle East. The US Christian Right research also led me to be interested in the mass media, persuasion, and religious conversion.

This century I have published extensively on the nature of the New Age spirituality that some scholars believe is growing to balance the decline of Christianity in the West. In particular I have been interested in the ways in which themes and practices borrowed from eastern religious cultures have been 'westernized' and secularized, so that yoga has become light exercise and meditation has become mindfulness. Encouraged by my colleague Marta Trzebiatowska, I have also spent some time trying to answer the fascinating question of why women are more religious than men.

Much of my career has been concerned with describing and explaining secularization. In the early 1970s, there was a general consensus among social scientists that the changes we gloss as 'modernization' (increasing prosperity, the growth of literacy and egalitarianism, democratization, greater social and geographical mobility, and the resulting growth of cultural diversity) were undermining the power, persuasiveness, and popularity of Christianity in the West. Over my career the popularity of the secularization thesis and the popularity of religion have shifted in a manner so paradoxical as to be ironic. The secularization thesis has lost favour at the same time as the continued decline of religion—which it attempts to explain—has demonstrated its accuracy. Since Bryan Wilson published *Religion in Secular Society* in 1966, every measure of religious interest and activity has continued to decline, and broadening the definition of religion to include amorphous expressions of spirituality makes no difference to those plummeting trend lines. Yet it has become increasing popular to argue that religion is not really declining; it is merely shape-shifting. My frequent presentations of evidence to the contrary caused me to inherit Bryan Wilson's role as the main spokesman for a now frequently caricatured and derided thesis. I am happy to apologize for my unmerited status as Wilson's equal, but, as the evidence in this book amply demonstrates, I have no need to apologize for continuing to argue that the modernization of the West has weakened religion.

A student of religion who wishes his books to be read widely, yet who fulsomely documents the demise of his subject matter, might seem as foolish as the huntsman who shoots his fox, but the secularization of the West should still fascinate social scientists, if only because its deviation from the record of religion's importance in most societies demands explanation. And even within largely secular societies there are important counter-trends to evaluate and explain. Clearly the various elements of modernization do not impact on all sections or regions of societies evenly or equally. Many Britons have been content to drift into religious indifference, but some have struggled to revise their beliefs and practices to make them more popular, some have retreated into isolated sub-societies, and yet others—Muslims who have argued for religious exemptions from equality legislation or members of the Christian People's Party, for example—have worked to reverse religion's marginality.

The starting point for this book's composition was a series of local 'then-and-now' studies funded by the Leverhulme Trust. As the primary funder of small-scale research, the Trust deserves the gratitude of all British academics and I now use only the soap products of Unilever, the shares of which fund the Trust. From the late 1940s to the 1970s, British anthropologists and sociologists produced a large number of very detailed accounts of particular places. Although none was primarily concerned with religious belief and practice, most contained enough detail about the religious life of those communities to serve as a baseline for assessing and explaining subsequent changes. From 2007 to 2014, I regularly visited Gosforth in Cumberland; Northlew in Devon; Banbury; Little Munden, Hertfordshire; Staithes, North Yorkshire; the mining areas of County Durham, Northumberland, and Yorkshire; Bolton in Lancashire; High Wycombe in Buckinghamshire; four parishes in North Wales; and Eskdalemuir and Mid-Argyll in Scotland. In all of those sites I was greatly assisted by the generosity of local clergy and church people who talked to me at length and provided me with information about their areas and their congregations.

This book has two overlapping structures: a series of places and a series of themes. Most chapters start by documenting the changes in the religious culture of some locale and then segue into a general topic; examples are the collapse of elite support for religion, the role of community structures in supporting or undermining shared religions, the nature and popularity of folk religion and superstition, the social-class bases of classic spiritualism and contemporary spirituality, the decline of Britain's stock of religious knowledge, the nature of religious identity, the role of the charismatic movement in modernizing the faith, and the effects of immigration and violence on public perceptions of religion. As written texts must necessarily be linear, and repetition and omission are undesirable, some of the locale–theme links are a little clunky, but that structure does allow me to illustrate national and international trends with considerable local detail.

Sceptics often assert that we cannot know if people are 'really religious'. Perhaps, but I hope this book better supports the counter-assertion: because religion used to matter a great deal, and because religious organizations have generally been good at keeping records, we know more about religion than about most other social phenomena. A great deal of statistical information on religious belief and practice is regularly published by churches, sects, and denominations, and nationally representative sample surveys often ask about religion. I have been involved in analysing three waves of British Social Attitudes data, and I am grateful to John Curtice and the staff of NatCen for those invitations and for access to the data.

Change over time can be tracked in considerable local detail because individual churches and chapels usually deposit their records with local archives. For forty years I have collected and collated such data and in the course of the local research that informs this book I have been greatly helped by the staff of the local records offices in Kirkwall, Lerwick, Whitehaven, Durham, Ashington, Wick, Banbury, St Albans, and Exeter, and by the special collections staff of many universities.

For forty or so years I have routinely clipped stories about religion from three or four daily newspapers and from such periodicals as *Spectator*, *New Statesman*, *Listener*, *The Economist*, *London Review of Books*, *Prospect*, *The Week*, and *Private Eye*. As well as providing a deal of illustrative anecdote, such sources often inadvertently reveal much about what their writers and editors think of religion and about what, rightly or wrongly, they suppose their readers think.

One relatively novel source of information is the self-published pamphlet. The reduction of printing costs towards the end of the twentieth century allowed cheap production of local histories (such as centenary histories of congregations) and autobiographies of ordinary people. A surprisingly large number of such works have been written by well-informed local historians, but even the most narrow and amateurish autobiography often well describes the author's childhood experience of religion.

Another novelty is the online source. David Voas, Clive Field, and Siobhan McAndrew created the wonderful *British Religion in Numbers* (or BRIN) website—a mine of valuable historical data and of summaries of one-off surveys and reports. There are also a number of sites (such as *Ship of Fools*) that display reports of church services and lengthy discussions of religious topics. Unfortunately websites lack the longevity of the printed word and many of those cited in the notes will already have died or migrated. The reader will simply have to trust that, at the date I accessed them, I noted accurately their content.

Because much of my published work has had a national focus or has involved international comparisons, and because I often use large-scale data,

I have sometimes been criticized for a lack of fieldwork. For an unbeliever I actually spend an inordinate amount of my time attending church services and other religious events. Forty years of that has exposed me to a wide variety of religious activities. That many congregations now follow their services with social refreshments has also allowed me to strike up casual conversations with thousands of churchgoers.

Although I am far from being persuaded that New Age spirituality is sufficiently popular to counterbalance the decline of conventional religion, I have learnt much about what a certain sort of Briton finds offputting in the mainstream churches by mixing with people who have rejected their conventional childhood religious socialization in favour of combining an interest in the supernatural with a variety of human potential psychologies and alternative medical therapies. Visits to such New Age centres as the Findhorn Foundation in Moray and Glastonbury in Wiltshire have been augmented with innumerable sessions of meditation, healing, hypnotherapy, divination, lifestyle counselling, rebirthing, and the like.

One of the joys of social research is that, with very little manipulation, everyday social interaction can generate rich data. With the right prompts, most people (taxi-drivers and bed-and-breakfast hosts especially) have stories and impressions they are happy to share, and I have filled many notebooks with such comments and observations.

In brief, this book is informed by a lifetime's immersive study of most of its subject matter. The exceptions are Judaism, West African Pentecostalism, and Islam, all of which I know only second hand. Those gaps are natural, given the relatively small numbers, and the geographical concentration, of their adherents in the UK. Fortunately there is now a considerable body of detailed ethnographic, autobiographical, survey-based, and journalistic work on all three populations.

Precisely how we handle such data is discussed at length in *Researching Religion: Why We Need Social Science*, which answers the myriad criticisms, most unfounded, of conventional social science that have been advanced by a variety of postmodernists and other relativists.[2]

Which brings me to my final sort of source material. Research is cumulative and I have been inspired and informed by a great deal of excellent work done by predecessors and colleagues. The notes at the end of each chapter document my debts, but here I would like to acknowledge Bryan Wilson, David Martin, Roy Wallis, Eileen Barker, Jim Beckford, Grace Davie, Paul Heelas, Matthew Wood, Robin Gill, Stephen Hunt, Alan Gilbert, Hugh McLeod, and Callum Brown. I am also greatly indebted to Peter Brierley, who has spent half a century conducting regular censuses of British churches, and to Clive Field, who has spent a lifetime collating and analysing religious data. In making sense of such material I have been greatly helped by the statistical prowess and good sense of Tony Glendinning and David Voas.

Notes

1. The following data are taken from S. Bruce 'Appendix Two', in B. R. Wilson, *Religion in Secular Society: Fifty Years on* (Oxford: Oxford University Press, 2016), and from the many sources listed in the endnotes of subsequent chapters.
2. S. Bruce, *Researching Religion: Why We Need Social Science* (Oxford: Oxford University Press, 2018).

Contents

List of Tables

1

The Big House

Elite Patronage of Religion

The Ingleborough estate in Clapham, North Yorkshire, was owned by the Farrer family. It was renowned for its gardens and its engineering: an artificial lake, apparently derelict follies, a pioneering hydroelectric scheme, an astonishing array of rhododendrons brought from the Far East by Reginald Farrer, and a tunnel to prevent a public right of way from spoiling the effect of the exotic planting. The Farrers paid a large part of the costs of rebuilding the parish church in 1815 and built the village school in 1865. In 1873, they gave the site for a new church in Keasden and paid all the costs of its erection. They wired the Clapham church to their power system. Even those family members who were not themselves enthusiastic members of the Church of England supported the local church. James Anson Farrer, who succeeded to the estates in 1889, was a rationalist. His *Paganism and Christianity* argued that pagans were happier and holier than Christians. His wife, Bessie, was a staunch churchwoman, and 'he followed her to church, at least in his later years, although at the same time he continued to write for the Rationalist Press Association'.[1] Bessie refurbished the church at the end of the nineteenth century. She raised the floor, renewed the pews, and fitted new windows, one of them a large stained-glass memorial to previous Farrers. After her death in 1937, the estate was much reduced and financial support curtailed, but the family continued its moral support for the church: for example, Dr John Anson Farrer served as a churchwarden from 1953 to 2005.

Social research often finds what it seeks, so it is striking when an unexpected thought occurs. In researching the background to the churches, chapels, and congregations of the sites in my religious-life-then-and-now project, I found myself repeatedly drawn to one specific overlooked (by me at least) change. In the nineteenth century and the first decade of the twentieth century, local magnates—landowners in the country, industrialists in the towns—had been important patrons of religious activity. And such involvement was almost entirely absent after the First World War.

Since at least 1851 (the date of the only government-organized count of church attendance), religion in the UK has been declining in popularity, prestige, and power. If we are interested only in the big picture of secularization, local detail is irrelevant. It is enough to show that there is a more-than-coincidental connection between modernization and the decline of religion in all the advanced industrial democracies.[2] By modernization I mean, among other things, the increasing complexity of social organization as life becomes organized into discrete spheres (such as the economy and the polity), each informed by its own distinct values; the increasing fragmentation of communities into classes; the rise of individualism and egalitarianism; and the gradual displacement of supernatural remedies by scientific-based technological solutions and an attendant growth of a positive view of human power and potential. Such basic changes in the nature of society have been accompanied by the growth of religious diversity, the liberation of human rights from religious rectitude, and a shift from an imposed religious conformity (typically embodied in a national church) to a voluntary 'free market' in religion. In thus changing, religion has lost much of its power and prestige. Its reach has shrunk so that it now commands only those who voluntarily submit to its discipline, and it has little control over even them. The state and such major social institutions as education and public broadcasting have become religiously neutral. Very large numbers of people are now religiously indifferent, and many of those who continue to be religious have become increasingly liberal and tolerant. Dogmatism and certainty have either declined or are largely confined to the small world of the private family and the domestic hearth.

Few people now doubt the basic fact of decline, and many of the causes I have just listed have been well established by detailed comparisons of societies and regions. However, even for those who accept the general secularization approach, there remains a considerable problem in demonstrating specific causal connections, which is why the weasel phrase 'has been accompanied by' appears in the abbreviated account I have just given. The various local studies that I have drawn on in this book were all intended to put flesh on the bare bones of the secularization thesis and in the course of those studies I was surprised by how often the religious patronage of the wealthy came to my attention.

Big House Patronage

The multinational and multi-religious nature of Britain means that the history of landowner obligation and its precise legal basis varied considerably with time and place, but for centuries there was a general burden on landed and wealthy parishioners to support the local parish of the state church.[3] In nineteenth-century England and Wales, the 'patron' (the person or entity who owned the advowson or legal right to choose the parish's cleric) was responsible for the fabric of the chancel (the part nearest the altar reserved for clergy and choir), while the parishioners were responsible for maintaining the nave (the main body of the church). In Scotland, the 'heritors'—usually the major landowners—were liable for 'public burdens', which, in addition to support for the poor and road repairs, included providing the minister with a church, a manse, and land that could either be farmed for produce or let for income. Not surprisingly, those who funded religion expected to manage it. Writing of England, G. E. Mingay said: 'Not infrequently church and manor house lay cheek by jowl, the slender spire of one overshadowed by the bulk of the other, symbolising both the affinity and the relationship of power spiritual and temporal.'[4]

Not all Big Houses accepted their responsibilities, but, as the examples given here show, financial and moral support for the respective state churches often went well beyond what was minimally required by law. Some grandees supported only the state churches, but very many were also happy to fund dissenters, as though Christianity in general was a common good. The Farrers of Ingleborough have been mentioned. In 1850, the parish of Ashbury, West Devon, had only 65 souls and 1,560 acres of land, mostly the property of John Woollcombe of Ashbury House, 'where his family has been seated since 1685'.[5] The small neat church was given new pews by the Woollcombes in the 1850s, and, twenty years later, Henry Woollcombe, the Archdeacon of Barnstaple, who was both a close relative of the Ashbury Woollcombes and the parish's incumbent, personally paid for the church to be rebuilt. Like many improving nineteenth-century landowners, the Dukes of Devonshire created a model village to complement their great house, and the seventh duke paid to replace the parish church of Edensor with one fitting the improved village. To ensure that it matched his status, he employed the famous architect George Gilbert Scott.

In the late nineteenth century, the Hertfordshire village of Little Munden had two Big Houses—Dane End and Green End—which, with two smaller houses, employed most of the parish. The Chauncys, who made their money from West Indies plantations, dominated the village and spent most of the nineteenth century buying up the area. Elizabeth Chauncy married Henry Surtees from Durham in 1843; he used his new connections to become the local MP. The Chauncys spent heavily to renovate the church, 'mainly for their own benefit in the form of family pews and, later, a vault.[6] Elizabeth's granddaughter inherited the house and married William Gladstone's son Herbert, who was Home Secretary from 1905 to 1910 and then Governor-General of South Africa. In 1914, he retired to Dane End. A keen Anglican, he was a parish councillor from 1917 to 1928. When he died in 1930, the parishioners, preceded by the church choir, carried his coffin from the house to the church. Children from the local school lined the route for Gladstone's last church visit.

The parish of Llanuwchllyn, to the south of Lake Bala, benefited considerably from the beneficence of the Williams-Wynn family.[7] When the church was replaced in 1872, half of the costs were born by Sir Watkin Williams-Wynn, sixth baronet and MP for Denbighshire, who also augmented the vicar's income. The recipient of that generosity handsomely repaid his patron. Sir Watkin's daughter died young, and she was commemorated with a stained-glass window in the church. At the 1883 dedication service, the Revd William Hughes, echoing Revelations 18:22, eulogized the deceased:

> You will see no more her well-known form, so familiar to all, so dear to many. No more will her cheerful voice and her kindly greeting be heard. No more will she cross the threshold to visit the sick and dying; the cottage of the poor will know her no more; her welcome visits have ceased for ever.

Hughes even managed to work praise for the still-living Sir Watkin into the eulogy for his daughter:

> Yet every cloud has a silver lining. While we then wept with those that wept, we also rejoice today with them that rejoice, in having among us once more, this year, restored to his usual health and vigour, the generous patron of this benefice and great benefactor of this parish.[8]

The religious life of the lead miners and small farmers of upper Teesdale in County Durham was well served by the Vanes, the major landowners, who were variously Lords Darlington, Dukes of Cleveland, and Lords Barnard. The church of St James-the-Less, at Forest, was rebuilt by Lord Darlington around 1803. In the 1840s, and against the wishes of the Bishop, who felt the sparse population did not merit the expenditure, the Duke of Cleveland sponsored a further rebuild of the church and the building of a parsonage. He gave the land and lent his architect. After considerable argument between the Duke's agent and the diocese, the Church of England, via the Incorporated

Church Building Society, paid £165, and the Duke paid ten times that amount. The London Lead Mining Company (of which more later) also made a substantial contribution. The Duke also paid for the prefabricated church of St Jude and its adjoining schoolhouse at Harwood, about halfway between Forest and Middleton.

Whether bishop or duke was right about the need for provision is not obvious. According to the 1912 visitation return, 5 per cent of the population of the upper dale attended holy communion, 10 per cent attended morning prayers, and a third attended evening prayers. Given the popularity of Methodism in Teesdale, the Duke may well have felt that his investment had helped preserve an Anglican presence. The curate added: 'dissent in Upper Teesdale had always been of a bitter political type...I think that there is a now a much more kindly feeling towards the Church and less bigotry.'[9]

For a Scottish example we can turn to Ford in Mid-Argyll. Poltalloch, the largest of three estates in the area, was the home of the Malcolm family. Like Little Munden's Dane End, it was heavily subsidized from Jamaican sugar plantations. The Malcolms spent much of their year in London but took seriously their obligations as heritors. Although there was a parochial school in Kilmartin, they erected two other schools at the extremities of the parish for younger children (who found the distance to the village too great) and paid the masters. In addition: 'A school of industry for girls has recently been established within a mile of Kilmartin, for the tenants on the Poltalloch estate, and for which Mr Malcolm has built a handsome house, at a cost of £1,000.'[10]

The Church of Scotland church at Ford, designed by the Poltalloch estate architect, was built in 1849 on land rented from Poltalloch for one shilling per annum and with a gift of £50. The second largest estate, Ederline, provided three beautiful stained-glass windows showing women epitomizing Faith, Hope, and Charity.[11] Although the Malcolms funded the local kirk, they were Episcopalians. In 1854, Neil Malcolm erected a substantial Episcopalian church beside Poltalloch House and settled an endowment that funded an incumbent until 1934. From then till the war there were regular services, conducted by visiting clergymen, only in August and September, when the Malcolm family was in residence. For three years from the outbreak of war in September 1939, Sir Ian Malcolm, an Anglican lay reader, every Sunday led Evensong, preaching the sermon and playing the organ.[12] The church was unused from 1943 to 1947, when it was taken over by the Rector of Christ Church, Lochgilphead; since then it has been used for two services a month.

The second half of the nineteenth century saw a major programme of church building after the Free Church split from the Church of Scotland in

1843. It set about matching the structural resources of the national Kirk and raised very large sums for churches, schools, and manses. This was not difficult in the urban lowlands, where it recruited the prosperous middle classes, but in poor areas, especially in the peripheries, dissenters had to be subsidized. Some assistance was channelled to remote areas. Uyeasound on the Shetland island of Unst owed its church to the Countess of Effingham, who was persuaded by Thomas Chalmers to give £600 to the building costs, and she later funded a number of churches in the remote highlands and islands.[13] However, the major donor was usually the local grandee. The Glenlyon, Perthshire, congregation were keen but poor:

> the Marquis of Breadalbane came to their aid by placing at their disposal a vacant crofter's house, barn, and byre, at Balnacraig, a mile below the deserted [parish] church, on the opposite side of the river. He also gave them timber from Drummond Hill, and window-frames which had been taken out of the old Taymouth Castle and stored when the new one was built. They pulled down the crofter's buildings, quarried and carted in more stones, and set themselves methodically to build a roomy church, made without lime or mortar except about doors and windows.

But they could not afford a manse or a clergyman. Hence when 'John Stewart Menzies of Chesthill, proprietor of the lower part of the Glen, joined them and gave them a feu for church, manse, and school, at Camusvrachan, they at last saw a clear way out of their long troubles and struggles'.[14] When the majority of the Free Church united with the Seceder Presbyterians to form the United Free Church (UFC), a protracted legal war over assets ensured, and the House of Lords eventually awarded much of the property to the tiny conservative rump. So, yet again, a church building programme was needed, and, yet again, a local grandee stepped in: Sir Donald Currie MP of Glenlyon House (who also completely rebuilt the Fortingall parish church) gave a site and a prefabricated building to the UFC.[15]

In Strathpeffer in 1882 the Duchess of Sutherland (who was also Countess of Cromartie) built an Episcopal church and gave a site in the main square for the Free Church.[16] In Upper Glenlyon, the parish church at Innerwick was supported by the Bullough family, Lancashire cotton millionaires who in classic Victorian fashion bought social status via the highland shooting estate of Meggernie Castle. When, in the 1920s, John Bullough sold the estate to concentrate on racing cars and London showgirls, the new owners—the Wills cigarette magnates—continued their support and donated a stained-glass window 'To the glory of God and in memory of Ernest Wills, 3rd Bart of Meggernie, died 1958, and of his wife Maud, died 1953.'[17]

In addition to building and maintaining the infrastructure, Big House families performed innumerable small acts of generosity towards church and chapel groups and activities. They were the honoured guests at church and chapel socials, and they reciprocated by hosting picnics and parties. J. C. Ley, a Devon Methodist farmer, reports that in the 1900s the annual Sunday School picnic took place in the grounds of Castle Hill, the home of Lord and Lady Fortescue. At Christmas, Lady Poltimore gave the children of the parish a Christmas tea and a present.[18] The historian A. L. Rowse, writing of his childhood in Cornwall at the time of the First World War, reports his church choir touring the houses of the minor gentry around St Austell: 'Our furthest journey was to Carthew...on the afternoon of Boxing Day: here we were shown into the low old-fashioned dining room, sang our best and received 10s. or £1.'[19] The wife of Sir Donald Currie of Glenlyon funded an annual 'Christmas Treat' for the local children and, though she did not attend the party herself, she paid for each child to receive a book.[20]

Industrial Paternalism

In the nineteenth century, lead mining dominated Upper Teesdale. The London Lead Mining Company (LLC), a Quaker concern, took its first leases in 1753 and bought a large estate in Middleton in 1823. At its mid-century peak, half the dale was directly employed in lead mining. A model of progressive paternalism, the LLC provided smallholdings for families in the dale and good bunkhouses for workers at the mine sites. It reacted to rapid rises in bread prices by forming a non-profit flour-importing company. Rather than lay off workers when demand for lead fell, it employed them on such maintenance work as dyke-building. It also took a very direct interest in religious and moral education. Youths who wished to be hired by the company had to pass a literacy test, and, to ensure they passed, the LLC built schools. It also required the schoolchildren to attend worship every Sunday: 'Steady persons are stationed by the Company's agents at the door of every place of public worship, from whom the pupils of the Sunday schools received tickets on entrance.'[21]

R. W. Bainbridge, the LLC's chief agent in Teesdale, added his own prestige and wealth to the encouragement of religion. He largely financed the building of the dale's two Baptist chapels. The Methodists originally shared a Baptist chapel, but when in the early 1890s they decided to build their own, the Duke of Cleveland gave the land at a nominal rent, and Bainbridge paid one-tenth of the building costs, as did the LLC.[22]

The LLC was not sectarian in its patronage of religion. Though a Quaker company, it did not confine its beneficence to dissenters. It built a parish church for its new model village at Nenthead, shared the costs of restoring St James-the-Less in Forest, and paid £20 per annum to the curate of the chapel-of-ease at Harwood.

When in 1851 Titus Salt built his village of Saltaire in Shipley, he created factories and houses that were models for the time. He also gave £1.5 million at 2017 prices to build a splendid Congregational chapel. Forty years later, soap manufacturer William Lever (later Lord Leverhulme) gave similar facilities to his model village of Port Sunlight.

The chapels of the Durham pit villages owed much to the colliery-owners. Commonly, the founding members of each local dissenting 'society' proved demand by meeting in colliery offices, in an empty colliery house, or in the schoolhouse (which the colliery had built). Then land was given or leased for a nominal sum, and the colliery provided the building materials. For example, Wingate's New Connexion Methodist chapel was built in 1886 with '49,350 bricks, 470 cwt lime, 51 tons of sand, [and] 77 loads of stone' given by the colliery-owners.[23] The Bearpark Colliery Co. paid almost half of the costs of Bearpark's 1883 Wesleyan chapel; the following year it paid £200 of the £900 costs of a Primitive Methodist chapel.[24] A. B. Cochrane of Eshwood Hall hosted the Deerness Valley Methodist Sunday school picnics. Johnson and Reay, which owned the Hamsteels colliery, gave the land and £100 for the erection of the Primitive Methodist chapel at Quebec in 1876, while Reay and his son each gave a further £52 each; in total, the company and its owners covered more than half the costs of the chapel.[25] Malton Colliery gave the sites and paid one-fifth of the costs of the Malton Wesley and Primitive Methodist chapels.

Joseph Love was the doyen of Durham mining paternalists. Born in 1796 in a pit village near North Shields, Love worked as a collier, hawker, and trader before marrying the daughter of a wealthy timber merchant and building a chain of shops. He lost one fortune when the Newcastle District Bank collapsed and he went back to work for Strakers of North Shields. The company of Love and Straker bought the coal royalty for New Brancepeth in 1840 and made a fortune converting the soft coal to coke and making bricks from the waste clay. Love was a committed New Connexion Methodist—a lay preacher from the age of 23. His obituary notes that: 'He lived plainly and was utterly devoid of pride or ostentation....Perhaps Mr Love was never more at home than in presiding over an anniversary meeting at Bethel Chapel.'[26]

Love paid for the erection of Bethel, near his home in Durham, and for the chapel at his pit in Cornsay Colliery, but he also contributed to the building of many others. His generosity was literally commemorated in the brickwork: the white bricks for the 1885 Wesleyan chapel at Esh colliery bore the name 'Ferens and Love'. Love also supported temperance causes. *The British Workman* was a periodical that encouraged the creation of alcohol-free social clubs. Love paid most of the costs of converting a Durham pub into a *British Workman* house. When colliers asked for land at Shincliffe Bank Top for an Oddfellows Hall, Love quizzed them about the Oddfellows and, once satisfied as to their temperance principles, gave them the land and paid the cost of building the hall. His widow continued his work. She paid for the short-lived Hamilton Row New Connexion chapel (which closed in 1910 and became the Gaiety Theatre) and, in a neatly reciprocal move, maintained the local balance of sin and salvation by converting a cinema in Langley Moor into a New Connexion chapel.

Despite being a committed Methodist, Love was happy to allow his Catholic employees to use the Ferens and Love private railway to transport building materials for the 1871 construction of the Our Lady Queen chapel at Newhouse. J. B. Johnston, the owner of Hamsteels Colliery, insisted that his domestic servants join his family in attending the Church of England, but he provided the stone for the Catholic church.

The other major employer in the Deerness area was Pease and Partners. The Peases of Darlington were Quakers with interests in the railways of the north-east, the port of Middlesbrough, the wool trade, and ironstone and coal mining. In the villages built for the ironstone mines, Joseph Pease 'provided a school and a chapel'.[27] By the 1890s, the family owned the third largest colliery in the north-east. The Peases rarely gave money for Anglican church building, but they gave land, paid much of the costs, and laid foundation stones for chapels at 'Ushaw Moor, Waterhouses, Hamsterley, Crook, Cockfield, Shildon, Spennymoor and West Auckland'.[28] They also funded missionaries in their villages, the last being one James Dack, who worked in Waterhouses from 1881 until his death in 1924. The New Brancepeth Colliery Co. funded the Church of England: its £500 donation to the 1890 building of St Catherine's matched that of the Ecclesiastical Commissioners, and the colliery owner, A. B. Cochrane, paid for most of the interior finishing.

E. P. Thompson remarks that the colliery-owners of the Deerness valley were unusual in their religious paternalism, but the villages that surrounded the deep pits of the Durham east coast were also provided with their churches and chapels by mine-owners.[29] Wingate has already been mentioned. Wheatley Hill was built with 20,000 bricks given by the colliery company.[30] Colonel Burdon, owner of the local collieries, built the very large neo-Gothic St Mary's church in Horden in 1913. Nor is there any reason to suppose religious industrial paternalism was confined to Durham. The pit village of Bowers Row in Yorkshire was ably described by Jim Bullock, a miner who rose to be a senior colliery manager.[31] Its mission hall was built in 1886 on land leased from Sir Charles Lowther, the third baronet, who also built the Anglican church in Great Preston, and made considerable contributions to the Swillington church.

Other Quaker industrialists were similar to the Pease family in their support for religion. When George Cadbury built the model village of Bourneville for his workers, he built an Anglican parish church as well as leaving a site and money for the expected Quaker meeting house. William Isaac Palmer (of Huntley and Palmer's biscuits) employed a full-time social worker and missionary to promote his religious and temperance principles among his Reading workers.[32]

The religious life of the Bolton area owed much to local industrialists. John H. Ainsworth, who ran the family bleaching firm from 1833, erected two Anglican churches and encouraged attendance at them: 'I spoke to some of the men about going to church.'[33] He also monitored attendance. His diary notes that, of 321 employees, 123 said 'they attended no place'. A similar number attended the Church of England. There were also 35 Primitive Methodists, 22 Congregationalists, 8 Baptists, and 7 Catholics. That almost half his workforce did not go to church shows it was not a condition of employment, but he was a staunch enough Anglican to sack a man who spoke against the Church of England: the offender apparently said 'he could not worship there...thus casting a reflection on the manner of conducting the service in church'.[34] The Egerton Dyeworks was owned by just two families from the 1850s to the First World War and both built chapels: the Ashworths paid for a Wesleyan Methodist chapel and the Deakins funded the Egerton Congregational chapel.[35] Another Congregational chapel, in St George's Road, Bolton, was funded by Lord Leverhulme, whose Port Sunlight chapel has already been mentioned. The Bairds of Gartsherrie, colliers and ironmasters, built a 'commodious' parish church for their workers and paid the minister's salary. When George Baird died in 1870, he left £25,000 (well over £3 million in 2020 money) to religious and charitable causes. Three years later James Baird gave double that to the Church of Scotland. He also gave £7,500 towards the erection of five churches in Aberdeen and bought and endowed a church in Bath Street, Glasgow.[36]

Sometimes old and new aristocracy combined. The church in the model village of Cresswell was built by the Duke of Portland, but the Bolsover Colliery Company paid for it to be electrified.[37]

Motives

As people often present themselves in the most flattering light, there is a natural debunking tendency in social science, but we need to be careful of undue cynicism. No doubt much patronage was self-aggrandizing. The parish church of Great Lever, Bolton, was created in the 1840s on the initiative of George Piggott, the local agent for Lord Bradford's estates who persuaded his master to stump up by telling him: 'the church should be considered, as it were, your Lordship's own church.'[38] The Duke of Devonshire hired Gilbert Scott to create a church that would match his family's exalted image of itself (and incidentally house a massive Jacobean monument to the first duke).

Much patronage was political. Many of the Big House families and the industrial paternalists who sponsored religion intended to strengthen the ties that bound the lower orders to their superiors and to imbue their tenants, servants, and employees with suitably conservative values. When the Marquis of Normanby laid the foundation stone for the Wesleyan chapel and Sunday School in the fishing village of Staithes, North Yorkshire, in 1865, his reported remarks were clear about the influence he expected the chapel to exert: 'He trusted that the children might learn in the schoolroom lessons of veneration and subordination which would be of benefit to them even in this life.' The Marquis was himself a believer: he 'was at pains to point out that as a member of the established church, he entertained a sincere veneration for the Anglican tenets, but he did not think it proper to interfere with those who sincerely differed from him in their mode of worshipping God' and he was sure that 'in the chapel they would be instructed in the truths of our common Christianity.'[39] That Sir Ian Malcolm shared the Christianity his family promoted by funding the local parish church and the family's chapel is clear from his work as lay reader and organist. In funding churches and chapels, the Durham colliery-owners were generally promoting a religion they themselves shared. The owners' preferences were often reflected in the activities of their senior managers. Henry Mein was manager of the Victoria Colliery, Howden Le Wear, in 1890s; he was also Superintendent of the Howden Le Wear Sunday

School.[40] The founding trustees of the New Brancepeth Wesleyan chapel included the managers of the colliery and the associated brickworks.[41] Bullock reports the tensions between the colliery bosses and the men who attended the Bowers Row mission hall—especially during the all-too-frequent industrial disputes—but he does not doubt the sincerity of the colliery general manager, who played the organ and led the choir, or of the under-manager, who led the Band of Hope and the Men's Bible Classes. Bainbridge, the London Lead Company's agent in Teesdale, clearly shared the company's religious ethos. When his eldest son came of age in 1849, Joseph Pease led a prayer meeting with his miners at the Adelaide Colliery and asked them to 'unite with me in humble desires—in prayers—that...he may fulfil his duties by the help of God as a true Christian and a true patriot'. Gurney Pease ran a Bible class for ironstone workers. Arthur Pease not only led Quaker worship but also conducted services in mission halls and chapels of other denominations.[42]

Where the paternalists were themselves pious Christians, as in the example of Love, this is well documented. What is not usually recorded, and has to be inferred, is the *noblesse oblige* support that continued when the *noblesse* were not particularly religious. We know that J. A. Farrer was a rationalist. The later Williams-Wynns were not known for their personal piety. The Marquis of Normanby was articulate about his willingness to support a competing branch of Christianity for its social benefits. For the various Durham colliery-owners who supported sects with which they had little affinity and which were well known as breeding grounds for troublesome trade unionists, or for the Vane family in Teesdale and Viscount Boyne (who owned much of the land on which chapels were built in the Deerness valley), we can only suppose that such support was in part a fulfilment of a general obligation that came with social status.

The Value of Paternalism

Paternalistic support for religion was intended to benefit the churches, but, as intentions are not consequences, it is worth itemizing the likely effects of such support. Some infrastructure provision may have made little difference. A local historian dismisses the Chauncy family's renovation of the Little Munden church as a vanity decorating project.[43] Poltalloch's private chapel mainly served the family and their English visitors and thus did little to advance the Christian cause in Mid-Argyll, but then the estate also funded the local kirk.

Sir Joseph White Todd was a wealthy Victorian merchant banker and founder of one of Britain's biggest insurance companies. The Morenish, Loch Tay, chapel built in 1902 by his wife, Aline, was an intensely personal memorial. The beautiful sandstone design, with its Arts and Crafts feel, is alien to its Scottish surroundings. Even more out of place is the stained-glass window, made by Tiffany of New York, which mourns the death of Todd's only daughter in childbirth. And, while the chapel lies between two distant parish churches, its provision was probably of little value because by then motor cars and better roads had put the Killin parish church within easy reach of those who lived in Morenish. But it was an additional adornment of the faith, and a century later still attracts visitors and admirers.

A memorial stained-glass window or new pews may have promoted the provider more than the faith, but the public still benefited from such vanity projects when they made the building more attractive and comfortable. And there is no doubt about the value of the County Durham church plant provided by the industrial paternalists: at the lowest it was a fifth of the costs and at its greatest—as with Horden's large church—it was the full cost. Without the combined generosity of the Raby estate and the LLC, there would have been no Anglican outlets in upper Teesdale and few dissenting chapels. At the very least, continuing support in one form released scarce congregational funds for other Christian works. For example, by providing coal to all four chapels in its village, the Bearpark Colliery Company allowed those chapels to spend the money thus saved on other chapel activities.

Religious paternalism certainly increased the number of full-time Christian workers. By paying the incumbent of St James the Less in Upper Teesdale when the Church of England declined to do so, the Duke of Cleveland created a church presence where there would otherwise have been none. Ditto the LLC's funding of the Harwood curate. When the Peases, the Bairds, and the Palmers employed missionaries for their workers, they increased the level of evangelistic work.

The British state gave up coercing church involvement in the eighteenth century, but, as we saw with Ainsworth of Halliwell and the Teesdale LLC, some paternalists continued to press their employees well into the nineteenth century. So he could badger his tenants about their church attendance, novelist Rider Haggard's father, the squire of Bradenham in Norfolk, would not let anyone leave the church until he was stationed at the door to count them.[44] In insisting that his servants accompany his family to the parish church, Johnston of Hamsteels was unusual only in persisting with a practice long after others had given it up.

It is impossible to be sure how effective was such social pressure. The 62 per cent of the Ainsworth bleaching company workforce that regularly attended church was well above the 27 per cent noted for the area in the 1851 Census of Religious Worship, which suggests provision and encouragement may have had some effect. Even if coercion bred resentment, it did at least keep a larger part of the population in contact with organized religion: Ainsworth's diary notes that almost half of his workers who did not attend church nonetheless sent their children to its Sunday School. So his work did something to preserve the stock of religious knowledge.

Even if some of those so press-ganged were sufficiently resentful to abandon church attendance at the first opportunity, some must have voluntarily continued what was initially an imposition. Others will have taken their Christian knowledge into a more positive commitment to a chapel or church of their preference. If nothing else, they would have had some religious capital to pass on to their children. And it does not follow that class tensions always tainted religious patronage. Bullock's account of Bower's Row shows conflict between colliery officials and miners in the mission hall: during periodic labour disputes, miners used extempore prayer to condemn quite openly the owners and managers. But the targets of such criticism remained members and continued to run the Men's Bible class and the choir.

The most important possible consequence of elite support for religion is the most difficult to evaluate: the persuasive power of legitimation. In the absence of opinion polls, we can only speculate. Did the presence of the Big House family in its reserved pews at the front of the church or in its own balcony—with its implication of divine favour for social hierarchy—strengthen the faith of the common people? In the Ashbury example, the church was renovated by the Big House because the incumbent is himself a family member. The church, like Poltalloch's, functioned like a medieval private chapel, with the celebration of the family's piety a principle if not primary object. But, even if the audience for such celebrations was small, the churches themselves were significant marks on the landscape, and the additional clergy funded by paternalism increased the amount of home visiting and provided additional religious offices. It seems reasonable to suppose that, had there been fewer churches and fewer clergy, Christianity would have been the weaker.

A more negative view of patronage is possible if we start with the divide of France at the time of the 1796 Revolution into pro-church supporters of the old order and anti-clerical progressives. US sociologists have taken Alexis De Toqueville's contrast of the vitality of America's voluntary religion and the moribund state of Europe's religious establishments to justify the general proposition that elite support weakens the appeal of religion by tying it to unpopular politics. While that generalization has some validity for Catholic countries with their monotone religious culture, it has little application for Protestant Britain, because, since the Reformation, it has had many alternatives that people could join if they came to resent the elite voice of the state church. When the people of Sutherland in the north of Scotland came to resent the Church of Scotland clergy for their often-sycophantic support for oppressive lairds, they could join the Seceders or the Free Church.[45] If the people of Teesdale disliked the Church of England because they disliked the Raby estate that funded it, they could attend the Methodist chapels that the estate had also helped to erect. If the people of Llanuwchllyn found the rector's attitude to the Big House overly oleaginous, they had five chapels of three sects to choose from.

Though the matter cannot be settled in this short space, it seems reasonable to suppose that the active support of the local Big House or the major local employer, if such people or organizations were popular, strengthened the plausibility of Christianity and thus helped to promote it. And, even if one particular patron of one expression of religion was unpopular, as we will see in Chapter 10, the religious make-up of Britain was sufficiently varied to allow class resentment to be expressed in dissenting religion rather than dissenting *from* religion.

The End of Paternalism

The death of paternalism is complex in detail but simple in essence: it was killed by democracy. State-sponsored welfare as a right ended the need for personal philanthropy.[46] The more power the common people acquired, the less they sought charity from their superiors, and the less those superiors felt obliged to provide it. The rise of the trade-union movement, the extension of the franchise, the growth of a working-class element in first the Liberal Party and then the Labour Party—all played their part in a blanket rejection of philanthropy. As the social demand for paternalistic welfare declined, so too did the ability of paternalists to provide it.

The Edwardian era was the zenith for the Big House, undermined by those two certainties of death and taxes. The high casualty rate among junior officers in the First World War meant unusually frequent demands for death duties. The 1919 budget raised inheritance tax on estates over £2 million to 40 per cent: 'By the end of 1921 the *Estates Gazette* concluded that a quarter of

England had changed hands.' By 1936, returns from agricultural land had reached their lowest point since 1870.

> The real losers in this process were the landed gentry, a group whose fortunes had been in decline since the agricultural depression of the late nineteenth century. Without the spread of resources and means to diversify of the larger landowners, the inter-war years took a heavy toll of smaller long-established families. It has been estimated that of the gentry families existing in Essex, Oxfordshire and Shropshire in the 1870s only a third retained their country seat by 1952.[47]

The Woollcombes' Ashbury estate was sold in the 1930s and the manor house demolished in 1934. The Williams-Wynn Llanuwchllyn estate was accepted by the state in lieu of death duties in the 1940s. The endowment that funded the incumbent of Poltalloch's Episcopalian chapel ran out in 1934; the estate sold much of its land in Kilmartin before eventually abandoning the mansion house in 1954. In the Scottish highlands, the government in the form of the Board of Agriculture bought up estates to provide land for crofters. A few families clung on. In Little Munden, Dane End did not sell its properties and land until the late 1950s. In 1954, the Loders village fete was still being hosted by Sir Edward and Lady Le Breton.[48] But across the country, the mansions of the gentry became hotels, hostels, or hospitals, or crumbled, or were demolished. The farm land was sold to its tenants; the large gardens covered with bungalows.

Industrial paternalism largely ended with the death of the locally owned and managed family firm, killed by amalgamation and by joint stock status. Companies increasingly answered to shareholders and to remote owners who had no personal ties to the place where the factories or mines they part owned were located. We can contrast the small family firms of the Vale of Leven in the nineteenth century, where the owner was often an elder of the church, an MP, or councillor, and a leading light in the Orange Order or the Masons, with the huge Singer factory in Glasgow's Clydebank. It was American owned and 'run by a professional manager who could be recalled to the USA at any time... [hence] there was little or no room for religious instrumentality'.[49]

Religious diversity played its part in undermining religious paternalism. The obligation of the wealthy to support the church made sense where there was just one church. It became less useful and more controversial the more that schism divided the people into competing alternatives. As we saw with the Marquis of Normanby, one possible response was to broaden the range of churches and sects supported, but that quickly turned into a decision to support none of them. In a religiously diverse world, paternalists who sought the improvement or loyalty of their tenants or employees were on surer grounds with secular forms of improvement: hence the Cadbury's Bourneville model of gardening societies, sports clubs, and concert halls. The colliery Peases made generous donations to homes for retired miners long after they gave up funding chapels and home missionaries.

Religious paternalism in England and Wales was also undermined by a small but significant change in the nature of ecclesiastical patronage. In the nineteenth century there was a concerted effort to shift the right to appoint clergy from individual landowners to either the diocese or to some national religious interest group. There were sound reasons for this. Controlling appointments allowed the diocese to shift resources to adapt to population movements. Theological interest groups became involved because owning advowsons was the simplest way of ensuring jobs for their type of cleric. Roughly speaking, two-thirds of advowsons were in private hands at the start of the nineteenth century; at its end, the bishops controlled about half, and most of the rest were held either by the Crown or by religious interest groups such as the Church Society. While this change protected parishes from the sometimes idiosyncratic choices of landowners and improved diocesan resource management, it also freed local landowners from the role that had been one of the main sources of a sense of obligation to the church. The mechanisms in Scotland were different. There, challenges from the schismatic Seceder and Free Churches led to the national church removing the right of heritors to impose ministers and vesting the right 'to call' entirely in the hands of each congregation. But the effect on the obligations of the wealthy was the same.

In the case of the coalfields, the owners' sense of obligation was gradually weakened by the ingratitude of workers who preferred the protection of trade unions to the charity of their employers, but it was killed by the Mining Industry Act of 1920. The work of Liberal MPs from mining constituencies, this created a welfare fund for miners, with its income provided by a levy of a penny per ton of saleable output. If a tax could be delivered by the political power of the workers, there was little need for the charity of their masters. And in the few cases where paternalistic arrangements survived joint stock status (as they did with the Bearpark Coal Company's heating of all the chapels in the village), they ended abruptly with the nationalization of the industry in 1946.

The end of Big House and local industrialist support for religion is clearly a symptom of secularization, but did it also hasten decline? The end of paternalism did not, of course, stop personally religious rich people promoting religion. If Love had felt no particular burden for the souls of his workers, he would still have given his fortune to chapel building. Banbury benefited from a similar figure in the person of Sir William Mewburn, who made his money in railway stocks before retiring to Banbury in 1865 and subsequently funding Methodist chapel building in his adopted home town. A study of business leaders shows that those who were Christians continued to give generously to religious causes and some of the very wealthy rationalized their charity by leaving their assets to a charitable trust.[50] The crucial point is that the breaking of *local* ties of responsibility reduced the subvention of religious life. When the church that needed renovation was just outside the gates of the Big House, the obligation was difficult to avoid.

> By the 1930s it was not uncommon for a local aristocrat to sit on the board of a London-based company…but have only marginal involvement in the affairs of his locality…Local landowners and manufacturers were more and more drawn into a wider world of business.…the kind of political and social domination exercised by many men of wealth before 1914 was being undermined…First-generation businessmen such as William Morris were prepared to act as local benefactors…by and large the very wealthy saw their role in a national context.[51]

The increasingly rare wealthy church members presumably still supported the church or chapel they attended, but they no longer felt uniquely obliged to provide such support and they were less pressingly confronted with specific needs. Their support for religion was now a choice rather than an obligation.

It is difficult to quantify the financial loss to the churches, but, unless my study areas are grossly unrepresentative (and that is unlikely), it must have been considerable. As the Scottish bourgeoisie demonstrated when it funded the post-1843 Free Church to replicate the parish structure of the Church of Scotland, the urban middle classes could afford to make their own provision but many rural and working-class areas were either too poor or insufficiently interested to support an effective infrastructure. The relationship between poverty and interest is complex. One might suppose that the basic needs of reformed Protestantism could have been supplied by any group of committed Christians but, as we will see in Chapter 2 with examples from Orkney and Shetland, there were parts of the country where the common people were too poor to build and maintain even the meanest chapel. Moreover, even those Protestant sects that had no ideological commitment to an ordained ministry in practice relied on full-time workers, and suffered from their absence. In Shetland, the main difference between those Independent and Baptist congregations that did or did not last more than one generation was the presence of a full-time resident pastor.[52] In Orkney, a number of Seceder congregations died because they could not provide a stipend that would sustain a minister.[53] As alternative provision was scarce in these places, we have to suppose that the failure of every such congregation was a net loss to the Christian churches.

If there is any value in the long sociological tradition that supposes that ideologies are strengthened not just by the mass of social support but also by the quality of that social support, then the upper classes abandoning their obligation to organized religion must have reinforced the trend towards individual freedom of choice. That is, the end of an association between social status and piety marked a clear acknowledgement that religion was now a matter of personal preference and that no stigma adhered to those who were not religious.[54]

Conclusion

One way of thinking about secularization is to see it as a gradual expansion of the freedom to choose. The first stage was the release of people from the obligation to attend the state churches; the next was the end of their obligation to fund churches they did not attend. Both formally (through the obligations of ecclesiastical patronage in England and Wales and through the heritor system in Scotland) and informally (through the sense of social honour), the wealthy were the last to be thus freed.

As the capacity of places of worship exceeded demand by the end of the nineteenth century, we might suppose that the end of religious paternalism made little difference to church effectiveness.[55] However, even leaving aside the fact that much giving was for running costs, there was still a need for new build and renovation. As people moved to take advantage of new industries and as new towns were built, new churches and chapels were needed. And where the old provision was in the right place and excessive, it still needed renovation and replacement. The local councils and private developers who took over the supply of housing often left spaces for church building, but that was the extent of their support. The chapels in the old pit villages of the Easington area were at least part-funded by the collieries. The Methodist chapel for the new town of Peterlee, planned to replace those pit villages, had to be funded by members themselves. By the end of the twentieth century, the churches and chapels built by the Victorians were reaching the end of their natural lives, and neither landowners nor major employers felt any obligation to replace them. In 2010, both the Anglican church and Methodist chapel in Middleton-in-Teesdale required expensive renovation and were far too large for their reduced congregations. With the LLC long gone and the Raby estates no longer in the church-building business, the two tiny congregations were left to their own insufficient devices. That subtle social forces (such as the growth of effective science-based technologies) were steadily reducing the plausibility of religion might imply that local circumstances were irrelevant, but it remains the case that adequate resources could always slow the rate of decline by making churchgoing easier and more pleasant. If we can agree that only the most committed churchgoer is not dispirited by being part of a small group occupying only the choir stalls in a damp and frigid building designed for six hundred people, then the decline of patronage clearly hastened decline.

Notes

1. P. J. Winstone and J. Hall, *A History of the Church in Clapham* (Clapham: St James' Church, 2007), 44.
2. S. Bruce, *Secularization* (Oxford: Oxford University Press, 2011).
3. R. M. Morris, *Church and State in 21st Century Britain* (London: Palgrave Macmillan, 2009), 61–90; M. H. McQueen, *Parson, Parish and Patron: Appointments to Benefices in the Church of England* (Appleford: Marcham Manor Press, 1968).
4. G. E. Mingay, *The Gentry: The Rise and Fall of a Ruling Class* (London: Longman., 1976), 134
5. W. White, *History, Gazetteer and Directory of Devonshire* (Sheffield: Robert Leader, 1850), 103.
6. A. Rowe, *The Protected Valley: A History of Little Munden* (Buntingford, Herts: Hamels Publishing, 1999), 10.
7. T. M. Owen, 'Chapel and Community in Glan-llyn, Merioneth', in E. Davies and A. D. Rees (eds), *Welsh Rural Communities* (Cardiff: University of Wales Press, 1960), 185–248.
8. W. Hughes, *A Short History of the Parish of Llanuwchlyn* (Bala: Davies and Evans, 1898), 23.
9. R. A. Bell, *St James the Less, Forest and Frith: A History of a Dales Church and Community* (Teesdale: self-published, 1995), 16.
10. S. Lewis, *A Topographical Dictionary of Scotland* (London: S, Lewis and Co., 1846), http://www.british-history.ac.uk/report.aspx?compid=43452 (accessed April 2008).
11. J. B. Stephenson, *Ford: A Village in the West Highlands of Scotland* (Edinburgh: Paul Harris Publishing, 1984).
12. Diocese of Argyll and the Isles, *Kilmartin—St Columba*, http://www/agyllandtheisles.org.uk/kilmartin.html (accessed April 2008).

13. M. Hunter, *Uyeasound Church 1848–1995* (Unst: Isles Telecroft, 1996), 2.
14. D. Campbell, *Reminiscences and Reflections of an Octogenarian Highlander* (Inverness: Published to a list of private subscribers, 1910), ch. 27, http://www.glenlyon.org/rroh_ch27.php (accessed August 2017).
15. A. Stewart, *Daughters of the Glen* (Aberfeldy: Leura Press, 1986), 33.
16. C. Finlayson, *The Strath* (Edinburgh: Saint Andrew Press, 1979), 68–9.
17 A. Scott, *Eccentric Wealth: The Bulloughs of Rum* (Edinburgh: Birlinn, 2011).
18. J. C. Ley, *The Story of my Life: Recollections of a North Devon Farmer, Preacher and Family Man* (Ilfracombe, Devon: Arthur H. Stockwell, 1978), 21.
19. A. L. Rowse, *A Cornish Childhood* (London: Jonathan Cape, 1942), 147.
20. Stewart, *Daughters*, 36.
21. C. J. Hunt, *The Lead Miners of the Northern Pennines in the Eighteenth and Nineteenth Centuries* (Manchester: Manchester University Press, 1980), 223.
22. H. L. Beadle, *Forest Methodist Chapel* (Forest: Forest Methodist Church, 1993).
23. United Methodist Church, *Circuit Schedule*, Durham Record Office M/DCP 109. I am grateful to the staff of the Durham Records Office for their assistance in accessing records of Methodist chapels in County Durham.
24. H. L. Neal, *The Story of Bearpark* (Durham: self-published, 1956), 21.
25. R. Moore, *Pitmen, Preachers and Politics: The Effect of Methodism in a Durham Mining Community* (Cambridge: Cambridge University Press, 1974), 83.
26. Anon, 'Death of Joseph Love Esq', *Durham Chronicle*, 26 February 1875, 7.
27. A. Orde, *Religion, Business and Society in North-East England: The Pease Family of Darlington in the Nineteenth Century* (Donington: Shaun Tyas, 2000), 44.
28. Orde, *Religion*, 49.
29. E. P. Thompson, 'On History, Sociology and Historical Relevance', *British Journal of Sociology*, 27 (1976), 387–94.
30. Anon, *Wheatley Hill Methodist Chapel 1904–1954 Jubilee Handbook* (Wheatley Hill, Co. Durham: Wheatley Hill Methodist Church, 1954).
31. J. Bullock, *Them and Us* (London: Souvenir Press, 1972), and *Bowers Row: Recollections of a Mining Village* (Wakefield: E. P. Publishing, 1976).
32. S. Yeo, *Religion and Voluntary Associations in Crisis* (London: Croom Helm, 1976, 93–4).
33. P. N. Dale, *Many Mansions. The Growth of Religion in Bolton 1750–1850* (Bolton: self-published, 1985), 90.
34. Dale, *Many Mansions*, 91.
35. G. Darley, *Villages of Vision: A Study of Strange Utopias* (Nottingham: Five Leaves, 2007), 129.
36. The records of the main Baird family company are held in the Special Collections of Strathclyde University, http://gdl.cdlr.strath.ac.uk/100men/gm05.htm (accessed 18 October 2003).
37. Darley, *Villages of Vision*, 98.
38. Dale, *Many Mansions*, 101.
39. J. Howard, *Staithes: Chapters from the History of a Seafaring Town* (Scalby, N. Yorks: self-published, 2000), 17.
40. W. Stokes, *Henry Green: Memoirs of a Primitive Methodist. Eventide Memories and Recollections by Henry Green 1855–1932* (Durham: Durham County Local History Society, 1997).

41. J. Atkinson, *New Brancepeth Methodist Church 1877–1977* (New Brancepeth, Co. Durham: New Brancepeth Methodist Church, 1977).
42. Orde, *Religion*, 99.
43. Rowe, *Protected Valley*, 69–70.
44. Mingay, *Gentry*, 174.
45. F. Bardgett, *North Coast Diaries: Strathy at the Time of the Great War* (Edinburgh: Birlinn, 2006).
46. See C. D. Field, *Secularization in the Long 1960s* (Oxford: Oxford University Press, 2017), 223, and F. Prochaska, *Christianity and Social Service in Modern Britain: The Disinherited Spirit* (Oxford: Oxford University Press, 2006).
47. J. Stevenson, *British Society 1914–45* (Harmondsworth: Penguin, 1984), 333.
48. M. Willmott (ed.), *The Parson Knows: From Parish Notes 1953–1968* (Gloucester: Bishop Street Press, 1999), 90–2.
49. D. J. Jeremy, *Capitalists and Christians: Business Leaders and the Churches in Britain 1900–1960* (Oxford: Clarendon Press, 1990), 130.
50. Jeremy, *Capitalists*.
51. Stevenson, *British Society*, 355.
52. W. D. McNaughton, *Early Congregational Independency in Shetland* (Lerwick: Shetland Times, 2005); G. Yuille (ed.), *History of the Baptists in Scotland from Pre-Reformation Times* (Glasgow: Baptist Union Publications Committee, 1926).
53. W. McKelvie, *Annals and Statistics of the United Presbyterian Church* (Edinburgh: Oliphant and Co. and Andrew Elliot, 1873).
54. Paternalistic support for the Catholic Church has been passed over for two reasons: when paternalism was most relevant, there were relatively few Catholics in Britain, and, because the Catholic Church was largely urban and more often organized around a few big churches rather than on the local parish model, the few Catholic grandees tended to support the church generally as 'missionary work' rather than as local obligation.
55. The case is made in detail in R. Gill, *The 'Empty Church' Revisited* (Aldershot: Ashgate, 2003).

2

Ties that Bind

Community Cohesion in Scotland and Wales

Understanding social change is much aided by structured comparison. Social scientists can rarely construct experiments to manipulate the variables that interest us, but we can sometimes find naturally occurring contrasts that perform a similar function. Why, even within a small society, are some places more religious than others? One important argument over the causes of religion's decline in the West concerns the impact of diversity.[1] On one side, we have the case that beliefs are most plausible, persuasive, and powerful when they are widely shared. People born into societies where everyone supports the same religion, and where frequent interaction reinforces a faith that is deeply embedded in social norms, acquire their religion in the same taken-for-granted way they acquire their language. In a mono-religious world, the propositions of that religion are hardly beliefs; that suggests choice. Rather they are accurate description of this world and the next. Such logic suggests that diversity weakens religion by showing it could be otherwise. The fact that believers now have to pick their religion (and are only too well aware that they are a minority) makes dogmatic certainty difficult.[2] We manage potential conflict by confining faith to ever smaller areas of life, by supposing that apparently contradictory beliefs are in some vague sense equally true, and by tolerating an ever-greater range of religions (including the option of unbelief). At the level of social structure, religious diversity, when it is combined with the modern notion that all people are in some sense of equal worth, forces the state to stop promoting one particular faith. That, in turn, reduces the frequency and the extent to which people are brought into contact with religious officials, institutions, offices, and rituals.

An alternative view supposes that, for religion, as for car production, competition is virtuous because it increases diversity, which in turn allows more people to find some variety that suits. Second, a competitive free market allows innovation and forces providers to work hard to attract customers, thus overcoming two major defects of a religious monopoly (especially one that is state backed and funded from taxation): clerical sloth and poor provision. Why should the clergy work hard to be popular if they get paid as much to be unpopular? Third—a problem raised in Chapter 1—diversity prevents religion becoming suspect because the clergy are closely allied with the elites and with the political status quo.[3]

If the consensus-gives-strength view is correct, then the most religiously diverse places should be the least religious. If the alternative is correct, diverse societies will be more religious than those with little variety. This chapter tests those alternatives with two sets of comparisons: between three Scottish islands and between four Welsh parishes. Those comparisons will be bookended by brief examination of two sorts of industry-based communities—fishing and mining villages—that have traditionally been taken as unusually religious and superstitious, and with a very brief consideration of religion in post-war new towns.

Fisherfolk

Fishing communities have long been regarded as unusually religious and superstitious. The classic text is Bronislaw Malinowski's study of the Trobriand Islanders: *The Argonauts of the Western Pacific*.[4] The men of the islands fished in two very different contexts: interior lagoons and the open sea. Malinowski observed that, while fishing in the open sea was surrounded by a variety of magic rituals, such ritual was largely absent from fishing in the lagoon. The difference was the degree of unpredictable danger involved in the two activities. The same explanation has been applied to twentieth-century New England fishermen.[5] Writing of the nineteenth century, a Scots folklorist said: 'They are a truly religious community, our fisherfolk. The dangers of their calling make them realise how unstable is their tenure on this life.'[6] A study of fishing villages in the north-east of Scotland was entitled 'Faith, Fear and Folk Narrative'.[7] An anthropology of one village noted: 'fishermen were said to be uniquely aware of their own mortality and thus their dependence on God in times of peril.'[8]

The last religious revival in Britain significant enough to be suitably so-called occurred in 1921 and it was confined to two fishing areas: East Anglia and the north-east of Scotland. It began in Lowestoft, where the local herring fleet was joined for the herring season by some 400 Scottish drifters.[9] While the coastal villages of Aberdeenshire were strongly affected, this interest in enthusiastic religion had no resonance a mile inland. Beyond being confirmed in their suspicion that fisher people were queer folk, the farmers and farm-workers were untouched.[10] Peter Anson, who wrote extensively on fishing folk from the 1930s to the 1960s, explicitly linked danger and superstition: 'When I first began to be interested in fisher folklore, the capture of fish still depended to a great extent on the moods of the winds and the waves...Life both ashore and afloat was still surrounded by fears and forebodings....There was still mystery on every side.'[11]

While it may seem sensible to suppose that unpredictably dangerous work causes people to seek non-material ways to control their environment and makes them mindful of their mortality, there are two potential weaknesses of using danger to explain receptivity to supernaturalist beliefs. The first is that we place too much weight on the psychological states or the needs of individuals taken severally rather than jointly. A very large body of evidence shows that few people's religious beliefs (and even more their superstitions) are the result of conscious adult choice. Mostly we believe what we were raised to believe and what was reinforced in interaction with like-minded others. If it is the case that people who work in unpredictably perilous circumstances are unusually receptive to religious or superstitious solutions to their problem, this will not appear as a series of separate adult choices. Rather it will have become a feature of a shared culture: the product of generations of choices distilled into common understandings that are passed down the generations along with the fishing tackle and techniques for its use.

The second problem is that some perilous occupations do not encourage unusual piety. Soldiering is a case in point. Despite their periodic vulnerability, British soldiers have not been known for their interest in religion. One obvious difference between the combatants of twentieth-century wars and fisherfolk is that the former did not generally form a stable community. People normally served in the forces for short periods and they were frequently posted from one unit to another. Because we have been fortunate enough to fight our recent wars overseas, our combatants were mostly removed from their families. In contrast, British fishing villages were generally isolated. By definition, they were on the coast, and so opportunities for social contact were only half those of inland settlements. Their economies had little connection with the farming hinterlands, and fishermen's working lives were unusually structured: they spent long periods at sea and they worked in teams, usually based on the extended family. Those families were directly involved in the business, women and children often being responsible for finishing and marketing the catch. Gardenstown, with its tightly packed houses pressed against the cliffs behind, is typical of fishing villages, and its physical structure produced the social counterpart: 'this gave rise to a strong sense of the community living in each other's pockets.'[12] The prying eyes of neighbours could not be avoided. Those who failed to attend chapel or to observe expected rituals such as the churching of women were immediately known to their neighbours as deviants and could be disciplined by shunning and by being excluded from economically important networks of mutual support.

If it is the case that community cohesion is the key to enduring religiosity, this should be visible in comparisons of places that are similar in most respects other than cohesion.

Scottish Islands

The impact of community structure on religious vitality is clear when we compare three Scottish islands (or, more precisely, one island and two island groups): Lewis, the outermost of the western isles, and the Orkney and Shetland islands to the north of Scotland. The three islands have much in common. All belong to the same nation state and hence share the same legislation, administrative structure, and history of church–state relations. Until the discovery of North Sea oil in the early 1970s brought prosperity to the northern isles, their economies were similar. All were 'crofting counties': a distinctive status based on nineteenth-century legislation to protect the rights of subsistence farming tenants. Most islanders lived by crofting and fishing. The three islands are also similar in religious culture: they were overwhelming Presbyterian and, until 1843, almost everyone belonged to the state Church of Scotland. At the start of the twentieth century, the three islands were similarly religious; by its end they were very different. While Orkney and Shetland had secularized at much the same rate as lowland Scotland, Lewis had become a byword for sabbatarianism and piety. That divergence invites explanation.

Dissent, Diversity, and Competition

In the first half of the nineteenth century, most Orcadians were members of the national Kirk. and the largest body of dissenters were Seceder Presbyterians: liberals who rejected the right of landowners to impose ministers on reluctant congregations and the right of the state to impose religious conformity. In Shetland, the Seceders had very little impact: the main dissenting body was Methodist. Lewis was the odd one out: as the minister of Lochs smugly asserted in 1833: 'There is not a single dissenter from the established Church in any part of the Lewis islands.'[13] Ten years later, that situation was dramatically changed when the evangelical third of the Church of Scotland clergy walked out to form the Free Church. The 'Disruption', as it was known, turned Lewis into the poster boy for dissent: almost everyone joined the Free Church. Because the Seceders in Orkney and the Methodists in Shetland were already strong dissenting presences, the Disruption had relatively little immediate impact in Orkney and Shetland.

Over the next fifty years, the Free Church in the urban lowlands of Scotland came round to the notion that religion should be chosen rather than imposed. It also became theologically more liberal, and in 1900 the Free Church and the largest Seceder bodies joined together to form the United Free Church. Twenty-nine years later, the vast majority of the UFC rejoined the Church of Scotland, which was once again a truly national church. But, in the highlands and the western isles, the majority rejected the liberal direction and continued as the Free Church.[14]

In the short term, competition improved religious provision. In all three islands, the Kirk's effort had long been woefully inadequate, largely because it was funded from local land taxes, and the land was poor. In Lewis in the early nineteenth century the 250 people who lived at Tolsta, for example, were 12 miles from the nearest parish church and, had they made the journey, they would have had to stand: the building seated less than a third of the parish's adult population. Orkney and Shetland ministers served very large areas, and all had at least two preaching stations; many served four congregations and so could officiate only once a month in each of their outlets. The minister of Dunrossness was expected to serve Fair Isle, which 'lies at a distance of 30 miles from the nearest point in Shetland' with 'a very rough and dangerous sea intervening.'[15] The Yell minister lived on Fetlar and had preached on Yell only three times in the previous five months. That left plenty of space for dissenters to fill, and so we can say that, in the short term, competition improved the supply of religious offices.

Competition also had an indirect effect in forcing the Kirk to up its game. For example, in the Orkney parish of South Ronaldsay, the Kirk had allowed one of its churches to fall into decay. Locals repeatedly argued that the intact church was too far away, but the Kirk did nothing for over a century. Only when a Baptist congregation was formed did the Kirk renovate its church and arrange regular services.

However, over the long run, any beneficial effects of competition appear to be swamped by a stronger association between consensus and religiosity.

Arguably church attendance offers a better measure of religious interest than church membership, but statistical data on attendance are sporadic. Using records of individual denominations, it is possible to calculate a rate for church members as a proportion of the adult population for the three islands from 1885 to 2011, and this is presented in Table 2.1. In 1885, Lewis was the least religious of the three islands. By 1901, it was slightly ahead. Fifty years later, in 1951, it was clearly ahead, with Shetland having slipped a long way. By the end of the twentieth century, although Lewis had become markedly less religious than it was, it was markedly more religious than Orkney and Shetland.

Local histories and biographies are clear that the strength of religion in Lewis owed much to the way in which it became embedded in the norms of shared everyday life. The sabbath was strictly kept. Most people attended church at least twice and filled the space between with family worship or the reading of religious texts. Secular activities were kept to such a bare minimum that children who broke the rules were not punished until Monday. Almost every household held daily Bible readings and prayer meetings. And that remained the case well into the twentieth century. The parish entry for Kinloch in the *Third Statistical Account of Scotland*, written in 1953, notes that 'the Sabbath is strictly observed in the parish' and that 'family worship...in Gaelic is daily observed in most houses'.[16]

Table 2.1. Church membership in Lewis, Orkney, and Shetland, 1885–2011 (as % of adult population)

Year	Lewis	Orkney	Shetland
1885	60	61	63
1901	61	56	59
1931	59	57	63
1951	62	58	49
1971	71	55	35
1991	n.a.	36	23
2011	35	22	14

Note: n.a. = not available.

Sources: Data compiled from a wide variety of congregational histories and denominational yearbooks kindly made available by the staff of the local records offices in Lerwick, Stornoway, and Kirkwall. Episcopal church data were provided by the Diocesan Registrar. Lewis Free Church data were kindly provided by the clerk of the Presbytery. A number of clergy in the three areas assisted with congregational figures. If there is a weakness in the figures, it is not in the church statistics but in the estimates of adult population used to calculate percentages. However, the relative differences are sufficiently large that we can have confidence in the basic patterns.

Accounts of Orkney and Shetland suggests a rather different culture. The diaries of preachers and denominational histories show a paradox. On the one hand, there was considerable general interest in religion. For example, every child was baptized, even when that meant making the hazardous sea crossing from Fair Isle to the Shetland mainland. Itinerant evangelists often found their arrival drew the entire free population of the area, even when it was unexpected, as, for example, when sea and wind conditions forced them to make land somewhere other than where they were headed. However, Orcadians and Shetlanders were very reluctant to make their own religious provision. The chapel in Sullom would attract two hundred people if a clergyman was preaching, but average Sunday attendances when a layman took the service was only twenty-five. Dissenting preachers found it easy to attract large audiences but very difficult to persuade those who heard them to establish and maintain their own fellowships. Small numbers of enthusiasts formed Baptist and Brethren fellowships, but few lasted.

This combination of keenness to consume religion and reluctance to exert themselves to sustain an enduring presence is odd, because a key characteristic of Protestantism is the equality of believers. In theory, Protestants have no need for clergy leadership. Any godly person, filled with the Holy Spirit, can preach, lead in prayer and song, and read the Bible. In rural England, the Methodists had little difficulty building congregations on the labours of members and lay preachers. In Shetland, the inertia of the people was a constant source of frustration. Writing in 1867, William Grigg noted that most of the seven Methodist chapels he superintended did not have viable weekly meetings and 'were not opened unless on the occasion of the minister's visit— say, once in six weeks, and so people were left to wander where they would, attending the ministry of other churches or none'.[17] In brief, in the nineteenth century in Shetland, and to a slightly lesser extent Orkney, we have almost universal willingness to consume religion but little active commitment.

It is difficult to untangle cause and effect. That all three islands were poor explains why, so long as it had to rely on local land taxes for funding, the Kirk's provision of religious offices was poor. It also explains the slow progress of dissent in Orkney and Shetland. Both the Seceders in Orkney and the Methodists in Shetland relied heavily on external subsidy: subventions from denominational national headquarters in the case of the Seceders and gifts from prosperous southern well-wishers in the case of the Methodists. Baptist and Brethren congregations were led by people who had to make their own precarious livings from crofting and fishing, which constrained their activities. To an extent the same was true of the people of Lewis. At its formation, the Free

Church adopted the principle of pooled funding: congregations would give to a central fund according to their abilities, and all clergy would be paid and churches maintained to a common standard from that fund. Nonetheless there is a clearly identifiable difference. Despite enjoying a standard of living no higher than that common in the northern isles, post-1843 the people of Lewis took great pride in raising enough to fund their dissent from the Kirk.

Structural Bases of Community Consensus

If it is the case that the greater piety of Lewis is to be explained by the strength of its shared religious culture, we can go one step back and consider how the underlying structural base helped maintain social cohesion. What is it about the social life of Lewis that explains why it had far less dissent than Orkney and Shetland? Or, to be more precise, why, when the people of Lewis did dissent, did they do so, not as individuals, but en masse?

Lewis had a narrower range of economic circumstances than the northern isles. The typical smallholding in Orkney was twenty-one acres; in Lewis, it was under ten (and in the northern part of the island, under five) acres. In Orkney, two-thirds of smallholdings were owner-occupied; in Lewis, none was. In Orkney and Shetland, less than 10 per cent of grazing was common land; in Lewis, more than half the grazing was common pasture. The small farmers of Orkney and Shetland could be neighbourly if they wished, but those of Lewis, where livelihood depended on the successful communal management of shared grazing, had no choice but to cooperate. That people labour in similar ways, enjoy a similar standard of living, and work cooperatively does not guarantee that they will think alike, but it much increases the odds.

As does proximity. In Orkney and Shetland, crofts were scattered thinly across the countryside. In Lewis, they were grouped in townships of twenty or more croft houses side-by-side. Living cheek-by-jowl does not ensure that neighbours will press each other to conform to the community's standards, but it is a precondition for such mutual encouragement, and it was more often absent in Orkney and Shetland than in Lewis.

A third difference concerns language. Like room temperature, community cohesion depends on insulation from the wider environment. Lewis was Gaelic-speaking; Orkney and Shetland were Anglophone. An 1825 survey showed that few Lewis families understood English better than Gaelic, and they were concentrated in Stornoway—the small cadre of professional people and incomers who dealt with the wider world.[18] Even those Lewis people who could understand English well enough to follow sermons preached in that language disliked it because it was the tongue of their masters and of the decadent mainland. The language barrier alone explains why the Seceders, a popular movement in urban Scotland, could recruit well in Orkney but manage only a short-lived toehold in Stornoway. More generally, the language barrier helped keep secular cosmopolitan culture at bay for a long time. That insulation gradually broke down from the 1950s as Gaelic-speaking declined. And, as Lewis became less isolated, so it became less religious.

From 1843, evangelical Presbyterianism enjoyed an unusual status in Lewis. It drew much of its strength from being a culture of opposition. The Lewis people had thumbed their noses at the establishment. They had rejected the religion of the upper classes and the landowners. They had made their own provision and they revelled in the fact that they were different. The lowlands might be going to hell, but, as an elderly resident put it to me in 1970, 'Lewis would remain the last stronghold of the pure gospel'. At the same time, that dissent was consensual and did not fragment the religious culture. It was a creed shared by the vast majority of the people, and its vitality rested on features of the economy and social structure that allowed the majority to monitor and censure the weakly committed and indifferent. In short, the evangelical religion of Lewis enjoyed the unusual combination of being sufficiently rebellious to enthuse the people but sufficiently widely shared to form the new 'taken-for-granted' reality.

Welsh Villages

We can pursue the effects on religious vitality of internal community cohesion and relative isolation by comparing four North Wales parishes that were studied in great detail in the late 1950s and early 1960s. For each I summarize what was said in those reports about the then popularity of the Church in Wales and the various Nonconformist chapels and present what I found when I restudied them in 2008 and 2009.

Llanfrothen Ffestiniog, Gwynedd

Llanfrothen Ffestiniog, an upland rural area of Merioneth (since 1974, Gwynedd), north-east of Porthmadog, was the site of Isabel Emmett's doctoral research. Its people were distributed between four small settlements (Garreg, Rhyd, Tan-lan, and Croesor) and the surrounding countryside. The majority at the south and middle of the parish worked in agriculture. At the north of the parish, the houses, chapel, and school at Croesor were built by men who, for a century from the 1830s, worked in the local slate quarries. Although the years since the end of the Second World War had seen a marked increase in average earnings, Emmett described the parish as relatively poor. More than two-thirds of employed people were manual workers: small farmers or agricultural labourers. There were schools in Garreg, Rhyd and Croesor, shops and post offices in Garreg and Croesor, and a hotel/pub in Garreg; most residents worked in the parish, and few had any reason to leave it.

Llanfrothen was primarily Welsh-speaking, and class, language, and national identity were closely linked. Small farmers, shepherds, quarrymen and estate workers spoke Welsh; major landowners were English and English-speaking, as were the few white-collar workers. Emmett describes a strong sense of Welsh identity among the locals, which, with Plaid Cymru not yet a significant electoral force, took the form of supporting the Labour Party.[19]

Although she had good reason, it is unfortunate that Emmett downplayed the most interesting thing about Llanfrothen. She was training as an anthropologist and wished to make general social-scientific observations about rural North Wales. She also wished to disguise her location and that could only be done by hiding the identity of the major landowner: Clough William-Ellis, the architect and pioneer conservationist who created the Italianate village of Portmeirion.[20] In 1908, William-Ellis inherited the Plas Brondanw estate and subsequently bought much of the surrounding property to preserve it from schemes for mineral extraction. He rented out many of the cottages—they were of such poor quality the locals preferred the new council houses in Garreg—to English intellectuals who were friends of his wife, Amabel (a member of the Strachey family). Among those who stayed were philosopher Bertrand Russell, social historian E. P. Thompson, the literary critic Christopher Wordsworth, and novelists Frank Showell Styles and Patrick O'Brien. Edith Young, now best known as the mother of Michael Young, sociologist and founder of the Open University and the Consumer Association, had a holiday home there. Philip O'Connor, who achieved short-lived fame as 'the tramp writer', rented the cottage next to the chapel in Croesor in 1959 and described (or more probably caricatured) many inhabitants in detail in *Living in Croesor*.[21]

Population fell in the 1960s and 1970s. Like most rural areas, Llanfrothen lost jobs with the decline of extractive industries and the mechanization of farming. Ambitious young people moved out, and the vacant houses were bought by outsiders as second homes. In 1973 and 1975, the Welsh Language Society demonstrated in Rhyd, where all but two of the seventeen houses had become holiday homes. Those protests (and the later cottage-burning campaign of the Sons of Glyndwr) played some part in reversing the trend, but the fact that half of the houses in Rhyd and three-quarters of those in Garreg are now occupied all year probably owes more to the same force that depopulated the area in the first place: the motor car. From the 1980s, population grew: Rhyd's 2003 population of thirty-seven was almost back to its 1944 level of forty-four. A large number of new houses had been built in Garreg, and most incomers were white-collar workers who commuted to well-paid jobs outside the area. Only 14 per cent of residents were now employed in farming; more worked in trade, in education, and in health and social work. Now owned by a local cooperative, the shop in Garreg was thriving, and, although the parish contained fewer shared facilities than in 1960, the residents of the southern end were prosperous and fully integrated into the social and cultural mainstream. Because the single-track road made access to Croesor difficult, its population had continued to decline; there was no longer any shop and the school closed in 2008.

There was considerable in-migration after Emmett's time. The 2001 census showed that 27 per cent had been born outside Wales and that has impacted on language use: only 69 per cent of residents said they could speak Welsh.

Emmett had no difficulty ascribing a religious identity to most of 241 adults of Llanfrothen. Calvinistic Methodists were 60 per cent; 17 per cent identified with the Church in Wales; and 8 per cent were Baptists. There was a handful of other Christians, and some 10 per cent had no religious affiliation. In 1960, the parish contained six Christian worship outlets, of which five were in fairly regular use; any one of them could have accommodated all the parish's churchgoers. Two were Episcopalian churches: St Brothen's, which gave the parish its name, and a nineteenth-century building in Garreg. Both had regular services, but they were already reduced from the normal schedule. Three chapels had two Sunday services every week: Siloam in Llanfrothen, Carmel in Croesor (both Calvinistic Methodist), and Ramoth, a Scotch Baptist chapel halfway along the narrow road from Garreg to Croesor. Two other chapels had recently cut back services (the Methodist chapel in Rhyd was by then used only for a Sunday school), and the Tan-lan Calvinistic Methodist chapel had closed in 1952.

Emmett did not give attendance figures for all the chapels, but her scattered remarks make it clear that there had been considerable decline from the time when the chapels were built (in respectively 1833, 1863, 1872, and 1904). She said of Siloam that attendances were sometimes so low that the services were held in the vestry.[22] Ramoth regularly attracted just six people (one of whom came from outside the parish). Nonetheless she believed that the culture of Nonconformist Christianity was important to most residents: 'the chapel was woven through it all in a way that gives it distinction.'[23] The Bible was sufficiently well known that its texts formed the basis for many casual discussions.[24] Although there had been some harvesting work done on farms rented by English people since the Second World War, the sabbath was still distinctive, and drinking alcohol was rare. O'Connor says that only two people in Croesor ever took a drink, and their consumption—a modest pint or two at the end of the working week—fell far short of his own.[25]

Croesor respondents recall that in the 1930s everyone in the hamlet belonged to the chapel and almost everybody went three times on the Sunday; some of the older people might miss the afternoon Sunday school. In Emmett's time, the remoter north end was still markedly more pious than the south end. As a very elderly Croesor man told me: 'The people down in Llanfrothen might have been a bit less religious because there were more English incomers there.'

Table 2.2 describes the decline in religious attachments between 1962 and 2009. The 2019 provision is even easier to describe: there is none. The Garreg church had become a private house and St Brothen's stands empty and unused. The parish is joined with Penrhyndeudraeth, Maentwrog and Beddgelert, and only one person from the parish is on the electoral roll of the new combined unit. Siloam is a storage shed and Ramoth a private house. The Croesor chapel is for sale.

Some residents may have pursued their religious interests outside the area, but those I interviewed could think of no one who did, and neighbouring parishes showed similar patterns of decline. Half the chapels of Blaenau Ffestiniog to the east were closed. Of three chapels in Maentwrog active in

Table 2.2. Church and chapel affiliation, Llanfrothen, 1962–2009 (as % of adult population)

Affiliation	1962	2009
Calvinistic Methodist	60	6
Baptist	8	0
Episcopalian	17	<1
Other	7	0
Total	92	6

Sources: The 1962 figures are from Emmett, *North Wales Village*, 90. The 2009 data were provided by local clergy and chapel stewards. (The figures in an earlier report of this research—S. Bruce, 'Religion in Rural Wales: Four Restudies', *Contemporary Wales*, 23 (2010), table 12.1—are mistaken, because of an error caused by using total, rather than adult, population as the base.)

the 1960s, two were private houses and the third had services only rarely. Penrhyndeudraeth, the small town to the south, had six chapels in the 1960s. In 2018 it had just two.

Chapel culture endured longer in Croesor than in Garreg. Croesor was more Welsh, in language, in national origins, and in national pride. The quarrymen, who in the 1870s had built the chapel, also built a school to save their children going to the Anglophone church school in Garreg. Croesor's isolation preserved its distinctive culture, but it also prevented its regeneration. While Garreg and Rhyd restocked with affluent commuters with young families, Croesor aged. Of those left in the village in 2009, most of the Welsh people—about half of the residents—were chapel members, but they were all elderly. Hence its subsequent closure.

Llanuwchllyn, Gwynedd

In 1949, Trefor Owen was employed to produce a social survey of the Glanllyn estate, which had been given to the state in lieu of death duties. 'Glan-llyn consists of the two parishes of Llanuwchllyn and Llangywer, together with small portions of adjoining parishes.'[26] Llanuwchllyn, which lies at the southwest end of Lake Bala and has a good road northwards to Bala and south to Dolgellau, was the focal point of the area. The smaller settlement of Llangower on the south-east side of the lake had diminished in size and importance since the nineteenth century. In what was primarily a farming area, the population had fallen from a peak of 1,852 in 1821 to 887 in 1951.

According to Owen, almost all inhabitants were Welsh-speakers: 'Formal social life within the community, including that of the chapels, is entirely in Welsh.'[27] It was also strongly nationalistic, and local clergy played small parts in two well-known expressions of national sentiment. In November 1956, Revd Gerallt Jones, the Independent pastor of Llanuwchllyn, led a protest outside the Liverpool city council chambers against a decision to flood Capel Celyn to create a reservoir to water Liverpool.[28] When Owen Williams was tried with attempting to sabotage the dam, the Revd Euros Bowen, the vicar of the parish, spoke on behalf of Williams and made his sentiments clear by insisting on his right to take the oath in Welsh.[29]

In numbers, the population is much as it was in Owen's study: it fell to 808 in 1981 and then rose to 831 in 2001. Although far fewer people worked on the land, agriculture remained the largest sector of employment. Increased ease of commuting was reflected in the spread of the rest across trade, education, construction, and manufacturing. Although Lake Bala remained a popular holiday resort, Llanuwchllyn saw fewer incomers than my other three research sites: 77 per cent of the 2001 residents were born in Wales. And that stability was reflected in language: in 2001, 79 per cent of residents were described as speaking Welsh, and Bala recorded the largest proportion of children speaking Welsh of any Welsh town.

Owen identified fifteen Christian places of worship in the Llanuwchllyn and Llangower area: the respective parish churches and thirteen chapels, of which one was Baptist and the remaining twelve were divided between Independents and Calvinistic Methodists. Two of the more remote chapels had closed before Owen began fieldwork. Most people had a nominal affiliation, and at least 60 per cent of the population regularly attended; the few non-churchgoers were English-speakers or incomers. That high degree of church adherence was still something of a decline from the mid-nineteenth century, when Yr Hen Gapel recorded 300 and Pandy had 211 at their most popular services on the day of the 1851 Census of Religious Worship.[30] In 1950, Sunday school rolls were already declining, and midweek meetings were poorly attended. Already there were many joint services.

I was not the first scholar to update Owen's study: Robin Gill details the decline he found in 1990 and 2002. As Table 2.3 shows, between 1950 and 1990 membership fell in tandem with population. Active participation fell faster: people attended less often and there was an increasing number of joint services. Gill estimates churchgoers in 1990 at 18 per cent of adults. Twelve years later that fall in interest was showing through in membership; now down from 80 to 61 per cent, with attendance at 11 per cent. The contraction

Table 2.3. Church and chapel affiliation, Llanuwchllyn–Llangower, 1950–2007 (as % of adult population)

Affiliation	1950	1990	2002	2007
Episcopalian	13	10	3	1
Independent	38	36	31	31
Calvinistic Methodist	31	33	26	22
Baptist	<1	1	1	1
Total	82	80	61	55

Sources: 1950 data are from Owen, 'Chapel and Community'. 1990 and 2002 data are from Gill, *The 'Empty Church' Revisited*, 48–52; as Gill does not provide a denominational breakdown of the 2002 figure, I have estimated it from the proportionate decline in the overall membership, moderated by the recollections of informed local respondents. The 2007 Independent and Calvinistic Methodist figures were compiled by Beryl Griffiths from chapel annual reports. The 2007 Episcopalian figure was provided by the Church in Wales priest-in-charge.

was apparent in the number of chapels (now down to five) and in the deployment of clergy. In the 1950s, there were two Episcopalian priests and two dissenting ministers. By the 1980s, Independents and Calvinistic Methodists were sharing a pastor, and in 2003 the Llanuwchllyn chapels were added to the charges of a Calvinistic Methodist minister in Bala.

A far-reaching change in chapel life is visible in the recent and marked fall in the number of young people involved in the chapels. Between 1945 and 1990, the number of junior members recorded in the annual reports declined in tandem with adult membership. In nine out of ten five-yearly points between 1945 and 1990, the number of children was between 28 and 35 per cent of adult membership. The one rogue data point was for 1945, which is explained by wartime dislocations. But, in 1995, the percentage of child members fell to 16 per cent, and by 2005 was down to just 12 per cent. Like the British churches generally, the chapels were ageing.

The greatest change for the Episcopalians came shortly after Gill's second study. The remaining Episcopalians of Llanuwchllyn, Llangower, and Llanycil were persuaded to close their churches, sell the properties, and invest in the dramatic and beautiful refurbishment of the parish church in Bala. But the people did not move with the assets: in 2009, only eight people on the electoral roll of the new combined parish resided in Owen's original research area. There were then still four chapel buildings in use, but in reality there were just two congregations. The Independents met in the village hall in Llanuwchllyn in winter and in the cavernous and hence hard-to-heat Yr Hen Gapel during the summer. Occasionally there were services in the Carmel and Peniel chapels, but these were attended by the same people as attended the village hall and Yr Hen Gapel. The Calvinistic Methodists had one chapel.

Llanfihangel Yng Ngwynfa, Powys

My third research site is the civil parish of Llanfihangel yng Ngwynfa, the subject of Alwyn D. Rees's celebrated *Life in a Welsh Countryside*.[31] It covers about 15 square miles of upland country in northern Montgomeryshire (now Powys), bounded by the Berwyn hills to the north and the River Vyrnwy to the south. When Rees studied it, Llanfihangel was a largely self-contained parish in which most of the 500 or so inhabitants were engaged in farming. Nine-tenths of the population lived in scattered farms and cottages, and the rest were in three hamlets: Llanfihangel, Dolanog, and Pontlogel (now known as Llwydiarth).

The population had long been in decline by 1940, when it was only half its 1841 size. That decline continued so that the 1981 census showed only 381 people. However, it then grew, and by 2001 was over 800 again. In growing, it became more diverse. In 1940, nine out of ten heads of household had been born in the parish. In 1997, only 61 per cent were born in the parish or a neighbouring parish. The 2001 census showed 44 per cent of residents born outside Wales and that was reflected in language use. In 1940, everyone spoke Welsh, and more than half said they spoke nothing but. In 1997, 65 per cent said they were fluent and 19 per cent had some Welsh.[32]

Although the numbers involved in farming had been greatly reduced, farming and forestry still formed the largest employment sector (with over 25 per cent in 2001). Car ownership and greater economic integration had combined to remove most of the shops. As Victoria Morgan summarizes: 'The facilities of the parish are declining, with only one shop left and reduced post office facilities, yet the present-day parish has an air of quiet prosperity about it,' a considerable contrast with the poverty and decay that Rees found.[33]

Rees readily ascribed a church or chapel affiliation to every resident in the parish (and, remarkably, included maps with lines linking individual farms with the chapels at which their inhabitants worshipped). In 1940, there were four Episcopalian churches that together claimed some 170 people. There were four Independent chapels to which some 152 people were affiliated. Three Calvinistic Methodist chapels had the allegiance of twenty-six families. Two Wesleyan chapels were supported by seventeen families. Finally, there were two Baptist families; their chapel closed while Rees was doing his fieldwork.

Llanfihangel had already seen a significant decline in attendance at the chapels since the majority were built (usually between 1820 and 1850) or expanded (in the last quarter of the nineteenth century). This is part explained by the halving of the population, but there was also a visible decline in levels of commitment. 'Practically all the inhabitants have retained their membership of chapels and churches, but only half of them attend services regularly.'[34] None of the chapels held midweek meetings and 'at least three of the smaller chapels' had no Sunday school.

By 1997, there had been some rationalization. Ten chapels had become six, but only two had services every week; the rest rotated services in a mini-circuit. By 2008, only one chapel had weekly services, the time of which varied depending on which preacher was available when, and services were suspended for the lambing season. There had also been considerable rationalization of the churches. Llanfihangel parish church was now part of the benefice of

Table 2.4. Church and chapel affiliation, Llanfihangel, 1940–2008 population

Affiliation	1940	1997	2008
Episcopalian	34	14	10
Independent	30	17	12
Calvinistic Methodist	21	20	10
Wesleyan Methodist	13	2	1
Baptist	2	0	0
Total	100	53	33

Sources: 1940 data are from Rees, *Life in a Welsh Countryside*, 112. The 1997 data are from Gilbert, 'Religion', 105–8. The 2008 figures are from local clergy.

'Garthbeibio with Lannerfyl with Llangadfan with Llanfihangel yng Nghwynfa with Llwydiarth'. Pont Robert and Dolanog were part of the benefice of 'Meifod with Llangynyw with Pont Robert with Pont Dolanog'. Typical attendance at all four churches combined was only thirty-one.

There had also been a significant shift in the age profile of churchgoers, with the almost complete collapse of the Sunday school system. A member of Sardis remembered that in the 1960s almost every child in the local primary school was also a member of the Band of Hope and regularly attended the chapel's Sunday school, where they were led by the same teachers who taught them secular lessons during the week. In 2008, the one viable Sunday school attracted fewer than ten children.

The change in the religious culture of Llanfihangel can be summarized thus. In 1940, everyone had some church or chapel connection and around half the people typically attended services. In 2009, affiliation was around a third and attendance typically less than half that.

Llansantffraid Glyn Ceiriog, Wrexham

About 20 miles north of Llanfihangel lies the Ceiriog valley. Despite its proximity to England and its natural beauty, relative inaccessibility has prevented it from becoming a popular tourist resort like the Vale of Llangollen to the north: the road through the valley is a dead end. In 1861, the population was 738, and by the time of Ronald Frankenberg's fieldwork it had grown to around 1,000, mostly employed in, or in servicing, agriculture and quarrying. In 1923, it was proposed to flood the valley to form a reservoir to supply Warrington; as the town was known for its breweries, opponents were able to

Table 2.5. Church and chapel affiliation, Llansantffraid Glyn
Ceiriog, 1905–2008 adult population

Affiliation	1953	2008
Episcopalian	10	5
Scotch Baptist	3	0
Welsh Baptist	54	6
Wesleyan	2	0
Calvinistic Methodist	7	6
Total	76	17

Sources: The 1953 data are from Frankenberg, *Village on the Border,* 57–8.
The 2008 figures are from local clergy.

campaign against 'Taking the W out of Wales to make Ales'. The valley was
saved by the opposition of Welsh MPs, who cited the judgement of David
Lloyd George that the area was 'a little bit of heaven on earth, which must be
preserved at all costs'.[35]

Glyn Ceiriog lost residents through the 1960s and 1970s but then grew
again to around 1,300 in 2008 as it experienced an influx of incomers from
England. Only half the 2001 residents had been born in Wales (as compared
to 77 per cent for Llanuwchllyn). The closure of the quarries, and the attendant
decline of rail traffic, removed the major source of male employment, but the
closeness to Chirk and Wrexham allowed commuting to work, which was
reflected in sectoral distribution. Health and social work was the largest
sector, with wholesale and retail trade second, and manufacturing third.
Owing to the proximity of England and the high proportion of incomers,
Glyn Ceiriog was linguistically the least Welsh of the four sites: only 35 per
cent are described in the 2001 census as speaking Welsh.

Frankenberg listed five sites of worship in 1953: the parish church of
St Ffraid and the Sion (Baptist), Salem (Scotch Baptist), Soar (Calvinistic
Methodist), and Bethel (Wesleyan) chapels.[36] There were two full-time resident
clergy: the parish priest and a Baptist minister. When asked by Frankenberg,
most people claimed a religious affiliation. As Table 2.5 shows, two-thirds
of the village belonged to one of its four chapels. Frankenberg describes the
remainder as Episcopalian. His comment that some people responded to his
'What religion are you?' with something along the lines of 'Nothing, really.
But you'd better put "Church", hadn't you?' suggests a degree of nominalism.
As if pre-empting the criticism that the figure of 300 members claimed by
the Welsh Baptist chapel was implausibly high, he adds: 'I have seen congregations of at least 150 attend on important occasions.'[37] If only half the

membership turn out on special occasions, then typical weekly attendance might have been as little as a third.

By the time of my restudy, church or chapel participation was rare. The parish church was united with St Garmon's in Llanarmon Dyffryn Ceiriog to the south and Pontfadog to the east, and all three were served by one vicar. The electoral roll showed thirty-seven members, and typical attendances were around half that figure. A joint service in St Garmon's in November 2008 was attended by only eighteen people, and a third of them were tourists staying in the hotel opposite the church. Only two of Frankenberg's four chapels remained: Soar and Sion. Bethel had been demolished and Salem was for sale. Of the chapels outside the immediate village, one had become a private house and the other alternated services with the Pandy chapel. All the extant chapels (and four others) were in the charge of one supposedly retired Calvinistic Methodist minister.

That the collapse of the village's religious life is neither unusual, nor explained by villagers worshipping further afield, is clear if we extend our survey. Three chapels in Pandy and Nantyr that in 1905 had claimed some 200 members now had fewer than 20. The Tregeiriog Calvinistic Methodist chapel, with 135 adherents in 1905, was a private house. In 1905, the three chapels in Llanarmon drew 234 adherents from a population that was barely higher; in 2008 the last extant chapel had twelve attenders, all elderly. Of the seven chapels along the road from Glyn Ceiriog to Chirk that were active in the 1950s, only one was still open, and it had fewer than ten members.

The Big Picture

In writing a 1948 accompaniment to the drawings of Kenneth Rowntree, Gwyn Jones said of the chapels: 'today their power weakens, but for three Welshmen out of four the gleam of the varnished pew, the smell of the polished linoleum, the ecstatic rustle of a rising congregation, and maybe the taste of a hymn-book cover, are unforgettably part of those childhood years when in sensuous innocence we stood a rung nearer heaven.'[38] Jones is right about the weakening power of the chapels (and churches); all four of my original authors note major declension since the nineteenth century and that continued. Well over half the places of religious worship open in the late 1950s have now closed and few of the remaining ones offer a regular weekly service. The decline in affiliation has been severe, and the fall in attendance worse, but worst of all is the disappearance of the Sunday schools. As well as losing their schools, Sundays have lost their distinctive and oppressive stillness. Even chapelgoers are no longer much constrained by sabbatarianism. In the 1950s, two services and an intervening Sunday school would consume most of the day. Now, with just a single, usually morning, service, churchgoers can spend the rest of the day in secular leisure. One final change: teetotalism is known now only (if at all) as a source of humour.

In metropolitan Britain, the decline of the mainstream denominations has been slightly offset by the growth of the charismatic and independent evangelical fellowships discussed in Chapter 5. There was little or no sign of this in my four sites. A few people in Llanfrothen attended an evangelical church in Penrhyndeudraeth that was somewhat charismatic, but that interest was too weak to disrupt the conclusion reached by analysing the distribution of what Peter Brierley calls 'New Churches': the appeal of such innovations fades as one moves further from the affluent urban south of England.

To introduce a theme taken up in Chapter 4, it is noticeable that the collapse of churchgoing has been accompanied by greater interdenominational cooperation. In all four sites, Independents, Baptists, and Calvinistic Methodists shared pastors and alternated services. Unlike the situation in Devon and in Cumbria (see Chapter 3), there was little or no cooperation between the chapels and the Church of Wales. Methodism in Wales has always been further in ideology and ritual from Episcopalianism than its English counterpart. That divide was deepened by the social class and nationalist associations of Welsh dissent. After it lost its 'established' (and taxpayer-funded) status, the Church in Wales did its best to stress its Welsh identity, but for many it remained the church of the English.[39] It is certainly the church of the English language. In my research areas, the chapels operated primarily in Welsh, while the Church in Wales services were generally in English, with a smattering of Welsh to placate local sensibilities.[40]

One of the trends suggested by national surveys since the 1980s is a deepening rift between churchgoers and the rest of the population, and we can see that in the introversion of the chapels. Many lacked notice boards to inform the passer-by of service times. Even members could become confused; as one said: 'Miss one Sunday and you don't know what's happening the next.' The Church in Wales buildings did have freshly painted signs, but potential customers would have been put off by the elaborate pattern of service rotation between underused sites. Despite their best evangelistic efforts, the churches and chapels served only their own small tiny memberships. Beyond attending funerals and weddings, most people had no contact with this world. Thirty years before my research, Daniel Jenkins said of many small chapels that they 'have come to think of themselves as virtually private affairs, more like families or at most clubs than public institutions open to all'.[41] As congregations shrank further, casual attendance became ever more daunting. That the chapels conducted services in Welsh excluded the growing English-speaking population, but the Church in Wales has in many areas declined faster than the chapels, which suggests a general lack of interest in Christianity.

Many of those to whom I talked in North Wales seemed reluctant to accept this obvious explanation of chapel decline: their preferred cause was demographic. They cited general depopulation or referred to the disappearance of a local industry that had once employed chapel members: the closure of the Glyn Ceiriog or the Croesor quarries, for example. Although the decline in chapel membership from the nineteenth century to the period of the initial studies could be blamed on depopulation, its continued fall over the period covered by my restudies generally cannot—Llanuwchllyn is the exception—because, in three of the four areas, population in 2008 was much as it was in the 1950s.

However, the demography explanation is correct in one important respect: the people might be as numerous but they were very different people. William-Ellis's policy of encouraging intellectuals and artists was unusual in the 1950s, but from the 1960s the lure of cheap property and beautiful scenery attracted the university-educated middle-class English. The old mill in Pandy became the studio-saleroom of an artist who worked in glass. One of the Llanarmon chapels became the studio of an archaeological illustrator. If they were typical of their class, such people will not have been churchgoing Christians; such spiritual interests as they did bring are likely to have been more New Age than chapel.

Immigration compounded a familial change. Like the rest of Britain, rural Wales has experienced a fundamental change in class structure, with white-collar work replacing manual work in extractive industries and manufacture. Many of the carriers of this change were the children and grandchildren of locals, but they left for higher education and they returned with more cosmopolitan outlooks. Especially if they had children, they valued the peace, the lack of crime, the clean air, and the scenery, and they had a sentimental attachment to the idea of community, but they did not share the faith of the chapels that had once been at the heart of those communities.

Religiosity, Cohesion, and Isolation

To summarize, at the starting points for my comparisons (which range between 1940 and 1962), over three-quarters of the adults of my four parishes claimed church or chapel affiliation; when I updated the figures, they ranged from 55 per cent for Llanuwchllyn, 33 per cent for Llanfihangel, 17 per cent for Glyn Ceiriog, and just 6 per cent for Llanfrothen. As both local sources and analysts (me included) used some imaginative estimation to construct these data, we should not make too much of the specific figures, but the relative differences are large enough to be reliable. Religion is now moribund in Llanfrothen, weak in Glyn Ceiriog, healthier in Llanfihangel, and most robust in Llanuwchllyn.

What explains this pattern? It is certainly not the case that, by providing everyone with some form of worship that suits their preferences, a high degree of religious diversity made a difference. The Church of Wales was proportionately stronger in Llanfihangel, but all four areas initially offered the same alternatives. Furthermore, to take up a theme developed in Chapter 4, interest in the theological disputes that divided the chapels in the nineteenth century had waned to the point where they were almost interchangeable. In particular, only their formal denominational titles maintained the Calvinism of the Scotch Baptists and the Calvinistic Methodists. If not diversity, then what?

Data from the 2001 census allow us to compare various social indices such as age, levels of education, importance of agriculture to the local economy, and social class: none is strongly correlated with the differences in religious vitality. Were it not for Llanfrothen (which is furthest from the border), distance from England, which in the pre-electronic media age is a decent surrogate for the press of cosmopolitan culture, would be a strong variable. The strongest variable (again if we leave aside Llanfrothen) is language. The gradient for Welsh-speaking (with Llanuwchllyn at 79 per cent, Llanfihangel at 59, and Glyn Ceiriog at just 35) not surprisingly mirrors that for the proportion of people born in Wales, and it matches that for religious vitality. As with our three Scottish islands, it looks as though a minority language retarded secularization. The anomalous status of Llanfrothen is almost certainly due to population size and churn. It was the least populous parish to begin with and the family stability that best reproduces any distinctive culture was undermined by William-Ellis's policy of encouraging English intellectuals and by the popularity of holiday home ownership.

Even in the 1960s, when sociologists began to write extensively about secularization, it was common to contrast the piety of the British peripheries with the secularity of the cosmopolitan centre. Wales, like Scotland, was markedly more Christian than England, and, within Wales, Welsh-speaking rural areas were more religious than the urban areas. That more than half the people of Llanuwchllyn retain some sort of chapel affiliation still sets them well above the national average, but the period covered by my restudies has seen the gap close. Two underlying trends—attendance falling faster than affiliation and a relative failure to recruit children—suggest that the peripheries are no longer that isolated. Improved transport links, mass communication, the decline of local media, greater occupational mobility, regional development policies, and the centralization of productive enterprises have all made everywhere in Britain more like everywhere else. The second great strength of Welsh religion—the strong association between chapel and Welsh identity—has also been sapped by the success of the campaigns to promote the Welsh language and create a devolved assembly. The stronger the secular base for Welshness, the less need for a religious version.

Miners

As for fishing, the unpredictably dangerous nature of mining is commonly assumed to encourage religiosity and superstition. All miners risk rock falls, but, because bituminous mines were pervaded by flammable gases, liable to be ignited by sparks from metal implements or by the explosives used to loosen the coal, colliers constantly faced the possibility of mass fatalities. For miners, 'intimations of their mortality were an ever-present reality as they worked in the mine, sensed in every creak of timber, fall of stones, or flicker of the lamp'.[42] John Harvey rightly notes that Nonconformity became the religion of the Welsh coalfields in the nineteenth century and that 'the culture of the collier was thus largely that of the chapel'.[43] Colliers praying and singing hymns underground provided one of the motifs of the 1904–5 Welsh revival.[44] And the extraordinary preponderance of Methodist lay preachers among the founders and first officials of colliers unions (especially in Durham and Northumberland) is sometimes expanded to imply widespread piety in the coalfields.[45] As I noted at the start of this discussion, to the extent that unpredictable danger plays any part in encouraging piety, it is not because individuals respond to fear by becoming religious, but because long-term living with threat creates a corresponding culture, which is passed from generation to generation. Social responses to any new stimulus will be shaped by the general extant culture and that requires a stable community base. What sets mining and fishing apart is not directly the vulnerability of the workers but the internal cohesion of the communities based on those industries. In explaining the appeal of the Brethren to the fisherfolk of the north-east of Scotland, Dickson notes that 'the communal nature of fishing way of life was a factor here'.[46] Webster makes the same point for Gardenstown.[47] The social structure of fishing and mining communities provided a bulwark against secularization and thus allowed attitudes that were once far more widespread to survive in those isolated pockets. Pit villages were hastily thrown up around mine workings, and miners lived in colliery property, so that almost everyone in a crowded confined area worked in the same pit. Because pit villages were densely populated and isolated, collier families intermarried. Colliers worked in teams that shared the profits of their labours. Thus not just their safety but their incomes rested on mutual reliance. The result was an unusually high degree of social integration and the possibility of close monitoring. The internal cohesion of mining and fishing communities was reinforced by the hostility of the wider society: fisherfolk were often regarded as queer by their farming neighbours and 'coal-mining communities were generally regarded with some distrust and suspicion by other workers'.[48]

The importance of community structure can be seen when we look at the religious culture of a body of Canadian miners. From 1895 to 1966, iron ore was extracted from Bell Island, Newfoundland, and, through extensive interviewing with former miners, Gail Weir was able to reconstruct the culture of Wabana in some detail.[49] The contrast with the Durham miners is considerable. Weir makes almost no mention of folklore or work-related superstition, and her only mention of religion concerns the international Catholic custom of not eating meat on a Friday. The contrast with the pious Methodists of the Durham coalfields might be explained by the work being considerably safer. Because the iron ore mines were not gaseous, there was a low accident rate, and such injuries and fatalities as did occur were correctly blamed on human error. But there are also considerable differences in community structure. Many miners lived off Bell Island and travelled to it for the working week. Very many had worked in other jobs in towns and cities in mainland Canada. British miners tended to move between pits as the economics and geology made some unviable, but they stayed in the industry and often in the same small area. The Wabana miners moved in and out of the industry depending on its health and prosperity. And they were a small proportion of the total population of Bell island. Thus, even if iron-ore mining had been as dangerous as coal mining, it was not rooted in a stable social structure that could create and sustain a distinctive common culture.

New Towns

One final set of examples will reinforce my point. One government response to Britain's growing population and decaying housing stock was the creation of planned settlements. Under the 1946 New Towns Act, twenty were built in England. Stevenage, Welwyn Garden City, Hatfield, and Hemel Hempstead in Hertfordshire; Harlow and Basildon in Essex; Crawley in Sussex; Newton Aycliffe and Peterlee in County Durham; Bracknell in Berkshire; and Corby in Northamptonshire were in the first wave. They were followed by Skelmersdale in Lancashire; Dawley New Town in Shropshire; Redditch in Worcestershire; Runcorn in Cheshire; and Washington in Tyne and Wear. The third wave consisted of Milton Keynes in Buckinghamshire; Peterborough in Cambridgeshire; Northampton in Northamptonshire; Warrington in Cheshire; and Telford in Shropshire.

As one observer put it, 'denominations struggle to connect with these new town communities'.[50] We can see this in a Durham coalfield example. Named after Peter Lee, a Primitive Methodist, trade unionist, and leading local Labour politician, the new town of Peterlee was constructed to replace the crumbling housing stock of a number of colliery villages, but membership of its new Methodist church was never more than half that of the old chapels it replaced. A similar divide can be seen in the more prosperous south of England. In the 2011 census, 25 per cent of the people of England and Wales said they had 'no religion', but the corresponding figure for Milton Keynes was 34 per cent. One of the first new towns—Hemel Hempstead—had a below-average church attendance rate despite its prosperous class base.[51]

In part, the relative irreligion of the new towns is a predictable result of their novelty: their first residents were migrants, and the very act of moving makes people reassess their commitments. It could be loyalty to the chapel your grandfather built, or the need to take an elderly parent to church, or nostalgic fondness for childhood routines, but staying put allows inertia to sustain churchgoing. Migrants must make a conscious effort to find a new church or chapel; in an-increasingly secular society, it is easy not to bother.[52] But there is also an important point about the social structure of new towns. They were not 'communities' in the sociological sense; they were commuter dormitories, and many of their residents worked, and shopped, and spent their leisure time elsewhere, and with other people. Hence there was no society to sustain a shared religious culture and few effective mechanisms to pass on traditional attachments or to press people on the fringes of organized religion into more active involvement.

Conclusion

Social research rarely produces the neat results of the successful laboratory experiment, but these comparisons of Scottish islands and Welsh rural parishes, augmented by the observations about fishing and mining communities, and new towns, strongly suggest this simple conclusion: distinctive religious cultures are best maintained by the twin forces of internal community cohesion and external isolation. If we then return to the abstract question posed at the top of the chapter, we can reasonably conclude that diversity weakens, rather than strengthens, religion.[53]

Over the twentieth century, growing prosperity has given the vast majority of the British people greater freedom from the need to conform to community expectations. The national institutions of the welfare state have reduced reliance on neighbours; the motor car has made travel easy and cheap, and electronic mass media have brought new cultures to the remotest of places. In the background we have the most general and abstract causes of secularization: a growing egalitarian ethos that prevents the imposition of religious conformity, the growing neutrality of the state, diversity narrowing the reach and the dogmatism of religion, and religious solutions to practical problems being displaced by more effective ones based on scientific technology. But such changes work through local levers. The comparisons explored here strongly suggest that, in the second half of the twentieth century, resistance to secularization rested on the internal cohesion of communities and their relative isolation from the cosmopolitan culture of the outside world.

Notes

1. S. Bruce, *Secularization* (Oxford: Oxford University Press, 2011).
2. P. L. Berger, *The Social Reality of Religion* (London: Faber and Faber, 1967).
3. This is the supply-side, religious-market, or rational-choice approach promoted by Rodney Stark, Roger Finke, and Laurence Iannaccone. It is discussed at length in S. Bruce, *Choice and Religion: A Critique of Rational Choice Theory* (Oxford: Oxford University Press, 1999).
4. B. Malinowski, *The Argonauts of the Western Pacific* (New York: E. P. Dutton, 1961).
5. J. Poggie, 'Ritual Adaptation to Risk and Technological Development in Ocean Fisheries: Extrapolations from New England', *Anthropological Quarterly*, 53 (1980), 122–9.
6. E. B. Simpson, *Folk Lore in Lowland Scotland* (Wakefield: E. P. Publishing, 1976), 142. Of the nine chapters, eight are organized around material objects or superstitions; the only occupation that gets a chapter to itself is fishing.
7. F.-J. Brown, 'Faith, Fear and Folk Narrative: Belief and identity in Scottish Fishing Communities', Aberdeen: University of Aberdeen, Ph.D. thesis, 2010. A history of the Brethren in the same area wrote: 'The perils the men were exposed to at sea certainly had an influence on their piety' (N. Dickson, 'Open and Closed Brethren and their Origins in the North East', in J. Porter (ed.), *After Columba after Calvin: Religious Community in North-East Scotland* (Aberdeen: Elphinstone Institute, 1999), 161).
8. J. Webster, *The Anthropology of Protestantism: Faith and Crisis among Scottish Fishermen* (London: Palgrave Macmillan, 2013), 5.

9. Providence Chapel, 'Forgotten Revival of 1921', http://providencechapel.blogspot. co.uk/2009/12/forgotten-revival-of-1921.html (accessed May 2013).

10. I heard this sort of comment from my father, who was a child of local farmworkers, and from other very elderly relatives.

11. P. F. Anson, *Fisher Folk-Lore* (London: Faith Press, 1964), 11–12.

12. Webster, *Anthropology of Protestantism*, 5.

13. R. Finlayson, 'Parish of Lochs', in *New Statistical Account of Scotland: County of Ross and Cromarty* (Glasgow: William Blackwood and Sons, 1845), 159. The complete texts of this and the original *Statistical Account of Scotland* are available online at http://edina.ac.uk/stat-acc-scot/ (accessed April 2017).

14. The post-1900 Free Church should not be confused with the much smaller Free Presbyterian Church, which split off earlier, in anticipation of the changes that created the larger dissenting rump.

15. *Specimens of the Ecclesiastical Destitution of Scotland in Various Parts of the Country* (Edinburgh: Church Extension Committee of the General Assembly of the Church of Scotland, 1835), 51.

16. A. McKillop, 'Parish of Kinloch', in A. S. Mather (ed.), *Third Statistical Account of Scotland: County of Ross and Cromarty* (Edinburgh: Scottish Academic Press, 1987), 412.

17. H. R. Bowes, '1867 William Grigg', *Quantum Sufficit; Know Your Heritage*, 9 (2010), 16.

18. *Moral Statistics of the Highlands and Islands Compiled from Returns Received by the Inverness Society for the Education of the Poor in the Highlands* (Inverness: Society for Educating the Poor in the Highlands and Islands of Scotland, 1826), 49–50.

19. L. McAllister, *Plaid Cymru: The Emergence of a Political Party* (Bridgend: Seren, 2001).

20. C. William-Ellis, *Architect Errant: The Autobiography of Clough William-Ellis* (Portmeirion: Portmeirion Ltd, 1991); J. Jones, *Clough William-Ellis: The Architect of Portmeirion* (Bridgend: Seren, 1998).

21. P. O'Connor, *Living in Croesor* (London: Hutchinson, 1962).

22. I. Emmett, *A North Wales Village: A Social Anthropological Study* (London: Routledge Kegan Paul, 1964), 99.

23. Emmet, *North Wales Village*, 11.

24. Emmet, *North Wales Village*, 77.

25. O'Connor, *Living in Croesor*, 99.

26. T. M. Owen, 'Chapel and Community in Glan-llyn, Merioneth', in E. Davies and A. D. Rees (eds), *Welsh Rural Communities* (Cardiff: University of Wales Press, 1962), 186.

27. Owen, 'Chapel and Community', 190.

28. J. Humphries, *Freedom Fighters: Wales's Forgotten 'War' 1963–1993* (Cardiff: University of Wales Press, 2008), 18.

29. Humphries, *Freedom Fighters*, 40.

30. R. Gill, *The 'Empty Church' Revisited* (Aldershot: Ashgate, 2003), 42–4.

31. A. D. Rees, *Life in a Welsh Countryside: A Social Study of Llanfihangel yng Ngwynfa* (Cardiff: University of Wales Press, 1950).

32. V. Morgan, 'Introduction', in V. Morgan (ed.), *A Welsh Countryside Revisited: A New Social Study of Llanfihangel yng Ngwynfa* (Llanfihangel yng Ngwynfa: Llanfihangel yng Ngwynfa Social History Group, 2003), 11–4. Details of the chapels in 2002 come from S. Gilbert, 'Religion', in Morgan, *Welsh Countryside Revisited*, 101–14.

33. Morgan, 'Introduction', 10,

34. Rees, *Life in a Welsh Countryside*, 118.

35. J. A. Lewis Jones, *A History of Llanarmon Dyffryn Ceiriog and Tregeiriog* (Llanarmon: Lewis-Jones, 2000), 17.

36. The term 'Scotch' in this title refers, not to ethnicity or geography, but to theology. It means Calvinistic as opposed to Arminian. That is, rather than being universal, the Christian offer of salvation was confined to those whom God had, from creation, chosen. This was the position of the Church of Scotland and other Presbyterian churches until the mid-nineteenth century and can still be found in Baptist churches with 'Grace' in their title.

37. R. Frankenberg, *Village on the Border: A Social Study of Religion, Politics and Football in a North Wales Community* (London: Cohen and West, 1957), 45, 57.

38. G. Jones, *Prospect for Wales* (London: Penguin, 1948), 24.

39. C. Harris and R. Startup, *The Church in Wales: The Sociology of a Traditional Institution* (Cardiff: University of Wales Press, 1999).

40. Although it apparently solves the language problem, bilingualism irritates some Welsh speakers. When I heard her, I was impressed by the Vicar of Bala's fluency in shifting back and forth between Welsh and English, but after the service a group of locals complained to me that any use of English was a betrayal of the area's Welsh heritage.

41. D. Jenkins, *The British: Their Identity and their Religion* (London: SCM Press, 1975), 47.

42. J. Harvey, *Image of the Invisible: The Visualization of Religion in the Welsh Nonconformist Tradition* (Cardiff: University of Wales Press, 1999), 35.

43. Harvey, *Image of the Invisible*, 33. In the 1970s, the Calvinistic Methodists changed their name to Presbyterian. Rather than strictly using the time-appropriate formal title, I have used whichever is clearer in the context.

44. C. R. Williams, 'The Welsh Religious Revival, 1904–5', *British Journal of Sociology*, 3 (1952), 242–59.

45. R. F. Wearmouth, *The Social and Political Influence of Methodism in the Twentieth Century* (London: Epworth Press, 1957); T. Mason, 'Lee, Peter (1864–1935), Trade Unionist', in *Oxford Dictionary of National Biography* (Oxford: Oxford University Press, 2004).

46. Dickson, 'Open and Closed Brethren', 161.

47. Webster, *Anthropology of Protestantism*, 5–6.

48. P. F. Mason, *The Pit Sinkers of Northumberland and Durham* (Stroud: The History Press, 2012), 98.

49. G. Weir, *The Miners of Wabana* (St John's, Newfoundland: Breakwater, 1989).

50. C. Baker, 'Religious Faith in the Exurb Community', *City*, 9 (2009), 110.

51. C. D. Field, *Britain's Last Religious Revival* (Basingstoke: Palgrave Macmillan, 2015).

52. P. J. Richter and L. J. Francis, *Gone but not Forgotten: Church Leaving and Returning* (London: Darton, Longman & Todd, 1998).

53. Bruce, *Choice and Religion*, makes the same case with comparisons of the Baltic states and the countries of Scandinavia.

3

Social Roles of the Clergy

Cumbria and Devon

At the end of every year the Queen honours people who have performed some outstanding public service. In 2002, she made the Revd Tim Alban Jones a 'member of the British Empire' (or MBE) in recognition of

> the eloquence with which he spoke on behalf of a community haunted by the murders of Holly Wells and Jessica Chapman...the Prince of Wales, the Prime Minister and the new Archbishop of Canterbury are all known to have been impressed by the way he took on the role of unofficial spokesman for the town.[1]

Holly Wells and Jessica Chapman were 10-year-old girls from the small Cambridgeshire village of Soham. Their bodies had been found near RAF Lakenheath in Suffolk on 17 August 2002 by a local farmworker. They had been murdered by Ian Huntley, a local school caretaker. Jones counselled the victims' parents, helped the friends of the dead girls come to terms with their loss, and acted as spokesman for the parents and for the village. His response to his honour was typical: 'This has come completely out of the blue. I wasn't expecting it one little bit...I feel greatly privileged, but I must stress that I was only doing what priests who are not in the media spotlight do every day of the year.'[2]

This chapter has two purposes. First, it adds local detail to our understanding of the changing status of religion in Britain since 1945 by updating the two classics produced by W. M. 'Bill' Williams, the doyen of British community studies; in particular it demonstrates the consolidation of the churchgoing community, as fewer people attended but did so more consistently and frequently. It then considers why the clergy continue to play important social roles despite the unpopularity of the faith they represent. That task is framed as a test of the salience of what Grace Davie has called 'vicarious religion'.[3]

Gosforth 1951

In the early 1950s, Williams spent three years in the civil parish of Gosforth, an area of just over 11 square miles on the 'western fringe of the Lakeland fells of Cumberland'.[4] His main focus was the link between forms of agriculture and social structure, but he reported a considerable amount of statistical and impressionistic material about religion.

In 1951, the nuclear energy facility at Windscale (later renamed Sellafield), which had begun construction four years earlier, was providing well-paid labouring work, but most people in Gosforth still worked on or close to the land. Just under half of the parish's inhabitants were employed adults and, of those, a third worked on farms (half as owners; the rest evenly divided between their sons and their wage labourers). Retail was the next largest sector, and construction work at Windscale came third.

Although almost everyone identified with the Church of England, participation rates were low, and this was not new. Williams calculates that between 1890 and 1895, excluding Easter, Whitsun and Christmas, on average fewer than seven people took communion on a Sunday. In the first decades of the twentieth century that figure rose to just under ten, but then fell back to just under eight in 1950. This is striking because of its contrast with the almost universal uptake of Anglican offices for rites of passage. Apart from the few dissenters—there were thirty-six in 1950—everyone was baptized, wed, and buried by the Church. Yet weekly church attendance was very low. The tension between the expectations of the people and the Church were most apparent in the ritual of confirmation. Apart from those who had died or left the parish, everyone who was baptized was later confirmed. However, while the Anglican incumbent saw confirmation as the start of adult involvement in the life of the Church, his parishioners saw it as a celebration of maturity and as an end to the churchgoing that was imposed on children. In July 1950 the Bishop of Penrith confirmed thirty-five candidates, but only six made their first Communion on the following Sunday.[5]

Unusually, the incumbent was unpopular. Some parishioners were offended by his frequent soliciting for church funds and his equally frequent criticism of their reluctance to attend church, keep the Sabbath, or observe Lent. As the low rates of church attendance pre-dated the incumbent, we may suppose this was more excuse than explanation. Some non-attenders were honest: Williams notes that 'most people admitted that they did not go to church "like we ought to", and conceded that the few regular churchgoers "are better folk than us likely" '.[6]

While Methodism had been strong in the urban and mining areas of Cumberland, it was relatively weak in the farmlands. Methodist membership in Gosforth peaked in 1879, five years after the chapel opened, at thirty-three. By 1918 it had fallen to ten and it stayed there.[7] The Williams study coincided with the chapel's low point. Its membership was kept from single digits only by the unusual longevity of the female members of the Barnes family, the village's main shopkeepers. In 1917, Robert P. Barnes was chapel steward, secretary, and treasurer. In 1951, one of his daughters held those three offices and another was completing her forty-fourth year as organist. However, the chapel had one asset: a popular Sunday school run by three young women who taught at a girls' boarding school in nearby Seascale. In addition, there were five Quakers who worshipped with the Methodists. There were eighteen Roman Catholics, descended not from old English Catholic families but from nineteenth-century Irish immigrants; they worshipped in Egremont. There was also one Christian Science couple and a lone Presbyterian.

Not surprising given the relative unpopularity of church and chapel-going, religiously inspired social mores had little or no impact on Gosforth. The people were not puritanical. Illegitimacy was commonplace and sabbatarianism almost unknown. 'In general... religious beliefs have little restrictive effect on social life. Indeed Sunday is the most important day of the week for those interested in football and cricket.'[8] Despite the rector complaining about it in his parish newsletter, dances were held during Lent. The lack of religious enthusiasm had one benefit: there was no hostility between Anglicans and dissenters. Methodists and Catholics sent their children to the local church primary school and routinely supported parish fund-raising events and Anglicans responded by sending their children to the Methodist Sunday school. Such amity existed despite church and chapel recruiting from different constituencies. While the farmers were Anglicans, the Methodists were mostly tradesmen. In 1895, only four of eleven chapel trustees were farmers. In 1920, only one of sixteen was a farmer. In the 1950s, the trustees comprised two spinsters, two married women, one widow, a storeman, a wholesale grocer, a grocery manager, a schoolmaster, an ironmonger, a retired truant catcher, a local government civil servant, a chemist, a gardener, an accountant, and an insurance agent.

Gosforth 2010

The area around Gosforth is now the Lake District national park and the village 'has a distinctly more genteel feel, being largely inhabited by members of the "service classes" rather than agriculturally-oriented professions'. [9] In 2010, farming employed few people: at 9 per cent, less than manufacture

(28 per cent) and real-estate sales (12 per cent), and barely ahead of hospitality and education (both 8 per cent).[10] Although the disappearance of tradesmen and craftsmen from the village might suggest economic decline, it actually reflected the greater mobility afforded by prosperity: van-owning skilled workers could serve a very large area.

Gosforth's geographical remoteness explains its ethnic homogeneity. In the 2001 census, less than 1 per cent of residents identified with a non-Christian religion and 84 per cent chose the Christian label. However, active participation in church or chapel had declined from its already low 1950s level. One inadvertent mark of the change is that, simply by asking a few well-informed people, Williams was able to assign a denominational affiliation to every family in the parish. My attempts to repeat that exercise failed completely for two rather different reasons. First, the growth in commuting meant that residents—especially those without children in the local school—were less well acquainted with each other than they had been in Williams's day. Second, most parishioners were not known to have any affiliation or that affiliation was not known, which may be much the same thing.

There had been some rationalization of the clergy. Since the 1970s the Gosforth benefice has included the small remote churches of Wasdale Head and Nether Wasdale, and the incumbent was expected to spend one day a week on diocesan work: in total an effective halving of the time available to Gosforth. The parish church still provided rites of passage, but these were much less popular than in 1951. Then all babies were baptized in the church; in the period 2005–10 only half were. It is difficult to use church weddings as an index of popularity because there are now so many other permitted venues and because many people chose to be married in places such as Wasdale Head, which are especially attractive or to which they have some link other than residence. One couple whose banns were read in the Gosforth church lived 30 miles away and had no church connection, but the bride-to-be had sung in the choir as a teenager. The incumbent still officiated at most funerals, though he noted that the families now often wanted him 'not to overdo the religion bit'.

For estimating the popularity of religion, the two most significant changes were in confirmation and church attendance. With only eight confirmations in the period 2005–8, it is clear that this was no longer a communal rite of passage but was closer to entry to membership; that is, as it had lost popularity, confirmation had regained its original religious significance. Gosforth had reduced the number of its services, but, unlike many rural parishes, it still had a mid-morning service every Sunday. A 'traditional language' *Book of Common*

Prayer communion was celebrated at 8.00 a.m. once a month. Every Sunday there was a 10.00 a.m. communion using *Common Worship*. Once a month the service was followed by prayers for healing. Sunday attendance was usually around fifty, with fifteen people attending the early communion and between thirty-five and forty at the family service. The congregation had very few young members; the typical attender was a woman in her sixties.

We have accurate measures for two weak indices of Anglican involvement: the electoral roll and Easter communication. Electoral roll figures are not available for the 1950s, but the three decades since 1981 showed a decline from 18 to 12 per cent of the adult population.[11] Easter communion has also declined: from around 20 per cent in the 1950s to some 10 per cent in 2011. However, there was a counter-trend in the numbers taking communion every week. In 1951, taking communion at Easter (the minimum qualification for good standing in the Church of England) was more than ten times as popular as that of any other Sunday; in 2011, it was only twice as popular, and that was the result of the numbers taking communion on an average Sunday rising as the Easter communicants fell.[12] Appearances can deceive, but the suggestion that the numerically diminished church core was in good heart is reinforced by my impressions of the church building: notice boards were neat and provided necessary information for occasional visitors, and the church was well decorated and in good order. Whether this was a consequence of the nuclear industry providing the area with well-educated professional people or the parish having a popular resident incumbent is hard to know; I was offered both explanations.

Methodism had also declined, though it was in such a weak condition when Williams lived in Gosforth that there was little scope for further shrinking short of closure: the fate of half the twenty-three chapels in the Whitehaven circuit in 1940. The chapel now had only an evening service on Sunday, and that was generally attended by fewer people than were notional members. As with the parish church, there was a discernible Windscale effect, with numbers in the 1960s going up as middle-class professionals moved into the area. But the boost was short-lived; by 1991 membership had fallen back to its 1951 level of just twelve people and by 2010 attendances were often in single figures. However, the chapel served a variety of largely secular purposes: one day had a late afternoon 'tea and chat', another had an 'armchair Pilates' class for the elderly, and its 'messy church' (essentially a fun Sunday school) attracted children whose parents were not members.

For completeness I should add that none of the decline in churchgoing in Gosforth was offset by any significant number of people travelling out of the area to attend the sort of charismatic fellowships discussed in Chapter 5. In summary, if we combine Anglican Easter communicants and Methodist members to create a category of 'more than nominally Christian', for Gosforth that figure was 20.0 per cent in 1951 and 11.5 per cent in 2011.

Northlew 1958

Williams followed his Gosforth research with a similar study of Northlew, a Devon farming community that he anonymized as *Ashworthy*. Seven miles west of Okehampton, Northlew was, like Gosforth, a remote farming community, but its religious culture was different. While Gosforth was overwhelmingly Anglican, Northlew, like most of the south-west of England, was strongly affected by Nonconformity. Indeed, it can claim to have had one of the first societies of the Bible Christian strand of Methodism. These were the work of William O'Bryan, an itinerant Wesleyan Methodist preacher who, in 1815, broke with the main body over much the same principles that, outside the south-west, produced the Primitive Methodists.[13] He was invited to Northlew shortly after its chapel had been built, and, as a result of his enthusiastic revival preaching, the local society split. The chapel became the property of the Bible Christians, and the Wesleyans met in private houses until they erected their chapel in 1860. There was a third chapel on the edge of the parish at Widdon. At the time of the 1851 Census of Religious Worship, the parish was fairly evenly divided between Anglicans and Methodists. There were 203 attendances recorded for the two Anglican churches in the parish (Northlew and Ashbury) and 174 attendances at four Methodist sites: the Bible Christian and Wesleyan societies in the village, Providence chapel at Whiddon, and a private house at Higher Goruish.[14]

In 1958, almost everyone in Northlew claimed a religious identity. Only 14 per cent of families were not associated with either church or chapel. Of the remaining 158 households, 47 per cent were Anglican and 38 per cent were Methodist. Williams notes that religious loyalties were sufficiently strong that intermarriage was the subject of some disapproval, but it was nonetheless common: 15 per cent of all households were mixed. Methodists attended Anglican social functions and vice versa, and there were occasional joint services. That mixed-religion families were common in Northlew but rare in Gosforth probably has more to do with the fluidity of Northlew's economic base than with any difference in religious tolerance. In Gosforth, the farmers were Anglican, while the Methodist chapel drew its support from the village's shopkeepers and tradesmen. Most of the farmers had worked the same land for generations, and there was little or no shifting between that class and ancillary occupations. In Northlew, there was far greater movement in and out of the area, between farms, and between occupations. There is also a difference in the county-wide associations of religious identity and occupation. In West Cumberland, Nonconformity was closely associated with mining and heavy industry. In Devon, Methodism recruited well among farmers. So, although Northlew's Anglicans and Methodists had long-standing family loyalties they were reluctant to see abandoned, their affiliation was not reinforced by religious affiliation coinciding with employment.

However, Northlew's church and chapel divide did coincide with other social divisions. Some leisure activities followed denomination lines: the football team and its supporters club, for example, were Anglican. And, as in Banbury (discussed in Chapter 5), the great late-nineteenth-century political division was still in evidence. The Liberal Club officers were nearly all Methodists, while the Conservative Association officers were Anglicans.

Of course, for some people church and chapel ties were weak. As Williams put it: 'the affiliation is given as stated by informants; it is not always supported by attendance at Church or Chapel. Ashworthy has its share of "indifferent believers"'.[15]

The most visible impact of religion in general was keeping the sabbath, which 'makes Sunday a very quiet day in the parish, in contrast to the bustle of weekdays', and the most obvious denominational difference was that 'the Methodists still live according to many of the precepts of their nineteenth-century predecessors. Only a tiny minority ever enter the bar of the village inn.'[16]

Williams does not document church attendance, but from the Registers of Services for St Thomas of Canterbury we know that 9.1 and 10.0 per cent of the adult population took communion in the parish church at Easter in 1951 and 1961 respectively. This was only half the corresponding figures for Gosforth, which reflects the relatively greater popularity of Methodism in Northlew. Although Methodism had been declining since the Edwardian era, it was still a presence at the time of the Williams study: around 20 per cent of adults were members, and, although he does not give attendance figures, if they were comparable to those for chapels elsewhere, more than 10 per cent of the people of Northlew regularly attended the chapel.

Northlew 2011

The Northlew I visited in 2011 had a very different economic base. Numbers working on the land had more than halved, while the service sector had grown almost threefold. Many of the trades present in the 1950s had gone, but new ones—grass engraver, leather worker, mobile hairdresser, interior designer and picture framer, and chartered accountant—had arrived.

Mechanization had already reduced the population before Williams began his work: from 762 in 1881 to 565 in 1951. It fell further through the 1960s and 1970s, but growth in car ownership allowed people working in Okehampton and further afield to stay in the village, and by 1991 the population was above the 1951 level and it remained so. Because it is significant for community spirit, it is worth noting that the high degree of commuting meant that, although the resident population was now as large as when Williams lived in its centre, the village was as quiet on a weekday as it would have been on a Sunday during the *Ashworthy* study. Villagers talked of it as a friendly place, and its silver band and football team were still active, but many residents worked outside the parish and had few strictly local ties.

Not surprising given its location, Northlew remained ethnically 'white British' and nominally Christian. In the 2001 census, less than 1 per cent identified with a religion other than Christianity and only 21 per cent claimed no religion or did not complete the question.

In the late 1960s, active membership of the Church grew. The retiring incumbent noted in 1969: 'This is a closely knit community with a good Church tradition. Lately a number of retired people from London and elsewhere have come into the village and bought old cottages for modernisation. Several of them are instructed Church people.'[17] Their presence was visible in the growth in Easter communicants from 1951 to peak in 1971 before falling steeply and then rising in the first decade of the twenty-first century. Nonetheless, the proportion of active Anglicans in Northlew has grown, largely because the Methodist alternative has declined more quickly.

As with Gosforth, we can see a significant change in attitudes to communion. In 1951, less than 1 per cent of adults communicated on a typical Sunday; in 1981 the figure was 7 per cent and in 2011 it was only 1 per cent lower. The weaker measures of electoral roll registration (from 11 per cent in 1981 to 6 per cent in 2011) and Easter communicating (from 17 per cent at its 1971 peak to 10 per cent in 2011) both show the Gosforth pattern: occasional attendance had declined but the core was relatively more committed. .

When Williams was in Northlew, it had a full-time rector who was also responsible for a second church a mile away at Ashbury (mentioned in Chapter 1). In January 2012, Northlew was one of thirteen parishes in the charge of the Northmoor team ministry of three full-time clergy and a curate: an average of just over three churches per cleric.

Methodism has also lost presence since the 1950s and has similarly responded by reducing clergy and broadening their responsibilities. In 1958, there was a full-time resident minister. In 2005, the minister was responsible for three chapels, and by 2009 he had seven: Chilla, Eworthy, Madworthy, Boasley Cross, Bridestowe, Broadley, and Northlew. When he retired in 2010, he was not replaced (though, as he remained in the village, he continued to take services periodically), and the West Devon circuit spread the work of superintending twenty-two chapels around two full-time and two-part time clergy.

The decline in chapel membership has been considerable: from 20 per cent in 1951 to 4 per cent in 2011. Unlike the parish church, the chapel did not benefit from the growth in population that resulted from immigration. Hence its decline, relative to adult population, accelerated. Or, to put it another way, Methodism had been steadily losing presence among the indigenous population, but its overall penetration has declined precipitously in recent decades because that general unpopularity was reinforced by a lack of appeal to newcomers to the area, who were less chapel-minded than the natives. This reflects their cultural backgrounds. Middle-class town-to-country migrants are now often what one called 'arty kind of people', more likely to describe themselves as spiritual than as religious. For those whose interest in Christianity is more aesthetic than theological, an ancient Anglican church has more appeal than a spartan Nonconformist chapel, because its rituals allow a greater degree of idiosyncratic interpretation than does the praise song, hymn, and sermon service of the Methodists. And the architecture has heritage appeal: if one is going to attend church in order to feel some sense of belonging to a community, the older and more ornate the building the better.

To complete the picture I might add that, as with Gosforth, I could find no evidence of village residents attending services outside the area.

To summarize, in both sites of Williams's community studies, the half-century since his fieldwork had seen a halving of church adherence. Combining the Anglican and Methodist figures can give us a rough-and-ready index of 'more than nominally Christian'. For Gosforth, that figure was 20 per cent in 1951 and 12 per cent in 2011. For Northlew, it was 29 per cent in 1951 and 13 per cent in 2011.

Consolidation

National data for the Church of England confirm the general pattern of consolidation. In 1931, 63 per cent of those who could be troubled to put their names on the electoral roll took communion at Easter. By the 1960s, the ratio had improved to almost three-quarters. In every year of the first decade of the twenty-first century, there were far more Easter communicants than names on the electoral roll: 120 per cent is the average.[18]

This is what we would expect. The churches' decline in popularity has very different effects on the periphery and on the core. In a society where most people attend church, those who are not particularly religious are under considerable pressure (often from family members) to attend at least occasionally. Those who wish to be married in church, to have children baptized, or to have their relatives buried may well feel obliged to support the church before and after to avoid the charge of cynicism. Once churchgoing becomes rare, those whose faith is purely nominal are released from the obligation of pretending otherwise, and the pressure on occasional attenders evaporates. It becomes acceptable not to accompany a churchgoing spouse, and the declining popularity of church weddings, baptisms, and church funerals further reduce reasons for occasional participation.[19]

At the same time, those who are committed to church or chapel feel pressed to attend because they appreciate that they are now an endangered species. Methodist chapels have been known to struggle on for decades with attendances in single figures because the remaining members are acutely aware that only their weekly participation keeps the chapel open. The chapels in Upper Teesdale survived a decade after any rational analysis would have seen them close because people who had moved to Barnard Castle or Middleton returned to attend Sunday services. One woman told me that she would prefer to attend the chapel just across the road from her house in Middleton, but she drove 20 miles every Sunday to a small chapel at the top of the dale because it was the spiritual home of an elderly lay preacher who had given sterling service to the cause: 'if the few of us who live down here don't go, it would be shut and where would that leave him? I'll keep going so long as he does and when he dies, we'll put the keys through the letter box and walk away!'

In brief, the shift from a largely religious to a largely secular society frees those on the fringes of Christendom from any obligation to support a faith they do not embrace. It also increases the pressure on those who wish to maintain the churches to attend more regularly.

Clergy Status and Organization

The Anglican Church's decline in popularity has had its counterpart in four important changes in the clergy. They are no longer drawn from a social class distinctly higher than that from which Nonconformist chapels recruit their pastors. They are now more likely than was previously the case to have entered full-time ministry as a late-life second career. They may well be women. And, to introduce a point pursued in Chapter 4, many now cooperate with clergy from other denominations to maintain a Christian presence where individual denominations are no longer popular enough to stand alone.

With Lew Trenchard only a short drive from Northlew, it is tempting to use the social class of its most celebrated incumbent, Sabine Baring Gould (1834–1924), as a contrast with that of the contemporary rural Anglican cleric. The composer of 'Onward, Christian Soldiers' and 'Now the Day Is Over' owned 3,000 acres and the gift of the living of Lew Trenchard parish to which he appointed himself. And he was wealthy enough to remodel the family manor house and to restore the church. He had a Northlew counter-part in Henry Woollcombe, a member of the local Big House family who was also Archdeacon of Barnstaple and who paid for the rebuilding of the Ashbury church in the 1870s. When Williams studied Gosforth and Northlew, the status of the clergy had been significantly eroded, but the Gosforth incumbent still inhabited the second largest house in the parish, kept a stable of horses, employed servants, and scolded his reluctant parish-ioners. The rector of Gosforth in 1951 was an Oxford graduate. Northlew's Henry Geipel was a graduate of University College, Durham. Both were career clerics. The Northlew incumbent in 2010, like a large proportion of recent ordinands, became a full-time clergyman in midlife. And—an even bigger change—his successor was a woman. The Anglican Church has also changed its structure. Now largely dependent on its current members for financial support, the Church has increasingly abandoned the resident incumbent in every parish model for something closer to the circuit system of the Methodists: a small number of full-time clergy superintending a large number of churches that increasingly depend on lay members and retired clergy to lead worship.[20]

Chapter 4 will consider in detail the growth of ecumenical cooperation that has been forced on the British churches by their decline. Here I note only that in 2010 the superintendent minister of the West Devon Methodist circuit was actually a minister of the United Reformed Church who also worked with the Anglican diocese in training clergy. In Northlew, Anglicans and Methodists cooperated closely and frequently shared services: a relationship aided for a period by the fact that the Anglican priest and the Methodist minister were friends with remarkably similar backgrounds as late entrants to the full-time ministry who had previously worked in agriculture.

Secondary Functions and Vicarious Religion

There is always a danger of oversimplifying when we break time into discrete epochs, but we can appreciate a significant change in the status of religion if we describe the Church as first losing secular roles as the remit of religion narrowed and then trying to find new secular roles as the appeal of the core business of religion declined. In the Middle Ages, in good part because the clergy were often the only literate and educated people in a parish, the Christian Church provided a wide range of services beyond religious offices: it was government administration, welfare provider, educator, major landowner and employer, and doctor and chemist. As societies became more affluent, they also became more differentiated, with religion losing many functions to secular alternatives. In the nineteenth century, the British churches became much narrower, especially after the state took control of education.

What we have seen in the late twentieth century is local congregations consciously seeking secular roles. Much of that revolves around the building.

Cafes and Community Centres

In 2007, *Country Life*, the house magazine of the rural upper classes, ran a competition for the best example of a church being remodelled for secular community use. Very many congregations have made a virtue of necessity by building new community roles into the renovation of unhelpfully large churches. In towns it is common for the worship area to be moved to a newly inserted first floor while the downstairs is converted into flexible multi-purpose space, often incorporating some sort of cafe. Although their new community activity was physically separate from the refurbished chapel, the Northlew Methodists combined providing a new community resource with renovation. Despite a small membership, in 2001 the trustees of the chapel decided to raise funds to refurbish it: 'chapel members started up a 50/50 shop in an unused, but very ancient shed behind the post office, opening for trade for two hours a week every Saturday morning. This was very successful, and even after the first flush of enthusiasm had passed, the money continued to come in.'[21] The shop moved to an area behind the chapel, and it was decided also to provide teas and cakes: 'this has become the focus for an increasing number of people to meet on a Saturday morning. Now, two years later, about 30 to 40 people come through our "café" on an average Saturday. Many come just for a chat and a cup of coffee and enjoy the friendship offered.'[22] Like secular charity shops, church-based community cafes offer opportunities for the active elderly who work in them to do something useful 'while getting out of the house for a few hours', as one elderly lady put it while serving my lunch. In Erdington, Birmingham, an evangelical pastor opened a restaurant; as well as providing food, Oikos arranged exhibitions of work by local artists and ran fund-raising events for local charities.[23] In the Norfolk village of Booton, St Michael the Archangel offered hostel facilities.

After the financial crash of 2008, a large number of congregations started food banks to assist the local poor. One form of social service common to many primarily urban churches was the provision of advice on managing debts. Six Ways Baptist Church in Birmingham provided free English-language classes for immigrants as well as a food bank: as the black pastor—who had previously worked as a nurse—put it: 'We are Christians and we can't just stand by and do nothing.'[24] The Church in Wales has closed many tiny churches, but it has also renovated many remaining ones to provide meeting facilities and kitchens to cater for social events. Port Quay, near Welshpool, divided its high-ceiling nave into two floors to reduce the worship space so that its much-reduced congregation did not feel oppressed by the rows of empty pews but also to provide meeting rooms and a tearoom to serve passing motorists.[25]

Community Identity

Graveyards are obviously repositories of community memories, but many church interiors, with their faded militia flags, war memorials, and plaques testifying to the virtues of long-deceased local grandees, also serve as sites for nostalgia. When the Stocks reservoir in the Forest of Bowland, Lancashire, was created in 1926, the original village disappeared under the water. Some 150 bodies were exhumed and reburied in a new graveyard on higher ground. Although the population was too sparse to justify regular services in the area, some local people expressed a wish to be buried there, and the Fylde Water Board rebuilt St James as a 'Mortuary Chapel'.[26] Its walls are decorated with enlarged photographs of the original village and accounts of local history. People come to seek their ancestors and periodically services are held in summer.

There is a neat symmetry in the fate of the Primitive Methodist chapel in Staithes, North Yorkshire. It is now a museum celebrating the lost culture of what in 1900 was a busy fishing village. A large collection of sepia photographs shows the fisherfolk at work; it also shows the congregations of the village's three chapels: they were the same people. A once-popular institution, having lost its congregation, now serves as a memorial to their work and way of life, which have also ended.

Community Spokesmen and Women

As public spaces that are usually empty most days and times, church buildings provide an important venue for people to respond to local disasters. Even those who become interested in life after death only at times of crises recognize the propriety of expressing their sentiments in buildings that once had a monopoly of managing death. When in 2011 four men were killed at Gleision colliery in Gilybebyll, the church of St John the Evangelist was opened for people 'to light candles, write condolences and sit in quiet reflection'.[27]

The clergy have always been asked to serve the not-particularly-pious, either because their theology saw them as mediators between the entire people and God, or because the church was so popular that the deficiencies of the minority could be overlooked. Now, as we saw with the example of the Soham murders at the start of this chapter, the clergy are often invited to perform largely secular social roles. A few evangelical clergy think that offering their services to those who patently do not take their religious content seriously is to insult their faith, but most clergy will baptize, marry, and bury irrespective of the church attachment of those who solicit or receive such services. Even if the motives of those asking are largely secular, such ceremonies provide a rare opportunity to bring 'a word of God' to people who would otherwise never hear it. As one incumbent explained to me: 'Of course I know that very few people at a funeral actually believe the words I am saying but it still provides the bereaved with some comfort. OK. Social worker rather than priest. But still a good thing.'

Both Northlew and Gosforth offer examples of the clergy responding to a local crisis: an outbreak of foot-and-mouth disease in Devon and mass murders in Cumbria. As one dairy farmer said:

> Before foot-and-mouth in 2001 it was something that happened in the 1960s in Yorkshire. Nothing had happened down here. It was a disease that had been wiped out if you like. It would almost be akin to the Black Death coming back in London. It was something that was not going to happen. Then we heard one of our neighbours had gone down. It was the middle of April when it hit.[28]

All movements of beasts was frozen, families were confined to their farms, thousands of animals were slaughtered, and livelihoods were severely damaged. Practical problems aside, the slaughter caused significant psychological distress. With their background in farming, both the Anglican incumbent and the Methodist minister worked to counsel and comfort those who suffered in the crisis. John Peak, the Methodist, took to the airwaves. A one-off service for Radio Devon, in which he spoke of his own family's experience of losing stock to brucellosis, developed into a regular half-hour monthly slot, shared with the vicar of Hatherleigh: 'The response I got was greater than anything I've ever done. If you had told me that two years ago, I wouldn't have believed you.'[29]

In June 2010, Whitehaven taxi-driver Derrick Bird went on a shooting rampage across west Cumbria. He killed twelve people and wounded a further eleven, some seriously. The rector of Gosforth had the duty of officiating at the funeral of Garry Purdham, a popular local farmer and amateur rugby enthusiast. When the Gleision miners died, it was the local cleric who spoke to the press: 'it has touched a nerve and the community has been so good in the way it has rallied round the families of the four miners. What it has also done is reawaken the sufferings of the past because there will have been people over the decades who will have suffered in various ways as a result of working in mining.'[30]

A Bishop of Liverpool, James Jones, became involved with the families of the football fans who died at Hillsborough in 1989 when he was asked to preside over a tenth-anniversary service. In 2012, he was invited to chair an independent panel inquiring into the causes of the disaster. The Archbishop of York, John Sentamu, when he was vicar of Stepney, was invited to be a member of the Macpherson inquiry that in 1999 reported on the circumstances surrounding the murder of black teenager Stephen Lawrence and on the subsequent police investigation.

It is worth adding that, while some (usually young evangelical) clergy in large towns resent serving people who make no pretence of interest in religion, most clergy are only too happy to perform secular functions. Unlike commercial organizations, which try to confine their benefits to those who pay for them, churches actively encourage what economists call 'free riding'. Churches do not charge an entry fee, and most go out of their way to encourage visitors. They hope that initial contact may turn into supportive involvement, but they do not make their work conditional on such returns. There is an additional reason for the clergy accepting work beyond the narrowly religious: extending their secular roles partially offsets the gloom created by the unpopularity of their primary task. One clergy wife wrote of her husband: 'For 363 days a year he feels a failure, and if numbers are any indicator, he is.'[31]

Such extension is possible only because large parts of the public welcome it. That is, there is still considerable receptivity among the religiously indifferent to secular activities performed by church people. What is at issue is whether this is, as Grace Davie has suggested with the phrase 'vicarious religion', people being religious in a roundabout way.[32] The idea of vicarious religion (that is, some people commissioning others to do religion *on their behalf*) is entirely sensible. Most of the major world religions permit the especially pious to transfer earned religious merit to the less Godly. It is the wish to benefit from the piety of others that explains the medieval Christian practice of paying others to say masses for one's soul postmortem. Wealthy people concerned about their souls founded schools whose pupils were required to pray periodically for their dead benefactors; hospitals and chantries likewise. In the Middle Ages, almost everyone left money to be spent on altar clothes, candles, and masses for their souls. That is clearly vicarious religion, as is the Buddhist convention of lay people feeding the monks in return for the monks earning transferable religious merit on their behalf. Likewise, the Hindu, Taoist, or Buddhist who pays temple or shrine officials to make offerings to the Gods on their behalf. However, in such examples, almost all of those who wish to benefit from the piety of others are themselves believers. There will have been some who cynically used their wealth to compensate for their irreligion, but even they must have believed in the supernatural, in the promises of a life after death, and in the ability of the pious to impress God on their behalf.

The examples I have presented above are importantly different in that it is patently the *secular* functions of the churches, not their religious activities or the beliefs that inform them, that are appreciated or accepted by the non-religious. The poor and indigent who accept alms from the Salvation Army may feel some gratitude that the faith of the Salvationists' causes them to be compassionate, but that is no more evidence that the poor are being 'vicariously religious' in accepting such help than is the willingness of non-religious people to put money in a Salvationist's collecting tin.

Davie uses the idea of vicarious religion to expand the numbers of people we can sensibly describe as religious (and thus to suggest that secularization is not as extensive as it appears), but an almost opposite interpretation is more plausible. It is precisely because few people now take religion seriously that the churches can play secondary roles.

To the extent that the churches and their officials continue to be viewed positively by the general public (and that is considered in detail in Chapter 11), it is not because that public is subconsciously, implicitly, or vicariously Christian; it is because the clergy of the state churches and the larger Nonconformist denominations form the only professional group of people who are experienced and fluent in public speaking, who are expected to care for their 'neighbours' irrespective of their social worth, wealth, charm, or power, and who are generally not self-interested. Any politician setting up a counselling service for farmers affected by foot-and-mouth would have been suspected of partisan self-interest. The MP for Soham could not have acted as community spokesperson after the Huntley murders because the supporters of other parties would have resented their opponent 'feeding off disaster like a shark', as one local churchgoer put it to me. Although organized religion enjoys considerably less prestige than it did in 1900 or 1950, church people are still taken to be honest, decent, caring, and non-partisan. And, even if such qualities have religious origins, it is for those secular characteristics, rather than for any religious underpinning, that the clergy are respected and found useful. Were the churches still powerful, more people would resent them and would object to their attempts to advertise themselves.

Conclusion

This chapter has used the pioneering community studies produced by Bill Williams as the starting point for documenting the decline of the churches in two rural areas on England. It also noted the process of consolidation mentioned in other parts of this study: as churchgoing has become less common, populations have divided more clearly into church and non-church. An entirely unexpected outcome of my restudies of Gosforth and Northlew was having my attention drawn to the continued public role that clergy play in local (and for that matter national) life. Grace Davie and others have argued that, in allowing religious officials to perform such roles, the apparently religiously indifferent majority of the population is being vicariously religious. According respect to the clergy shows that we really appreciate their religious work on our behalf. I have argued that this is a complete misreading. Like eunuchs working in a harem, the clergy are invited to play significant social roles because they are impotent. If contemporary Britain was like Franco's Spain in being divided into pro- and anti-Church factions, then the willingness of apparently anti-Church people to use the Church's resources or to have a cleric represent them might indeed be a sign that they are not as thoroughly secular as they appear. However, Britain's secularization has been driven by indifference rather than by hostility. Because they do not much matter and most of us do not much care, the churches are able to function as vaguely benevolent honest brokers.

Notes

1. D. Thompson, 'MBE for Vicar who United Soham', *Daily Telegraph*, 31 December 2002.
2. Thompson, 'MBE for Vicar'.
3. G. Davie, 'Vicarious Religion: A Methodological Challenge', in N. Ammerman (ed.), *Everyday Religion: Observing Modern Religious Lives* (New York: Oxford University Press, 2006), 21–35.
4. W. M. Williams, *The Sociology of an English Village: Gosforth* (London: Routledge and Kegan Paul, 1956), 1.
5. Williams, *Sociology of an English Village*, 182.
6. Williams, *Sociology of an English Village*, 197.
7. J. H. Tonkin, *Methodist Chapel Gosforth 1874–1974* (Gosforth: Gosforth Methodist Chapel, 1975).
8. Williams, *Sociology of an English Village*, 197.
9. B. Wynne, C. Waterton, and R. Grove-White, *Public Perceptions and the Nuclear Industry in West Cumbria* (Lancaster: Lancaster University Centre for the Study of Environmental Change, 2007), 8.
10. Data on employment and religious identification have been extracted from the NOMIS website presentation of the 2001 census.
11. Anglican communicant data are from various Registers of Services in the Whitehaven Records Office and from the incumbent; electoral roll figures are from respective issues of the *Carlisle Diocesan Directory*; and population data are from Williams and from the *Vision of Britain* website. Methodist data are from circuit plans in the Whitehaven Records Office.
12. Williams has an average of 7 or 8 communicants on a typical Sunday in 1951. In 1961 the figure was 34 and, although it peaked in 1981 with 62, in 2011 it was still 56.
13. Tonkin, *Methodist Chapel Gosforth*.
14. M. J. L. Wickes, *Devon in the Religious Census of 1851* (Exeter: Self-Published, 1990).
15. W. M. Williams, *A West Country Village Ashworthy: Family, Kinship and Land* (London: Routledge and Kegan Paul, 1963), 185.
16. Williams, *West Country Village*, 8–9.
17. The incumbent, 'Articles of Visitation and Inquiry: Northlew with Ashbury', Diocese of Exeter, Bishop's Visitation, 1969.
18. These figures are calculated from R. Currie, A. Gilbert, and L. Horsley, *Churches and Churchgoers: Patterns of Church Growth in the British Isles since 1700* (Oxford: Oxford

University Press, 1977), table A1, and from P. Brierley, *UK Church Statistics 2005–2015* (Tonbridge, Kent: ABCD Publishers, 2011), table 2.7.

19. My colleague Tony Glendinning's analysis of 2001 Times Use Diary survey data (available from the UK Data Archive) shows that, of those adults with a spouse or resident partner who attended church, half were not accompanied by their partner.

20. The Church has successfully plugged some of the gap, especially in rural areas, by offering free accommodation and expenses to retired clergy in return for them conducting Sunday worship.

21. J. Peak, 'Northlew: Small but Significant', *Presence Papers: Stories of How Christian Congregations Have Made a Difference In Their Rural Communities*, 1 (2004), 7, http://content.yudu.com/Library/A1rw2n/ThePresencePapers/resources/3.htm   (accessed February 2011).

22. Peak, 'Northlew', 7.

23. N. Parveen, 'Birmingham: Each Year the Benefit System is More Heartless', *Guardian*, 15 May 2017.

24. Parveen, 'Birmingham'.

25. S. Williams, 'A Church Closed Monday to Friday is "Worst Advert for Christianity"', *Western Daily Mail*, 14 April 2008.

26. To quote local historians: 'Dalehead is the smallest of all the Craven churches, but the fact that it is there at all in this remote location, creates a sense of continuity and survival')V. Leigh and B. Podmore, *Outstanding Churches in Craven* (Settle: Val Leigh Publications, 1985), 77).

27. R. Hall, 'Mine Victims Remembered at Church Services', *Guardian*, 19 September 2011.

28. 'How Two Devon Farmers Fought Foot-and-Mouth', *BBC News*, 10 February 2011, http://www.bbc.co.uk/news/uk-england-12392311 (accessed February 2011).

29. M.-V. Parr, 'Prayer Qualities', *Daily Telegraph*, 18 July 2011.

30. Hall, 'Mine Victims'.

31. 'What I Am Really Thinking: The Vicar's Wife', *Guardian Weekend*, 12 April 2014.

32. Davie, 'Vicarious Religion'.

4

Old Rivals Merge; New Divisions Emerge

In the winter of 1998 hurricane-force winds removed much of the roof of the Methodist chapel in the Devonshire village of Bratton Fleming. The Anglicans of St Peter's offered their church as a temporary refuge. The two congregations had long been on good terms: they held joint services for Remembrance Day and for pre-Christmas carol singing, they shared a Bible study group, and they jointly managed the Christian Aid collection. With the Anglican service ending around 10.30 and the Methodist service starting at 11, the two congregations often passed in the churchyard: one going and the other coming. Once the repairs were complete, the Methodists returned to their chapel, but the experience of sharing caused many churchgoers to consider their long-term future. In 2001, they began to alternate: the Methodists joining the Anglicans on one Sunday and hosting them on another. The Methodists drank from the traditional chalice on the first Sunday of every month, and on the third Sunday the Anglicans learnt to take their communion from small glasses handed around on a tray. After two years of switching, they took the next step: a 'covenant' formalized the joint arrangements, and then the Methodists decided to close their chapel. Bratton Fleming now had just one worshipping congregation: St Peter's Anglican–Methodist Church.

Slow National Progress

Particular splits and mergers always have specific and local reasons, but from a distance a pattern is clearly visible. When Christianity was popular, the Protestant churches split into competing fragments, and, when it declined, they reunited. During the nineteenth century, Scottish Presbyterianism experienced numerous schisms, with Reformed Presbyterians, Seceders, and Free Church either challenging the legal status of the national church or hoping to replace it. In addition, there were incursions from the south: most English sects managed to establish at least a toehold in Scotland. The fragmentation was reversed at the end of the century with the various Seceder fractions first forming the United Presbyterian Church and then joining the bulk of the Free Church in 1900. In 1929, almost all of the congregations of what was now the 'United Free Church' returned to the Church of Scotland. The trajectory of English Methodism is similar. In the nineteenth century, when Methodism was growing, the movement divided into Wesleyan, Primitive, Bible Christian, Free Methodist, and Countess of Huntingdon's Connexion elements. In the first decades of the twentieth century, after growth had turned into patent decline, they gradually reunited, so that, by 1932, almost all strands were part of a single Methodist Church. It is paradoxical but understandable that such reunions increased rather than decreased the number of sects and denominations. As there were almost always some congregations that rejected merger, the union of two major denominations resulted in three organizations: the large new body and two small groups of refuseniks claiming to embody the ethos of the originals.

As merger, with its promise of reducing spare capacity and costs, became more attractive as Christianity declined, it is tempting to accept the cynical interpretation that paying bills trumps principles. But a more complex reading is better: failure to triumph over the opposition prompted a revaluation of tolerance. Few of the sects formed before the mid-nineteenth century were initially more liberal than the church they had left and few argued for toleration. Most shared the prevailing view that, as there was just one God, there was only one true religion, and the state was obliged to impose that truth on all its citizens. The typical schismatic group was initially inspired by the conviction that it had a much better grasp of God's will than the corrupt and corpulent establishment it wished to supplant. But, when growth stalled, the sectarians realized that they were destined to remain a small minority. Then they started to reconsider their claims to unique access to the mind of God. Partly from self-interest and partly because their own stance had increased rather than decreased religious diversity, they gradually persuaded themselves that imposition was a bad thing. Their wish to become the state-enforced church was reduced to a demand for the establishment to be stripped of its privileges and for fair competition between alternative religious organizations. As the state churches lost their advantages, they too scaled back their claims to unique legitimacy and came to see themselves as just one (albeit the best one) of a number of equally God-pleasing bodies. In sociological language, we can say that the second half of the nineteenth century saw both sects and churches gradually evolve into denominations.[1]

That convergence allowed cooperation. At the level of formal institutions, the ecumenical movement was driven by a combination of declining sectarianism and pragmatic cooperation. Especially in the mission fields of India, Africa, and the Far East, where non-Christians were often baffled by the ill-feeling between what to them seemed like very similar faiths, Anglicans, Presbyterians, and Methodists found it increasingly difficult to justify their divisions. Inter-church meetings designed to address common problems (such as the 1910 Edinburgh World Missionary Conference) led to the formation of standing bodies, and in turn these led to the formation in 1948 of the World Council of Churches and its national subsidiaries.[2]

However, although there were notable mergers in mission fields—the 1947 formation of the Church of South India, for example—talks about merging major denominational traditions in Britain made little headway. In the 1950s, progressives in the Church of Scotland bravely produced a scheme to insert some sort of bishop into their Presbyterian structure, but a spirited campaign of opposition by the *Scottish Daily Express* scuppered that deal.[3] In the 1960s, the Church of England was involved in discussions with bodies to the left and the right. The 'low-church' Anglican clergy wished to see closer ties with the Methodists, Congregationalists, and Presbyterians. The 'high-church' clergy wanted closer bonds with Rome. Given the difficulty of reversing the Reformation, it is no surprise that the second strand of talks got nowhere, but the first strand was hardly more successful. Although there was steady growth in active cooperation in local church councils and the like, the only major reunion in the second half of the twentieth century was the 1972 formation of the United Reformed Church from the Presbyterians and Congregationalists in England.

For reasons pursued shortly, there has long been a popular current in favour of ecumenical cooperation. A Gallup poll of 1949 asked for reactions to the Church of England merging with such Nonconformists as the Methodists: 45 per cent were in favour, 24 per cent did not mind, 12 per cent had no firm view, and only 19 per cent were opposed. The same question posed in 1961 showed those against down to 15 per cent and those in favour grown to 54 per cent.[4]

Unfortunately, such polls did not seek the reasons for divergent views, but we can guess one connection: the most committed members of any organization were likely also to be the most committed to its distinctive characteristics. This produces a paradox that may well explain why high-level talks between officials made only slow progress. When the clergy of competing churches met to discuss their differences, they did so as representatives of those very differences, and they were often expected to exemplify them.[5] The Methodist or the Quaker or the Catholic was chosen for his denominational identity and invited fully to represent it. And, even if the selection of representatives and the expectation that they defend their defining characteristics did not prevent some radical clergy from deciding to seek common ground, such schemes had to be ratified by general assemblies and synods composed of the most active and committed members of the respective churches. The gradual loss of members over the first half of the twentieth century gave the major churches good reason to cooperate in such public ceremonies as Remembrance Day services and in the sharing of such privileges as chaplaincies and BBC broadcasting opportunities, but the greatest changes came from the grass roots.

Local Merger

Buildings seem permanent, and, because of their status as houses of God, churches have usually been among the costliest structures of their time and place. But even the best buildings require regular maintenance, and many Nonconformist chapels were not the best; they were hastily thrown up by enthusiastic volunteers working with cheap materials. In the second half of the nineteenth century, schism, population growth, and Victorian overconfidence produced a spate of chapel and church construction. A century later those structures would have needed repair and refurbishment, even if generally improving standards of lighting and heating had not created a demand for upgrading.[6] As other public buildings such as cinemas, schools, and hospitals, and private homes, became more comfortable, worshippers came to expect more of their chapels. Yet, as expectations went up, congregations went down, and the increasing costs had to be borne by ever-smaller numbers. In England in 2015, 13 per cent of churches had congregations of ten or fewer and a further 23 per cent numbered between eleven and twenty-five. That meant a third of churches are used by too few people to fund their clergy, let alone finance buildings repairs.[7]

With local variations, the Bratton Fleming example has been repeated across the country. Some cooperation was peripheral. For example, when the Methodists of Eynsham, Oxfordshire, gave up their chapel, the local Anglican priest invited their weekly women's group to meet in the vicarage.[8] But much cooperation was close to merger. The decades around the end of the twentieth century in the Durham Methodist circuit provide many examples. In Sacriston, three Methodist chapels and two Anglican parish churches agreed to sell their buildings and pool resources to build a modern church and a block of sheltered housing. Initially Anglicans and Methodists held separate services on three Sundays and joined together for one Sunday a month, but periodic shortages of clergy led to more joint services, and gradually the two congregations became in effect one. The Anglican parish of Bowburn had a spectacular modern building that combined a pineapple-shaped dome for the worship area with a rocket-shaped steeple. Its novel structure and building materials attracted considerable admiration from architects; its persistent leaking impressed the users less. After two decades of failed repairs, the Anglicans gave up and moved in with the local Methodists. In Crook, the United Reformed Church congregation moved in with the better-housed Methodists. The Gilesgate Methodists gave up their building and moved in with their Church of England neighbours.

Given their national presence, it is no surprise that Church of England con-gregations figure in many de facto mergers. The Embleton, Northumberland, parish church took in the United Reformed when their chapel degenerated beyond repair. The same merger took in Horwich.[9]

Like lending a lawnmower, sharing a building can be just good neighbour-liness. But it opens the way to solving the often-coincidental problem of ministerial supply. In 1983, the Methodist and Anglicans of Filleigh, Barnstaple, began to hold their services in a single building, and they also alternated clergy. Two Sundays a month an Anglican service was led by an Anglican priest. On the other two Sundays, when the priest was officiating elsewhere, the services were taken by a Methodist preacher. One building, two ministers, but only one at a time: the next step was obvious: 'the distinctions are now hardly noticeable.'[10]

The Methodist–United Reformed combination is common: we find it in Barnstaple, Devon, in Ware, Hertfordshire, and in Scunthorpe, Yorkshire.[11] As the churches have continued to decline, theologically more remote bodies have been drawn in. The Baptists, who are distanced from the Protestant mainstream by their opposition to infant baptism, joined with the local Church of England to form a single congregation in Ware. In Cumbria, they merged with Methodists. In 2009, the Anglicans of St Augustine's in Northampton experienced what was a common trigger: 'we had an architect's report on the building which said it needed a lot of money spending on it.' They moved in with the local Baptists.[12] Four-way combinations are not unknown. In Cambourne, Cambridgeshire, a new congregation was formed from Church of England, Methodist, United Reformed, and Baptist groups. The congregation of St Thomas Philadelphia, Sheffield (discussed in Chapter 5) was a joint enterprise of Anglicans, Methodists, URC, and local charismatics.

The sheer number of such local initiatives is striking; they are now to be found in almost every town, village, and suburb where religion's declining appeal has not been offset by net population growth. More significant than the fact of merger is the theological distance now being spanned. In all the examples just given, the differences that are being set aside could be described (by an outsider at least) as relatively small. With good will, small reinterpretations can resolve many of the organizational disputes that separate Presbyterians, Methodists, Baptists, and Congregationalists. Precisely what sacramental powers (if any) are possessed by the ordained clergy but absent from the laity loses importance when all churches are finding it increasingly difficult to recruit full-time clergy. In many parts of the country, Anglican priests are having to supervise four or five separate congregations and can provide regular services only with the assistance of retired clergy and committed lay people. And that structure is little different from the circuit system of the Methodists, with an ordained minister who supervises a number of congregations and many services led by local lay preachers. The argument over infant baptism was once extremely important, because it signified the difference between two very different views of the offer of salvation. In the organic community model of religion promoted by the Orthodox, Catholic, and Lutheran strands, a single church represents an entire nation to God (and vice versa), and salvation is presumed to be available to pretty well all of those who do not explicitly reject it. In that view, it makes perfect sense to baptize infants: the newborn are accepted into the nation's church at the same time as they are accepted into the nation. But many Protestants take an individualistic view of salvation. Each of us must consciously 'decide for Christ'. The piety of one's nation or even one's family makes no difference. In that view, only people old enough to understand the commitment they are making can be baptized. However, Christian baptism of any sort has become unpopular, and it is obvious than many people regard it as a social rather than a religious ritual. The churches that do baptize infants also have a confirmation ritual in which the teenager or young adult augments the commitments made by parents and godparents with his or her own commitment. With just a little repositioning, the communal church and the individualistic sect views can be reconciled: the sect can have a 'naming' ceremony for babies that is not quite a baptism and the church can downgrade infant baptism slightly and put more stress on adult confirmation and education. In Teesdale, a number of adult Methodists who had not been baptized as children decided they would like to be baptized by full immersion: a considerable deviation from traditional Methodist practice. The superintendent minister was keen to oblige, and the local Baptist chapel, which has a tank under the floorboards, was happy to lend its facility.

In short, we can see how, in a largely secular society, the merger of Protestant sects and denominations can be relatively painless.

In the 1960s, relations between the Catholic Church and Protestant churches were so cold that, when a few activists on each side wanted to discuss the possibility of a joint mission in the north of England, they felt obliged to keep their meetings secret. It took five years to plan the coordinated events, and, even with every effort to placate possible participants, the Catholic clergy of Hexham and Newcastle voted five to one against involvement, and many conservative Protestant churches stayed aloof.[13] Half a century later, local cooperation and combination include Catholics. In 1990, the worshippers at the small Catholic church of the Holy Family in Kirkby Stephen found that they could no longer afford to repair their crumbling building and moved in with the Church of England. Although the formal arrangement was confined to sharing facilities, over two decades the congregants gradually came to form pretty much one homogenous group. When the Catholics of Portland, Dorset, faced similar repair problems, the local Anglicans offered them a similar arrangement.[14]

Decay of Religious Capital

As noted at the start of this chapter, the declining popularity of Christianity was the main driver of merger, but we can elaborate the causal connections a little.

I noted that Gallup polls from the 1940s and early 1960s showed a generally positive attitude towards closer church cooperation. As the data were either not collected or not reserved, we know nothing of the churchgoing habits of the various categories of respondent, but I strongly suspect that the positive responses reflected benign indifference rather than a principled commitment to ecumenism. As the number of people who regularly attend church has declined, so has the society's stock of religious knowledge. A tiny handful of those who assert that they are really Christian despite never going to church may be well-informed self-taught critics, but the vast majority will have little knowledge of the key themes of the Christian faith and (beyond some possible recognition of differences in building style or music) absolutely no idea of what distinguishes the many different Christian churches.[15] In those circumstances, religion is reduced to ethics. Christians are supposed to be nice people and religion is about being nice. And making a fuss about small details, such as the precise meaning of baptism, or wishing to preserve the integrity of an organization, is not nice.

The following is a tiny selection from just one year's news reports. At Easter 2017, Tesco, one of the UK's largest supermarket chains, issued a public apology for promoting 'great offers' on beer and cider with the slogan 'Good Friday just got better!'. It took church leaders to point out to Tesco that, while Christians might rejoice in Christ's resurrection from the dead, it was unseemly to use his crucifixion to punt cheap drink.[16] On 15 September 2017, a number of London Underground passengers were injured when a bomb partially exploded at the Parsons Green station. A fortnight later, people on a tube train at Wimbledon panicked and fled the carriage when a man began to read aloud from the Bible: they thought he was a Muslim terrorist.[17] The *London Evening Standard* mangled a number of important distinctions in a space-filler prelude to the wedding of Prince Harry and Megan Markle. It announced that Ms Markle would have to be baptized before the wedding because she was a Protestant, which demonstrated that the journalist (and the sub-editors who checked the text) did not know that Harry's grandmother was the titular head of the Protestant Church of England. It further described the putative baptism with text cut and pasted from a Catholic website: so Markle becoming a 'Protestant' would actually involve her taking the Roman 'mass'.[18]

In the first half of the twentieth century some knowledge of Christian beliefs and rituals was still widespread because both populations and practices have residues. In the 1920s, almost half of all children in Britain attended Sunday school. By 1961, it was 20 per cent. Now only the children of regular churchgoers go to Sunday school. The children of the 1920s became the adults of the 1960s, and hence twice as many people as then attended church had experienced some contact with Christian teaching and ritual. If nothing else, hymn singing was still familiar. As anyone who has recently attended a Christian wedding or funeral will appreciate, that is now no longer the case.

The way schools treated religion changed markedly over the twentieth century. In 1900, almost all schools began the day with collective act of Christian worship. Children in my local school were set a Bible verse to memorize each day and were instructed in the Shorter Catechism. Schools unashamedly took the view that children should be instructed in the key principles of the one true faith, and alternatives were considered, if at all, only to dilate on their errors. From the 1960s onwards, the teaching of religion first broadened to become inclusively comparative, and then it became entirely non-partisan.

The precise details of those changes differed for the constituent nations of the UK, and there was a brief hiccup when the Conservative governments of the 1980s tried to bolster the presence of Christianity in state schools, but the direction of drift was common. Where religion has not entirely disappeared from the curriculum, it has been subsumed in general ethical discussion. A syllabus introduced in 2009 for the Religious Studies GCSE in England offered homosexuality, binge drinking, drugs in sport, and conservation as study topics and was modularized in a way that would allow pupils to avoid the more traditional subjects of worship and theological ideas.[19]

Schools in England are still legally obliged to 'provide religious education and daily collective worship for all registered pupils' and that worship should reflect the fact 'that religious traditions in the country are in the main Christian'.[20] The vast majority either ignore the requirement or reduce it to something so pallid that many churches would rather see the charade dropped. In Scotland, for example, the national church and the Humanist Association have agreed that such rituals need to be brought into line with popular attitudes.[21] In 2015, the Welsh Assembly decided to scrap religious instruction and collective acts of worship in Welsh schools.[22]

Every Oxford and Cambridge college established before the 1980s has a college chapel, and in the 1950s large numbers of their students worshipped in them. It is no surprise that student teachers being trained in Church of England colleges were required to attend services, but for a long time after the state took over funding such colleges and employed most of their alumni, such colleges encouraged (if they could no longer require) church involvement. Now the vast majority of higher- and further-education students have no contact with institutional religion. Even within the few theology programmes that remain (and many have closed), Christianity is in retreat. Where a century ago such degrees taught only Christianity, now it is just one of a number of options, alongside all the other major religions and New Age spirituality.

From its inauguration in 1922, the British Broadcasting Company (later Corporation) regularly broadcast church services, despite the opposition of some clergy who worried that working men might listen in pubs without removing their hats! Initially divine worship was the only thing broadcast on a Sunday morning, and, in the 1950s, over a third of British people claimed to listen to such services.[23] When television was invented, the holders of government licences (the BBC and the various local independent TV companies) were legally obliged to make and air religious programmes in a preserved early Sunday evening 'God-slot', and the ITV companies refrained from sullying the hour with advertisements.[24] The popularity of the BBC's *Songs of*

Praise and ITV's *Stars on Sunday* declined in tandem with the decline in churchgoing, and, by the 1980s, television companies were aggressively lobbying the government to remove the requirement. A prime slot was being wasted on small audiences and, worse, in the days before various forms of TV-on-demand, if viewers switched off one programme they did not like, they might well not return for a number of hours, and so the despised God-slot depressed total viewing audiences. It was dropped.[25]

Another obvious mark of the secularization of broadcasting is the change in staffing. Initially the BBC's religious programmes were made by clerics. Like college chaplains, they were often more liberal and ecumenical than their parish counterparts, but they were well versed in the Christian faith. When I worked for the BBC in Northern Ireland in the early 1980s, that model still obtained: the department head was a Catholic priest, the producer was a Presbyterian minister, and the main presenter was a Church of Ireland priest. By the end of the twentieth century, such staff positions had either been removed or were filled by non-Christians. In 2009, the first Muslim was appointed as Head of Religion.

In 2012, ITV produced just two hours of religious programming where it had managed 104 hours in 2004.[26] When they did not entirely abandon their traditional obligations, broadcasters pretended to meet them by making programmes that critically analysed, rather than promoted, religion or by describing as religious programmes that touched on faith only tangentially. For example, a 2017 drama about a Sikh journalist telling his parents of his engagement to a non-Sikh was described by the BBC's head of religious programming as 'an exemplary piece of integrated religious programming'.[27] In March 2018, the BBC billed a routine travelogue of seven minor celebrities (four of them avowed atheists) talking about themselves while walking in Spain as 'Pilgrimage: The Road to Santiago'. In brief, the removal of the religion requirement in the twenty-first century saw pretty well the end of the promotion of religion in the national electronic mass media.

The proliferation of alternative forms of broadcasting that came with satellite TV, television-on-demand, and digital programmes accessed through various forms of personal computer caused the national audience to fragment. The very small number of people who wanted religious programmes could access them and avoid the more critical treatments of religion in what remained of mainstream broadcasting. An evangelical Christian can now watch American or Nigerian Pentecostal preachers on high-number satellite TV channels. The religiously indifferent can now entirely avoid any religious knowledge.

Beyond such public promotion of Christianity as we find in education and broadcasting in the 1950s, there was also a large amount of what David Voas has usefully called 'ambient religion'. The Crieff Hydro hotel was entirely conventional in having short daily services morning and evening for staff and guests.[28] Very many public events and proceedings contained some affirmative reference to Christian ideas and rituals. Public bodies (local councils, for example) often began their proceedings with prayers and even with a reading from scripture. By 2013, less than a quarter of councils still began their deliberations with a prayer or Bible reading.[29] Almost all acts of communal eating—formal company dinners, school and college meals—were once sanctified by someone saying grace. In 2009, after requests from students at Newnham College, Cambridge, for an alternative to the Christian grace in Latin, a secular Latin text was composed: translated, it read 'For food in a hungry world, for companionship in a world of loneliness, for peace in an age of violence, we give thanks'.[30] It is worth pondering that change. The college thought it appropriate to replace Christian words (because very few of the hearers believed them) with secular words, but it translated them into a language that has been dead a lot longer than Christianity. Both the Christianity and the Latin are part of the heritage of Oxbridge colleges—outdated but arguably worth keeping because they remind the current generation of the past of their institution. But the old language was retained, while the old religion was dropped.

Despite its name and original purpose, Christmas has now become secular. This can be illustrated with the poignant, almost ironic, fate of Gorton monastery in Manchester. Designed by E. W. Pugin in the neo-Gothic style in the 1850s, the abandoned building was bought in 2006 by a local businessman who restored it as a wedding, conference, and party venue. It advertises Dickensian Christmas events—'come back with us in time by joining one of our Victorian talks and lunches'—and, like the works of Dickens, it makes no reference to religious themes.[31] A 2010 survey of 2,100 designs of Christmas cards on sale in major retailers revealed that fewer than 4 per cent showed a nativity scene or any reference to the Bible. Most depicted secular elements of the holiday (such as decorated Christmas trees and Father Christmas) or generic winter images (such as snowmen and robins).[32] The disappearance of Christ has been noted by Christian organizations, which have reshaped their products and their activities to deal with widespread ignorance. In 1995, the Churches Advertising Network devised a national campaign to promote Easter that deliberately omitted the Cross: 'We are trying to reach those who are currently not interested in the churches or the Christian faith. We are trying to meet them where they are.'[33] In 2014, the Synod of the Church of England approved new versions of the baptism service that removed any mention of the Devil; parents had previously been required to 'reject the Devil and all rebellion against God'.[34] As is customary when ideologies are altered, the change was presented as merely making clear what the Church had always believed, but, even were such changes merely terminological, they are clear testimony to the country's loss of Christian capital. In 2017, the Scripture Union responded to surveys that showed that a third of children aged 10 to 13 did not know that Christmas celebrates the birth of Christ by slimming down its annual summary of the Christmas story. It removed references to biblical texts: 'When we realised that children don't even know the basics of what they are celebrating then the traditional simple story is the best way.'[35]

Because the current state of religious knowledge is important for the argument of this book's final chapter, it is important to distinguish well-informed universalism from ignorance. There have long been religious activists and officials who make the principled and informed case that all religions are equally valid. An example would be the Anglican parish priest of Whalley Range, Manchester, who in 1992 said: 'People often ask me "Has Christianity got anything distinctive to offer?" I say "No. It hasn't." I see no difference between Jesus and Mohamed in terms of the message they bring us.'[36] He made a point of visiting the mosques, temples, and gurdwaras in his parish and had well-informed views about the teachings of non-Christian religions. While such universalists are significant in providing post-hoc justifications for change, what better explains the current spate of de facto local mergers is the lack of understanding of (and interest in) those key disputes that formed the twentieth-century landscape of competing churches, denominations, and sects. Those outside the realm of organized religion know nothing, but even most regular churchgoers would now be hard pressed to explain why the people who built their chapel disagreed with the people who built the one across the road.

Formal Ecumenism in the Twenty-First Century

By the start of the twenty-first century, the plethora of ad hoc local mergers, reunions, and accommodation-sharing had created sufficient momentum, and the problems of decline had grown such, that high-level institutional talks began to produce results. In 1972 and again in 1982, the Church of England rejected schemes devised in negotiations with the Methodists.

Matters looked more hopeful in 1995 because by then the Church of England had followed the Methodist lead in ordaining women and thus removed a major difference between the two organizations.[37] Still the talks foundered. In 2010, the President of the Methodist Conference went so far as to declare that the Methodist Church was willing to dissolve itself in the interests of reunion, but it was not until 2017 that the Church of England and the Methodist Church agreed fully to recognize the validity of each other's clergy and to remove all obstacles to the Anglican priests taking services in Methodist chapels and vice versa.[38] The infamous 'Bishops in Presbytery' scheme for reconciling the Church of Scotland and the Church of England had been torpedoed in the 1950s, but various forms of cooperation were developed, and, although the plans that came out of formal talks in the 1990s between the Church of Scotland, the Scottish Episcopal Church, the Methodists, and the URC were rejected, in 2016 the two national churches endorsed the Columba Declaration. It accepted that holy communion was 'rightly administered' in both churches and thus removed the final barrier to clergy-swapping.

These major official decisions have been augmented by a very wide variety of small changes in local practices. Church of England, URC, and Methodist clergy now cooperate in ministerial training programmes. In places, URC and Methodist clergy serve each other's chapels; in the first decade of the twenty-first century, the superintendent minister of a Devon Methodist circuit was actually a URC pastor. Anglican cathedrals, which enjoy a considerable degree of autonomy, have often led in small but symbolically important gestures. For example, in 2008, Ripon Cathedral appointed as canons a Roman Catholic priest and a Baptist pastor, to add to the Methodist minister who already held such a post. In 2017, Southwark Cathedral similarly honoured Steve Chalke, a well-known Baptist minister.

New Divisions: Women Clergy, Worship, and Sexuality

There is an alternative to the mergers and reunions described above. Instead of becoming ever more ecumenical, liberal, and tolerant, some Christians argue for a last-ditch stand to maintain the 'old paths in perilous times', as a popular early twentieth-century phrase put it. But even the traditionalists have been affected by secularization in the sense that what they now oppose are not relatively small differences of theology or ecclesiology but major changes in social mores, mostly concerned with sex and gender.

Women Clergy

The gradual expansion of women's rights over the twentieth century and their increasing role in the labour market affected most British churches, albeit with some considerable time lag. The Roman Catholic and Orthodox Churches still reject female clergy, but it is now commonplace in all but the smallest and most sectarian Protestant bodies. In 1917, Constance Coltman become the first women ordained by the Congregational Union (most of which later became part of the URC). The Methodists, having had women preachers since the eighteenth century, introduced deaconesses in 1890 and ordained women as presbyters from 1974. The Church of Scotland commissioned women as deaconesses from 1888, and from 1949 allowed them to preach. Mary Levison was ordained as a 'Minister of Word and Sacrament' (that is, she could administer communion as well as preach) in 1978.

The Church of England's General Synod voted in 1992 to ordain women to the priesthood, the necessary two-thirds majority being achieved in the House of Laity by the thin margin of five votes.[39] That decision was met with excited predictions of mass defection to Rome. In April 1996, a former head of the Walsingham Shrine (long a centre for high Anglicans) was received into the Catholic Church along with thirty-five of his South Kensington parishioners, but such group conversions were rare. However, the number of clergy departures was significant: between 1993 and 2004, 512 clergy left the Church of England's active ministry under the legislation. Of these, 260 became Roman Catholics and 30 Orthodox. By 2004, 72 (including 33 who had become Roman Catholics) had returned to ministry—31 of them to full service, 14 to unpaid ministry, and 20 as retired clergy.[40] A few prominent conservative politicians also converted. Although the Catholic Church did not overtly tout for business, in 2011 it did facilitate defection (in preparation for the decision, eventually taken in 2014, to ordain women as bishops) by establishing the 'Ordinariate of Our Lady of Walsingham' as a semi-autonomous unit within the Church and by creating a liturgy for its services that drew heavily on traditional Anglican rites in the language of Thomas Cranmer. But that halfway house was not terribly popular. By 2014, it included 85 priests (many of them retired) and around 1,500 laypeople.[41]

In 2004, a decade after the first women were ordained to the priesthood, public debate about the ordination of women as bishops began. This time, the loudest and most bitter argument was not so much about whether women could become bishops but about how—if at all—those who, for theological reasons, could not receive their ministry could continue within the Church of England. To the outsider, letting women enter the profession but barring them from promotion seems like naked sexism, but there are important theological arguments here.[42] The thoroughly Protestant Presbyterian, Baptist, or Congregational churches, for example, suppose that ordination confers no symbolic significance: the clergy are distinguished from the laity (who select them) only by knowledge, expertise, and personal piety. For the Catholic Church and the Church of England, however, bishops are the successors of the Apostles. Through that succession, symbolized by the laying-on of hands, they receive power to ordain priests, who in turn can consecrate the bread and wine of the Eucharist so that it becomes the body and blood of Christ, and have the power to absolve sin—two roles beyond the most pious lay person. In addition to serving as a conduit for the transmission of sacramental power, bishops are the focus of their diocese's unity, and the clergy minister on their behalf. Those who oppose the ordination of women to the priesthood, for example, because Christ called only men to be his Apostles and because in celebrating the Eucharist the priest represents Christ, could live with women priests because they could avoid their services. But, if women became bishops, traditionalist clergy and laypeople would be unable to accept their oversight or their sacramental ministry. Further, they could not accept the ministry of clergy, female or male, whom women bishops had ordained.

In brief, if a church has a ministry to which it accords sacramental significance and is hierarchically ordered, with an order of ministry the remit of which extends beyond the local congregation, allowing women to occupy the top posts has a much wider impact than is the case when women's ministry is exercised only within individual congregations. Hence the ordination of women as bishops was far more problematic for those of traditional views than the initial entry of women into the priesthood.

In the Church of England, traditionalists mostly accepted that ordaining women as bishops was a logical consequence of ordaining them to the priesthood. Therefore, whereas in 1992 they had sought—but narrowly failed—to prevent the ordination of women as priests, twenty years later their efforts were directed not towards preventing women from becoming bishops but towards achieving a settlement that would mitigate the difficulties just described. In this, they were much more successful, securing the defeat of the initial legislation in 2012 and its replacement in 2014 with provisions that they supported—while still voting, as a matter of principle, against the ordination of women as bishops that those provisions made possible.

That women priests have been almost universally accepted shows both the power of popular ideas and the consequence of decline. It is now almost impossible for anyone in public life openly to argue that women are less capable than men and hardly easier to argue that religion justifies exemptions from widely accepted norms. It would also now be very difficult for any major Christian organization in the West to survive without the large number of women clergy. In 2017, just over half of the 544 people who began training for the Anglican ministry were women.[43]

Worship

As visible as the gender of the officiating clergy is the style of worship. Changes in church decor, furnishings, liturgical language, and music will be discussed in detail in Chapter 5. Here it is enough to note that, as one North Yorkshire rector who superintended seven congregations serving areas with very distinct social-class profiles, put it: 'Nobody gets excited by doctrine but, God love them, do they get heated over pop music versus Victorian hymns, and chairs versus pews, and casual dress versus Sunday best.' His solution was to let each congregation maintain its own preferred format and to tailor his officiating style appropriately; as most people drove to church, his adherents could attend the outlet that best suited them. Other churches try to serve a range of tastes by having different sorts of services at different times of day, and the Church of England has facilitated such variation by allowing a range of alternative liturgies. Digital technology has helped that process by allowing clergy to download and alter online Orders of Service to suit their tastes and those of their congregants. Although innovations initially associated with the charismatic movement have now, in watered-down form, become widespread, the tone and tenor of church services have almost certainly displaced theological argument as an important factor in the movement of British Christians between different organizations.[44]

Sexuality

All the major faiths have devoted considerable effort to monitoring and policing human sexuality, but who can do what to whom under what circumstances has come to consume an ever-greater part of the public's perception of religious ethics as the remit of the churches has shrunk. Churches now have little or no control over the economy or the polity; they still pronounce on major issues, but they are entirely ignored. That leaves the family and sexuality.

That church records from previous centuries are replete with the details of parishioners being disciplined for various forms of immorality and licentiousness reminds us that popular behaviour has long fallen short of church standards, but for a long time the churches were sufficiently popular and powerful that those who offended against their standards felt obliged to hide the fact. The 1960s saw an abrupt change in public attitudes. Roy Jenkins, as Labour Home Secretary from 1965 to 1967, ended capital punishment, relaxed the divorce laws, abolished theatre censorship, and gave government support to the legalization of abortion. He also decriminalized homosexuality at a time when 25 per cent of people thought it should be punished, 22 per cent thought it should be condemned though not punished, and only 36 per cent thought it should be tolerated.[45] Compared to contemporary politicians, who seem perpetually terrified of the press and public opinion, Jenkins was a man of enormous self-confidence: he dismissed criticism of the so-called permissive society by responding that it was in reality the civilized society and that homosexuals paid taxes too.

The prominence of gay rights in Christian arguments is an extension of the last-skittle-standing principle that explains the shrinking of Christian ethics to sex. Conservative Christians have usually been puritans. Sex is fun and fun is bad because it distracts us from glorifying God. Were it not required for the continuation of the species, many Christians would ban sex altogether and many more permit it only for the purposes of reproduction, which is why the Catholic Church is so firmly opposed to artificial contraception and why 'spilling one's seed' (that is, masturbating or ejaculating outside the vagina) is a sin. Homosexuals, because their sexual activity cannot produce offspring, are therefore very bad. Conservative Christians have lost most of their wars on sex. Easy contraception has allowed the pleasure of sex without the fear of pregnancy, and no amount of church criticism has prevented even masstaking Catholics making use of it. The prohibition on sex before marriage is a complete washout. In the 1970s, the phrase 'living in sin' was still used and not always ironically. Now couples living together, as either a prelude or an alternative to marriage, is unremarkable, as is illegitimacy. In 2012, for the first time since records had been kept, more babies in Scotland were born to unmarried than to married women.[46] Which leaves homosexuality as one of the very few items on the list of battles not yet entirely lost.

The march of gay rights has been long, and it has suffered setbacks. Most notable was the Conservative government's infamous Section 28 of the

Local Government Act 1988 (and section 2a of the corresponding Scottish legislation): a local authority 'shall not intentionally promote homosexuality or publish material with the intention of promoting homosexuality' or 'promote the teaching...of the acceptability of homosexuality as a pretended family relationship'.[47] But gay rights triumphed, immeasurably helped by the HIV/AIDS crisis. The inhibition on an effective public-health response caused by the climate of secrecy and denial encouraged many gays to come out. Where studio managers and agents fearful for the public reputation of their charges had once pressed gay actors into fake marriages, well-known artistes were now declaring their sexuality with very few negative consequences. Classical actor Ian McKellan, who late in his career reached new audiences as Gandalf in the *Lord of the Rings* films, came out in 1988 and co-founded Stonewall, an organization that campaigned for gay rights. In 1984, Chris Smith became Britain's first openly gay MP when during a rally against a possible ban on gay employees by a town council, he began his speech: 'Good afternoon, I'm Chris Smith, I'm the Labour MP for Islington South and Finsbury and I'm gay.'[48] He was later promoted to the Cabinet. Eventually even homosexual professional sports men and women went public.

The election of the Labour government in 1997 was a watershed. Same-sex partners were recognized for immigration purposes. The ban on gays serving in the forces was lifted. The age of consent for gay and heterosexual sex was equalized at 16. In 2003, Section 28 was repealed, and it was made illegal to discriminate against people in the workplace on grounds of sexual orientation. In December 2005, the Civil Partnership Act—which gave gay couples a legal standing similar to that of married couples—came into force.

Those changes were consolidated by homophobes losing their political home. When David Cameron, forty years younger than Thatcher, was elected leader of a Conservative party that had lost three successive elections, he set out to rid it of its image as the nasty party. He appointed gay MP Alan Duncan to his front-bench team and, in 2008, declared that he was thrilled that Duncan was to became the first Conservative MP to enter a civil partnership. The following year Cameron addressed a Gay Pride meeting and assured his audience that homosexuals could feel at home in the modern Conservative party. By 2013, the governments of both Scotland and the UK were legislating for gay marriage.

In 1983, just over half the public thought that homosexuality was 'always wrong' and only one in five respondents said it was 'not at all' or 'rarely wrong'. In 2000, over a third of Britons said that 'sexual relations between same-sex adults' were 'not wrong at all'.[49] A 2007 Scottish poll showed that over two-thirds of Scots supported civil partnerships. Five years later, a similar proportion approved of gay marriage.[50]

That gradual acceptance of homosexuality was opposed every single step of the way by the churches. For example, in 2008 'nearly 800 clergy and lay leaders met in All Souls, Langham Place' to sign a declaration against the ordination of homosexuals.[51] But gradually the churches came round.[52] Official blanket condemnation of gays was gradually tempered and evolved into official neutrality combined with support for the 'rights' of the homophobes within their ranks. Hence the otherwise curious wording of a 2012 statement from the Church of Scotland:

> we cannot support the Government's proposals on celebrating civil partnerships or same sex marriage. We have also expressed concerns about the speed with which the Government is proceeding with this and what we fear will be inadequate safeguards for religious bodies and ministers and people of faith who view this as being contrary to their beliefs.

The irony of Christian churches objecting to gay rights is that there are almost certainly more homosexuals in their ranks than in other establishment organizations. One senior Church of England cleric reckoned that a quarter of the men he trained with were gay.[53] There has always been a quietly acknowledged presence of gay men at the 'high' or Anglo-Catholic end of the Church of England and in the Catholic Church.[54] Like the theatre and other performing arts, ritualistic churches seem to attract cultured men who are, in the contemporary language, 'in touch with their feminine side', and whose sensitivity makes them excel in the pastoral role. Some manage their sexuality by becoming celibate; some simply lie about it and maintain discreet relationships.[55] Gene Robinson, the Episcopalian Bishop of New Hampshire, in 2007 said of his visit to Britain:

> I have met so many gay partnered clergy and it is so troubling to hear them tell me that their bishop comes to their house for dinner, knows fully about their relationship, is wonderfully supportive but has also said if this ever becomes public then I'm your worst enemy. It's a terrible way to live your life and I think it's a terrible way to be a church.... If all the gay people stayed away from church on a given Sunday the Church of England would be close to shut down between its organists, its clergy, its wardens...it just seems less than humble not to admit that.[56]

Edging forward brings its own absurdities. While we can see the logic in distinguishing between homosexuality as a preference and homosexual acts, accepting one but not the other forces people into demeaning degrees of disclosure. 'The Bishop of Exeter has given his blessing to our civil partnership because, although we are extremely close and have a commitment to each other, we are not lovers. We have satisfied the Bishop we do not have a sexual relationship'—that was said by a Canon Emeritus of Southwark Cathedral in explaining the precise nature of the event that the bishop had agreed to bless.[57] Other clergy just ignore the rules: the Anglican vicar of St Hywyn's in Aberdaron held a church service to bless the civil partnership of two gay women.[58] As an increasing number of senior clergy now acknowledge their gay relationships, the church's position begins to look not just out-of-touch but downright hypocritical.

It is no surprise that organizations that claim to represent the unchanging will of God are slow to change, and there is serious heft on the conservative side from the African churches in the worldwide Anglican Community; the Episcopalian churches in the US and Scotland were suspended from membership for permitting gay marriages.[59] But there is an additional demographic reason why the British churches have generally opposed increasing liberalism in matters sexual. The main cause of church decline is not adult defection: it is the failure of 'cohort replacement'. Or, to put it less formally, the churches have declined because they have not recruited young people at the rate needed to replace the dying. Hence churchgoers are older than non-churchgoers. Even if their faith had no independent effect on their attitudes to abortion or homosexuality or divorce, they would need only to have maintained the attitudes they acquired in childhood to be significantly more conservative than the population at large. In 1983, people aged 65 and over were 80 per cent more likely than young adults to believe that homosexuality was always wrong. By 2000, they were 300 per cent more likely to feel that way; not because they had changed but because younger age cohorts had become more liberal and tolerant.[60]

Even with that demographic conservativism built in, the churches have gradually come round. And in some cases the change has been rapid. In 2013, 47 per cent of Anglicans were against gay marriage and 38 per cent in favour; three years later, 43 per cent were in favour and only 35 per cent thought it morally wrong.[61] Conservative sects such as the Brethren remain resolutely Victorian, but the major churches and denominations have largely accepted the changed climate. And even large parts of the charismatic movement have moved with the bulk of British opinion. The Pentecostal churches, which recruit entirely or largely from Caribbean and African migrants, remain homophobic (which explains the over-representation of black clergy in the Christian political parties discussed in Chapter 10). But the dire predictions of a great schism turned out to be false prophecy. When the Church of Scotland debated the ordination of gay clergy, the press ran stories announcing 'a fifth of elders ready to leave Church of Scotland?' and 'up to 150 ministers might quit Church of Scotland'.[62] In the end only a handful of congregations and ministers quit.

Conclusion

It is harder to measure British Christianity's loss of influence than to estimate its popularity, but the above examples of the churches being forced to accept changes they initially bitterly opposed clearly demonstrate its current impotence. To gender equality and gay rights, we can add the other battles—constraints on the sale and consumption of beverage alcohol and on gambling, the legal protection of the sabbath, the availability of divorce and abortion—that have been lost. In brief, the churches have failed to resist social change. Some small sects continue to suppose that the Christian life should be fixed where it was in the 1950s, but, as we will see in Chapter 5, even charismatic and independent evangelical congregations have moderated their conservative social mores.

To return to this chapter's opening theme, the secularization of Britain has been accompanied by growing cooperation between most Christian bodies and a considerable degree of de facto local merger. Those grass-roots changes are now working through to significant changes in the relationships between the national headquarters of the major churches and denominations. While this is obviously a direct rational response to decline, it is facilitated by more subtle consequences of secularization. As the number of well-informed committed Christians has fallen, so has government and major social institution support for Christianity. Those two changes have combined radically to reduce Britain's stock of religious knowledge. As ever-fewer people (even inside the churches) know about or care about the arguments that shaped the organizational landscape of the nineteenth and twentieth centuries, it has become both more important and easier for once-antagonistic bodies to share dwindling resources and present a common front.

Notes

1. For a detailed discussion of the sociological categories of church, sect, denomination, and cult, see S. Bruce, *Religion in the Modern World: From Cathedrals to Cults* (Oxford: Oxford University Press, 1996), ch. 4.

2. For detailed histories of church mergers in mission fields, see E. M. Jackson, *Red Tape and the Gospel: A Study of the Significance of the Ecumenical Missionary Struggle of William Paton (1886–1943)* (Birmingham: Phlogiston Publishing, 1980); E. M. Jackson (ed.), *God's Apprentice: The Autobiography of Stephen Neill* (London: Hodder & Stoughton, 1991); and S. Neill, *A History of Christian Missions* (Harmondsworth: Penguin, 1974).

3. For details of the campaign, see S. Bruce, *Scottish Gods: Religion in Modern Scotland, 1900–2012* (Edinburgh: Edinburgh University Press, 2014), 105–7.

4. C. D. Field, *Britain's Last Religious Revival? Quantifying Belonging, Behaving and Believing in the Long* 1950s (London: Palgrave, 2015), 83.

5. P. L. Berger, 'A Market Model for the Analysis of Ecumenicity', *Social Research*, 30 (1963), 77–93.

6. R. Gill, *The 'Empty Church' Revisited* (Aldershot: Ashgate, 2003).

7. The problem is compounded for the Church of England by the age of many of its churches. It owns 44 per cent of the Grade 1 listed buildings in England; J. T. Brown, 'Church Upkeep Leaves Vicars Hot under the Dog Collar', *Financial Times*, 5 November 2016.

8. M. Harris, *From Acre End: Portrait of a Village* (London: Chatto and Windus, 1982), 92.

9. United Reformed Church, 'Reports: General Assembly 2006. Resolution 5 New Churches', http://www.urc.org.uk/assembly/assembly2006/churches_changes.html (accessed January 2018).

10. St Paul's Church, Filleigh, http://www.filleighchurch.org.uk (accessed March 2010).

11. *Scunthorpe Telegraph*, 5 December 2007.

12. *Northampton Chronicle*, 24 April 2009.

13. I cannot credit the source of this story (who was active in organizing the mission) because it comes from an article I refereed anonymously for the journal *Northern History*.

14. *Dorset Echo*, 1 November 2007.

15. This can be demonstrated from British Social Attitudes (BSA) survey data from 1983 onwards. Those people who identify as 'Christian—no denomination', but who do not regularly attend church, do not generally score high on traditional Christian beliefs and attitudes.

16. *The Week*, 22 April 2017.

17. *BBC News*, 2 October 2017.

18. *Private Eye*, 1459, 15–22 December 2017.

19. J. Henry, 'Religious Studies GCSE to Have Questions on Homosexuality, Binge Drinking and Drugs', *Sunday Telegraph*, 1 February 2009.

20. Department of Education, 'Collective Worship in Schools', https://www.gov.uk/government/publications/collective-worship-in-schools (accessed July 2018).

21. 'Humanists' Legal Challenge to School Religious Observance', *BBC News*, 12 September 2016, https://www.bbc.co.uk/news/uk-scotland-37336340 (accessed April 2019).
22. R. Garner, 'Philosophy and Ethics Replace Religious Education in Wales', *Independent*, 4 August 2015.
23. *Religious Broadcasts and the Public: A Report on a Social Survey of the Differences between Listeners and Non-Listeners to Religious Broadcasts* (London: BBC, 1955).
24. K. M. Wolff, *The Churches and the British Broadcasting Corporation 1922–1956* (London: SCM Press, 1984).
25. K. Burgess, 'Songs of Praise Shunted to Earlier Slot', *The Times*, 19 February 2019.
26. I. Burrell, 'Religious Broadcasting Needs to Cover More than Extremism', *Independent*, 25 August 2014.
27. K. Burgess, 'BBC to Give All Religions Primetime TV Boost', *The Times*, 20 December 2017. Between 1987 and 2007, the BBC's total output doubled, but the number of religion hours fell from 177 to 175, and much of that was only tangentially religious; J. Wynne-Jones, 'Church is Living in the Past, says BBC Chief', *Daily Telegraph*, 7 February 2010. For further data, see K. Knott, E. Poole, and T. Taira, *Media Portrayals of Religion and the Secular Sacred* (London: Routledge, 2013), 52–4. The word 'sacred' in that title is profoundly misleading: it usually describes mentions of good luck and fortune in stories about gambling.
28. G. Christie, *Crieff Hydro* (Edinburgh: Oliver and Boyd, 1967), 100.
29. 'Prayers Now Axed in Most Town Halls', *Daily Mail*, 26 October 2013.
30. 'God Falls from Grace at Dinner in Cambridge', *Daily Telegraph*, 15 May 2009.
31. The Monastery website, http://themonastery.co.uk/the-venue/christmasgiftthateveryoneshouldget/ (accessed January 2016).
32. B. Leach and A. Jamieson, 'Religion is not on the Cards at Christmas', *Daily Telegraph*, 19 December 2010.
33. R. Gledhill, 'Church's Easter Message Dispenses with the Cross', *The Times*, 10 March 1995.
34. A. Brown, 'No Devil in the Detail of Church of England's New Baptism Service', *Guardian*, 20 June 2014. The change was signalled a decade earlier in Church of England Doctrine Commission, *The Mystery of Salvation* (London: Church House Publishing, 1995).
35. O. Rudgard, 'Bible References Dropped from Nativity Tale', *The Times*, 18 November 2017.
36. M. Handscomb, 'Praise him with Cymbals and Sitars', *Independent*, 13 July 1992.
37. *Guardian*, 18 December 1995.
38. K. Burgess, 'Churches to Heal 200 Year Rift by Sharing Clergy', *The Times*, 28 June 2017.
39. Church of England General Synod, *Report of Proceedings*, 23 (1992), 775.
40. Church of England, *Church Statistics, 2003/4* (London: Church House Publishing, 2005), 43.
41. *The Tablet*, 19 April 2014, 44.
42. Public incomprehension is clear from survey data. One poll showed 74% of people in favour of female bishops and only 12% against; ComRes, *Women Bishops Survey* (July 2012).

43. K. Burgess, 'More Women Inspired to Become Priests', *The Times*, 19 June 2017.

44. I would not make too much of this, but I suspect both a cohort and an age effect in such movements. Clearly each new cohort is attracted to innovations that claim to remedy the defects of the previous generation's worship style. But it also seems that many people who were attracted to the livelier worship of charismatic and independent evangelical congregations in their youth drifted towards more formal liturgical styles as they aged.

45. Social Surveys (Gallup Poll) Ltd, *Television and Religion* (London: University of London Press, 1964).

46. The proportion of births to unmarried parents (including those registered only in the mother's name) was 29% in 1991, 43% in 2001, and 51% in 2011; M. Wade, 'More Children Born to Unwed women than to Married Ones', *The Times*, 18 December 2012.

47. M. R. T. Macnair, 'Homosexuality in School—Section 28 Local Government Act 1988', *Education and the Law*, 1 (2006), 35–9.

48. D. Campbell, 'The Pioneer who Changed Gay Lives', *Observer*, 30 January 2005.

49. A. Crockett and D. Voas, 'A Divergence of Views: Attitude Change and the Religious Crisis over Homosexuality', *Sociological Research Online*, 8 (2003), http://www.socresonline.org.uk/8 (accessed May 2004).

50. Ipsos MORI, *Statement on Same-Sex Marriage Poll in Scotland*, 18 June 2012, http://www.ipsos-mori.com/newsevents/latestnews/1098/Ipsos-MORI-statement-on-samesex-marriage-poll-in-Scotland.aspx (accessed July 2012). An ICM poll for the *Guardian* where the question was the more specific—'Do you support the move to legalise for gay marriage'—produced similar proportions, http://www.guardian.co.uk/society/2012/dec/26/voters-back-gay-marriage-poll (accessed January 2013).

51. R. Gledhill, 'Evangelicals Sign up to a "Church within a Church"', *The Times*, 2 July 2008.

52. A symbolically important date was 2014, when the Association of Christian Counsellors, Britain's leading body of Christian therapists, instructed members to stop trying to 'pray away the gay' (P. Studwick, 'Christians Counsellors Ban Therapy Aimed at "Converting" Gay Patients', *Guardian*, 14 January 2014.

53. R. Gledhill, 'Friend of Dr Rowan Williams Feels "Betrayed" by his Stance on Gays', *The Times*, 8 December 2009, http://www.thetimes.co.uk/tto/faith/article2100871.ece (accessed June 2013).

54. On the Catholic clergy, see F. Martel, *In the Closet of the Vatican: Power, Homosexuality, Hypocrisy* (London: Bloomsbury, 2018).

55. Kevin McKenna raises the possibility that the Catholic Church might have inadvertently encouraged gay men to join the clergy. The Church treats homosexuality as a vile sin. Young Catholic homosexuals are told to control their urges. Celibacy is one way to suppress sinful urges. Joining the clergy thus offers a worthwhile career, an expression of piety, and a way to resolve, through repression, the gay man's identity problems; K. McKenna, 'Unfit for Purpose and in Denial: A Church that has Lost All Authority', *Observer*, 2 March 21013.

56. R. Gledhill, 'Without Gay Priests Church would Be Lost Claims Bishop Gene', *The Times*, 27 July 2007.

57. *Daily Telegraph*, 2 August 2008.
58. M. Beckford, 'Vicar Defies Rules to Carry out Church Blessing of "Lesbian Wedding"', *Daily Telegraph*, 23 September 2008.
59. For a review of the international Anglican communion's divisions over homosexuality, see C. G. Brittan and A. McKinnon, *The Anglican Communion at a Crossroads: The Crises of a Global Church* (Philadelphia: Pennsylvania State University Press, 2018).
60. Crockett and Voas, 'A Divergence of Views'.
61. Data summarized by Jayne Ozanne, who commissioned the YouGov poll, https://jayneozanne.com/2017/09/12/attitudes-to-same-sex-marriage-yougov-poll/ 30 January 2016 (accessed January 2019).
62. 'A Fifth of Elders Ready to Leave Church of Scotland?', *British Church Newspaper*, reprinted in *Scottish Protestant View* (June 2011); S. Carrell, 'Church Braced for Mass Walkout over Gay Clergy', *Guardian*, 15 November 2011.

5

Modernizing the Faith

The Charismatic Movement

In 1999, Revd Martin Down, the incumbent of the joint charge of Ashill and Saham Toney in the diocese of Norfolk, resigned. This was the culmination of a long rumbling dispute between innovators and traditionalists in the Ashill congregation. Soon after his arrival, Down decided that Sunday worship at the ancient church of St Nicholas's and St George needed to become a lot less ancient if it was to become popular. He proposed removing pews to create a flexible space for lively worship.[1] The chairman of Ashill parish council complained: 'The normal Sunday morning services are now very happy-clappy, with people diving around and getting "messages". It's alien to what we're used to, and a bit off-putting.'[2] Down tried to defuse tension by postponing any decision for six months but eventually concluded the way to resolve it was 'by moving the people rather than the pews'. So he held charismatic services in the local community centre and continued the more traditional forms at the parish church. The orthodox were not placated. As one put it: 'We traditionalists rely on solemnity to a great extent to offset the fast pace of our inventive, ephemeral lives. We prefer a ceremony that trickles with unguent to the Hallelujah-all-fall-down service that is increasingly in vogue.'[3] They voted to remove Down.

The Church of England is usually keen to defend its hierarchical structure, so it is telling that the Norfolk diocese overlooked what was in effect a schism to classify Down's followers (now meeting as 'The Fountain of Life') as a mission church. It further conceded the appeal of this upstart competitor by appointing Stephen Mawditt, the successor to Down, as one of the diocese's evangelistic outreach specialists. Remarkably, Mawditt seemed unaware of that status when I interviewed him. He rather ruefully noted that his charismatic congregation took very little inspiration from the Church of England though it made one of the highest per capita contributions to the diocese's coffers.

The effects of the dispute on the Church's popularity are pointed. In 1990, before the split, 5.9 per cent of the area's adults were Anglican members. That rose to 7.1 per cent in 1997 and then fell back to 6.7 in 2000 and declined further to 4.4 in 2005. But the point is even clearer if we take the two congregations separately. Saham Toney, which was not directly involved, showed a steady decline: from 5.1 per cent of village residents in 1997 to 3.0 per cent in 2005. But Ashill's electoral roll leapt during the dispute (adding twenty-one members to a base of eighty-three) and then fell.[4] The Fountain of Life probably had about fifty members in 2005, so arguably the total churchgoing population of the parish had increased, but this was largely because the new congregation was attracting people from a wider area.[5]

Growth

The Fountain of Life is a local instance of a national movement that represents one of the few growth spots in post-war Christianity. The charismatic movement was sufficiently complex for Peter Brierley, the UK's premier church statistician, to give up trying to find a more specific designation and call its separatist congregations simply 'New Churches'. He estimates that, from small beginnings in the 1960s, the movement grew by 144 per cent between the church censuses he conducted in 1979 and 1989.[6] By 1991, New Churches accounted for just over a quarter of all English church attendance.[7] More importantly, two in five charismatic congregations were growing, while most every other variety was declining.[8] The movement was also influencing older denominations. Baptist, Methodist, Anglican, and URC congregations that were strongly affected by it also affiliated to one of a number of charismatic networks. And, while the typical congregation in those denominations was declining, the charismatic ones were likely to be growing. Finally, as we will see, many aspects of charismatic style influenced even those congregations that did not accept its distinctive theological principles.

Viewed from afar, the history of the Christian Church exhibits a wave pattern. Periodically, enthusiasts attack the dominant church for dull conformity and campaign for a return to the vigour of the days of the Apostles. One recurrent theme is the possibility of deriving energy and confidence from the supposedly neglected third part of the Trinity: the Holy Spirit. Traditionally, Christians have supposed that the supernatural gifts displayed by the Apostles at Pentecost—healing, prophecy, and speaking in the tongues of men and angels—were intended for only the foundation of Christianity and that they were thereafter embedded in the structure and rituals of the Church. Pentecostalists are those who suppose such gifts are still available to those who seek them and, further, that such gifts will reverse the decline of Christianity in the West. That was the basis for the early twentieth-century Pentecostal movement that became institutionalized in new sects: the Elim Pentecostal Church, the Assemblies of God, and the Church of the Nazarene.[9] That wave recruited best from the top end of the working class and was thus popular in the north of England. The charismatic renewal movement of the 1960s was different in that it attracted a more middle-class base from the affluent south of England and, because the general climate was considerably more secular, it was both less theologically and socially conservative.

The history of charismata in the late twentieth century is complex, but it can be simplified into two strands. Many charismatics 'came out' of their previous sects and denominations to form new ones—generally as networks of semi-autonomous congregations linked to some dominant personality. Examples include the Newfrontiers network led by Terry Virgo and the Vineyard churches led by John Wimber. The second strand was formed by clergy of mainstream churches (largely the Church of England though some Catholic congregations were also influenced): Ashill's Fountain of Life is an example.

The separatists were initially called the 'house church movement' after their most obvious characteristic: small groups meeting in private homes.[10] But many grew rapidly and either moved into redundant churches or, more often, rented flexible spaces such as school halls or empty shops and factories. Just as annual events such as the week-long camp meetings of the Keswick Convention were important in spreading new ideas outside the formal denominational structures in the nineteenth century, so the camping holiday was an important part of the early spread of the charismatic movement. In the early 1980s, the brothers Bryn and Keri Jones, who led the Harvestime groups in the Bradford area, ran Dales Bible Week on the Harrogate Showground.[11] Similar events were organized in Sussex and in the New Forest.

To give some flavour of a later charismatic congregation, it is worth quoting at length from the 'Mystery Worshipper' section of the excellent *Ship of Fools* website.[12] This invites anonymous contributors to describe, under a standard set of headings (in italics), church services they attend. That for 'St Thomas, Philadelphia Campus, Sheffield' is as follows:

Denomination: A local ecumenical project between the Church of England and the Baptist Church.[13]

The building: There's a good reason why this church calls itself a campus! It occupies several old converted warehouses in the central industrial district of Sheffield; I counted at least four of them. It was rather confusing, actually. I ended up accosting some people who looked likely to be Christians—or at least looked suspiciously middle class for this part of town—to find out which building we were actually meeting in.

The church: Well, they're an official Church of England Fresh Expression of Church, if that counts! They're a mission church, founded by a large local church, St Thomas Crookes, to reach people in Sheffield's city centre.

The neighbourhood: Sheffield is a city in the north of England once known as a steel production centre. It is home to the University of Sheffield. The church is based in Sheffield's industrial district, so there are a lot of warehouses nearby, but not very much else, though there is some housing maybe a quarter of a mile away. It makes one wonder where the congregation actually come from; further investigation revealed that they're from a fairly widespread area.

The cast: The service was led by the Rev. Steve Cockram, a Baptist minister at the church. On sermon duty we had Richard England, who I found out later was their student worker.

The date & time: Sunday, 23 April 2006, 10.30 a.m.

What was the name of the service?: Sunday Celebration.

How full was the building?: I'd estimate there were maybe 300 to 400 people there. The building could have held more, but it was about 80 per cent full.

Did anyone welcome you personally?: I was greeted at the door by a guide who handed me a 'welcomer' and said that as a first time visitor I was entitled to a free book. He passed me on to someone named Paul, who explained the church's various groupings called lifeshapes, clusters, focuses, triangles, etc. I was beginning to get lost in the jargon. 'You see,' said Paul, 'Some have a geographical focus and some have a more mission-oriented focus, like outreaches to prostitutes or the homeless or something.' The book he gave me is supposed to explain all this. I actually enjoyed my conversation with Paul despite the jargon!

Was your pew comfortable?: It was a stackable plastic chair, exactly the sort you get in schools. My backside remembered those schooldays well and accommodated itself nicely to the contours of the 'pew.'

How would you describe the pre-service atmosphere?: It was a busy hustle, as people chatted to their friends, browsed the bookstall, or sampled the pre-service coffee and pastries. Sadly, I hadn't been able to get any pastries, since I'd spent so long being told about lifeshapes, clusters, focuses and triangles. I did have a bit of time to chat with the person sitting next to me before the service began.

What were the exact opening words of the service?: The guitars had already started playing for the first chorus when the leader said, 'All right, could you be making your way to the seats, please?'

What books did the congregation use during the service?: No books were provided. Many brought their own Bibles, and the readings and songs appeared on an on-stage data projector screen. Though I didn't have a Bible with me, the reading sounded like it was from the New International Version.

What musical instruments were played?: Acoustic and electric guitars, a bass guitar, a drumkit, and lead and backing singers. The classic Christian rock lineup.

Was the worship stiff-upper-lip, happy clappy, or what?: Philadelphia is the happiest, clappiest church I've ever been to. My ears actually had to adjust to the volume. The air was a forest of hands—they even had people waving streamers at the front! (Why is it always women that wave streamers, by the way? I've never seen a man do it, ever.)

Exactly how long was the sermon?: 40 minutes.

On a scale of 1–10, how good was the preacher?: 7—I felt the sermon could have been shorter without losing anything. Richard England told too many anecdotes for my liking. He made some good points, though, and was lively and engaging.

In a nutshell, what was the sermon about?: 'No prize, no price'—1 Corinthians 9. Some people are running nowhere, but just running. We've got to pay the price, to train hard, and get out of our comfort zones for Jesus. We wouldn't race if we didn't have a prize to aim for, and that's eternity with Jesus. Jesus also had to pay a price, which was death on a cross. His prize is us, every single one of us.

Which part of the service was like being in heaven?: Being in a church where people were so obviously enthusiastic. I could see that this wasn't just a church for Sunday pew-pushing, it was a church you could plant your roots in, and you wouldn't be the only one doing so.

And which part was like being in...er...the other place?: The preacher seemed to inject 'Y'know' into every other phrase. 'No, I don't know!' I wanted to scream. 'Get on with it and tell me!'

What happened when you hung around after the service looking lost?: I continued my conversation with the person sitting next to me. Eventually I wandered off to sample the coffee.

How would you describe the after-service coffee?: It was bog-standard instant in a cardboard cup. I needed it too—the service had left me feeling rather tired.

How would you feel about making this church your regular (where 10 = ecstatic, 0 = terminal)?: 9—The style isn't really for me. I prefer smaller churches and I'm not all that keen on 40 minute sermons. All these are minor points, though, since this was definitely a church where I could see Jesus working. I'd need to read the jargon-busting book first!

Did the service make you feel glad to be a Christian?: Most definitely.

What one thing will you remember about all this in seven days' time?: The volume.

Characteristics

The movement overall had a number of distinctive features. The most obvious innovations were in worship: classic Victorian hymns replaced by contemporary pop songs, and the organ replaced by the rock band format of drums, keyboards, and guitars and vocalists using hand-held microphones. That the new songs were initially unfamiliar and the meetings intended to attract outsiders were reasons for the format of simple lyrics being repeated six or seven times. Sometimes, in the manner of black American church services, a chorus was repeated twenty or thirty times as the preacher declaimed short prayers or slogans over the swelling anthem. Members of the congregation stood with arms raised, as if to draw down the Holy Spirit, and they spoke in 'the tongues of men and angels'.[14]

Critics were quick to claim that such services were mere entertainments that, if they had any effect, were generating 'a bizarre pseudo-ecstatic state' or 'an intensity of emotion' rather than proper spirituality.[15] In its North American form, the movement's services were often accompanied by extravagant responses. In the style associated with the Vineyard congregation near Toronto airport (hence the term 'Toronto Blessing'), congregants barked like dogs and prostrated themselves. The British were generally more reserved, but in the early 1990s enterprising journalists could always find congregations where people fainted, groaned as if in pain, writhed on the ground, or drummed their feet like demented rabbits.[16] Of itself there was nothing new in using secular entertainment to attract the ungodly. The Salvation Army did it in the nineteenth century with the now-passé brass band. The large 'Central Mission' halls built by the Wesleyan Methodists attracted labourers in their work clothes to musical entertainments with a religious subtext; they even permitted pipe-smoking. However, those examples involved augmenting traditional services with additional formats rather than drastically altering the standard worship formats.

Like its nineteenth-century Holiness movement predecessor, the charismatic movement promoted a special 'executive class' of Christian. Being baptized of, in, or by (all three prepositions have been used) the Holy Spirit conferred a status higher than that enjoyed by the ordinary converted Christian. And speaking in tongues was a sign of that status. The more thoughtful were nuanced and ambiguous about such assertions, but for many charismatics their claim to the gifts enjoyed by the early Apostles was a warrant for seeing themselves as better than others. Not surprisingly, this elitism provoked fierce opposition from mainstream Christians.

The movement also developed a novel form of leadership. To outsiders there might seem little peculiar about Arthur Wallis, Bryn Jones, and Terry Virgo claiming to be apostles or prophets; they assume such terms are used metaphorically. But the leaders of the charismatic movement did think that they enjoyed a status similar to that of Peter and those who had known Christ personally. It is a characteristic of formal organizations such as the Church of Scotland or the Methodist Church that roles are well defined and officials are thus constrained in what they can do. It is also the case that, in a society where religious involvement is a free choice, churches can demand very little of their members; if they find the expected commitments irksome, they simply walk away. That the house churches were small and, in the first generation, composed of enthusiasts who had voluntarily committed themselves meant that leaders who could claim the justification of divine prophecy had considerably more authority and control over their members than had the mainstream clergy. Add to that a lack of formal controls or constraints and one has a recipe for manipulation and bullying. In its early house-church phase, many leaders promoted the idea of 'shepherding', which essentially boiled down to the leader claiming the authority to direct members' lives with guidance on marriage partners, residential location, job choices, and—most self-interestedly— tithing.[17] Members were instructed that the true Christian gives a tenth of their income to God, which usually meant to the leader.

A fourth characteristic of the charismatic movement was self-confidence. No innovation attracts people with promises of failure, but the charismatic leaders were unusually fond of grandiloquent predictions of success. God was about to send a great deliverance and the leaders knew this because the Holy Spirit had given them the gift of prophecy. They were, of course, not alone in presenting hopes as predictions. Most political movements gain confidence from the belief that history is on their side. Wallis was fond of the idea of 'latter rain': God was ready to deliver a great revival of Christianity, but it would require an entirely new structure, which he and his disciples would produce. In 1974 he wrote: 'I see no future for denominations but a glorious future for the Body of Christ.'[18] Build it and they shall come. Wimber claimed to see 'Signs and Wonders'.

The final notable characteristic is an unusual stress on personal experience. Many of the traditionally important elements of Christianity were neglected: 'the concept of sin, the Bible, heaven, grace and salvation are less frequently dealt with.'[19] Many charismatics were dismissive of the controversies around which the mainstream denominations and established sects had been created. The leaders may have been theological aware; the rank-and-file wanted assurance and a spiritual high. Hence the general tone was resolutely upbeat. In various forms, many recruits to the charismatic movement have told me they left sects such as the Brethren because they were fed up being constantly nagged about sin and they were repelled by threats of eternal damnation. They wanted the assurance of sunlit uplands and they wanted to enjoy themselves.

Sheffield: Charismatic Abuse

Most British people paid no attention to the charismatic movement beyond learning the dismissive adjective 'happy-clappy', but one extreme expression did briefly attract a deal of public attention. What happened in Sheffield was not at all typical, but the scandal caused by the Nine O'Clock Service (NOS) floridly illustrates two of the characteristics just mentioned: liturgical innovation and abusive leadership.

In the early 1980s, Chris Brain moved to Sheffield, formed a band, started to attend the Anglican congregation of St Thomas, and impressed the vicar enough to be appointed leader of a house group.[20] About ten other young people joined him in what became a commune. The band performed at the Greenbelt Christian Arts festival and got 'a reputation for being provocative, both theologically and sexually'. In November 1985, members of the commune attended a Signs and Wonders conference at Sheffield City Hall and become enthusiastic Wimber supporters. The vicar had a vision of 'several hundred young people' being attracted to his church and encouraged Brain's commune to set up an experimental service for their kind of people. One young woman who joined the commune told me:

> Sheffield in the 1980s was an amazing place. The electronic music scene. The social justice stuff. The super trendy look. They were very attractive people. And I was attracted by the idea of living as a community. They were the antidote to Thatcher's Britain. They were into Liberation Theology…They were a living example, something exciting. Sex was not an issue then: people

had affairs all the time. Smoking fags and a bit of pot. We all got married then. There were about twelve marriages. There was a lot of pressure because people started complaining about the sex and the promiscuity and we got the word to straighten up our act so a lot of us got married. It was a big mistake.[21]

Unlike the usual charismatic service, with its repetitive singing over an amplified soft-rock format, the NOS was based on

choppy mid-eighties goth rock, unremarkable in [local clubs] but spine tingling in a church environment. The lyrics were projected at the front, letrasetted white on a black background, a world away from the marker pen and [overhead projection] of the normal services, and even further from the dusty hymnals that I remembered from my childhood.[22]

To heighten the dramatic effect, the organizers and regulars all wore black.

Theologically speaking, NOS was initially mainstream charismatic, but its core membership was unusually elitist and selective: 'People were interviewed and counselled before being admitted into membership, and then assigned several ministries ranging from roadie type duties, through arts and media, to healing and intercessory prayer.'[23] Through the late 1980s, NOS evolved with the city's youth culture: acid house music and style were adopted, and a greater emphasis was placed on dance, performance, and multimedia in the services. A communion service (grandiosely entitled the Planetary Mass), which combined incense, elaborate light shows, Gregorian chant, and ambient music, was devised and proved sufficiently popular that NOS moved out of a traditional church and into a warehouse.

In August 1995, tabloid newspapers broke the story that Chris Brain had financially and sexually exploited his colleagues and followers. He and his closest lieutenants had used the claim that they were the vanguard of the Lord's work to intimidate the rest, often by public humiliation: 'The staff meetings were terrifying. You'd have an agenda but we never got through the items because someone would get picked on and mercilessly hammered. And you'd be sitting there rigid hoping that it wouldn't be your turn next. The fear was absolutely phenomenal.' Brain had turned the commune into his private service organization.

One reason Chris got away with the exploitation was that it came gradually. At first he just had the car because he needed it for his role and then he needed a mobile phone. Great brick of a thing it was in those days but he needed it and so he had it. And then he needed more time than everyone else so other people sorted his house for him. My husband was responsible for Chris's clothes and for designing and decorating his house. He was a very talented decorator but he wasn't allowed to decorate our house because that was a distraction from the mission. He had to minister to Chris.

As well as doing his domestic work, Brain had attractive young women help him 'relax' from the stress of his Herculean task with rather personal massages. Although the sex element was what attracted the tabloid press, and a number of women later came to see him as having been a groomer and predator, the sexual abuse was not the primary cause of unhappiness. After all, the commune members were closer to the sexual mores of Sheffield's youth culture than to the puritanism of the typical evangelical church.

> The biggest thing wasn't the money or the house or even the sex; it was Chris's wife getting pregnant. About fifteen of us had agreed we would not have children because we were to give ourselves completely to the group and to Jesus and that was a huge loss for some of us and then she gets pregnant and has a baby.

To an outsider it seems obvious that, if he was not plain mentally ill, Brain was suffering from megalomania: 'Getting near the end you could see Chris was dropping hints that he was Christ. He never said it but it was absolutely clear that he was a superior being. At one meeting we all had to draw ourselves and Chris drew himself in the Garden of Gethsemane!'

It may seem strange that the Church of England was so accommodating—Brain was offered a short cut to ordination—but it was desperate: only too well aware that its congregations were shrinking and its members ageing. In 1881, around 12 per cent of the people of Sheffield regularly attended the Church of England; a century later the figure was around 1 per cent.[24] In 1881, there were forty-three Anglican outlets; a century later only eleven. And the people in the pews were patently well above the average age, especially for a university city. In that context, the ability of the NOS to attract young people did seem a Godsend.

Banbury: Religion and Cultural Currency

Banbury was the site of one of the first major community studies in modern British sociology.[25] After three years of fieldwork between 1949 and 1952,

Margaret Stacey detailed the tensions between the traditional economy, society, and culture of a small market town and the world of the new industries and Labour politics that had arrived post-war. In 1966, a team of three fieldworkers began a follow-up study under Stacey's direction, and in 2010 I spent some time in the town.[26] I will briefly describe the major changes in Banbury's religious culture and then consider in some detail one of the major features of Christianity in modern Britain: the deliberate abandoning of distinctive features of the faith in pursuit of cultural relevance and hence, its advocates hope, renewed popularity.

Banbury of the 1950s was typical of most small English towns in that the vast majority of churchgoers were Anglican and most of the rest were Methodist. The Church of England and the Methodists each had four congregations; there were two Baptist congregations; and one each for the Roman Catholics, Congregationalists, Salvation Army, Open Brethren, Closed Brethren, Unitarians, Four Square Gospel, Quakers, Jehovah's Witnesses, and Christian Scientists.[27] A total of 20 worship outlets served a population of around 18,000: one church for every 900 people. In total, about 21 per cent of adults were church members: half of them Anglican and the rest divided pretty evenly between Catholics and Methodists, with the others being tiny.[28] Stacey tried to estimate churchgoing. A survey of just over 2,000 residents asked if they attended church and—quite implausibly—most claimed so to do. Stacey herself queried these data: 'When...interviewers asked a respondent whether he attended a place of worship, they were faced with the problem of deciding whether he was telling the truth. Even allowing for the fact that a man who went to church at Christmas or Easter only was classed as an attender, it is certain that interviewers gave too many respondents the benefit of the doubt.'[29] The problem was 'compliance effects': in the 1950s, churchgoing was still sufficiently popular that many non-attenders felt obliged to pretend otherwise.[30]

Stacey's church membership data are more reliable because they came from the clergy, and, for Nonconformists such as the Methodists and Baptists, the clergy would have had little trouble providing accurate figures for what most of us would think of as 'members'. For Anglicans it is the figure for those interested enough to ask for their names to go on the parish electoral roll, which in the 1950s was generally a little smaller than our current notions of membership.[31]

Twenty years later, the town's religious complexion had changed slightly. There were still four Anglican churches, but the Methodists and the Catholics had each added one. The Full Gospel Testimony church had joined the Elim

Pentecostals, and there was now a Mormon tabernacle.[32] In total, 22 outlets served a population of 26,000: at one church or chapel per 1,182 people, that was a significantly reduced presence. While the number of worship outlets had grown by 10 per cent, the population of the town had grown by over 40 per cent. There was a corresponding decline in church membership between 1950 and 1967: from 24 to 15 per cent of the adult population.

The second Banbury study was an improvement on the first in one respect: instead of asking people about their churchgoing, the researchers counted attendances at all the town's known churches and chapels. This showed roughly 7 per cent of the town's adults in church on a particular Sunday, with the Catholics (at 3 per cent) easily ahead of conservative and evangelical Protestants and Church of England (both at 1 per cent).[33] And, although the charismatic movement was still in its infancy, its outlets already had as many attenders as the Methodist chapels.[34]

By 2010, the religious life of Banbury had changed dramatically. Both a symptom and a cause of the other changes I will mention shortly, there had been a marked decline in nominal attachment to Christianity; some of this represented a real change in attitude but much will have been simply the decline in compliance effects. Fewer committed Christians meant less reason for anyone else to pretend to some attachment.[35] In 1950, all but 3 per cent of Stacey's survey respondents claimed to attend church. In the 2011 Census of England and Wales, only 54 per cent of Banburians claimed to be Christian, and 28 per cent said they had no religion.[36] The number of worship outlets was slightly higher than in 1967, but the population had grown much more: there were now 25 sites for 41,815 people or 1 per 1,672 people.

There had been some change in the composition of the church milieu. Two fringe sects—the Christian Scientists and the Christadelphians—had gone, as had the Elim Pentecostalists. Liberal Protestantism, already weakening in 1967, had continued to shrink. The Unitarians, who had been third in popularity in 1851, had all but vanished by 1967; two years later they disbanded and their chapel was demolished.[37] The Congregationalists (who merged with the Presbyterians to form the United Reformed Church in 1972) had given up their premises and moved into St Mary's with the Anglicans. The conservative Protestant block had changed slightly in composition and grown equally slightly. To broaden its appeal, the Brethren meeting had rebadged itself as the Southam Road Evangelical Church. The main Baptist congregation had renamed itself the People's Church. The Banbury Evangelical Free Church had been founded in 1984, and the tithes of its largely middle-class members permitted the employment of a trainee pastor, but its 2010 membership was down from its 1990s peak to just twenty-five and typical attendances was around forty. The new Grimsbury Baptist congregation numbered around twenty.

The most obvious change was the growth of two charismatic congregations. The Banbury Community Church (an independent body affiliated to the Evangelical Alliance) was founded in 1995, and Jubilee (part of the Newfrontiers network) began regular services in 2003. Neither had acquired its own premises: one met in the local secondary school; the other in a community hall.

Although the Church of England had initiated outreach services in the new housing estates, both it and the Methodist church had seen a considerable decline in members and attendances. That change and migration from Eastern Europe—in 2011, 7 per cent gave their main language as Polish—had seen the Catholic Church become Banbury's largest Christian body.[38] But the change that rivals the growth of the avowedly non-religious was the growth of the Muslim community. In 2011, 8 per cent of Banbury residents described themselves as Muslim: a growth of 303 per cent on the 2001 figure. They had a choice of two mosques. The smaller was named after a leading Saudi Wahhabi scholar Sheikh Abdul Aziz ibn Bazz.[39] The Banbury Masjid was based in a converted house when I visited in 2010, but two years later it acquired a very large purpose-built mosque, and it was running a school for girls.

To summarize, the history of religion in Banbury in the second half of the twentieth century is typical of English towns of its size. Relative to the growing population, the Christian churches lost more than half their membership; new charismatic fellowships grew at the expense of the traditional denominations; and migration vastly increased the proportion of Catholics in the town.

Table 5.1. Christian church membership, Banbury, 1950, 1967, and 2010

Church and membership	1950	1967	2010
Anglican	1,138	854	356
Roman Catholic	560	700	1,392
Methodist	448	455	220
Baptist	90	180	170
Salvation Army	72	120	70
Congregational	68	70	50
Other	66	200	723
Total adherents	2,442	2,579	2,981
Estimated population over 17	10,000	17,100	30,000
Members as % of adult population	24.4	15.1	9.9

Source: Technical details of how these figures were generated from census data and from clergy estimates are provided in Bruce, 'A Sociology Classic Revisited: Religion in Banbury'.

And, where there were no Muslims in 1950, by 2010 they were a sizeable proportion of the town's residents.

Decline and Cooperation

As noted in Chapter 4, a common response to Christianity's decline is increasing cooperation between churches. Stacey remarks on the frostiness of relations in the 1950s. There was a 'Clergy and Ministers Fraternal', but the Anglican clergy (who were better educated and of higher social status than their Nonconformist counterparts) rarely attended; the Catholic priests never did. There were no united services, not even on Armistice Day. The 1967 restudy noted that a local Council of Churches had been formed in 1965 and that the clergy were generally more likely to see each other as colleagues in a common enterprise. In 2010, the main churches advertised each other's events and cooperated in presenting a united Christian front to the town. Even the Southam Road Evangelical Church and the Salvation Army joined in such activities as 'Banbury Christians Praying Together'—a 'prayer walk' around the town. The weekly local paper carried a church column, authorship of which is rotated around the churches and, in 2010, coordinated by the Methodist minister.

The coincidence of dwindling congregations and ageing buildings had prompted much local improvisation. The largest Anglican church—St Mary's— was now shared with the URC. Though the two congregations maintained separate structures and meet sequentially most Sundays, they periodically shared services. Another Anglican church, St Francis's, became a 'local ecumenical partnership'. Initially involving the United Reformed Church, Southam Road Evangelical Church, and the Catholic Church, three services a month were run by the Anglicans with the Methodists leading worship on the fourth Sunday. The third venture was the most radical. In the Grimsbury area of town, the Methodists replaced their inappropriately large chapel with a block of sheltered housing that contained a small chapel, shared by the Methodists and the Baptists.

Although the new charismatic fellowships presented themselves as a radical alternative to the other churches in Banbury, they were helped by the Methodists. Jubilee borrowed the large Marlborough Road Methodist church for special events such as the weekend of prayer held in May 2010. The Methodists also lent Marlborough Road to the Banbury Community Church for weddings and the Methodist minister acted as registrar.

Disguising Religion

Banbury churches exemplify an important trend in British Christianity: the deliberate secularization of what Erving Goffman called 'the presentation of self'.[40] As noted in Chapter 4, few people now know what distinguishes Congregationalists from Presbyterians from Anglicans or what explain why Methodists divided into Wesleyan, Primitive, New Connexion, or Calvinistic Methodists. Many churchgoers are themselves hardly well informed and that makes it possible for them to see theological and ecclesiological differences as minor. This, in turn, permits the argument that the best way to recruit outsiders is to play down any feature that can plausibly be regarded as non-essential. As the pastor of the People's Church put it: 'I want to try and create a church for people who aren't used to coming to church. It's more about the people outside than inside.'[41]

Many churches have rebranded. In some cases a specific identity has been replaced by a vaguer or more abstract tag: a Pentecostal Apostolic Church in the Inner Hebrides now calls itself the Skye Bible Church. Banbury Jubilee's self-description is vaguer—to non-Jews and non-Christians, a jubilee is just a commemorative celebration—and its website describes it simply as 'a small Christian community'. The Banbury Brethren went for the broader 'evangelical' label. Some names were changed to remove reference to passé theological argument: so Banbury's adult dippers dropped 'Baptist' in favour of the aspirational 'The People's Church'. 'Community' is a popular title adjective for three reasons. It avoids theological arguments, it asserts a mission to the local people, and it implies that it already has the support of the community. 'Life' (as in the River of Life in Dumfries or the Fountain of Life in Norfolk) is another popular tag. 'Hillsong', the name of a large congregation in London and an international network of affiliates, nicely avoids any suggestion of religion and aims instead for the same vaguely inspirational territory as gyms, dating websites, and health spas. The Richmond Pentecostal Church is now 'Influence'; 'XCEL' has congregations in Glasgow, Newtown Aycliffe, and Portree. 'Destiny' is a very popular tag.

The secularization of presentation can be seen in the choice of new premises and in the refurbishment of existing ones. The Southam Road Evangelical Church looks like a school hall, and one of Banbury's charismatic congregations meets in a school hall. Baptist churches were hardly ornate before, but the People's Church looks like a conference centre lecture room: a projection screen in place of stained glass; moveable chairs in place of fixed pews, a lectern in place of an altar, no Bibles in the back of chairs, and a distinct absence of religious decoration.

Although the website of the People's Church has links that make clear its evangelical Protestant theology, the most obvious message of its public face is the fun aspect of its worship: 'What happens on a Sunday? Loud and clear. It's different, you won't be bored, it's not for very long and you'll leave with a smile on your face. Every Sunday the worship is inspiring, the prayers are real and the talks speak directly to you. We're a church for people who aren't used to coming to church and so your experience will be different.'[42]

Fun as the selling point is often conveyed in the photographs used on the websites of New Churches and those that have been influenced by their demotic style. The sidebar for the website of the King's Community Church, Braintree, is decorated with generic photographs of attractive (but not offputtingly so) men and women in their 40s grinning with their mouths wide open.[43] The same photo stock could easily be (and probably has been) used to advertise dating, exercise, holiday, food supplement, mobile phones, and life insurance.

Christian churches differ in the extent to which they employ a formal prescribed liturgy or set of rituals form for worship. The Catholic and Orthodox churches regard their liturgies as 'sacred'. The clergy say and do things, and the congregation say and do things, because those things contain sacramental power: they change our being and our relationship to God. Protestants reject that view of liturgy, but most enduring Protestant denominations have developed set forms for the conduct of services (psalm, hymn, prayer, Bible reading, hymn, prayer, end) and have scripts that the clergy routinely follow. The Church of England has its Book of Common Prayer. The original 1549 version was the first prayer book to include complete forms of service for daily and Sunday worship in English, and it had services for baptism, confirmation, marriage, and funerals, and prayers for the sick. It also included weekly variations appropriate to the Christian calendar and the seasons of the year, and it specified which Old and New Testament texts should be read each week. With various modifications, the Book of Common Prayer remains in use to this day, not just in the Church of England, but in Anglican churches throughout the world.

Irrespective of whether the language used in divine worship is seen as divinely inspired and sanctified or merely conventional, alterations to it are often as contentious as related arguments about which translations of the Bible best represent the word of God.[44] The arguments on either side are reasonable. Traditionalists take the view that Thomas Cranmer's sixteenth-century prose is as clear as anything more recent. Initial unfamiliarity is not a problem, because people are always learning new words and phrases and hence should have no difficulty learning some old ones. And having a distinctive language is good because it reminds people that divine worship is set apart from the secular life; it is not a chat with friends around the kitchen table. Equally sensibly, modernizers suppose that outsiders will not be persuaded to believe things they do not understand and that Cranmer was writing in the demotic prose of his day; he was not imitating the archaic style of the tenth century.

Both sides were well represented in arguments over the 2012 decision of the-then-Education Secretary to mark the 400th anniversary of the King James translation of the Bible by having a copy sent to every school in England and Wales. This was obviously a sop to the Conservative party's nostalgia-and-heritage wing of elderly voters. Non-Christians were perplexed, and Christians who actually worked with children were annoyed by the pointless gesture: as one priest reasonably asked: 'Has Michael Gove actually met a child recently?'[45]

Like most New Churches, Banbury's Jubilee and the Southam Road Evangelicals now use rock bands for their worship, and, lyrics apart, the songs they sing are often indistinguishable from the soft rock of 'drive-time' radio programmes. Actually, even the lyrics often obscure the purpose. Very many use a personal (my mother would have said 'over-familiar') style of addressing the deity and avoid themes such as hell and damnation that clearly separate a Victorian Presbyterian hymn from a love song.[46]

Innovation in church music has always been contentious. Even when the norm has obviously secular origins, later generations often take the preferred style of their grandparents to be especially pleasing to God.[47] Scottish Presbyterian churches initially sang unaccompanied, because they could not afford instruments. Yet, when conservative factions resisted the general trend to increasing liberalism and toleration in the nineteenth century, they insisted that only the Psalms of David could be sung (because they were written by God rather than by people) and then only unaccompanied.[48] The eighteenth-century hymns of Charles Wesley, and the late-nineteenth-century songs associated with the revival crusades of American evangelists Dwight L. Moody and Ira D. Sankey, were initially rejected as the devil's work. By the 1950s they were accepted by almost all Protestant churches as inspirational.

Some objections to the happy-clappy style are aesthetic. The Catholic Scots composer James Macmillan, for example, criticized 'aisle-dancing and numb-skull jogging-for-Jesus choruses, maudlin sentimental dirges, faux American folk music, and cod Celticness'.[49] But there is also a point of substance. When Ian Dury entitled one of his best-known songs 'Sex and Drugs and Rock-and-Roll' and followed those words with 'is very good indeed', he was only articulating the obvious connection. Modern amplified pop music celebrated the deviant lifestyles of the promiscuous drug-taking hippies of the late 1960s, and even country-and-western music (generally seen as a conservative alternative) is often morally ambiguous—giving rather too much loving attention to the sins and vices of which the singer intends to repent, some day. Hence, when Christians object to the appearance of drum kits, electric guitars, and hand-held microphones, they are not just being traditional because they suppose the past better than the present; they fear contamination. They are also concerned that the loud rhythmic music will 'brainwash' its hearers—human psychological contrivance replacing what should be the effects of divine inspiration.[50]

My impression is that, even if it were the case that people could be brainwashed by lively music (and there is no evidence of that), it would not happen in any charismatic meeting I have attended. Though this may seem like a racist generalization, it has to be said that British charismatic worship is often limp and tepid compared to the Black Pentecostal version. When I attended the Sheffield Philadelphia congregation already described in detail, my report would have been rather different from that of the Mystery Worshipper. The ad-libbed addresses were inarticulate and bumbling. The opening children's performance—with actions to match the lyrics—was inept and embarrassing: the words 'conquering sin' were accompanied with what were presumably intended to be martial arts postures but looked like an attack of hives. The rock band did not so much accompany the congregation's singing as club it into submission.

The New Churches' secularization of their public image can be seen in a radical attitude to dress and demeanour. The Catholic Church and the Church of England have always had distinctive uniforms for their officials: the robes, croziers, and mitres of bishops are intended—like their cathedrals—to signify the power and glory of God and of his earthly vicars. The black gowns worn by Nonconformist clergy were initially chosen because they were not church outfits, but when the clergy continued to wear them after university lecturers and schoolteachers had given them up, they became a clerical uniform. For centuries British Christians have worn their best (provided they were sombre) clothes to go to church. In nineteenth-century Shetland, one finds ministers soliciting funds to buy decent clothes for poor parishioners who could plausibly explain their absence from church by their lack of respectable apparel. As the phrase suggests, for the first three-quarters of the twentieth century churchgoers wore their 'Sunday best'. But from the 1970s an age difference emerged: old people still dressed up but young people dressed down. And, since the 1980s, casual dress has been an essential part of the appeal to people outside the traditional circle of churchgoers. The website for Banbury's Jubilee charismatic fellowship specifically says: 'Our meetings are friendly and lively, most people dress casually', and that for the Banbury Community Church says: 'Our communication style is very informal, jeans often being the order of the day.'[51] That trend is sufficiently powerful for the Church of England regularly to raise (but then dodge) the matter of clergy outfits.[52]

When religion was popular and important, the clergy enjoyed high status, and this was reflected in the respect they expected and received: in the 1920s, the Gosforth rector literally talked down to his parishioners from the saddle of a large horse. Exactly why the laity deferred to the clergy differs with tradition. Catholics admired their clergy for their sacramental power, piety, celibacy, and, in many cases, poverty. Protestant clergy did not claim sacramental power, but they often enjoyed the prestige that came with a considerable income, a large rectory, and a university education. Even in churches that reject a distinct clergy, those who preached and led in worship would normally be respected for their skills and piety, and thus were distinct from their congregants, in the business of religion if in nothing else. Church of Scotland ministers often had three degrees: they graduated in a wide variety of secular subjects before taking a theological degree, and many then studied for a doctorate.

Although charismatic group leaders often enjoyed exceptional power over their followers, they led the way in removing the outward appearance of high status. They, like their younger congregants, dressed casually; it is almost impossible to find a suit and tie in the smiling portrait photographs of the pastors and worship leaders on New Church websites. Some fellowships have gone further than encouraging casual dress: the senior pastor of River of Life in Dumfries said: 'Our presentation style was deliberate. We gave a lot of thought to this. We deliberately chose to wear casual clothes but in manly colours: blacks and greys. We did not want to seem feminine.'

One further mark of casualization is the abbreviated first name. Until the 1960s, clergy were addressed by their rank titles, and the notice boards outside their churches listed their credentials. Then first names become common. But even those, if they were too long, might be too formal for the unchurched. Hence, in 2005, St Thomas, Philadelphia, Sheffield listed the following abbreviated names in its ministry team: Mick, Tom, Dan, Jude, Andy, Malc, Becca, Al, Phil, Rich, Tricia, and Steve.

Speaking styles have also changed. Where nineteenth- and early twentieth-century preachers were admired for their rhetoric, modern charismatic and evangelical worship leaders seem determined to show that they are no more articulate than their audiences. The Mystery Worshipper whose review of the St Thomas Philadelphia congregation was quoted earlier in this chapter found irritating the repeated insertion of 'you know'. There is something more complex going on in the frequent insertion of the word 'just': as in 'We *just* want to say how fantastic it is to be able to just share with you all tonight' and 'I *just* want to bring a message from the Lord'. In part it is pleading; in part it conveys humility. But it also implies the speaker is so moved by God's love that the facility for concise speech has been lost. Emoting is more important than conveying ideas, and 'passion' is paramount. The website description of the leaders of Coventry's Jubilee Church tells us that 'Andrew is passionate about Christ', while his wife, Janice, is 'passionate about giving every child the opportunity to thrive'. Their colleague Paul 'has a passion for Jesus' and Hannah's 'passion is to give herself to people in need'.[53]

Modern politicians have made the same change. Tony Blair, premier from 1997 to 2007, pioneered a verbless sentence structure that conveyed the degree of his commitment and his emotional response to problems far better than it conveyed policy detail. He was a man of the people, and the people might be alienated by him reminding them that he had been to a good school and to a better university.

Sometimes the charismatic worship leader's style is so demotic that it could easily be heard as ironic distancing from the matter in hand; one charismatic worship leader said: 'if some of you need to do some repenting, then this is a chance to do it.'[54]

Alpha and Mainstreaming the Charismatic Movement

A number of Banbury churches had used the Alpha course as an instructional device, and a number of their websites linked to it. Alpha was the work of one of the main centres of the charismatic movement in the Church of England—Holy Trinity, Brompton (or HTB)—the incumbent of which had visited Canada to witness the Toronto Blessing. Alpha began in 1969 as an in-house programme but became known outside HTB when it was taken over by Nicky Gumbel. As Nicholas Gumbel, the Old Etonian had been a successful lawyer before he switched to the Anglican ministry as a second career and shortened his name. Small groups of people were invited to attend ten weekly sessions, each consisting of a video presenting and explaining a central Christian idea, and a subsequent discussion. The professionally made videos were accompanied by a plethora of instructional materials, intended both for the neophyte and for the instructor.

The programme was enthusiastically taken up by congregations across almost all the denominations because it provided a ready-made and field-tested tool for refreshing the faithful and evangelizing the ungodly.[55] Gumbel was a keen supporter of Wimber's Signs and Wonders, and the Alpha course was unashamedly charismatic. After the third or fourth week, participants would be invited to a 'Holy Spirit' weekend, where they would be presented with specifically charismatic teachings on the gifts of the Spirit. However, that topic was sufficiently well segregated within the programme that it could be dropped by mainstream congregations. At its formal launch in September 1998, over 4,000 congregations supported a £1 million Alpha Initiative, which included, among other forms of publicity, hiring over 2,000 billboards to advertise the programme. By 2000, over 7,000 British congregations had run Alpha courses.[56]

The widespread use of Alpha leads to a more general observation: the mainstream churches have adopted many of the stylistic innovations associated with the charismatic and independent evangelical movements.[57] It is impossible now to distinguish what part of that is direct influence and what is simply the coincidence of other Christians coming to similar conclusions about the need to modernize the faith to combat decline. Whichever, the accommodation of church life to secular norms is patent. Across the board, liturgies have been modernized: the Church of England regularly revises them and now, by making orders of service available online, allows clergy to modify them to suit their own congregations. Most churches use recent translations of the Bible. The pop music style of 'praise worship' is widespread. Almost all Protestant clergy dress down, and even Church of England bishops go by abbreviated first names.[58]

There has, of course, been a traditionalist reaction. At the same time as mainstream churches have adapted their services to the norms of popular culture, attendance at cathedral services has increased.[59] The beauty of traditional liturgies sung by a professional choir is a specific draw, but more general attractions are indicated in this explanation of why cathedral evensong was popular: 'This may be because it is read by a minister who understands the richness of the language and listened to by a congregation that knows it will not be asked either to shake hands or sing any verses of "Shine Jesus Shine". It's also done and dusted in 27 minutes.'[60]

That mention of shaking hands brings us to a subtle point about both the decline of mainstream congregations and the intrusive friendliness of the charismatic style. Many regular churchgoers like formality and social distance, preferring either to spectate or to have their contribution scripted. They do not want strangers to 'presume' by treating them like long-lost friends. A sparsely attended rural Anglican service offers no place to hide, and large charismatic fellowships task experienced members to meet and greet strangers. Like an experimental theatre production with audience participation, this may demand too much too soon of visitors who fear being embarrassed by being pressed into an excessive degree of commitment. Hence the appeal of the cathedral service both to traditionalists who want formality and to casual enquirers who want to ease themselves in gradually.

Stephen Hunt wrote: 'from the 1960s to the close of the twentieth century a preoccupation with religious experience and happy sing-along songs associated with the charismatic movement has dominated the evangelical world.'[61] There is no need to confine that observation to the evangelical world. Although such distinct beliefs of the charismatic movement as the current availability of spiritual gifts such as healing and speaking in tongues have had very limited appeal, those innovations in style and ethos that the charismatic movement pioneered have spread far beyond its separatist congregations.

Institutionalization and Stagnation

Over the late 1980s, the growth of the charismatic movement slowed, and some New Church congregations and networks even showed decline. This stagnation has three causes. Over-blown promises of growth were a threat to the reality they envisioned. The failure of secular hope reflects only on the calculations of those who made the predictions. The failure of divine prophecy, though it is not always damaging, may threaten the spiritual base of the credibility of the prophets. In April 1995, Gerald Coates, the founder of the Pioneer network, very publicly prophesied that Dr R. T. Kendall would see considerable growth in the congregation of his Westminster Chapel: 'in eighteen months, in eighteen months, in eighteen months, the Spirit of God...is going to come on that place.' It did not, and many of those who witnessed Coates's prophesy became disillusioned with him and with the Toronto Blessing.[62]

Second, growth reduced commitment. For all that the charismatic movement promoted spiritual elitism, once it moved from house churches to mega-churches, it lost much of its fire. In small groups, face-to-face interaction allowed the keenest members to cajole and coerce the least driven. Despite the just-mentioned efforts to welcome first-time attenders and draw newcomers into fellowship activities, few New Churches congregations are anything like as demanding as the nineteenth-century Methodist societies with their two services on a Sunday and two mid-week evening meetings, and none is led by a pastor as demanding as the minister of Uig in Lewis who refused almost his entire congregation the right to take communion because he did not believe them to be Christians.[63]

But the primary cause of the stagnation lies in the sources of initial growth. Most of those attracted to the movement—in either its separatist or its tendency-within-the-mainstream forms—were already Christian. A comparison of charismatic and conventional Anglican congregations showed that 82 per cent of the conventional congregations had been Christians for over ten years; at 71 per cent the charismatic groups were little different.[64] Only 1 per cent of those who attended the Alpha programme—supposedly the most successful recent evangelistic enterprise—had not at some time been regular church-goers.[65] A historian of the separatist Restoration strand of the movement estimated that 90 per cent of members were defectors from other churches.[66] It was, as Canadian sociologists dubbed it, a 'circulation of the Saints'.[67] Initially the decline of the mainstream churches helped the charismatic movement: as congregations shrank, the more mobile remaining members had ever stronger reason to defect to larger churches (especially ones with viable youth work). Conservative sects lost young people to the charismatic movement because it let them continue with Jesus while ditching the con-servative theology and morals of their parents. In both cases, defection reduced the pool of potentially defectors. Even if the charismatic movement had been as relatively popular with dissatisfied churchgoers in 2000 as it was in 1980, recruitment would have slowed because the number of the potentially receptive was declining rapidly.

Community, Consensus, and Commitment

We can now return to the theme of Chapter 2: the importance of community cohesion. Most New Churches have grown by attracting very small propor-tions of people from very large catchment areas. For centuries, religion in Britain was organized on the basis of the small parish with its resident clergy-man, its church school, and a centrally placed building to which most people could readily walk. That was the model for the state churches funded from local land tax, and it was copied by dissenters, such as the Methodist sects in

England and Wales, and the Free Church of Scotland, that sought a national presence. The New Churches of the late twentieth century were organized around the motor car. Like the massive supermarkets that were often their neighbours, the New Churches based themselves on edge-of-town ring roads or on run-down industrial estates with easily adapted warehouses and ample parking; a sensible response to their very shallow degree of penetration of a commuting world.

That location model combines with the individualism of New Church theology to create a voluntary association, the weakness of which is not disguised by frequent use of the term 'community' in self-description. True, most New Churches provide better social facilities than small parish churches (especially activities for children), but, when the congregants drive away from the warehouse where they worship, they disperse to places where they are an insignificant part of the population. Their children are in a very small minority in their schools. They work alongside, shop with, and live next to people who do not share their religious views. Hence, unlike that of the people of the island of Lewis or North Wales in the 1940s, their faith cannot become deeply embedded in everyday life, and the next generation cannot be raised in an environment where the faith is taken for granted and reinforced in everyday interaction.

Conclusion

Outsiders often failed to notice that the charismatics were considerably more socially liberal than the Protestant (especially Brethren and Pentecostal) sects in which many had been raised. A survey of Pentecostal clergy in the 1990s showed that, although there were denominational differences (with the Elim clergy being the most liberal), most still rejected smoking, gambling, homosexuality, and playing sport or trading on a Sunday, and more than a third were opposed to the consumption of beverage alcohol: the puritanical attitudes of 1930s fundamentalism.[68] The members of Chris Brain's Sheffield commune were extreme in their rejection of puritanism, but the young people who were attracted to the charismatic movement were generally far less conservative than their parents.

The rise of the charismatic movement is often presented as proof that the sociological assertion of a strong link between societies modernizing and becoming less religious is mistaken: here is a late-twentieth-century innovation that was successful despite, at least superficially, being more interested in the magical and supernatural than the declining churches. However, this is a mistake. While the charismatic movement brought back speaking in tongues, prophesying, and extravagant claims for the power of the faith, it also privileged personal experience over the objective reality of Christ's redeeming sacrifice. It made feelings, which are by definition subjective and individual, more important than the shared doctrines that could form the basis for social regulation. It abandoned the distinctive culture of church architecture, language, dress, and hymnody in favour of secular culture with a few words replaced. It was 'not strict about lifestyles or commitment' and it was 'often world-accommodating and open-minded, and did not demand a great deal of conformity'.[69] Although it would reject the parallel, it was similar to the New Age spirituality discussed in Chapter 9 in allowing adherents far greater authority and autonomy than did conventional Christianity. If we consider where its recruits came from, and where their children ended up, we can see the charismatic movement, not as an obstacle to secularization, but as a convenient halfway house en route from the religious to the secular. This is, of course, illustration rather than proof, but one of the key figures in Sheffield's NOS commune was the daughter of an Anglican bishop; she passed through the charismatic movement on her way to a liberal and unaffiliated Christianity, and none of her children grew up to share even that inchoate commitment.

To survive, any cultural product must be distinctive. The Protestant Reformation was already a secularizing force in that it largely abandoned the idea that religious activities (and the buildings and officials associated with them) enjoyed a distinctive sacramental status, and it abhorred visual aids to faith. The icons were smashed and the gruesome depictions of hell whitewashed. During the First World War it became common in the East End of London to erect small shrines to commemorate the dead. J. H. Kensit and his Protestant Truth Society objected to them because they might inspire Romanist idolatry; Kensit was himself assaulted at one protest.[70] For Reformed Protestants what mattered went on inside the head: in order to be saved, we must believe certain things and subsequently act in certain ways (none of them particularly obvious or memorable). But without associated symbols beliefs lose presence. As a farmer friend said of the redundant Presbyterian church he wished to buy: 'With the folk gone, it's just a tractor shed.' The Reformation insistence that the clergy were just ordinary people was based on the assumption (and hope) that the ordinary people would be pious and reasonably well-informed Christians. In a largely secular society, making the clergy more like everyone else reduces them rather than elevates the rest of us.

The clichés and stereotypes deployed by script-writers are often revealing, and it is no accident that, when any TV drama now wishes to show Christian religion, it uses a Catholic priest and a Catholic church. We may not know quite what crossing oneself, lighting candles, fingering rosary beads, dabbing one's forehead with holy water, whispering confessions to a person hidden behind a screen, or bowing before an altar represents, but we can recognize it as religious business. The words of the King James translation of the Bible or Cranmer's liturgy may be difficult, but they are recognizably religious. While it is understandable that many of the small Christian minority in our secular society wish to dispense with or downplay those elements of the faith that they suspect deter outsiders, their reforms make religion ever less visible.

In summary, the charismatic movement, and the innovations it pioneered, was intended to reverse secularization, but it actually facilitated decline by providing young members of conservative Christian families with a stepping stone on the road to religious indifference and by reducing the visible presence of Christianity.

Notes

1. On the history and significance of church seating, see T. Cooper and S. Brown (eds), *Pews, Benches and Chairs* (London: Ecclesiological Society, 2011).
2. C. McCrystal, 'The Church that Died', *Independent*, 19 December 1999.
3. McCrystal, 'The Church that Died'.
4. As is clear from the structured comparisons in Chapter 2, the benefits of competition are usually short-lived and localized. As we see here, a dispute causes people to take sides, which leads them to signal commitment by, for example, putting their names on the electoral roll, but, once the dispute is settled, commitment levels drop, and the long-run effect is to reduce the relative influence of organized religion on the surrounding population by changing it from a putatively community property to being a matter of individual preference.
5. These data are from my original research on churches in south Norfolk. I am grateful to Revd Mawditt for information on the Fountain of Life and to Revd Jane Atkins for access to the electoral roll data on which the Anglican calculations are based.
6. P. Brierley, *'Christian' England: What the English Church Census Reveals* (London: MARC Europe, 1991).
7. Brierley, *'Christian' England*, 159.
8. Brierley, *'Christian' England*, 121–2.
9. For a history of the Pentecostal movement in the UK, see W. K. Kay, *Pentecostals in Britain* (London: Paternoster Press, 2000), chs 1, 2.
10. For an early history of the house church movement, see W. Hollenweger, 'The House Church Movement in Great Britain', *Expository Times*, 92 (November 1980), 45–7, and J. V. Thurman, *New Wineskin: A Study of the House Church Movement* (Frankfurt: Verlag Peter Lang, 1982).

11. I was invited by the BBC to attend Dales Bible Week as an expert commentator for a documentary. I am grateful to the producer David Henshaw for that invitation and to the film crew and the management of the convention for making me welcome.

12. Mystery Worshipper 1276, *Ship of Fools*, 23 April 2006, http://www.shipoffools.com/mystery-worshipper/st-thomas-philadelphia-campus-sheffield-england (accessed February 2009).

13. This is slightly inaccurate: one component was a charismatic house church based in Nether Edge.

14. On glossolalia, see M. J. C. Calley, *God's People: West Indian Pentecostal Sects in England* (Oxford: Oxford University Press, 1965), 78–80, and M. J. Cartledge, *Charismatic Glossolalia: An Empirical–Theological Study* (Aldershot: Ashgate, 2002).

15. These judgements come from former charismatics discussing their experiences on the *Ship of Fools* website in 2009.

16. D. Thompson, *The End of Time* (London: Sinclair-Stevenson, 1996).

17. Further, some leaders taught that anyone not 'covered' by an approved 'shepherd' was 'out of God's will'; that is, they added acceptance of an unusual authority model to the normal Christian requirements for salvation.

18. Quoted in T. Tillin, 'Bread and Games: Reflections of the British Church. Part 3: The Latter Rain and the Restoration Movement in Britain', http://www.intotruth.org/res/restuk3.html (accessed January 2010).

19. D. Davies, 'The Charismatic Ethic and the Spirit of Post-Industrialism', in D. Martin and P. Mullen (eds), *Strange Gifts: A Guide to Charismatic Renewal* (Oxford: Blackwell, 1984), 145.

20. For a detailed account of the NOS, see R. Howard, *The Rise and Fall of the Nine O'Clock Service: A Cult within the Church* (London: Mowbray, 1996).

21. Personal interview, 2008.

22. Neil Hopkins, 'The Nine O'Clock Service', http://members.tripod.com/neil_hopkins/docs/nos.htm (accessed March 2010).

23. Hopkins, 'The Nine O'Clock Service'.

24. E. R. Wickham, *Church and People in an Industrial City* (London: Lutterworth Press, 1957), 169.

25. M. Stacey, *Tradition and Change* (Oxford: Oxford University Press, 1960). Its significance for British social science is discussed in M. Savage, *Identities and Social Change in Britain since 1940* (Oxford: Oxford University Press, 2010), 151–6.

26. M. Stacey, E. Batstone, C. Bell, and A. Murcott, *Power, Persistence and Change; A Second Study of Banbury* (London: Routledge and Kegan Paul, 1975). The second Banbury study seems to have been a less-than-happy experience; see H. Newby, 'Editorial Note', and C. Bell, 'Reflections on the Banbury Restudy', in C. Bell and H. Newby, *Doing Sociological Research* (London: George Allen and Unwin, 1977), i–ix, 47–62, and C. Bell and P. Thompson, 'The Second Banbury Study', *International Journal of Social Research Methodology*, 11 (2008), 114.

27. Although the designation of such groups as the Jehovah's Witnesses, Christian Scientists, and Mormons as 'fringe Christian' is casual, what distinguishes them from the Christian mainstream is not important here.

28. Stacey, *Tradition and Change*, 59.

29. Stacey, *Tradition and Change*, 57. Her certainty derives from the variation in data generated by interviewers. Six of ten interviewers had attenders outnumber non-attenders

by about two to one; three made the two groups roughly equal, and one made non-attenders outnumber attenders by three to two.

30. To give another example, in 1937 Mass Observation estimated Bolton church attendance at 13%, but when a Methodist minister canvassed an area of Bolton door-to-door he found 'near universal claims to church associations' (C. D. Field, 'Religion in Worktown', *Northern History*, 53 (2016), 121).

31. Stacey, *Tradition and Change*, 59. For reasons explained in S. Bruce, 'A Sociology Classic Revisited: Religion in Banbury', *Sociological Review*, 59 (2011), 201–22, I have considerable doubts about some of the data in the restudy report and have endeavoured to produce a more accurate estimate.

32. This may be more of an observer effect than a real change. Barrie Trinder's history of churches in Banbury lists a number of small Protestant groups that Stacey may have missed; B. S. Trinder, 'Banbury Churches', in A. Crossley (ed.), *A History of the County of Oxfordshire Vol 10* (London: Victoria County History, 1972), 95–120.

33. C. Bell, 'Church Attendance in a Small Town', *New Society*, 28 May 1968, 801–2. One has to say 'roughly', because we do not know how many people came from outside the town to worship. Presumably few Anglicans or Methodists did, because those denominations had many outlets in the surrounding countryside, but the smaller organizations could well have attracted their clientele from a 30-mile radius.

34. This may flatter the charismatics. Because such groups were rare in the countryside, they would have attracted attenders who did not live in Banbury, while Methodists who had recently moved to Banbury might have continued to attend their original chapels elsewhere.

35. In 2010, I visited Banbury twice, interviewed five clergymen and two lay church leaders, attended three church services, visited all the listed worship sites, corresponded with local experts, consulted library and archive sources, and read back copies of the *Banbury Gazette*—a time investment far short of the original Banbury studies but enough to be reasonably confident of the observations made here.

36. Oxfordshire Council, *Banbury, Grimsbury and Castle Profile—2011 Census* (Oxford: Oxfordshire Council, 2012).

37. They re-established a weak presence in 1994 with a weekly meeting of typically nine people in a rented room in the Town Hall.

38. Ethnicity is also relevant for the smallest sector. Web searches showed the spectral presence of two Pentecostal bodies: the Tabernacle of Faith and the New Anointing Apostolic Ministries. Both listed private houses as their addresses, neither advertised services, and none of the Banbury clergy had heard of them. We may assume these were embryonic African churches that failed to take off.

39. Wahhabism is a conservative form of Islam promoted by the Al Saud family.

40. E. Goffman, *The Presentation of Self in Everyday Life* (Harmondsworth: Penguin, 1984).

41. 'Welcome to People's Church', *Banbury Gazette*, 26 April 2010.

42. The People's Church, https://www.thepeopleschurch.org.uk (accessed July 2010).

43. The King's Community Church, Braintree, http://www.kccbraintree.org.uk/#/newfrontiers/4520165212 (accessed April 2010).

44. For detailed arguments about late 1970s changes to the language and structure of Anglican services, see D. Martin and P. Mullen (eds), *No Alternative: The Prayer Book Controversy* (Oxford: Blackwell, 1981).

45. Letter to the Editor, *Guardian*, 18 May 2012.

46. This is not unprecedented. Islamic God-addressing poetry (especially of the Sufi variety) has often been successfully reused by western pop artists to address this-worldly lovers.

47. For a general history of English church music, see A. Gant, *O Sing Unto the Lord: A History of English Church Music* (London: Profile Books, 2018).

48. In 2015, the Free Church of Scotland permitted the use of musical instruments in worship; the smaller Free Presbyterian Church of Scotland still maintains the old prohibitions.

49. J. Macmillan, 'Sweet Singing in the Choir', *Standpoint* (October 2017).

50. This case is made by William Sargant in two books that formed the basis for the common claim that religious innovations brainwash their converts: *The Battle for the Mind: A Physiology of Conversion and Brainwashing* (London: Heinemann, 1957) and *The Mind Possessed: A Physiology of Possession* (London: Penguin, 1977). The plausibility of brainwashing is examined in S. Bruce, *Researching Religion: Why We Need Social Science* (Oxford: Oxford University Press, 2018), ch. 7.

51. Jubilee Church, Banbury, http://www.jubileechurchbanbury.org.uk (accessed January 2010).

52. See, e.g., H. Sherwood, 'Church Heads off Discussion about Mitres', *Guardian*, 26 November 2015, and N. Hellen, 'Anglican Bishops Urged to Cast off "Daft" Mitres', *The Times*, 9 July 2017.

53. 'Leadership', http://jubileechurchcoventry.org/leadership-team/andrew-janice-simpkins (accessed August 2017). The website makes no reference at all to the theological training or qualifications of the leaders.

54. This quotation is from my notes of a service at St Thomas, Philadelphia, Sheffield, 3 May 2009.

55. For a excellent journalistic account of participating in the Alpha course, see J. Ronson, *Lost at Sea* (London: Picador, 2012).

56. S. J. Hunt, *The Alpha Enterprise: Evangelism in a Post-Christian Era* (Aldershot: Ashgate, 2004).

57. On its effect on Anglican congregations, see S. Hunt, 'All Things Bright and Beautiful: The Rise of the Anglican Charismatic Church', *Journal of Empirical Theology*, 13 (2000), 16–34, and L. J. Francis, D. W. Lankshear, and S. H. Jones, 'The Influence of the Charismatic Movement on Local Church Life', *Journal of Contemporary Religion*, 15 (2000), 121–30.

58. Diocese of Sheffield, 'Bishop Pete's installation', https://www.sheffield.anglican.org/blog/guest-blog/bishop-pete-s-sermon-from-his-service-of-installation (accessed September 2017).

59. Church of England, 'Cathedral Statistics 2016', https://www.churchofengland.org/sites/default/files/2017-11/Cathedral%20Statistics%202016_0.pdf (accessed January 2019).

60. Letter to the Editor, *Guardian*, 27 October 2012.

61. Hunt, *The Alpha Enterprise*, 45.

62. A. Howe, 'False prophesy today?', *Evangelicals Now* February 1997; http://www.e-n.org.uk/p-473-False-prophesy-today.htm. Accessed March 2010.

63. S. Bruce, *Scottish Gods: Religion in Modern Scotland, 1900–2012*. Edinburgh: Edinburgh University Press, 2014, 20.

64. Hunt, 'All things bright and beautiful', 23.
65. Hunt, *The Alpha Enterprise*, 171.
66. A. Walker, *Restoring the Kingdom: The Radical Christianity of the House Church Movement* (London: Hodder and Stoughton, 1988), 228.
67. R. Bibby and M. Brinkerhof, 'The Circulation of the Saints', *Journal for the Scientific Study of Religion*, 12 (1973), 273–83.
68. W. K. Kay, *Pentecostals in Britain* (London: Send the Light, 2002), 180–90.
69. S. J. Hunt, *Alternative Religions: A Sociological Introduction* (Aldershot: Ashgate, 2003), 80–1.
70. J. Winter, *Sites of Memory, Sites of Mourning: The Great War in European Cultural History* (Cambridge: Cambridge University Press, 1995), 80–2.

6

Migrant Christians and
Pentecostalism in London

London is quite unlike the rest of England in its size, prosperity, and ethnic diversity, and its citizens reflect that in their sense of self. A 2017 survey offered them a variety of identity labels: only 12 per cent chose 'English', 17 per cent chose 'British', and 46 per cent chose 'Londoner'.[1] The religious life of the capital has long diverged from that of the rest of England, but that difference has recently flipped. At the start of the nineteenth century, London was remarkably ungodly. Particularly in the Rookeries so colourfully described by Charles Dickens in *Oliver Twist*, and so feared by the respectable working class and the middle classes, the light of God was as scarce as the light of day. In 1859, the police knew of almost 3,000 brothels and suspected the total to be twice that number.[2] The social damage caused by gin was hardly exaggerated in William Hogarth's memorable 1751 *Gin Lane* cartoon. A century later the metropolis had both literally and metaphorically cleaned up somewhat, but the 1851 Census of Religious Worship still showed London (at 37 per cent) well behind the national average of around half the population attending.[3] An 1886 attempt to measure churchgoing concluded that 31 per cent attended, but that study did not allow for 'twicers' and thus will have exaggerated somewhat.[4] More reliable research in 1903—it deployed enumerators at church services—estimated that, once the roughly 66,000 people confined in various sorts of institution were removed from the base, about 19 per cent of Londoners attended church.[5] Helped by Catholic migrants from Ireland, the twentieth century saw some improvement; although the 14 per cent of Londoners who in 1978 claimed to attend at least weekly was a net fall, the decline was less than that seen by the rest of England. By 2000, London had the second-best churchgoing record of any English region.[6]

Twenty-First-Century Church Life

Peter Brierley called the report of his 2012 London church census *Capital Growth*, and he is not wrong. He found 9 per cent of Londoners attending church, well above the national average. Since his previous count in 2005, the number of churches had grown by 17 per cent and the number of attenders by 16 per cent. Much of that apparent expansion disappears when we set such figures against the total population that was available to attend church, because it had grown from 7.2 million in 2001 to 8.2 million in 2011.[7] But, even scaled down, such data show the extent to which, in terms of church-going, London and the rest of England have switched places.

Londoners had changed, but not in the manner hoped for by evangelical Christians keen to see mass conversion. Instead, many of the at-best-nominally-religious white British Londoners had moved out to be replaced by migrants from traditionally religious countries. While Africans were 1 per cent of the rest of England in 2011, they were 7 per cent of Londoners; people of Caribbean ethnicity were well below 1 per cent for the rest of England but 4 per cent of Londoners. Those migrants and their children are much more likely than the average white British Londoner to be religiously observant. Only 8 per cent of the white population attended church, but the figure for Chinese, Korean, and Japanese Londoners was 16 per cent, and for black Londoners it was 19 per cent.[8] To describe the link the other way round, almost half of church attenders in Inner London were black.[9] In sum, the change in religious climate had come, not from members of a static population changing their beliefs, but from movements of people who brought the religion of their homeland with them.

The most visible change brought by migration was the growth of Islam. Although only some 4 per cent of the English in 2011 were described in the census as Muslim, in some London boroughs the figure was almost one-third. Although much that is said here about the role of religion in the experience of migration applies every bit as much to non-Christian as to Christian religions, the impact of Muslims on Britain's religious life differs enough from that of previous waves of migrant to merit separate treatment, and it is the subject of the next chapter.

The effect of migration can be seen in the changing fortunes of traditions within Christianity. In 1979, there were just under 600 Pentecostal churches in London; in 2012, there were almost 1,500, and almost all of those were 'BMC' or 'black majority churches'.[10]

The Migrant Experience

A hint of the effects of migration can be seen in a small detail of a 1975 survey of Small Heath, Birmingham. While only one-quarter of white British people claimed to attend church or equivalent regularly—an undoubtedly inflated claim—Irish (at 66 per cent) and West Indian residents (at 30 per cent) exceeded the native English norm.[11] Part of the explanation lies in simple continuity. The Irish Catholics who settled in Britain at the end of the nineteenth and first half of the twentieth century came from a conventionally religious country, and it was two generations before they integrated sufficiently with the religiously indifferent among whom they settled to adopt their irreligion. Likewise, West Indians.

But it is often the case that migrants are *more* religiously observant in their new world than they were at home and that for two sorts of reason. First, we need to appreciate the difference in the place of the individual believer in majority and minority religion. When all the important social institutions of a society promote the same religion, and when almost the entire population is socialized into it in childhood, that faith that can be taken for granted; it is more a property of the society than of the individual. A minority faith, if it is not to be abandoned, must be embraced as a personal commitment. The second reason for migrants to be self-consciously religious is that religious institutions provide a variety of secular benefits that ease the stress of migration. Churches (and, as we will see in Chapter 7, mosques, temples, and gurdwaras) provide a variety of important resources for new arrivals.

International migration, even in this age of instant communications and inexpensive travel, can be a traumatising experience. Immigrants become strangers in a new land with the loss of familiar sounds, sights, and smells. The expectations of customary behavior, hearing one's native tongue, and support from family and friends can no longer be taken for granted. Even the most routine activities of everyday life...can be alienating experiences for many new immigrants who find themselves in strange settings that require constant mental strain to navigate and to be understood.[12]

Migrant churches are the obvious place to meet people from the old country and to reminisce in a familiar tongue about shared experiences. They are excellent venues for young people to meet potential marriage partners. They provide an environment that is comfortable, because either it makes a stigma vanish or it makes it a virtue. Black people stand out in a primarily white world, and the attention they receive is often negative. Black people in a black church are at home. An ethnic identity that may be devalued elsewhere there either is greeted as a valued characteristic or (often a greater psychological benefit) is ignored as people are judged more for their personal qualities than for their ethnicity. Hence the spread of Caribbean churches followed the West Indian settlement pattern: in 1965, there were thirty-seven in London, twenty-one in Birmingham, eight in other towns in the West Midlands, and only a handful elsewhere.

When the minority is disadvantaged, its faith can provide an important form of sustenance: consolation and encouragement in this vale of tears. The point was clearly made in a study of West Indian Pentecostalists in Bristol in the 1970s:

> If one cannot accept society or be aggressive towards it with a view to reforming it, then one can devalue the significance of this world by with-drawing from it in a community of like-minded individuals and projecting one's hopes into a supernatural and otherworldly Kingdom.[13]

The poor and deprived could try revolution. But the religion that West Indians brought with them laid considerable stress on obedience to authority, and England's social structure was hardly fragile. So what was left? The dispossessed could just feel miserable and inadequate. Or they could be attracted to a puritanical religion that told them that the meek shall inherit the earth and that it is easier for a camel to pass through the eye of a needle than for a rich man to enter the kingdom of heaven. The ascetic ethos of fundamentalism allows poor people to feel good about themselves by turning privations into virtues.

But it is also clear that, whether or not they intend to do this, puritanical 'religions of the oppressed' provide values and attitudes that help assimilation and upward mobility.[14] West Indian Pentecostal churches taught that God's grace and spirit cannot enter an unclean body. Hence drinking alcohol and smoking were prohibited, as were swearing and dancing, and mixing with sinners was discouraged. The churches encouraged men and women to dress as modestly as possible. Although many women wore brightly coloured clothes, the men wore dark suits, white shirts, and ties. In the late 1950s, Malcolm Calley observed a more subtle illustration of formality: the saints spoke in West Indian dialects among themselves and before and after the service, but when testifying or preaching they avoided their native speech in order to show the seriousness and importance of their worship.[15]

Sexual relations were permitted only within (hopefully) lifelong monogamous heterosexual marriage. For the late 1950s congregations studied by Calley, fornication (which included pre- and extramarital sex) was the greatest evil, and the goal of sexual continence survived the permissive society of the 1960s. As a 1970s Bristol pastor put it in a sermon:

> And one more thing before I stop. You don't go around giving your bodies to immorality either. Sexual relations outside marriage is an abominable and horrifying sin! Our bodies are the receptacles of the Holy Ghost and they are not to be pampered and petted, kissed and rubbed and inflamed in the erotic regions, to the point where you are afraid to stand up![16]

Puritanism offers a corrective to the behaviour patterns that prevent the poor dragging themselves out of poverty. The sanctity of the family is vital. Rich people can afford to see the break-up of the home, but being a single parent (and usually that meant a mother) was one of the major causes of poverty, and, for those already near the bottom, the collapse of the family was often enough to push them below the ice. And the classic vices of drunkenness, drug abuse, and sexual immorality were both directly and indirectly expensive. They cost scarce funds and they constrained opportunities for legitimate well-paid work.

For the West Indian Pentecostalists there was also a very specific ethnic reason for puritanism. They were only too well aware of racist stereotypes of West Indians as, at best, rather too racy and, at worst, feckless, unreliable, and criminal. Those stereotypes had some grounding in reality. In the 1950s, black men were popularly associated with jazz, calypso, drinking dens, sexuality, and drugs. By the 1970s, West Indian youth was strongly linked in the mind of the British public with reggae music, dance halls, yardie gangs, and 'ganga'. The hugely popular Bob Marley was an unashamedly heavy consumer of marijuana; his fellow Wailer Peter Tosh had a hit with his single 'Legalise it!'. Just as early nineteenth-century working-class people were attracted to Primitive Methodism and the Salvation Army as a way of putting clear blue water between themselves and their indigent neighbours, Caribbean Pentecostalists used their faith to distance themselves from popular stereotypes and to save their own children from a hedonism that often bordered on the self-destructive.

The adjective 'puritanical' is almost always negative; puritans are killjoys who condemn natural human appetites and harmless fun. But puritanism can be positive. Pentecostal pastors taught that the saints should avoid negative thoughts, constrain anger, and be diligent and trustworthy. The saints were individually responsible for their salvation, but there was nothing lonely about that individualism. As Calley put it: 'A Christian is enjoined to turn his back on the world but he must not turn his back on other Christians.'[17] Members sought out each other's company, welcomed each other into their homes, looked after each other's children, and helped with finding accommodation and work.

The structure of church services itself made individual members feel supported and loved. Everyone was expected to 'testify'. The frequency with which any one congregant stood to tell the congregation what the Lord had done in her or his life obviously varied with the size of the church, but between every fourth service and every second service was the norm. While the worship leader chose the hymns, the choruses (usually a couple of verses repeated ten or twenty times) were chosen by the congregants. Someone would start a familiar refrain and everyone else would join in. In Catholic and 'high' Anglican worship, the formality of the set liturgy reduces congregants to an audience or bit players, but West Indian worship was thoroughly participatory.

West African Pentecostalism

The West African story could be told in similar terms.[18] Between 1991 and 2001 the number of African migrants to England doubled: from 47,201 to 88,380. Like West Indians, the Ghanaians and Nigerians who changed the complexion of London's Christianity came from a strongly religious culture, and the first generation maintained the church involvement they had displayed in Africa, either by forming local branches of their previous denominations or by creating new churches in the familiar style.[19] Because such churches overwhelmingly recruited from one ethnie or nationality, the next arrivals of the same ethnie or nationality were drawn to them. As one Nigerian pastor in London explained, it is 'almost like a home away from home, a community away from home. Because once you find yourself here you don't have the support network that you once knew back at home. Therefore the church becomes a form of support network.'[20] And most BMC churches in London have teams of volunteers who help newcomers integrate.[21]

The largest African Pentecostal organization is the Redeemed Christian Church of God (RCCG), which was founded in 1952 in Lagos, Nigeria, by Josiah Olufemi Akindayomi. Enoch Adeboye joined the church in 1973, was ordained two years later, and succeeded Akindayomi on his death. The church in Nigeria became remarkably successful: in 2016, the weekly worship attendance of the church in Lagos averaged 50,000. And Nigerian migrants took it with them across the globe. The RCCG is in many respects conventionally Christian: most conservative Protestants of the 1950s would take exception only to its Pentecostalism (especially 'Holy Spirit baptism' and faith healing). What marks it out today is its social puritanism. It forbids 'worldliness' (a word seldom heard now in Christian circles): like the Bristol West Indian pastor, it opposes anything that suggests sexual promiscuity. It is opposed to gambling and to debt. And it is very much in favour of obedience. It promotes reverence for one's parents, one's elders, and the church.

Also unusual is the age and class composition of the RCCG and similar denominations. Not surprisingly, given that many Nigerians came to Britain for education and career advancement, RCCG congregants are unusual for Britain in being young (one survey put 90 per cent under 40) and unusual for Nigeria in being urban and middle class.[22] They also have a social-class profile markedly higher than that of the Caribbean migrants who made up the bulk of the black Pentecostal churches of the 1960s. Calley says that most members 'were unskilled workers, few were skilled workers, fewer still hold white collar jobs'.[23] In contrast, two-thirds of the West African Pentecostalists surveyed by Stephen Hunt in the 1990s were graduates.[24]

Most of London's megachurches are black majority Pentecostal. In 2015, only four of the eleven churches with congregations of over 1,000 were not overwhelmingly African, and two of those had a large Caribbean component. Kingsway International, founded by Matthew Ashimolowo in 1992, had congregations of over 5,000 meeting in a former warehouse in Walthamstow; New Wine Church had over 2,000 attenders. But the RCCG, while it had some very large congregations (Jesus House in Brent Cross, for example), also followed the West Indian model in favouring small congregations and planting new churches far and wide. About half of it over 700 congregations are in London and neighbouring counties, and there are concentrations in Birmingham and Manchester, but it has also planted fifty churches in Scotland, seven in County Durham, eighteen in Lancashire, six in Wiltshire, and seven in Yorkshire.

While the white charismatic churches discussed in Chapter 5 have followed the Tesco model of big sheds on ring roads, the RCCG has used the old parish model of a church within walking distance of members and potential recruits. In 2010, 39 per cent of RCCG pastors had attendances of less than 50 and two-thirds had congregations of less than 100. That difference is partly due to the social-service role of the migrant church. While the white middle-class charismatics talk a lot about community and try to provide a wide range of church-related activities for all ages, their members feel no sense of solidarity beyond their shared religion; they may, as all Christians should, think of themselves as 'sojourners in a strange land', but any sense of alienation they feel is the result of a chosen identity. BMC churches have a good reason to be local churches: they recruit people who share a minority social identity.

Material Success

The difference in social class between Caribbean and Nigerian Pentecostalists is reflected in the rather different attitudes towards material success.[25] Although the first wave of BMCs would be pleased if a congregant prospered, their puritanism tended to be reactive and protective: the pious person worked hard to glorify God and hoped that diligence, honesty, and frugality offered some protection against falling back into the morass of the undeserving poor (and particularly into the macho subculture of baby mommas and drug-dealing). Too great an interest in prosperity was suspect because it was 'of the world'. The West African churches seem less concerned about avoiding that sort of worldliness. Members are encouraged to be ambitious: 'I like the teachings on fulfilling potential. Everyone has at least one gift or talent, and if we all applied them then everybody would be a success. . . . God wants you to have a good career, good life and be happy.' Another said: 'The church motivates young people to follow their dreams.'[26]

Some Pentecostal pastors preach what in the United States is called 'Name it and Claim it' or 'Prosperity Theology'. This is an elaboration of various promises apparently made by God in the Old and New Testaments. For example, Luke 6:38 says 'Give, and it shall be given unto you', and 2 Corinthians 9:6 says: 'But this I say, He which soweth sparingly shall reap also sparingly; and he which soweth bountifully shall reap also bountifully.' Various verses in Proverbs suggest a similar return on investment: for example, Proverbs 11:24 notes: 'There is that scattereth, and yet increaseth; and there is that witholdeth more than is meet, but it tendeth to poverty.'

Most Christians suppose that such observations reflect the underlying moral order to God's creation and encourage generosity. The Health and Wealth gospel takes such promises literally and somewhat mechanically. As one Prosperity preacher put it:

God is releasing [his tenfold promise] once again to men and women who have eyes to see and ears to hear. He's releasing a fresh revelation on exponential kingdom growth according to the ways of heaven. He's releasing an upgrade to the prosperity movement in the body of Christ. I call it 'financial glory'!

Give £10 to the Lord and the Lord will give you £100 back:

> You create a favor storm that effectively enables you to step into everlasting harvest! This is the law of the tenfold return which God has given to me, which I now give to you. Begin using it, never let a seed sown go without an agreement with the power that is within that seed, and watch as your life forever changes. Watch as you walk through the rest of your life in a continual state of harvest and manifest blessing![27]

Pentecostalism is not the only religion to turn God into an ATM. Buddhists of the minority Soka Gakkai sect 'chant for' things. They believe that. if they hold in their thoughts some material object or some less tangible benefit (such as a job promotion) as they chant, their desires will be met. Many New Agers subscribe to the similar notion of 'visualization' or 'cosmic ordering': imagine what you want. and the universe will provide it. This is not the psychological reassurance trick of the athlete who gives herself confidence by imagining she has won the race; it is a belief that the divine DJ plays requests. Some Pentecostal Christians use the term 'positive confession' for saying aloud what you want to happen in the expectation that God will deliver. Words have actual power. Concentrate too much on the negative (poverty, privation, poor health) and you inadvertently turn down the health, wealth, and well-being that God has promised us.

Although Prosperity Theology is less popular in Britain than in the US, it has some appeal because it works. It certainly works for the pastors. The leader of a small West Indian church in the 1970s enjoyed a standard of living little better than his working-class congregants, but many West African pastors have prospered. For ease of calculation, assume that Pentecostalists conform to the expectation of 'tithing' (that is, giving a tenth of gross income to the church) and that overheads are low. A church with 100 members will provide its pastor with an income almost 10 times that of individual members; with 200 members, the pastor is 20 times as well off as his people. Even if some members do not tithe and overheads are considerable, pastors of successful churches will be much richer than their members. When Douglas Goodman of the Victory Christian Centre (VCC), north London, was investigated for sex attacks on members of his congregation (for which he received a three-year prison sentence), a large number of 'significant unauthorised salary payments' to him, his wife, and other trustees were discovered. He had built VCC into one of London's biggest black churches, with a 2001 income of £3.5 million and he had rewarded himself with an expensive house and a fleet of cars that included a Ferrari.[28] Bishop David Oyedepo, the leader of Lagos-based Winners International (which has more than 1,000 members in the Dartford area of Kent), received over £16 million in three years from the UK and spent some of that on a private jet.[29] In 2005, the Charity Commissioners ordered Matthew Ashimolowo of Kingsway International to repay £200,000 after it was discovered that he had used church funds to buy a timeshare in Florida and spent £120,000 on his birthday celebrations.[30]

Such openly high living is alien to mainstream churches—in 2013, the Archbishop of Canterbury was paid £75,000 plus free accommodation, and the average priest got half that [31] But there is little or no resentment of the black pastor's wealth, because it is seen as proof of God's promise, and members also feel it works for them. One survey of RCCG members found that 78 per cent thought their finances had improved and 67 per cent had enjoyed a job promotion since joining.[32]

Supernaturalism and Witchcraft

Neither West Indian Pentecostalism in the 1960s nor its West African successor fifty years later are homogenous enough to make too much of differences between them, but there is something of a contrast in expectations of the presence of the supernatural, and that separates both from native British Pentecostalists. Although the Elim Pentecostal Church and the Assemblies of God believe in faith healing, their claims for the presence of evil and their ability to direct divine power for good are muted and not that far from a secular view that a positive attitude may help heal certain ailments. Magic plays a far larger part in Caribbean than modern British culture, and even more so for Africans. In BMCs, exorcisms involving isolation, fasting, and violence are common. Psychiatric conditions—and sometimes just teenage rebellion—can be seen as devil possession, and such is the faith of many West African Pentecostalists in the spiritual power of their pastors that they will pay them handsomely to drive out evil spirits. Although all Christians believe God can cure, most suppose that we should have recourse to the scientific medicine that God gave us before we bother him with personal requests. Although it is very much a minority position even within BMCs, this is a sector in which preachers can assert that resort to conventional medicine betrays a lack of faith in God and in his earthly representatives. Hence the rare but attention-catching occurrence in the press of stories of black parents being convicted for failing to seek medical assistance for their children.[33]

Although West African Pentecostalists generally set themselves against the more barbaric parts of their heritage's attitude to magic, the press (and its popular reception) sees continuity in witchcraft and Pentecostal possession. In 2002, the mutilated torso of a boy was found in the River Thames. The police thought it was a *muti* killing, a South African practice that involves removing organs for use in tribal medicines. A specialist in African tribal religion took the nature of the wounds and that fact that the body was drained of blood as proof that this was a Nigerian human sacrifice. The boy's killers were never apprehended, but the police did discover a trafficking ring that smuggled African children to Britain for ritualistic abuse.[34] There is no suggestion that Pentecostalists were responsible, but that sort of story contributes to the general impression (important for the argument I will make in Chapter 11) that religion taken too seriously is dangerous.

The Limits of Attraction

Although the largest black majority churches have recruited in Britain only for some forty years, that 'black majority' still usually means 'almost entirely black' invites explanation. An obvious place to start concerns style. Black churches, whether American, Caribbean, or African, worship in a livelier and more demonstrative style than do traditional British churches. Black worship demands that congregants be involved; white worship invites the audience to spectate. Even the charismatic fellowships described in Chapter 5 are pallid in comparison. Where the black Pentecostal pastor preaches up a storm, hamming like a Victorian actor, the white charismatic preacher is often dull and tedious or trivial. Black singing is forceful, tuneful, vibrant, and emotional; white charismatic 'praise worship' is often tepid and lifeless. In contrasting them with Methodists, a woman raised in Newcastle in the 1940s said 'my parents—while they would certainly have classed themselves as Christians—were not keen on outward signs of religion, finding it off-putting and embarrassing.'[35] That attitude is still common today.

Black churches expect and receive much greater commitment in time and in money than white churches: services can stretch for an hour or more beyond their expected finish time, and members are expected to be deeply involved in small group activities and to give generously to the church's work.

Chapter 5 made a point about cathedral worship that applies even more strongly here. All churches face a dilemma in handling visitors. A complaint often made (especially by West Indians about British churches) when people explain why they did not join a church is that they were not made welcome.[36] Nobody greeted them at the door; nobody encouraged them to become involved. But, if a congregation demands too much of visitors, it risks scaring them off. Most of us like to slide gradually and unnoticed into some new activity, taking time to decide if it is the sort of thing we will like. Black worship expects participation, and a white person can hardly attend a black church service without being noticed and hence without their lack of enthusiastic participation being apparent.

The appeal of BMCs may also be limited by their social conservatism. We see this in the divisions in the worldwide Anglican communion over gay rights and the ordination of women: the British and North American churches are in favour, while the African churches are opposed. The 'spiritual father' of Greenwich's New Wine Church called being gay 'a warped sexual identity'; another pastor who was a regular preacher there called homosexuality 'evil'.[37] Many British Pentecostal pastors took prominent roles in the Christian party and the Christian People's Alliance (discussed in Chapter 10); their abysmal failure to attract voters had many causes, but the gulf between black Pentecostal culture and the mores of most British people must have been a factor.

The greatest obstacle to conversion beyond the African diaspora, however, is the one to which I will return in the final chapter: the importance of social similarity. One member of the RCCG, in explaining why she joined her church, said: 'Like attracts like. You go where you won't stand out. People from other cultures tend to pass through because they feel conspicuous.'[38] Africans were attracted to the RCCG and similar because they felt comfortable there. The same logic explains why very few non-Africans have joined.

Given the limited ethnic appeal, the future of the BMC sector depends on future migration and on the success of family transmission. The former slowed in the twenty-first century, and the BMCs appear no better at the latter than the average British Christian family. Hence the slowing-down of Pentecostal growth. In the 2000s, the sector grew by 5.8 per cent while the churches overall declined by 0.7 per cent. But growth in the 2010s was only 2.1 per cent, and, according to returns to the Charity Commissioners, it seems that a number of smaller churches closed.[39]

Isolation and Faith: The Irish in Britain

The discussion so far has identified two reasons why migrant religious minorities were more religious than the typical native of their new world: they came from a more traditionally religious culture and their religious institutions provided a wide variety of secular resources that assisted settlement. Both of these have a short shelf life. The second generation is one removed from the old country and, to the extent that the immigrants prosper in their new setting, they rise in social status, and on that journey they lose much of what initially distinguished them from the natives. In the process they tend to lose their faith.

This can be seen very clearly in the changes experienced by Irish Catholic migrants to England and Scotland. The 1950s wave of migration saw the Catholic population of England rise from 4.7 to 5.6 million. The number of parishes grew from 1,910 to 2,320, and there was a 25 per cent increase in the number of parish priests. Short of technical skills and capital, the Irish Catholics who settled in London, Liverpool, and Glasgow usually came into the labour market at the bottom, but over the second half of the twentieth century they prospered, initially by providing commercial services (such as pubs, bookmakers, printing businesses, building trades) to their own people but then, as the welfare state grew, through the opening-up of higher education and the massive growth in white-collar professional work. Initially much Catholic higher education was introverted: the Church's colleges trained bright Catholics in professions (such as the law and medicine but especially teaching) that would allow them to serve the Catholic population and preserve it from external influence, but ambition could not be so constrained for long. By the end of the century, Catholics in England and Scotland were as likely as non-Catholics to have well-paid, high-status jobs.[40]

As they prospered, the immigrant Catholics gradually dropped many of the social barriers that had kept the first generation relatively isolated and relatively close to their parish churches.[41] The urban regeneration that followed the Luftwaffe bombings of the Second World War saw large numbers move from Liverpool and Glasgow to new towns, and neither the rented council housing nor the private home-owner sectors reproduced the ethnic and religious composition of the city parishes that were abandoned.[42]

At the same time, the Catholic Church gradually become more demotic in a shift from the fortress mentality (seen, for example, in the insistence that the children of any mixed marriage be raised as Catholics) to a more open faith. The Second Vatican Council (1962–5) stimulated a variety of changes: the

Latin services were translated into English, lay readers became more common, and girls were permitted to act as altar servers. Congregants still attended mass, but they gave up confession of sins and periods of fasting and abstinence.[43] Conservative Catholics insist that the reforms caused decline; reformers argued that they retarded it.[44] That British Catholicism was topped up by Irish migration in the 1950s suggests that the reformers had the better case, but we can settle for noting that the reforms did nothing to reverse decline. In the 1960s, mass attendance peaked at around 2 million; by the 1990s, that had fallen to 1.1 million. Child baptism fell from 134,000 to 75,000. Conversions fell from 15,000 to 6,000. While there had been 46,000 Catholic marriages in the early 1960s (and half of those were between two Catholics), by 1999 there were only 17,000 and only one-third involved two Catholics.[45] Monastic vocations plummeted: in 1982, 207 people joined orders. In 2000, the figure was 42.[46] The fate of Manchester's Gorton monastery was mentioned in Chapter 4. Another magnificent Pugin building, Stanbrook Abbey in the Malvern Hills, was sold in 2006, and the remaining twenty-four nuns (with an average age of 65) moved to a house in South Yorkshire. The modernist classic St Andrew's teacher-training college in Glasgow was opened in 1969 and closed thirty years later. The award-winning Cardross seminary was opened in 1966 and closed in 1980. Despite the addition of a large Polish and Lithuanian Catholic population and the considerable increase in life expectancy, the number of Catholics in England had fallen to around 850,000 by 2012. Where there were just under 8,000 priests in England in 1965, a century later there were just over 2,000. Scotland saw a similar decline. Between 1982 and 2010, the proportion of Scottish Catholics dropped 18 per cent, baptisms fell by 40 per cent, and the number of Catholic church marriages fell by more than half. Although it is tempting to explain some of that fall in popularity as reaction to sex and child-abuse scandals, as with the assertion that the decline is a result of Vatican II reforms, claims that specific events have caused the decline are hard to reconcile with the fact that the downward trends had been evident since the 1960s.

At the end of the twentieth century, a local historian of Liverpool's Docklands—a Catholic stronghold in the 1950s—wrote: 'Catholics in the Vauxhall area have, in the past, identified closely with their parishes, and have looked with respect upon their priests and sought guidance from them. With very few exceptions, this tradition has died.'[47] Michael Hornsby-Smith comes to the same conclusion for the country as a whole: 'For all intents and purposes English Catholics are indistinguishable from other English people.' In a remarkably forthright interview in the 1990s, an elderly Scottish Catholic priest ruefully connected the social progress of his constituents and their declining interest in his church:

> When I was young the Catholic people round here really were my people. Not all of them were as observant as they should have been but all the children went to the parochial school, all prepared for first communion. I walked from door to door and was always welcomed. They didn't have much but they were a close community and they gave generously to the Church and they respected my views. Or at least they felt obliged to pretend! Of course it's grand to see many young folk getting on in life and getting wee houses out in the suburbs but they have lost the faith. I am just glad I am not starting out now. It is an uphill struggle.[48]

To summarize, as Britain's Irish migrant Catholics prospered, they lost much of their distinctive culture, they married out, and they lost interest in the shared faith that had sustained them when they were a disadvantaged minority.

That observation allows us to think about the subsequent waves of black immigrants and likely changes in their religious culture. A high level of religious interest is best maintained by a ghetto. Such social isolation may be a result of some distinctive characteristic (poverty in the case of Irish Catholics), and it may be reinforced by a frosty reception from the host majority. When English landlords sometimes posted 'No Irish. No Blacks' signs, it is no surprise that the migrants stayed close to their fellows.[49] What undermined Catholic solidarity was the upward mobility that resulted from improved education and the growth of white-collar professional work, and the urban redevelopment that moved people out of their immigrant communities.

Will Caribbean and West African Pentecostalism experience the same fate? One obvious difference concerns identification. For bigots to discriminate against some minority and maintain social distance, they need to be able to identify its members. Outside of their religious practices, there was little or nothing that marked out the second generation of Irish Catholics. But West Indians carried their identity on their skins. Nonetheless there has been a considerable growth in inter-racial partnerships. The number of people described on census forms as being of 'mixed' or 'multiple' ethnicity almost doubled from just 660,000 in 2001 to 1.2 million in 2011.[50]

Modern communication technology and cheap flights have reduced the finality of migration. If they wish to keep in touch with their old world, Caribbean and African migrants will find that much easier than did the Irish.

That makes the erosion of social networks and traditional culture less pressing and thus reduces the subtle pressures to assimilate, but the evidence of religious commitment among these populations declining is already visible.[51] To the extent that they prosper and intermarry with the most likely secular white British, social isolation will diminish and with it the faith.

Conclusion

The social geography of religion is complex. The social forces that weaken religion strike unevenly. We saw one pattern in Chapter 2: their geographical isolation meant that the people of the regional peripheries—rural North Wales, the highlands and islands of Scotland, the West Country, and East Anglia—were slower to be affected than the core of the country by the rationalization of life, by the universalizing ethos of modern industrial work, and by the need to rub along with people of very different religious backgrounds. Hence they remained traditionally religious longer. The effects of social class will be discussed in Chapter 9, but they can be summarized here as a paradoxical mix of opposing trends. Partly because the conservative upper classes are old-fashioned and partly because they benefit from stability, they tend to be more religious than the lower orders; hence a general class and religion correlation. However, the new university-educated professionals who work for the state in education, in welfare, in health, and in government—the sort of people who now staff the Labour Party—tend to be self-consciously irreligious (or prefer an amorphous spirituality to conventional religion). This creates a general pattern of the more prosperous parts of Britain being more religious than the poorer 'rust-belt' areas (such as the north-west and north-east of England), but there are pockets of professional middle-class irreligion and working-class sectarian religion. Layered on top of the class patterns are the effects of migration. Britain was one of the world's first industrial democracies, and it was one of the first largely secular societies. Some immigrants have been somewhat secular: the European émigrés who moved to Britain in the 1930s to escape the Nazis were often cosmopolitan liberals. Those who chose to stay in Britain after the Second World War rather than return to the central and eastern European countries under Soviet domination were often drawn from the least religious and traditional parts of the populations of their home countries. But the major waves of twentieth-century migration—Irish Catholics, Caribbean Pentecostalists, West African Pentecostalists, and Asian Muslims—shifted people from non-industrial societies to the secular 'First World'.

The effect of that can be seen on church growth in London. If we ignore entirely the migrant background of the newcomers, we could mistakenly conclude that secularization is now being reversed. This is very far from being the case. London has become more religious relative to the rest of the country because it has become home to people from more religious countries. As I will argue in Chapter 11, far from being a sign of religious revival, that change almost certainly reduces the chance of any reversal of secularization.

Notes

1. Bagehot, 'Podsnappery and its Reverse', *Economist*, 23 June 2018, 24.
2. R. Porter, *London: A Social History* (Cambridge, MA: Harvard University Press, 2001), 298–9.
3. B. I. Coleman, *The Church of England in the Mid-Nineteenth Century* (London: Historical Association, 1980), 40–1.
4. British Weekly, *The Religious Census of London* (London: Hodder and Stoughton, 1888).
5. R. Mudie-Smith, *The Religious Life of London* (London: Hodder and Stoughton, 1904). For an extraordinarily detailed social accounting of London, see the seventeen volumes of C. Booth, *Life and Labour of the People in London* (London: Macmillan, 1902–3). Much of his material is available online courtesy of the London School of Economics, https://booth.lse.ac.uk/ (accessed 4 August 2018).
6. C. D. Field, *Secularization in the Long 1960s* (Oxford: Oxford University Pres, 2017), 101. See also C. D. Field, 'Faith in the Metropolis: Opinion Polls and Christianity in Post-War London', *London Journal*, 24 (1999), 68–94.
7. Trust for London, 'London's Population over Time', https://www.trustforlondon.org.uk/data/londons-population-over-time/ (accessed July 2018).
8. These data are from P. Brierley, *Capital Growth: What the 2012 London Church Census Reveals* (Tonbridge, Kent: ABCD Publishers, 2013).
9. Brierley, *Capital Growth*, 3, and 'Immigrant Churches in Britain', *Future First*, 50 (April 2017).
10. Brierley, *Capital Growth*, 23.
11. Field, *Secularization*, 103–4.
12. C. Hirschman, 'The Role of Religion in the Origins and Adaptation of Immigrant Groups in the United States', *International Migration Review*, 38 (2004), 1210.
13. K. Pryce, *Too Much Pressure* (Harmondsworth: Penguin, 1979), 221.
14. V. Lanterni, *The Religions of the Oppressed: A Study of Modern Messianic Cults* (New York: Mentor Books, 1963).
15. M. J. C. Calley, *God's People: West Indian Pentecostal Sects in England* (Oxford: Oxford University Press, 1965), 73.
16. Pryce, *Too Much Pressure*, 214.
17. Calley, *God's People*, 62.

18. P. Kalilambe, 'Black Christianity in Britain', *Ethnic and Racial Studies*, 20 (1997), 308–19.
19. H. Osgood, 'The Rise of Black Churches', in D. Goodhew (ed.), *Church Growth in Britain: 1980 to the Present* (Aldershot: Ashgate, 2012), 107–26.
20. R. Burgess, 'African Pentecostal Growth: The Redeemed Christian Church of God', in Goodhew (ed.), *Church Growth in Britain*, 130.
21. Burgess, 'African Pentecostal Growth', 132.
22. S. Hunt, '"Neither here nor there": The Construction of Identities and Boundary Maintenance of West African Pentecostals', *Sociology*, 36 (2002), 147–69. See also his 'Deprivation and Western Pentecostalism Re-Visited', *Pentecostal Studies*, 1 (2002), 1–18.
23. Calley, *God's People*, 31.
24. Hunt, '"Neither here nor there"'.
25. Osgood, 'The Rise of Black Churches', 112–13.
26. Hunt, '"Neither here nor there"', 162.
27. S. Powell, 'The Tenfold Return', *Lion of Light Ministries*, http://www.lionoflight.org/writings/view/95-The-Tenfold-Return (accessed August 2018).
28. T. Shifrin, 'Church Charity Closed down', *Guardian*, 7 September 2004, https://www.theguardian.com/society/2004/sep/07/charities.charitymanagement (accessed August 2018).
29. R. Booth, 'Preacher Faces Scrutiny from Charities Commission over Church's Finances', *Guardian*, 18 August 2013.
30. R. Booth, 'Richer than St Paul's: Church that Attracts 8,000 to a Disused Cinema', *Guardian*, 11 April 2009.
31. J. Bingham, 'Church of England Officials on Six-Figure Salaries', *Daily Telegraph*, 20 November 2013, https://www.telegraph.co.uk/news/religion/10464070/Church-of-England-officials-on-six-figure-salaries.html (accessed August 2018).
32. Burgess, 'African Pentecostal Growth', 133.
33. For example, S. Tonkin, '"Emaciated" Baby Died with no Trace of Milk in her Stomach after her Religious Parents Left her with a Woman who Had "Supernatural Powers" because their Church Banned Modern Healthcare', *Daily Mail*, 10 November 2015.
34. R. Hoskins, *The Boy in the River* (London: Pan Macmillan, 201)2.
35. B. Fox and G. Gofton, *When the War is Over* (London: Sphere, 2016), 120.
36. Much research into why people gave up churchgoing is compromised by the high likelihood that some will give excuses rather than straightforwardly admit that they do not believe.
37. 'Wine Stains', *Private Eye*, 1450, 11 August 2017.
38. Hunt, '"Neither here nor there"', 157.
39. P. Brierley, 'Pentecostal Growth Slowing down', *Future First*, 52 (2017), 1.
40. While this is universally acknowledged for England, a few scholars insist that the descendants of Irish Catholics in Scotland are still the victims of systematic labour-market discrimination. That case is refuted in detail using survey and census data in S. Bruce, 'Sectarian Discrimination in Local Councils and Myth-Making', *Scottish Affairs*, 23 (2014), 445–53; S. Bruce and T. Glendinning, 'Sectarianism in the Scottish Labour Market: Census 2011', *Scottish Affairs*, 26 (2017), 163–75; and S. Bruce,

T. Glendinning, I. Paterson, and M. Rosie, *Sectarianism in Scotland* (Edinburgh: Edinburgh University Press, 2004). The gradual assimilation of Catholics is described in G. Scott, *The RCs: A Report on Roman Catholics in Britain Today* (London: Hutchinson, 1967). The first chapter that sets the base line for change with an account of the Catholic community in Cardiff in the 1930s is called 'Keeping themselves to themselves'.

41. M. P. Hornsby-Smith, *Roman Catholics in England: Studies in Social Structure since the Second World War* (Cambridge: Cambridge University Press, 1987).

42. On Liverpool, see C. Ward, *Priests and People: A Study in the Sociology of Religion* (Liverpool: Liverpool University Press, 1961), and J. B. Mays, *Growing up in the City* (Liverpool: Liverpool University Press, 1954).

43. *The Tablet* (19 July 2008) reported a Von Hügel Institute, Cambridge University, survey of 1,500 English and Welsh Catholics in which 89% said they took communion every Sunday they attended mass, but only 3% said they made their confession first.

44. For example, M. Davies, 'The Church in Collapse', Latin Mass Society, http://www.latin-mass-society.org/collapse.htm (accessed February 2007).

45. M. P. Hornsby-Smith, 'English Catholics at the New Millennium', in M. P. Hornsby-Smith (ed.), *Catholics in England 1950–2000: Historical and Sociological Perspectives* (London: Cassell, 1999), 295. A vast body of detailed statistical information is contained in A. E. C. W. Spencer, *Digest of Statistics of the Catholic Community of England and Wales 1958–2005* (Taunton: Russell-Spencer, 2007).

46. J. Petre, 'Monks and their Monasteries Go into Retreat as Recruits Dwindle', *Daily Telegraph*, 10 April 2006.

47. F. Boyce, 'Catholicism in Liverpool's Docklands: 1950s–1990s', in Hornsby-Smith (ed.), *Catholics in England*, 66.

48. Personal interview, Glasgow, 1997.

49. For a detailed study of the effects of racism on housing policy and settlement patterns in the 1960s, see J. Rex and R. Moore, *Race, Community and Conflict: A Study of Sparkbrook* (Oxford: Oxford University Press, 1967).

50. Office of National Statistics data reported in J. Bingham, 'Love across the Divide: Interracial Relationships Growing in Britain', *Daily Telegraph*, 3 July 2014.

51. Brierley, 'Pentecostal Growth Slowing down'.

7

Worktown and Muslims

In December 1988, members of the congregation of Bolton's Zakariyya Jame Masjid led a crowd of some 7,000 Muslims to the town centre and there burned a copy of Salman Rushdie's *The Satanic Verses*: 'It was a peaceful protest, and we burned the book to try and attract public attention,' said a supporter of the action.[1] Rushdie, an Anglo-Indian author, had previously won the Booker prize with his novel *Midnight's Children*, and the career of *The Satanic Verses* began well with it winning the Whitbread prize. Muslims complained that the novel insulted Islam, but its publisher strongly objected to any revival of the book censorship that had been hobbled by the *Lady Chatterley's Lover* trial of 1960 and killed off by the trial of *Oz* magazine in 1971. Lawyers were consulted about a blasphemy prosecution but correctly advised that the ancient laws protected only Christianity and that there had been no state prosecutions for over fifty years. India, Pakistan, and South Africa had banned the book within a few weeks of publication, but the infamy of *The Satanic Verses* was created by Ayatollah Khomeini, apparently at the suggestion of Kalim Siddiqui, a British Muslim activist and founder of the Muslim Parliament.[2] The religious and political leader of Iran issued the following fatwa (or legal ruling):

> I am informing all brave Muslims of the world that the author of The Satanic Verses, a text written, edited, and published against Islam, the Prophet of Islam, and the Qur'an, along with all the editors and publishers aware of its contents, are condemned to death. I call on all valiant Muslims wherever they may be in the world to kill them without delay, so that no one will dare insult the sacred beliefs of Muslims henceforth. And whoever is killed in this cause will be a martyr, Allah Willing. Meanwhile if someone has access to the author of the book but is incapable of carrying out the execution, he should inform the people so that [Rushdie] is punished for his actions.

As an incentive, Khomeini offered a bounty of $6 million on Rushdie's head. Britain broke off diplomatic relations with Iran, and Rushdie began a decade of life in hiding and protective custody.

Bolton seemed an unlikely place to prompt thirty years of conflict. It is a large 'rust-belt' town in the north-west corner of the Greater Manchester conurbation. Like its neighbours, Bolton thrived on cloth production: when the industry peaked in 1929, half the town worked in its cotton mills and bleaching and dyeing works. That prosperity was converted into magnificent civic buildings—town hall, library, art gallery and museum, and numerous large churches—but it also coated the town in thick black soot. One observer noted: 'a dully grey canopy hung over the densely packed cobbled streets.'[3] J. B. Priestley, who visited the town for his 1930s travelogue *English Journey*, said: 'The ugliness is so complete that it is almost exhilarating. It challenges you to live there.'[4]

The cotton industry declined after 1919, but even in the 1960s it was strong enough to attract workers from Pakistan to its mills. Bolton was poorer than many comparable towns. In 1950, about 17 per cent of Britons were in the top two of five social classes; for Bolton the figure was only 14 per cent. The proportion of graduates was always markedly behind the national figure: in 1960, it was 2 per cent for Bolton when it was 3.2 per cent for the rest of Britain. By the end of the century it was 15 per cent for Bolton but 20 per cent for the country as a whole.[5]

The neglect of the manufacturing economy in favour of promoting the City of London's financial institutions by the Conservative governments of the 1980s damaged Bolton as it did the rest of the north-west: the proportion employed in manufacturing fell from 30 per cent in 1960 to less than 10 per cent in 2011. However, the twenty-first century has seen something of a revival in fortunes, with the growth of the university playing an important role.

Religion in Mass Observation's Worktown

An editorial in the *Bolton Chronicle* of 1854 wrote:

> Bolton, if no worse, is certainly no better than the general run of manufacturing towns, and not withstanding all its seeming activity in works of religious, moral and intellectual improvement, there is, we regret to say, within its boundaries a floating population without the fear, if not the knowledge, of God in the world, intemperate and immoral, and who if they have acquired the arts of reading and writing, are certainly without the better part of education which consists in the development of moral nature.[6]

The Census of Religious Worship taken three years earlier offers some foundation for the editor's concern. Bolton had 36 churches for a total population of 86,000 or one worship opportunity for every 1,433 adults. As some of those churches were tiny, there was obviously considerable religious indifference. Church attendance—at 20 per cent of the total population or 33 per cent of people over 15—was below the national average. Almost half the churchgoers were Anglicans. A further quarter attended one of the town's four types of Methodist chapel. Catholics represented 12 per cent of attendances, but, because they did not attend twice, a greater number of churchgoers. Congregationalists accounted for 11 per cent, and no other group got over 3 per cent.[7]

That we know a lot about the religious life of Bolton in the twentieth century is due to the work of Mass Observation (or MO), which was founded in 1937 by Tom Harrison (an ornithologist turned anthropologist) and Charles Madge (a journalist who later became Professor of Sociology at Birmingham University).[8] Their aim was to describe the British, especially the working classes, in the sort of detail Bronislaw Malinowski had given to the Trobriand Islanders.

As usual, 'Britain' meant England: Bolton, rather pointlessly anonymized as 'Worktown' in MO's various publications, was one of two research sites; London was the other. The team collected a great deal of material on religion in Bolton, but it did so haphazardly, and the plans to produce a book based on the 1937 study came to nought. In part this was because the war gave the participants more pressing concerns, but mostly because, in the absence of any clear focus, the material could not be shaped into a coherent volume. Harrison returned to Bolton in 1960 to update the research and, with a small number of collaborators, collected the data that appears in *Britain Revisited*.

One weakness of the project was its initial insistence on unobtrusive observation. The American lady addressing the tiny congregation of the 'health and well-being' New-Age-before-its-time Mazdaznan meeting was 'about 5' 10" in height and has a perfect figure...dressed in a purple evening gown, covering in skin-tight fashion her bosom and posterior'. This sounds like a good advert for Mazdaznan's dietary principles, and the reporter's admiration hints at the gulf in health and beauty between affluent Americans and poor Boltonians, but it tells us nothing about the number or the sort of people who heard her.[9]

Another flaw is a lack of attention to representativeness. Lots of people recorded their impressions of elements of religious life as diverse as sermon themes, the contents of church notice boards, and the dress of church attenders, but we have no way of knowing whether what was observed was at all typical. It is certainly clear that the Mass Observers were not.

What was immediately obvious was the bulk of the panel was either living in Bloomsbury or Hampstead, were members of the Communist party, vegans, you name it. That is to say, wholly unrepresentative, very literate but very much concerned with their own personal, private political problems. That is, they were not members of the working class reflecting on their daily lives.[10]

However, there is some value in the lists of churches and estimates of church membership and attendance gathered by the MO team.[11] There are inconsistencies, but Clive Field has corrected the mistakes, and the results are displayed in Table 7.1.[12]

The Church of England dominated Worktown's religious scene. It had the biggest buildings and the largest total attendance. The Methodists had the largest number of outlets but that represented a considerable over-provision. In the late nineteenth century, the competition between Wesleyan, Primitive, and United Methodists meant often three buildings where, after the 1932 reunion, only one was needed. The MO commentators noted that, while the Protestant congregations were much smaller than their churches and chapels would allow, the Catholic buildings were often full.

Table 7.1. Places of worship, Bolton, 1851, 1937, 1960, and 2018

Places of worship	1851	1937	1960	2018
Church of England	9	38	41	22
Roman Catholics	2	13	14	17
Congregational/Presbyterian/URC	6	10	14	12
Methodist (inc. Independent Methodist)	11	44	34	14
Other Christian/Fringe	8	52	54	28
Total Christian/Fringe	36	157	157	93
Muslim	0	0	0	30
Other Non-Christian	0	1	0	5
Total	36	158	157	128

Note: As the differences are not important for my concerns here, I have lumped together small Christian bodies such as the Brethren, semi-Christian sects such as Christian Science, and 'New Age' bodies such as Theosophy and Mazdaznan. Other data are from Mass Observation documents corrected and kindly supplied by Clive Field.

Sources: The 2018 figures are from the websites of the Anglican Diocese of Manchester, the RC Diocese of Salford, the Bolton Circuit of the Methodist Church, and various smaller religious organizations.

MO made no systematic effort to count attendance, but, by taking the average of some patchy data and allowing for enthusiasts attending more than one service, Field guesses that about 13 per cent of the people attended church. That is down from the 1881 survey figure of 35 per cent but in line with other English towns in the 1930s. One important note about that estimate: it is incompatible with the almost universal claims to having some church association made to MO workers during the house-to-house canvasses.[13] Even more strongly than in Banbury twenty years later (see Chapter 5), the people of Bolton felt obliged to inflate their religious involvement.

Partly because legislation prevented some activities, the sabbath was quiet, and, even for the non-churchgoers, 'the influence of Sunday and its special habits is in itself enough to keep down over-drinking', as MO observed in its comparison of the appeal of the public houses and the churches.[14] One attempt to straddle those two worlds was the Victorian Methodist central mission, which, as well as church services and evangelistic rallies, hosted secular entertainments. MO noted fifty-seven different activities in one week's programme at Bolton's Victoria Hall, and its 1,800 seats were often full for Saturday evening concerts.

As Table 7.1 shows, there was little change in the supply side of Bolton's religious life between Harrison's two studies. The Church of England had slightly extended, with new churches in the growing peripheral housing estates. The Catholic population had almost doubled from 1937 and the Church had expanded its provision to cater both for increased numbers and for their wider dispersal. In 1937, the Methodist Church had just been formed out of the former Wesleyan Primitive and United Methodist strands and had not yet begun to rationalize its over-provision; by 1960, a quarter of its chapels had closed. The Victoria Hall was still extant, but the similar King's Hall in Bradshawgate had closed in 1958.

There was also little change in demand. Field suggests that some 16 per cent of Bolton's people regularly attended church in 1960. Superficially that represented a small growth in religious activity, but it was an aggregation of two opposing trends. The Catholic population had grown considerably—Irish migration, high birth rate, and insistence on children of mixed marriages being raised as Catholic—while the Anglican and 'Other' Christian presence had declined. St Paul's, Deansgate, for example, could seat 1,000 people but had an average turnout of 70 in the morning and 110 in the evening. Overall, there were about 12,000 Catholic and 5,500 Anglican attendances. We cannot know how many of the 9,000 attendances estimated for the other denominations and sects were by people attending twice, but most of these outlets were small. The most popular—a Salvation Army service—had only 150 people, and the Congregational chapel in Mawdsley Street, which could seat 700, had only 10 adults and 7 children at the service observed by MO.

The devout of the 1960s devoted less time to their faith than did their parents. Although Sunday was still quiet, churchgoers no longer gave up the whole day to religion. Protestants had adopted the Catholic pattern of attending just one service and spending the rest of the day on social and leisure activities. Most Protestant chapels had given up the afternoon Sunday school—central to the sex lives of parents of large families in small houses—and merged it into the main morning service. Adult Bible study classes had been largely abandoned, as had mid-week meetings. The history of St Luke's, Halliwell, notes that in 1952 'there were 250 scholars in the Sunday School, each of whom it is reputed could say the Lord's Prayer, the Creed and the General Confession at an early age...but in 1973 the number had fallen to about 50—the Sunday run in the family car has taken its toll'.[15]

Another mark of the shrinking reach of religion was its disappearance from the streets. In the late nineteenth century and first half of the twentieth, many churches and chapels displayed their popularity by holding parades (or 'Sermon Day Walks' or 'Wakes') as part of their annual prize-giving and picnic events. The pupils, often dressed in new clothes bought for the occasion, marched behind bands and ornate banners, similar to those used by trade-union branches, fraternal lodges, and mutual insurance companies. The Lee Clough Mission, Astley Bridge, banner depicted Christ ushering in sheep above the motto 'I am the door'. An old man who had attended the Mission in the 1940s wrote: 'I have lots of happy memories, "field days", walking on sermons day, playing on the slag heaps at the side of Hesketh's Mill, concert parties and prize day, when those who had not missed any Sundays got a book.'[16] By the 1960s such walks were rare, and they soon died out.

Fifty years on, Bolton's religious milieu has changed drastically. Liberal and mainstream Protestantism have markedly declined. There has been some shuffling in conservative sects, with the older ones declining or rebranding, and a few additions. Some of the more exotic fringe groups (the Swedenborgians and the Christian Scientists, for example) have gone. The Unitarian Church, once the home of posh liberal dissent, is now down among the exotics, both in size and in association: its Bank Street chapel rents its basement to Madame Blavatsky's Theosophical Society. The Church of England has closed half its outlets since 1960. The Methodists have been particularly hard hit. Including the Independent Methodists, the number of chapels fell from 34 in 1960 to 14 in 2018. Superficially, the United Reformed Church (URC) with twelve congregations has survived in better shape, but one is a joint venture with the Methodists and others are struggling: the Tonge Moor and Red Lane congregations gave up their churches and now meet in small halls. The Catholic Church grew and then shrank again, as Catholic migrants from eastern Europe added variety but failed to compensate for the decline in English numbers. Almost a third of the twenty-four outlets listed in 2008 were closed by 2018.

There has been some reorganization in the conservative Protestant sphere. The Elim Pentecostal Church seems to have disappeared, and two Assemblies of God congregations now 'present as' modern charismatic groups. The Brethren/Gospel Hall sector has shrunk somewhat and also been rebranded, so that it looks more like the independent evangelical churches associated with the Evangelical Alliance. Bolton has gained two black majority churches: New Testament Church of God and Redeemed Church of Christ. And a fair number of black people are now members of the two Church of the Nazarene congregations.[17]

None of these innovations comes close to stemming overall Christian decline. Bolton's Anglican attendance is slightly better than the Diocese of Manchester's average, but it is only about a third of the 1960 figure.[18] As we have seen elsewhere, the decline of the churches has been accompanied by an increase in the commitment of those still involved at all. In 2017, 87 per cent of the 885 members of the eleven Methodist chapels attended regularly—a considerable consolidation since the 1960s when membership was often twice attendance.[19]

The biggest change since Harrison's second period in Bolton is the growth of two non-Christian populations. The Hindu Shree Swaminarayan Mandir began life in 1979 in a small terraced house. Twenty years later it moved to a disused Unitarian chapel, and in 2013 it opened a major extension. Bolton became a focus for Hindus in the north-west; proportionately they were twice as numerous in the borough as in England as a whole.

Bolton welcomed its first Muslims in the late 1950s. Initially they were single men living in boarding houses:

> The first Bolton home known to have been bought by a Muslim family was 140 Deane Road. Ishaq and Yakub Bermat bought it in 1959, having arrived in the UK a year earlier. Gradually more families came over and distinct areas of settlement in Bolton emerged.... As the community expanded in the early sixties, the need for educational facilities arose for the children of newly arrived families. In 1962 the first committee, a nascent group which would eventually forge the Islamic Cultural Centre, was formed.[20]

The first madrasah (or Islamic school) was opened in 1965 but was closed down by the police, as was the first mosque—on Latham Street in the Blackburn Road area—because the premises were not licensed for public gatherings. For a time Friday prayers were held in a rented nightclub, and then in 1967 suitable premises became available when a redundant Methodist chapel and school in Peace Street was burnt out, and the site was bought for the Zakariyya mosque.

In the 2001 census, only 3 per cent of England, and of the north-west, identified as Muslim, but the figure for Bolton was 7 per cent. In 2018, there were thirty mosques in Bolton. Many were small, often converted houses, but, with a main hall capacity of 3,000, the Zakariyya building is twice the size of the central halls the Methodists built in their heyday.

Nativist Reaction: Identity and Schooling

The large number of Muslims in Bolton coincides with three related distinctions. The first is the high proportion of Boltonians who identified as 'Christian' in the 2001 and 2011 censuses. As we can see from Table 7.2, 71.8 per cent of the people of England and Wales but 74.6 per cent of the people of Bolton identified as Christian in 2001. The far lower attendance figures tell us that the vast majority of such identifiers were nominal; they were expressing an ethnic identity rather than a religious attachment. The census form used in England and Wales invited exactly that, because it immediately preceded the religion question with one asking the respondent to select an ethnic identity and—in contrast to the Scottish version, which offered denomination tags such as 'Church of Scotland' and 'Catholic'—the tick box options for religion were 'Christian' followed immediately by 'Muslim', 'Buddhist', and so on.

The north-west had reasons to be concerned about ethnicity. The area had long been characterized by racial tensions, which culminated in riots in 2001—just a month after the census forms had been completed and a few weeks before the fascist British National party (BNP) achieved electoral breakthrough by winning council seats in nearby Oldham and Burnley. At the time, the chairman of the Council for Racial Equality wrote to the Home Secretary calling for 'immediate measures for the summer to defuse the tension' and adding that 'Young Muslims who feel disenfranchised relate neither to white authority nor to the mosque or to their own "community leaders". We must—and can if we show we are taking them seriously—reach them, identify those with the talent for leadership, and draw them in.'[21]

Table 7.2. Religious identity, Bolton and England and Wales, 2001 and 2011 (%)

Religious identity	2001		2011	
	Bolton	England and Wales	Bolton	England and Wales
Christian	74.6	71.8	62.7	59.3
None/Not Stated	16.1	22.3	22.9	32.3
Muslim	7.1	3.1	11.7	4.8
Hindu	2.0	1.1	2.2	1.5
Other	0.4	1.8	0.6	2.1
Total	100.2	100.1	100.1	100.0

Note: Percentage totals are not always 100 because of rounding.

Sources: Office for National Statistics, '2001 Census: Census Area Statistics: Key Figures: Area: Bolton (Local Authority)' and '2011 Census, Key Statistics Table KS209EW', https://www.ons.gov.uk/peoplepopulationandcommunity/populationandmigration/populationestimates/datasets/2011censuskeystatisticsforlocalauthoritiesinenglandandwales (accessed September 2012).

It is difficult to be precise about the riot's causes, but those identified for the disturbances in nearby Oldham seem generally applicable. In the background is the deprivation caused by the loss of manufacturing. The south Asian migrants were residentially separate from the white British residents, and both developed victimhood myths. Asians feared white areas and believed that the council discriminated against them; they were certainly under-represented in council jobs. With less evidence, many white people believed the council invested disproportionately in Asian areas and curried favour with Muslims by removing emblems, such as flags, that supposedly offended them. In the year leading up to the riots, growing evidence of racial tension was exploited by the BNP and by the National Front, and the extensive media coverage attracted right-wing hooligans and their left-wing opponents in the Anti-Nazi League.

The third distinction is the popularity of voting to leave the EU. The 2016 vote in Bolton divided 58.3 per cent leave and 41.7 per cent remain.[22] As we do not know precisely what proportion of Muslims and non-Muslims voted, we cannot make any statistical adjustment, but, because Muslims UK-wide were twice as likely as non-Muslims to vote remain, and because Bolton has more than the UK average of Muslims, Bolton's white British population probably voted two-thirds to leave.[23] Of course, that vote had many causes, but we can suppose that the white people of Bolton were unusual in their wish to assert their Englishness.

As well as having a high proportion of nominal Christians, Bolton had a higher than average church attendance rate. The numbers attending church fell by a third between 1989 and 2018, but that still left Bolton as the only one of ten local authorities in the Greater Manchester area that recorded an above-the-national-average rate of churchgoing in Peter Brierley's 2012 clergy-based estimate of attendance.[24] Some of that may be explained by the presence of Catholics (traditionally better attenders than their Protestant counterparts), but a part of it may be an unintended consequence of changes in the English school system. One well-informed local—a schoolteacher who was also active in one of Bolton's largest Anglican congregations—said:

> the likeliest explanation is the existence of two officially 'outstanding' Church of England High Schools. Canon Slade and St James are both heavily over-subscribed. Their Admissions Policies give points for church attendance.... We have a large number of attenders at our church who seem to come along simply to get the points to get into a good school—after all, its cheaper than paying for independent school fees (and there's only one sizeable independent school in the whole of Bolton) or buying a house in the catchment area of a good school.

To understand that we must briefly review the recent structure of schooling in England.

An Aside on Faith Schools

Much of Britain's school system (especially in rural areas and small towns) was initially created by the Christian churches. The state Church of England and Church of Scotland aimed to provide a church and a school in every parish, and much additional provision in the nineteenth century came from other churches (especially Methodist, Free Church, and Catholic) following suit. The huge shifts and growth in population associated with industrialization, plus a growing appreciation of the need for an educated populace, led the state to recognize the poverty of private provision and to create nation-wide systems of taxpayer-funded state-managed schooling. In Scotland, the Presbyterian churches handed their schools to the state in 1872; the Catholic Church stayed out of that arrangement, because it gave insufficient guarantees about church control. It eventually joined in 1918, when it was offered what critics called 'Rome on the rates': full state funding but complete church control over staffing and curriculum. In England and Wales, the state assumed the financial burden of Church of England and Catholic schools but left the respective churches in charge. For a long time this was relatively uncontroversial, because the schools, especially the rural ones that unselectively accommodated local children, were not especially Christian.

From the 1980s the number of private faith schools grew from two sources. Some charismatic and evangelical Christians (usually members of independent churches) set up small schools to shield their children from secular culture. Many such schools used Accelerated Christian Education (ACE), an educational instruction package developed in the US. Because pupils effectively teach themselves and the curriculum is narrow (science and technology subjects are addressed almost entirely without practical work), ACE allows very small schools to operate with few trained staff. Oak Hill in Bristol began in 1985 with seven staff, of whom only four were qualified teachers.[25]

Members of minority religions started independent schools for much the same reasons. They wanted to indoctrinate their children in their distinctive faiths—many Muslim schools have been criticized by the Office for Standards in Education (Ofsted) for diverting too much time from conventional lessons to the study of the Quran—and they wanted to protect their distinct social mores.[26]

Those ambitions were accidentally encouraged by the Conservative Party's general aim to undermine left-wing politics. Councils in cities and large towns were often controlled by the Labour Party, and their education departments were staffed by professional teachers, whose support for trade unions and for progressive legislation offended Tory principles. The 1980s Thatcher government weakened local authorities by creating a new class of secondary school—the academy, which was taxpayer funded but answered to the national Department of Education rather than to the local council. Extant schools could opt out of local-authority control, and new schools (funded, it was hoped, by private enterprise) could be created. Labour governments continued the academy experiment, and the subsequent Cameron and May governments extended the programme by adding 'Free Schools'.

To justify these innovations without admitting the real purpose, the government required Free Schools to have some special focus (such as performing arts or technological subjects). Of the first twenty-four Free Schools, six were religious.[27] As the vast majority of state-funded faith schools were Christian, the government encouraged minority faiths to bid for Free Schools.

The differences between the types of state school need not concern us beyond the general observation that the voluntary-aided and voluntary-controlled faith schools are required to follow the national curriculum and to take all applying pupils without regard to faith unless they are oversubscribed, when they can apply religious tests (which leads to the hypocritical pretence described in the next section). Faith academies are free from the requirement to follow the national curriculum.

Liberals have fretted over faith schools, but there has been no great expansion of the more-than-nominally-Christian sector. The Christian Schools Trust, the main industry organization, had sixty-five schools in 1992 but only forty in 2000 and the same in 2018.[28] One block on growth has been that the charismatic movement has stagnated, its members have aged, and their children have graduated. The new faith schools are generally small and reliant on volunteer staff. Those Christian parents willing to fund-raise and teach to shield their own children from the world usually do not feel as strongly about children in general.

As Table 7.3 shows, the number of faith schools is large—37 per cent of primaries and 19 per cent of secondaries—but the overwhelming majority of these (and the largest) are Church of England or Catholic—a residue of the nineteenth century rather than a modern reaction to the secularity of state schools. Of the 28 per cent of primary schoolchildren who are in some sort of notionally faith school, 97 per cent are being taught in Anglican or Catholic schools. Of the 19 per cent of secondary school pupils in faith schools, 84 per cent are in Anglican or Catholic establishments. Especially in rural areas, these function as local comprehensives; their pupils, staff, and curricula are not distinguished by their religion.

Table 7.3. Types of school, England, 2017

School type	Primary		Secondary	
	Number of schools	% Faith schools	Number of schools	% Faith schools
Community	7,317	0	523	0
Voluntary-aided	3,031	99	267	93
Voluntary-controlled	2,115	95	42	52
Foundation	637	4	248	1
Academy (sponsored)	1,082	20	619	16
Academy (converted)	2,530	35	1,371	18
Free Schools	136	28	238	10
Total	16,848	37	3,308	19

Source: R. Long and P. Bolton, *Faith Schools in England: FAQ; House of Commons Library Briefing Paper 06972* (London: House of Commons, 6 June 2017).

The schools that are most clearly distinguished by their faith are largely invisible to all but their clients. When thirty-four boys and two adults had to be rescued from the foot of cliffs near Dover, it was found that they came from an unregistered 'yeshiva' in the borough of Hackney; the council estimated that some 1,000 Orthodox Jewish boys between 13 and 16 were missing from its school system.[29] Muslim communities also support an unknown (but probably large) number of unregistered schools that offer very little by way of formal education and exist primarily to prevent children from being corrupted by the culture and social mores of the secular world.[30]

The God Scam

The appeal of mainstream religiously tinted schools lies not in religion but in educational performance and social class (and those are closely related). The number of pupils entitled to free school meals is a good index of poverty. Faith schools that were permitted to apply religious tests because they were oversubscribed took 27 per cent fewer such children than did the other schools in their areas.[31] Some middle-class parents who are not themselves Christians pretend to be religious to save their children from mixing with poor people. As one journalist noted:

> every parent knows about the God scam.... It is almost a cliché, bumping into previously quasi-heathen parents, suddenly taking their child to church every Sunday. Some of them seem genuine. Others mumble furtively about 'being attracted to the sense of community'. Then there are those who are completely brazen about going through the motions purely to get their child into the good school or, as one parent put it 'You need a letter saying you're a regular'.[32]

Another quoted a newly minted churchgoer saying: 'Of course the vicar knows most of us are agnostics at best. His attitude is so long as there are bums on seats, who cares?'[33] When a popular Church of England primary school can insist that parents attend church 'at least twice a month, for at least one year before March 31 in the year in which the admission takes place', it invites what one parent called 'faith school cheating'.[34] Such deception is obvious to the churches, which are torn between wanting more rigorous proofs of faith and worrying that the religiously indifferent may tire of generously subsidizing organized religion.[35]

Religion in Bolton Summarized

In summary, Bolton's religious life has changed as follows. Christianity has lost popularity and influence since the mid-nineteenth century. That decline was somewhat retarded by Irish migrants boosting Catholic numbers. The period since MO's 1960 study has seen decline accelerate and it has also seen the growth of Hindu and Muslim populations. The coincidence of economic decline and the very visible growth of Islam seems to have produced a small but significant rise in the symbolic importance of Christianity, exhibited in two rather different class patterns.

The working class shows small but clear signs of hostility to, and resentment of, Muslims. A study of schools in Burnley (a town close and similar to Bolton) noted that 'Muslim students of Asian heritage...may be more willing than their White Christian and non-Christian counterparts to accept social diversity without feeling that their identities are being threatened'; for example, 30 per cent of the children in a mostly white mostly non-Christian school, but only 11 per cent of Muslim children, thought that one race was superior to another.[36] For the working class, ill-ease is expressed in street disturbances, Brexit voting, and the nominal assertion of Church of England identification. For the middle classes, it has taken the form of somewhat insincere church attendance designed to ensure children are admitted to good middle-class schools.[37]

Whether such shallow attachment to Christianity is likely to become something deeper and more sincere will be considered in the final chapter.

Muslim Growth and Demography

With 4.4 per cent of the population according to the 2011 census, Islam is the second largest religion in the UK. It is also the fastest growing: in the first decade of the twenty-first century the Muslim population increased almost ten times faster than the non-Muslim population. Little of that is due to conversion. The majority of the 179,733 people in the 2001 England and Wales census who described themselves as both Muslim and white chose 'Other white' rather than 'white British' as their ethnic tag; they were most likely from Bosnia and Herzegovina, Kosovo, Bulgaria, Chechnya, Albania, and Turkey. Hence we can guess an upper limit of some 60,000 converts, with a much lower figure being most likely.[38] Rather, the growth is biological: although the difference is eroding, British Muslims have larger than average families.

The Muslim presence in Britain is a result of the long backwash of empire. In the nineteenth century, the Indian subcontinent was under British rule, and, like the Caribbean, after the Second World War, it provided a ready pool of labour. Bolton's recruitment of Pakistani workers for its mills has been mentioned. Before the change in attitude that led to his 'rivers of blood' speech (see Chapter 10). Enoch Powell, as Conservative health minister, had recruited large numbers of doctors to staff the growing NHS.

British Muslims face some social disadvantage. They live in poorer housing, have lower levels of education, and experience higher levels of long-term ill health than the rest of the population. Much of that is explained by location: the mills towns of the north-west, such as Bolton, which once provided well-paid, if arduous, work, now have high rates of unemployment, for non-Muslims as well as for Muslims.

Another reason is the relative underemployment of Muslim women. In 2006, only 28 per cent of Pakistani women, as compared to the national average of 70 per cent, worked outside the home. Only a quarter of UK women in general, but two-thirds of Pakistani women, were voluntarily 'economically inactive'.[39] Those Muslim women who did seek full-time work did well. A quarter were in managerial or professional positions, which was markedly better than the 21 per cent achieved by Christian identifiers.[40]

The other exceptional pattern is the unusually high proportion of self-employed men. In the Scottish census of 2011, 28 per cent of 'Other religion' men aged 35–44 were own-account workers or small employers, as compared with only 14 per cent of 'Christians'.[41] As the Irish did a century earlier, Muslims responded to their lack of formal educational qualifications and technical skills by providing services to their communities: restaurants, clothes shops, travel agents, and taxi firms, for example. Although many self-employed men work in low-earning jobs, Muslim businesses have prospered; in 2008, the Home Secretary estimated that there were some 10,000 Muslim millionaires in the UK.[42]

Muslim Isolation

Like most migrant populations, Muslims cluster together—hence their markedly uneven distribution, with many parts of Britain having few Muslims and others with concentrations of over 25 per cent.[43] Such clustering is doubtless partly a reaction to hostility: 'institutional racism in both the public and private housing markets...together with popular racist sentiments expressed through racial harassment, continued to reinforce existing patterns of minority residential segregation.'[44] Racist right-wing groups such as the National Front and the BNP, and more recently the English Defence League, Britain First, and UKIP, have tried to mobilize anti-immigrant and anti-Muslim sentiment. And, though there have been few fatalities, there have been a significant number of acts of violence against minorities. For example, of 400 people detained in 2016 on suspicion of terrorism, 143 were right-wing extremists.[45]

But to stress the push factor of an unwelcoming environment neglects the greater importance in minority concentration of pull factors. Even without external pressure, migrants tend to cluster because they want to live alongside relatives and others who share their language and their background, and who are able to provide job opportunities. For some ethnic minorities, religion is an additional pull. Keeping dietary laws, worshipping at the mosque, and ensuring the children are socialized into the parents' religion are good reasons for Muslims settling among other Muslims. The just-quoted scholar who sees Muslim segregation as reactive misses the implication of her own observation that 70 per cent of Muslims 'valued living near to some other people of south Asian origins (preferably Muslims)'.[46] The Muslim who said 'We tell our children to make friends but make sure they are Asian friends and not white ones....Why? Because they have a different culture...drinking, partying, boyfriends, sex and tolerating things that are not allowed in Islam' was reasonably typical.[47] Muslims, like other religious minorities, understand the sociological principles demonstrated in Chapter 2: community cohesion (which is positively linked with a lack of integration with the wider society) is important for maintaining the taken-for-grantedness of their faith. They even justify their isolation with examples of faith groups that have been extensively studied by sociologists. Mohammed Khan, the leader of Blackburn council, said in 2018: 'in the US, Mennonites live quite separately, drive buggies, dress in black, and don't use electricity; and few consider this abnormal.'[48] Actually the Mennonites (better known as the Amish) are widely regarded as unusual; to pre-empt a point made later, they are just not seen as a challenge by their majority neighbours because they are so thoroughly introverted that they have no impact on anyone outside their community.

One symptom and cause of the relative isolation of many British Muslim communities is the strong prejudice against marrying out of the faith—a preference for endogamy explains why many British Muslim parents arrange for their children to marry partners from the home country. Another symptom of the interest that British Muslims retain in their old worlds is the scale of financial transfers: in the fiscal year 2017/18, remittances from the UK to Pakistan amounted to over £2.4 billion.[49]

Although most discussions of segregation concern geography, we should note that modern media make a degree of social segregation possible even for those who are not physically separate from the wider population. Until the invention of satellite TV and then the internet, electronic mass communication was confined to four TV channels, four national radio stations, and a handful of local radio stations. Most of that output was managed by the BBC, and all of it was subject to stringent controls on content. Print journalism was dominated by ten national newspapers and a number of local weekly papers (many of them owned by a few large companies). The raw materials for building an alternative culture were largely confined to imported videos and a few weekly newspapers. Now anyone with a satellite dish, a computer, or a smart phone can access news content from around the globe, and, instead of most of the nation consuming the same outputs, people can select the sources that fit and reinforce their existing attitudes and beliefs.

Even when there is little or no geographical separation and people do not bolster rather different worldviews by consuming very different mass media, a degree of social distance is created by the sorts of differences in personal value preferences that will be discussed shortly.

Muslim Distinction

Concern about segregation has grown with the rise of Islamic fundamentalism worldwide and with such local expressions as the Rushdie book-burnings and the later terrorist attacks in London. Although few non-Muslims are so bigoted as to suppose that all Muslims are jihadis, many see some looser connection between social isolation, unpopular attitudes, and hostility to the UK. Such suspicions are not entirely without foundation. British Muslims held far more negative views of the West than other European Muslims: almost half said that being a devout Muslim conflicted with living in a modern society, while only a quarter of French Muslims agreed.[50] In 2006, around 81 per cent of British Muslims thought of themselves as Muslim first.[51] However, while some of that may reflect dislike for Britain, more of it is probably caused simply by Muslims regarding their faith as more important than any nationality—an attitude one would expect from all seriously religious people. Had such surveys been conducted among Scots in 1800, I cannot imagine the answers would have been very different. When, instead of comparing the relative weight of different sorts of identity, we ask about citizenship, we generally find that Muslims are as likely as Christians to feel they belong to Britain.[52]

There have been innumerable polls of British Muslim opinion, and the results are often apparently incompatible, but the following summarizes the most consistent findings. A useful starting point is to note that in their day-to-day lives Muslims are mostly concerned about the same things as non-Muslims: jobs, housing, the state of the health service, the consequences of Brexit, the quality of their children's education, and drugs, street violence, and crime in general. British Muslims are distinctive in their piety. In 2009, 80 per cent of Muslims claimed to be religiously observant (as distinct from 32 per cent of Christians and 66 per cent of Sikhs). All these figures are inflated by aspiration replacing evaluation, but the relative differences are more important than the net figures.[53] A more realistic report has 78 per cent of Muslims saying that religion is very important but 48 per cent saying they never attended a mosque.[54] Among schoolchildren of the north-west, 81 per cent of Muslims claimed to attend mosque once a week or more often, while the figure for non-Muslims attending church was only 8 per cent. Only 10 per cent of Muslim children thought religion 'unimportant', while 59 per cent of other children took that view.[55]

That high degree of religiosity is associated with distinctly conservative attitudes. Segregating boys and girls in school was favoured by 40 per cent of Muslims but only 11 per cent of the general population.[56] Almost two-thirds of Muslim respondents agreed with the statement that homosexuality is wrong and should be illegal; not one thought homosexuality morally acceptable.[57] In 2013, just before same-sex marriages were legalized, over 400 leading Muslims published an open letter opposing the bill on the grounds that 'Muslim parents will be robbed of their right to raise their children according to their beliefs, as homosexual relationships are taught as something normal to their primary-aged children'.[58] When Birmingham primary schools introduced a programme to encourage inclusive attitudes to minority sexual orientations, Muslim parents demonstrated and withdrew their children.[59]

While most Muslim parents confine control of their children to more or less consensually arranged marriages, there is sufficient evidence of young girls being taken abroad and forced to marry their parents' choice (a crime since 2014) that Sajid Javid, the Home Secretary, ordered an official review in 2018.[60]

Muslims generally say they support the implementation of sharia law, although it seems more popular in the abstract than when presented as concrete propositions.[61] Islamic law is contentious because it enshrines attitudes common in the Arab world in the tenth century; in particular, it discriminates against women. In March 2014, the Law Society issued guidance to solicitors on drafting sharia-compliant wills that specifically said that male heirs should normally receive twice as much as female heirs.[62] The guidance was withdrawn following criticism by solicitors and by the Justice Secretary. Increasingly, informal sharia councils have been used to settle domestic disputes, usually to the advantage of men.

In essence there are two ways of getting married in the UK: local Registry Offices provide a brief secular civil ceremony to accompany the legal formalities and most major religious organizations register their clergy to record legally marriages they conduct as part of a religious ritual. The problem for Islam is that most imams do not register with the state to perform marriages and few Muslims follow the obvious alternative of getting married in a Registry Office before or after a religious ceremony.[63] Hence many Muslim couples (one estimate suggests two-thirds) are not legally married, and the wives have little or no legal protection against being impoverished by divorce.[64] The problem could be readily solved if Muslims followed the UK law, but instead some campaign to have the law changed to accommodate their preferences.

Another way in which British Muslims are unusual is in their views of international conflicts. That Britons travelled to Syria and Iraq to fight for Islamic State (ISIS) was often reported, and, while that degree of commitment to the politics of Muslim countries is rare, British Muslims are more likely than non-Muslims to oppose Western involvement in majority Muslim states, even when that involvement was solicited by factions within those countries.

One common consequence of social isolation is that it increases the plausibility of victimhood myths. Although the census data on social class and many large social surveys show that Scots Catholics are now of much the same social status as non-Catholics, it is still common for Catholics to claim that sectarian discrimination is rife. As with fears of being victims of violence, such claims are almost always second or third hand—justified with stories of the experiences of a distant relative or a friend of a friend.[65] One serious study of Muslims noted the same phenomenon: 'it is also notable how concerns about [bigotry and racism] were often relayed with reference to stories heard from friends, family or via the media.'[66]

The sense of being beleaguered is clear from polls such as one that asked British Muslims: 'If anyone is charged and put on trial in Britain in connection with the [London Transport] bombings of July 7, do you think they will or will not get a fair trial?': 37 per cent thought they would, but 44 per cent thought they would not. A 2016 survey asked British Muslims who was responsible for the Twin Towers bombing. Only 4 per cent accepted Al-Qaeda's boast of responsibility; 7 per cent thought it was the work of Jews, 31 per cent of the US government, and 52 claimed not to know who was responsible.[67]

That reference to Jews shows a general anti-Semitism that, while not confined to them—witness the problems of the Corbyn-era Labour Party—is common among Muslims. In 2013, Lord Ahmed, the first Muslim appointed to the House of Lords, was convicted of using his mobile phone while driving. In an interview with a Pakistani TV programme he said his conviction was the result of a Jewish conspiracy against him.[68] A former Lord Mayor of Blackburn claimed that the Sandy Hook, New Jersey, school shootings were the work of the state of Israel. Sheikh Riyadh ul Haq, a leading figure in the UK's Deobandi movement who ran a school in Leicester, thought that the Jews 'monopolised everything…money, interest, usury, the world economy, the media, political institutions'.[69] In a remarkably inapt comparison, Muhammed Abdul Bari, the head of the Muslim Council of Britain, said the UK's treatment of Muslims was comparable to the Nazi's treatment of Jews. For years his organization refused to attend Holocaust Memorial Day. Labour MP Naz Shah in 2016 had to apologize for anti-Semitic postings on Facebook.[70]

In summary, insofar as it makes any sense to generalize about very large numbers of people united only by a broad and variegated religion, Muslims are distinctive in their piety, in their conservative social mores, and in their international political sympathies. And those distinctions are to a large extent maintained by community isolation.

Competing Directions of Change

Recent changes in the attitudes of British Muslims are difficult to summarize because they are an amalgam of two broadly competing alternatives that have been made possible by local instability and international politics. The Burnley Muslim who said 'What's happening at the moment is that people are becoming either extremely religious or they're just going the opposite way and rejecting religion completely' was exaggerating, but he had a point.[71]

The local instability comes from children and grandchildren finding the attitudes of the first generation of immigrants unhelpful in making their way in the new world. Increasingly, the young find themselves alienated from the elderly Urdu-speaking men who run the mosques and the foreign-trained imams they hire. Migration always raises issues of identity. As W. I. Thomas and Florian Znaniecki demonstrated in their magisterial 1920 work *The Polish Peasant in Europe and America*, Poles who stayed in Poland did not need to think about how and in what ways they were Polish; those who migrated to the US had to consider which elements of their culture were important enough to maintain and which could be allowed to slip.[72] Will Herberg offered a generations model of what followed. The second generation generally rejected most of their parents' culture and did their best to assimilate. The third generation tended to be more selective: they retained those elements (such as food and music preferences) that did not inhibit getting on, celebrated their roots, and modified their Catholicism or Judaism to fit with the Protestant denominational model of religion in the US.[73] Obviously the American sequencing cannot be applied easily to the situation of Muslims in modern Britain. In religion and culture, the gulf between the largely secular British and the religiously observant south Asians is far wider than that between Herberg's European Catholic or Jews and the Americans among whom they settled.

The other big difference concerns the impact of political conflict. Few migrants to the US in the 1930s would have opposed their new home's involvement in foreign wars. The twenty-first century has seen marked changes in Islam worldwide, and those have repercussions for British Muslims.

> Because of the failure of pan-Arab nationalism, military defeats in the Middle East, the Iranian Revolution, and the successful ejection of Russia from Afghanistan, Islamism has created a stifling environment where dissent is rejected.... The Islam practised by first and second generation Muslim migrants to the United Kingdom has been transformed into a politically reactionary Islam.... a new generation of Muslims was exposed to Islamist views and opinions as though they were normal; local activities and events... regularly promoted views that Muslims were 'under threat'... The peaceful deeply introspective and reflective nature of Islam was overshadowed by angry, politicised and reactive responses of a younger generation of Muslims who saw Islam not as a personal belief system, but as a way of life that others must follow.[74]

That process has been partly driven, both directly and indirectly, by Saudi Arabian wealth. The direct influence comes from the Saudis promoting their conservative Wahhabi version of Islam by funding hundreds of mosques across Europe. One source reported that the number of such mosques in Britain had increased from 68 in 2007 to 110 in 2014.[75] Proving causation is always difficult, but there is a clear temporal association between Saudi influence and Saudi conventions (in what counts as religiously mandated dress codes, for example) displacing Pakistani norms. The indirect influence comes through Muslim wealth funding Al-Qaeda and other jihadi groups to foment conflicts that, though they often have local roots, can be interpreted as a grand 'clash of civilisations'.[76]

One mark of the increasingly sectarian nature of Islam is growing hostility to unorthodox Muslims. In 1984, Pakistan hardened its rejection of the Ahmadiyya community by making it an offence, punishable by three years in jail, for Ahmadis to call themselves Muslim. In 2016, Tanveer Ahmed, a Bradford taxi-driver, travelled to Glasgow to murder Asad Shah outside his Shawlands shop because he was an Ahmadi who had drawn attention to himself by using Facebook to send his best wishes to Christians celebrating Easter.[77] In 2016, Jalal Uddin, a Rochdale imam, was murdered by another Muslim who believed his teachings to be heretical.[78]

Quite why some Muslims choose to become more assertively and visibly Muslim, while others follow the general pattern in secular societies of confining their faith to the home and to leisure activities, is too complex to be considered here. It is enough for our purposes to note that many young Muslims are, as one Muslim journalist put it, 'more likely than their parents to assert their identity in the public sphere, express anti-Western feelings, and feel a strong sense of victimisation'.[79] The generational difference can be seen in polling data. In 2007, for example, only 19 per cent of Muslims aged 55 and over thought that apostasy should be punishable by death, but twice as many aged 16 to 24 did.[80]

There is also ample evidence of increasing assertiveness in twenty-first-century protests and court cases. A Muslim worker sued Tesco because he was asked to use his fork-lift truck to move pallets of beer.[81] Not surprisingly, given the chaos that would result if distribution workers could opt to move only those goods of which they personally approved, the case was lost, but the more interesting point is that I cannot imagine any such right being claimed fifty years ago, or, if it was, the claimant would have been ridiculed rather than supported in his court case. A Muslim scientist was barracked and threatened with murder after he gave a lecture on Darwinian evolution at his local mosque in Leyton.[82] Four men attacked and seriously injured a teacher at a north London school because he taught Muslim girls about religions other than Islam.[83] A young white British women who worked in a pharmacy was heckled and jostled by Muslim women in Whitechapel because she was not dressed in a manner of which they approved.[84] In Derby, five Muslim men handed out a leaflet calling for gay men to be executed.[85] A police cadet refused to shake hands with the male Police Commissioner congratulating her on completing her training.[86] A Muslim convert refused to stand in court because his religion apparently forbade showing respect to non-Muslim powers.[87] A Muslim taxi-driver in Oxford refused to take a passenger whose grocery shopping included alcohol.[88] A Muslim doctor wrote to the *Guardian* to argue that the use of body scanners in airport security 'should not be accepted by the Muslim community, and especially by our Muslim women'.[89] He repeated the unfortunate possessive when he added that scanning should be banned to 'make sure no man is looking at these private "naked images" of our Muslim women'. Press attitudes to Islam will be discussed shortly, but it is worth stressing here that, in all these examples (and they are just a tiny fraction of my news-cutting collection), the complainants justified their actions by their religion and, while those actions may not have been mandated by Islam, they were consistent with attitudes popular in the UK Muslim world.

A defining feature of liberal democracy is that all votes should count the same and hence religion cannot be played like a trump card. Given that Muslims are a very small minority of the electorate, they cannot hope that the state will support values that only they hold. That point is patently missed by some Muslim spokesmen who justify attitudes ranging from disdain to violence by claiming that their interests have been neglected. An example is the imam who said: 'For five years young Muslim people have been trying to influence a policy that they are profoundly opposed to without success. Naturally they are losing faith in the democratic institutions of the country.'[90]

Some recent conflicts stem not so much from a novel unwillingness to compromise as from the growth in Muslim numbers making previously overlooked differences more visible. One example concerns animals slaughter. Since 1933, UK law has required that animals be stunned before being killed. Jews were exempted, not because people liked kosher rules, but because the numbers of animals involved was small enough to pass unremarked, and the meat so produced was consumed only by Jews. Initially, halal meat was similarly tolerated, but, as the Muslim population grew, many organizations and institutions found it simpler to feed halal meat to all their hospital patients, prisoners, and school pupils, for example, than to maintain parallel supply chains. The Food Standards Agency reported that a quarter of the lambs slaughtered in 2017 had not been stunned.[91] This was enough to bring the issue to public attention, and professional bodies such as the British Veterinary Association condemned the growth in halal and kosher slaughter.

The visibility principle explains why other religious minorities, such as the Exclusive Brethren, attract far less opprobrium. Although Hasidic Jews share with Muslims unpopular attitudes and practices—sexism, hostility to homosexuality, endogamy, censorship of school curricula, ritual genital mutilation, and strict dress codes—they attract less criticism because they are much fewer in number. Outside of Stamford Hill in north London, they prefer to remain inconspicuous. Furthermore, because Judaism is an inherited religion that permits conversion only grudgingly, it is difficult (unless one buys anti-Semitic conspiracy theories) to see Jews as any challenge to British norms. Hence, although the press is thoroughly critical of the Exclusive Brethren or of Orthodox Jews if (as in the case of the yeshiva boys who had to be rescued in Dover) they become notable, they far less often come to public attention.[92]

What is also less apparent is the large number of British Muslims who are well integrated into British life and whose faith is a private matter. Large numbers of British Muslims have made successful careers in politics; examples include Sajid Javid, Home Secretary in a Conservative government, and Sadiq Khan, Mayor of London, both sons of Pakistani migrants who worked as bus drivers. At 2 per cent of Westminster MPs after the 2015 election, Muslims are still under-represented, but their 9 per cent of local councillors in 2018 is an over-representation.[93] Muslims are now found across all professions and occupations. The change is particular dramatic for women. Young Muslim women are much less likely than their mothers and grandmothers to accept the limitations of traditional gender roles. They are now performing well in schools and entering universities, and hence white-collar professions, in considerable numbers.[94] Involvement in conventional careers is not incompatible with strict religious observance, but it requires moving in a largely secular environment that makes the latter less attractive. The proportion of British Muslims who claim to be religiously observant varies considerably between surveys, but it is likely that about half of young Muslims are close to religiously indifferent.

For obvious reasons, those Muslims who become more assertive and extreme than their parents attract our notice far more than those who have become less religious, selectively dropped the more distinctive elements of their faith, or both. But there is little doubt that the second route is far more popular than the first.[95]

Islamophobia and the Media

It is now common for any criticism of Muslims to be dismissed as 'Islamophobia', and a number of organizations have argued that any negative response to Islam should be classified and punished as a 'hate crime'.[96] The term 'phobia' is unhelpful because it assumes, without persuasive argument, that the concern in question is irrational. If we are to understand reactions to the presence of Islam in the UK, it is better to consider than pre-emptively to dismiss those responses.

Islam is, in the strict sense of the word, unpopular. In 2008, those interviewed for the British Social Attitudes (BSA) survey were asked to 'rate that group using something we call a feeling thermometer. Ratings between 50 degrees and 100 degrees mean that you feel favourable and warm toward the group. Ratings between 0 degrees and 50 degrees mean that you don't feel favourable and don't care too much for that group.' Or you could pick the 50-degree point if 'you don't feel particularly warm or cold toward the group'. As we see from Table 7.4, less than half of respondents regarded Muslims favourably.

Three things should be noted. First, despite the rubric inviting respondents 'to use the entire extent of the scale', the typical response to all religions is not far from indifference: a 13-degree spread above and below neutral covers all the categories. Second, the British are hardly more fond of the 'deeply religious' than they are of Muslims. Third, as my analysis of links between attitudes and the religious practices of respondents shows, dislike of Islam is stronger among the religiously indifferent and the nominal Christians than it is among those who attend church regularly. Regular churchgoers in the survey sample

Table 7.4. Attitude towards religious groups, BSA 2008 (%)

Feelings towards...	Degrees of 'warmth'
Protestant people	62.6
Catholic people	60.9
People who are not religious	60.0
Jewish people	56.6
Buddhist people	56.1
NEUTRAL POINT	50.0
People who are deeply religious	50.0
Muslim people	46.8

Note: n = 2,236.

Source: author's analysis of British Social Attitudes, 2008 data.

Table 7.5. Attitude towards various groups, BSA 2018 (%)

	Attitude			
	Positive	Neutral? and Can't choose	Negative	Total
Christians	52	44	4	100
Buddhists	42	54	4	100
Atheists	40	55	5	100
Jews	38	57	6	101
Hindus	38	56	5	99
Muslims	32	51	18	101

Note: Totals vary from 100 because of rounding.

were more positive about all religious groups than were those who never attended church: just over half of churchgoers liked Muslims. The second and third points taken together point to an important possibility: that Muslims are disliked more because they take their religion seriously than because they have the wrong religion.

A slightly simpler version of the question in 2018 produced the results in Table 7.5.[97] Muslims are the least popular of the faith groups, but almost twice as many Britons like as dislike Muslims. More significantly, if we leave aside 'Christians' (who presumably win the approval of the Christians who form the largest group of respondents), there is only a 10-point spread in the positive rankings of the others. But most significant is the popularity of indifference: almost half the respondents do not care enough to have a positive or a negative view.

Clearly violence is a major concern. Irrespective of whether they support or regret such engagements, British involvement in wars in Afghanistan, Iraq, and Syria has made people only too well aware that our enemies (or the enemies of our Muslim allies) justify their violence by Islam. Muslims in the West have been responsible for a large number of terrorist attacks. Many British Muslims travelled to fight for ISIS in Iraq and Syria.[98] And the issue of how to deal with those who wished to return to Britain put that story back on the front pages in 2019.

Just how closely people associate Islam and terrorism depends on which way round they estimate the percentages. If they ask 'how many British Muslims support the use of terrorist violence for religious ends?', the answer must be 'very few'. However, 'what proportion of terrorist violence in the UK has been perpetrated by Muslims?' has a very different answer. Since the main combatants in Northern Ireland reached a ceasefire in 1994, almost all UK terrorist injuries and fatalities have been caused by Muslims. Between 2000 and 2009, there were six terrorist incidents. Four were instigated by Irish Republicans and caused no injuries. One was the work of a white British man and caused no fatalities. The sixth was a jihadi attack on London Transport; it killed 52 and injured over 700 people. Between 2010 and 2017 there were seven incidents with fatalities. Two were caused by white British people: Labour MP Jo Cox was killed by an English nationalist and a Muslim man died when a vehicle was driven into a crowd outside a Finsbury mosque. One fatality was the work of a Ukrainian who wanted to start a race war. Those events were overshadowed by four Muslim jihadi attacks that killed 34 people and injured 237 people, many seriously. Most of those deaths and injuries resulted from a bomb attack on an Arianna Grande concert in Manchester. As the bomber must have anticipated, most victims were young girls. Thus Muslims have been responsible for 96 per cent of the terrorist-related deaths in this century.[99] If we reason from the odds on any British Muslim being a violent jihadi, fear of Islam might indeed seem like a phobia, but it is clearly not groundless. Hence there is something slightly unhinged in one study of press reporting that complained of coverage of the car bomb attack on Glasgow airport in 2007: 'the actors were explicitly categorized as "bombers" and "terrorists"'.[100] How else should people using explosives with intent to kill strangers be categorized?

Just as news coverage of the Catholic Church in the twenty-first century has been dominated by clergy sex scandals, a series of convictions of south Asian men for the sexual exploitation of young girls has been extensively covered by the British press. In 2017, Nazir Afzal, a former chief crown prosecutor, described the religious and ethnic origins of men involved in sex-grooming scandals as 'a pattern we simply cannot ignore'.[101] Over the previous six years, gangs of men had been convicted of sexually exploiting underage girls in sixteen English towns and cities. In all but two cases, the men were Muslims of south-east Asian origin, and, in all but three, the victims were white teenage girls. The abuse was on an industrial scale. In 2011, a gang of nine men (all bar one Asian) were convicted in Derby of grooming over 100 young girls, most of them under the age of consent.[102] In the Rotherham case, the National Crime Agency estimated at least 1,400 girls were involved. In 2018, 20 men in Huddersfield were convicted of 120 offences against 15 girls aged 11 to 17 who were, according to the judge's summing up, 'plied with drink, drugs, and gifts before being "used and abused at will"'.[103]

The religion of the abusers might be irrelevant, their actions better explained by their occupations than by their motives. Almost all the abusers worked in the 'night-time' economy of takeaway restaurants, night clubs, bars, and taxi companies. They used their jobs to seduce young girls with free food, drink, drugs, and taxi rides. On the other hand, larger numbers of white men work in such industries and produce fewer examples of organized abuse. The main reason for thinking that religion is involved is that the perpetrators themselves used the victims' lack of the correct religion as justification. The girls were 'asking for it' because they were 'trash' and 'easy' and they were so because they were not Muslims. In this logic, irreligion led to a lack of morals that meant the girls were fair game. That many of the victims had been abandoned by their families and were in social care is further seen as proof of British decadence, again explained by the lack of the correct faith.

It is not hard to find malicious or incautious reporting of Muslim stories. As an example of the incautious, we might note the 2015 *Independent* newspaper report that 20 per cent of High Wycombe residents were Muslims, a figure widely repeated on social media. The actual figure was less than half that.[104] Slightly more malicious is a general willingness to believe the worst. For example, in 2016 the *Daily Mail* reported that school exams would be postponed to accommodate Ramadan. The Joint Council for Qualifications denied the story, and exam dates were not changed. But it is the way of such things that those who already suppose that Muslims are a nuisance noted the original report but not the later denial.[105]

Even the serious end of the British press is not above exaggeration. In 2017 *The Times* headlined a report on a legal battle over the placing of a child in care under the headline 'Christian girl forced into Muslim foster care'. The 'white Christian' girl had apparently been distressed by carers removing a crucifix from her, not speaking English, and encouraging her to learn Arabic. This provoked a considerable nativist reaction, with, for example, a former leader of the English Defence League tweeting that this was 'a disgrace and an outrage'. To illustrate the story, *The Times* used a photograph of a woman shrouded head-to-toe in black firmly gripping a small blonde-haired girl, as though dragging her away. It did not explicitly say it depicted the people involved, but that was the implication.

The picture was actually a stock photo originally entitled 'Happiness couple in Dubai park'. *The Times* had photoshopped a veil over the attractive face of the original model to make her look sinister and given long blonde hair to her dark-haired daughter.[106] It also turned out that the story was more complex than *The Times* had reported. The girl's grandmother, whom the parents had wanted as the girl's carer, was herself Muslim, though described as 'non-practising', and her English was very poor.

Sometimes the press simply inflate. The Aberdeen *Press and Journal* managed to get a half page under the headline 'Police dogs to don booties on searches of Muslim homes'.[107] The germ of the story was that the Association of Chief Police Officers was drawing up new guidelines to encourage cultural sensitivity and one possible inclusion was awareness that some Muslims think dogs are ritually unclean. That allowed an earlier non-story—the Dundee police had apparently apologized for using a cute photo of an Alsatian puppy sitting in a police hat in a crime prevention poster—to be rehashed and padded with, of all things, a solicited quotation from a Kennel Club spokesperson strenuously objecting to any curtailment of the rights of dogs.[108]

But there are examples of good practise. Most newspapers now complement their skating-choristers-at-Christmas pictures with minority-religion equivalents: an example is the *Financial Times* front page illustration of the end of Ramadan with a large photograph of young Muslims eating ice cream in a park in Small Heath, Birmingham.[109] The *Times* report of a pharmacist convicted of trying to recruit young lads for ISIS by showing them beheading videos made no reference to religion in its headline, and the word 'Muslim' appears only twice: once in a quotation from the convicted man telling the boys 'only [to] have Muslim friends' and once in the judge's summation that the man had 'caused offence to the vast majority of law-abiding Muslims'.[110] And in August 2018 the *Daily Mail* report of the Huddersfield grooming story made no mention of the religion or ethnicity of the accused.[111] The story under the heading 'Mother and daughter jailed for ISIS-inspired terror plot' did not mention their religion or ethnic origins at all.[112]

However, such reticence is not without its critics. As a letter to *The Times* put it: 'The formulation of your headline "Asian sex gangs are racist criminals" insults Asian Hindus, Sikhs, Buddhists, Christians, Confucians, secularists and those of other faiths living in the UK... Call things by their right names.'[113] That letter came from a Hindu.

Although it is usually assumed that poor reporting comes from animus against Muslims, some of it may be explained by structural problems. The growth of alternative news outlets since the 1990s has drastically cut radio, TV, and newspaper revenue. Between 2007 and 2017, revenues, and the number of journalists employed, both fell by 25 per cent.[114] One study showed that, of 2,000 new stories in British quality daily papers in 2005, only 12 per cent were composed of material that had been researched by the source's own staff. The rest were 'constructed from second-hand material, provided by news agencies or the PR industry, and showed no evidence of proper fact-checking'.[115]

The loss of expert knowledge has been accompanied by severe competition for a share of the dwindling audience: hence the growth of click-bait stories even in the quality press. Outlets such as the BBC (which does not directly rely on audiences for revenue) now exaggerate to attract attention to their websites. A typical example is the story under the heading 'Sharia law tribunal is proposed'.[116] At a glance that looked like some official body was considering a profound change to British law. It was actually a puff for a very thin BBC documentary programme that used the preferences of one Cardiff Muslim to solicit horrified responses from Christians, feminists, or secularists who could be goaded into protesting against a change that no one of consequence was advocating.

The problem with spotting media defects is that, like horoscopes readers who check only their own star sign and do not notice that many entries are similar, putative victims of bias notice only the slights to their faith. The media has not hesitated to report the Catholic Church's sex scandals or the preposterous claims for faith healing made in some Protestant churches. For example, *The Times* ran an item severely critical of Destiny, a Pentecostal sect, for hosting a preacher who said that true Christians should consult God about their illnesses first and 'then, maybe, confirm with the doctor, not the other way round'.[117] The report made no mention of the fact that the vast majority of British Christians would disagree; it thus implied that the views of a tiny minority were commonplace.[118]

To return to the question of Islamophobia, it is important to remember that, while many trivial stories come close to being made up, and such relentless snarking doubtless has some effect on public opinion, the press did not invent Islamic terror. The bombing of the Arianne Grande concert, the machete murders in Smithfield market, and the attacks on Glasgow airport and London Transport were real enough. And, as no one is suggesting such atrocities should not be reported, the main issue becomes how well or badly reports generalize from jihadis to Muslims in general.

This brings me to one final thought on British attitudes to Muslims: while some sections of the ruling elites happily encourage xenophobia, the party line of the ruling class is precisely that argued by most Muslims: that jihadism is a deviation from an otherwise peaceful and tolerant religion. I had an unexpected personal experience of this. When invited to address students at the Royal College of Defence Studies (all military officers, many from Muslim states) on fundamentalism, I argued that, while all religions are potentially flexible enough to justify any political position, there are small but sometimes significant differences between religions in the ease with which they either support theocratic imposition or accept being confined to the private sphere.[119] As someone familiar with the Crusades, the Wars of Religion, and the violence of the Scottish Covenanting era, I was hardly likely to argue that only Islam produces violent fundamentalists, but I was also not suggesting that all religions were the same. At the end of my talk, the College Commandment thanked me very much and summarized my lecture as meaning that all religions were indeed the same. That mishearing could have been a one off, but the following year I gave a similar lecture and a different commandant responded in precisely the same way. In sentencing a man for plotting to bomb Downing Street, a judge concluded: 'Let me say to you as I have said to other similar offenders. You will have plenty of time to study the Koran in prison in the years to come. You should understand that the Koran is a book of peace. Islam is a religion of peace.'[120] Even the Archbishop of Canterbury, who might be thought to be required by his position as head of the Church of England to favour Christianity, 'insisted that many faiths, not just Islam, had a problem with radicalisation'.[121]

Conclusion

Amidst all the noise about hate crimes and Islamophobia, it is easy to overlook the fact that, compared to every majority Muslim society, the UK is religiously tolerant: rights are allocated without reference to religion, major social institutions treat all religions similarly, religion barely affects socio-economic status, minorities are well represented in the polity, and most British people are religiously indifferent. Insofar as is compatible with liberal values, migrant religions have been readily accommodated. Even Muslim critics accept that they enjoy full citizenship rights.[122]

From the 1960s onwards, the arrival of significant numbers of Hindus, Buddhists, Sikhs, and Muslims diversified Britain's religious culture and increased the proportion of seriously committed believers. It also changed British religion by reopening the question that all democracies face: can religious liberty be extended to those who justify their illiberal values by religion? Unlike the US, which has a formal constitutional statement of the relationship between church and state, the UK gradually stumbled its way to the modern default position of permitting almost anything in private and excluding almost everything from the public arena. The Christian churches lost their social power but were allowed to retain a few symbolic advantages. Most people remained positive about religion in the abstract, though they had little time for it in practice. Islam, in particular, because it is the largest non-Christian faith and the one that presents the most apparent divergence from liberal values on such matters as gender roles and sexual orientation, has challenged that settlement. Some conservative Christians, often funded by Americans, have responded with 'me-too' demands for exemptions from public policy.

As the final chapter will show, the twenty-first century has seen a rapid increase in the number of British people who dislike religion and think it dangerous. Regular churchgoing Christians are more favourable towards Muslims (and to the seriously religious in general) than are those people who adopt the Christian tag as justification for their xenophobia. As we see in Bolton, a nominal identification with Christianity is associated with negative attitudes towards religious minorities. Such nominalism can be fairly benign, as we see with the journalist who clearly confused 'British' and 'English' when he wrote: 'I may no longer believe in God but I still feel I belong to the Church of England. It's called being British. One of Her Majesty's subjects.'[123] It can be malign, as in its use by the English Defence League, UKIP, and others as a justification for hostility towards Muslims.

It is hardly a surprise that the growing presence of a non-Christian faith should give some of those people who resent that change (among others) reason to claim a nominal attachment to the Christianity that characterized their imaginary Garden of Eden. Whether it can also stimulate a Christian revival will be addressed in the final chapter.

Notes

1. R. Lustig, M. Bailey, S. de Bruxelles, and I. Mather, 'War of the Word', *Observer*, 19 February 1989.
2. Whether from conviction, or from an appreciation of the damage the invited assassination was doing to the reputation of Islam in the UK, Siddiqui and his successor as leader of the Muslim Parliament, Ghayasuddin Siddiqui, adopted the weasel position of justifying the fatwa but arguing that it should not be enforced in the UK.
3. D. Hall, *Worktown: The Astonishing Story of the Project that launched Mass Observation* (London: Weidenfeld and Nicolson, 2015), 11.
4. J. B. Priestley, *English Journey* (London: Folio Society, 1997), 216.
5. GB Historical GIS/University of Portsmouth, 'Bolton', *A Vision of Britain through Time*, http://www.visionofbritain/org.uk/ (accessed September 2017).
6. R. Hargreaves, *Victorian Years Bolton 1850–1860* (Bolton: Ross Anderson Publications, 1985).
7. These data are from the Bolton entry in the 1851 Census of Religious Worship, England and Wales. It is available online at the UK Data Archive, University of Essex, http://www.histpop.org/ohpr/servlet/ (accessed January 2018).

8. On Mass Observation in general, see J. Hinton, *The Mass Observers: A History 1937–49* (Oxford: Oxford University Press, 2013).

9. Hall, *Worktown*, 197.

10. Hall, *Worktown*, 46.

11. C. D. Field, 'Religion in Worktown: Anatomy of a Mass Observation Sub-Project', *Northern History*, 53 (2016), 116–37.

12. I am perpetually obliged to Clive Field, in this case for providing his annotated list of 1937 and 1960 places of worship.

13. Field, 'Religion in Worktown', 121.

14. Field, 'Religion in Worktown', 121–2.

15. G. W. Gray, *A Brief History of St Luke's Church, Halliwell, 1860–1976* (Halliwell: St Luke's Church, 1976). St Luke's was torched by two young boys just after the centenary.

16. Bank Top URC, 'And the Banner Rises Again', Bank Top URC website, 30 September 2013, https://banktopurc.org.uk/and-the-banner-rises-again/ (accessed August 2018).

17. The Church of the Nazarene is a Wesleyan Holiness movement: 'Wesleyan', contrasted with 'Calvinist' or, in the case of Baptists, 'Scotch', signals belief that all people rather than just a preordained elite can potentially be saved. 'Holiness' means that its converts are confident of their saved status and claim spiritual gifts akin to those of the Pentecostal and charismatic movements.

18. Church of England, *Statistics for Mission 2015*, http://www.churchofengland.org/media/3331683/2015statisticsformission.pdf (accessed August 2017).

19. Figures calculated from Methodist Church website, https://www.methodist.org.uk/about-us/statistics-for-mission/district-circuit-and-church-reports (accessed August 2017). Anglican data for the Manchester dioceses suggest a similar consolidation, with Easter Day communicant numbers at 82% of the electoral roll membership and typical Sunday attendance at 78%.

20. Bolton Council of Mosques, *Muslims in Bolton*, https://www.thebcom.org/index.php/muslims-in-bolton (accessed August 2018).

21. A. Travis, 'Summer of Race Riots Feared after Clashes in 2001', *Guardian*, 28 December 2006.

22. C. Dobson, 'EU Referendum: Bolton Votes to Leave', *Manchester Evening News*, 24 June 2016.

23. For an analysis of voting by religion, see B. Clements, 'How Religious Groups Voted in the 2016 Referendum on Britain's EU Membership', *British Religion in Numbers*, 11 May 2017, http://www.brin.ac.uk/how-religious-groups-voted-at-the-2016-referendum-on-britains-eu-membership/ (accessed January 2019).

24. These data were kindly provided by Peter Brierley.

25. J. Judd, 'Here Beginneth the Lesson', *Independent on Sunday*, 25 March 1990.

26. C. Hughes, 'Inspectors Publish Scathing Reports on Two Islamic Schools', *Independent*, 4 September 1991.

27. J. Vasager, 'One-Third of Approved New Free Schools Are Religious', *Guardian*, 14 July 2012.

28. G. Walford, 'The Face of the New Christian Schools: From Growth to Decline?', *Educational Studies*, 27 (2001), 465–77.

29. K. Burgess, 'Rescued Jewish boys "Are Students at Illegal Faith Schools"', *The Times*, 5 July 2016.

30. In late 2017, Ofsted estimated between 45,000 and 50,000 children were being educated in unmonitored establishments; S. Griffiths and I. Ramzan, 'Hunt Begins for Legion of "Missing" Children Being Educated at Home', *Sunday Times*, 18 February 2018.

31. Anon., *Understanding School Segregation in England 2011–2016* (London: iCoCo Foundation, SchoolDash and The Challenge, 2017).

32. B. Ellen, 'Every Parent Knows about the God Scam', *Observer*, 28 June 2009. Many parents are entirely open about this; see, e.g., D. Runciman, 'A Change Is Coming', *London Review of Books*, 21 February 2019.

33. J. Llewellyn-Smith, 'The Old School Lie', *Sunday Telegraph*, 17 April 2009.

34. A. Griffin, 'More than a Question of Faith', *Daily Telegraph*, 13 March 2010.

35. M. Taylor, 'Two Thirds Oppose State Aided Faith Schools', *Guardian*, 23 August 2005. A quarter of respondents to the ICM poll liked faith schools in general, 8% favoured Christian schools but not those of other faiths, and 64% opposed all faith schools.

36. A. Holden, *Religious Cohesion in Times of Conflict* (London: Continuum, 2009), 53–7.

37. Measured as a significant deviation from the ethnic mix of the children of the surrounding area, 79% of Bolton's secondary schools in the period 2011–16 were 'segregated'; Anon, *Understanding School Segregation*.

38. Using a variety of assumptions, David Voas offered four possible extrapolations from 2001 census data for England and Wales: 7,500, 18,000, 29,000, and 33,000.

39. National Statistics Online, 'Religion: Labour Market', 21 February 2006, http://www.statistics.gov.uk/cci/nugget.asp?id=979 (accessed September 2012).

40. M. Mirza, *Living Apart Together: British Muslims and the Paradox of Multiculturalism* (London: Policy Exchange, 2007). See also C. Joppke, 'Limits of Immigration Policy: Britain and her Muslims', *Journal of Ethnic and Migration Studies*, 35 (2009), 459–60.

41. S. Bruce and A. Glendinning, 'Sectarianism in the Scottish Labour Market', *Scottish Affairs*, 26 (2017), 163–75.

42. J. Slack, 'Two Million Muslims Now Live in Britain and 10,000 Are Millionaires, Reveals Home Secretary Jacqui Smith during Visit to Pakistan', *Daily Mail*, 8 April 2008.

43. For analysis of patterns of segregation, see T. Cantle and E. Kaufmann, 'Is Segregation Increasing in the UK?', *Open Democracy* (November 2016), https://www.opendemocracy.net/wfd/ted-cantle-and-eric-kaufmann/is-segregation-on-increase-in-uk (accessed August 2018). And E. Kaufmann, 'The Demography of Religion in London since 1980', in D. Goodhew and A.-P. Cooper (eds), *The De-Secularization of the City: London's Churches, 1980 to the Present* (London: Routledge, 2018), ch. 2. Kaufmann shows that towns with low proportions of white British identifiers in 2001 had fewer by 2011. Blackburn, for example, went from 76% white British in 2001 to 67% in 2011.

44. D. Phillips. 'Parallel Lives? Challenging Discourses of British Muslim Self-Segregation', *Environment and Planning D: Society and Space*, 24 (2006), 27.

45. M. Evans, 'Surge in White and Female Terror Suspects Pushes up the Number of Arrests to Record High', *Daily Telegraph*, 7 December 2017.

46. Phillips, 'Parallel Lives', 33.

47. S. Manzoor, 'Divided Britain', *The Week*, 24 June 2017, 57.

48. J. Seabrook, 'The Town that Stopped Working', *New Statesman*, 27 July–9 August 2018, 47.

49. 'UK, US Contribute More as Pakistan's Remittances Increase 2.3%', *Express Tribune*, 10 March 2018, https://tribune.com.pk/story/1655847/2-foreign-exchange-uk-us-contribute-pakistans-remittances-increase-2-3 (accessed April 2019).

50. Pew Research Centre, *The Great Divide: How Westerners and Muslims View each Other* (Washington: Pew Center, 2006). The same paradox is noted by J. Klausen, *The Islamic Challenge* (Oxford: Oxford University Press, 2005), and Joppke, 'Limits of Immigration Policy'.

51. Pew Research Forum, *Muslims in Europe: Economic Worries Top Concerns about Religious and Cultural Identity* (Washington: Pew Center, 2006).

52 Department for Communities and Local Government, *Attitudes, Values and Perceptions: Muslims and the General Population in 2007–08* (London: Department for Communities and Local Government, 2010), ch 2.

53. C. Ferguson and D. Hussey, *2008–09 Citizenship Survey: Race. Religion and Equalities Topic Report* (London: Department for Communities and Local Government, 2010), tables 156, 157.

54. A. Wells, 'Muslim Polls' (August 2006), http://ukpollingreport/blog/archives/265 (accessed January 2007).

55. Holden, *Religious Cohesion*, 50–1. A 2001 survey offered respondents fifteen possible answers to 'Which of the following things would say something important about you if you were describing yourself?'. For 'White British' respondents, religion came tenth of fifteen; for 'Black British' respondents, it came third after family and ethnicity; for 'Asian British', it came second after family; M. O'Beirne, *Religion in England and Wales: Findings from the Home Office Citizenship Survey* (London: Home Office Research, Development and Statistics Directorate, 2004).

56. M. Frampton, D. Goodhart, and K. Mahmood, *Unsettled Belonging: A Survey of Britain's Muslim Communities* (London: Policy Exchange, 2016), 7.

57. R. Butt, 'Muslims in Britain Have Zero Tolerance of Homosexuality, Says Poll', *Guardian*, 7 May 2009.

58. Letter to the Editor, 'Muslim Leaders Stand against Gay Marriage', *Daily Telegraph*, 18 May 2013.

59. N. Parveen, 'Birmingham School Stops LGBT Lessons after Parents Protest', *Guardian*, 4 March 2019.

60. P. Morgan-Bentley, 'Forced Marriage: Sajid Javid Is Pressed to Review Cases and Give Anonymity', *Sunday Times*, 2 August 2018.

61. Frampton et al., *Unsettled Belonging*, 7.

62. M. Cross, 'Society Withdraws Sharia Wills Note', *Law Society Gazette*, 24 November 2014.

63. This is an English problem. Scots imams are registered celebrants.

64. According to a survey conducted for Channel 4, almost two-thirds of Muslim marriages were non-registered religious ceremonies; Channel 4, *The Truth about Muslim Marriage* (August 2017).

65. S. Bruce, T. Glendinning, I. Paterson, and M. Rosie, *Sectarianism in Scotland* (Edinburgh: Edinburgh University Press, 2004), ch. 3.

66. Frampton et al., *Unsettled Belonging*, 8.
67. Frampton et al., *Unsettled Belonging*, 9.
68. A. Norfolk, 'Muslim Peer Blames Jewish Conspiracy for Jailing him', *The Times*, 14 March 2013.
69. *The Week*, 15 September 2007.
70. *The Week*, 6 May 2016. For a discussion of Muslim anti-Semitism, see M. Hasan, 'The Sorry Truth Is that the Virus of Anti-Semitism Has Infected the British Muslim Community', *New Statesman*, 21 March 2013.
71. Holden, *Religious Cohesion*, 159.
72. W. I. Thomas and F. Znaniecki, *The Polish Peasant in Europe and America*, 5 vols (Boston: Gorham Press, 1918–20).
73. W. Herberg, *Protestant–Catholic–Jew* (Chicago: University of Chicago Press, 1955).
74. F. Mughal, 'Liberal Fall-Back: The Assault on Liberalism', in F. Mughal and A. Saleem (eds), *Leaving Faith Behind: The Journeys and Perspectives of People who Have Chosen to Leave Islam* (London: Dartman, Longman and Todd, 2018), 28–9.
75. J. M. Dorsey, 'Saudi Arabian Extremism in the UK: Inside the Henry Jackson Report', *Market Mogul*, 6 July 2017.
76. S. Huntington, *The Clash of Civilizations: The Remaking of the World Order* (London: Simon and Schuster, 2002).
77. A. Learmonth, '"Disrespect" Blamed for Shop Killing', *National*, 7 April 2016.
78. 'Jalal Uddin Murder: Syeedy Guilty over Rochdale Imam Death', *BBC News*, 16 September 2016.
79. M. Mirza. 'Being Muslim Is not a Barrier to Being British', *Guardian*, 1 February 2017.
80. Klausen, *Islamic Challenge*, 100.
81. The case was reported in media outlets on 29 September 2008.
82. *Sunday Times*, 13 March 2011.
83. *Daily Telegraph*, 22 February 2011.
84. *The Week*, 30 April 2011.
85. 'Derby Gay Death Call Leaflet "Was Muslim Duty"', *BBC News*, 16 January 2012.
86. 'Police Respond to Handshake Snub', *BBC News*, 21 January 2017, http://news.bbc.co.uk/1/hi/uk/6284231.stm (accessed January 2017).
87. 'Judge Orders Asbo Preacher Ricardo Macfarlane to Stand up', *The Times*, 30 August 2017.
88. 'Alcohol in my Taxi is against Religion, Woman Told by Driver', *Daily Telegraph*, 13 May 2010.
89. Letters to the Editor, *Guardian*, 7 January 2010.
90. J. Burke, 'Muslim Anger: The Real Story', *Observer*, 20 August 2006.
91. B. Webster, 'Concern over Rise in Animals Killed without Stunning', *The Times*, 9 September 2017.
92. For an example of press reporting of Hasidic Jews that is similar to hostile coverage of Muslims, see G. Pogrund, 'Meet the British Jews who Escaped from the Haredi Community', *Sunday Times*, 2 July 2017.
93. E. A. Buaras, 'Exclusive: 400 Muslim Councillors Elected', *Muslim News*, 8 June 2018, http://muslimnews.co.uk/newspaper/home-news/400-muslim-councillors-elected (accessed 10 March 2019).

94. H. Ranji, 'Dynamics of Religion and Gender amongst young British Muslims', *Sociology*, 41 (2007), 171–89; N. Khattab and T. Modood, 'Accounting for British Muslim's Educational Attainment: Gender Differences and the Impact of Expectations', *British Journal of Sociology of Education*, 39 (2018), 242–59.

95. D. Voas and F. Fleischmann, 'Islam Moves West: Religious Change in the First and Second Generations', *Annual Review of Sociology*, 38 (2012), 525–45.

96. Definitions of Islamophobia were much discussed in the media in April and May 2019.

97. These data were supplied by NatCen, the organization that runs the BSA survey. I am grateful to Sir John Curtice for inviting David Voas and me to analyse the religion data from the 2018 survey and to David Voas for statistical analysis drawn on here and elsewhere.

98. M. Townsend, 'Only "200 Britons" Remain in ISIS Combat Zones', *Observer*, 6 August 2017.

99. L. Dearden, 'Number of Far-Right Terrorists in UK Prisons Triples as Arrests Hit New Record. Islamists Make up the Majority of Terrorist Prisoners and Suspects Arrested in Britain', *Independent*, 14 June 2018.

100. K. Knott, E. Poole, and T. Taira, *Media Portrayals of Religion and the Secular Sacred* (London: Routledge, 2013). 82.

101. Anon, 'Child Sex Gangs: A Question of Race?', *The Week*, 19 August 2017.

102. *Daily Telegraph*, 8 January 2011.

103. G. Sweeting, 'Gang Convicted of Grooming and Raping Girls', *The Times*, 20 October 2018; J. Halliday, 'Twenty Men Convicted of Drugging, Trafficking, and Raping Girls as Young as 11', *Guardian*, 20 October 2018.

104. P. Gallagher, 'High Wycombe Muslims Defend Town in Face of Terror Arrests', *Independent*, 1 January 2015.

105. *Private Eye*, 1451 25 August–7 September 2017.

106. J. Grierson, 'Council in Fostering Row Hits at "Errors" in report', *Guardian*, 30 August 2017.

107. 'Police Dogs to Don Booties on Searches of Muslim Homes', *Press and Journal*, 7 July 2008. See also G. Smith, 'Police Sniffer Dogs to Wear Bootees during House Searches to Avoid Offending Muslims', *Daily Mail*, 17 September 2008.

108. For a running critique of press reporting, see the website run by Miqdaad Versi, who monitors UK mass media, https://about.me/miqdaad.versi (accessed June 2019).

109. *Financial Times*, 16–17 June 2018.

110. *The Times*, 7 October 2017.

111. *Daily Mail*, 15 August 2018.

112. D. Gardham, 'Mother and Daughter Jailed for ISIS-Inspired Terror Plot', *The Times*, 16 June 2018.

113. Letter to the Editor, *The Times*, 11 August 2017.

114. Department for Digital, Culture, Media & Sport, *Press Release*, 28 June 2018, https://www.gov.uk/government/news/tackling-the-threat-to-high-quality-journalism-in-the-uk (accessed January 2019).

115. N. Davies, 'Printing Stories that Just Aren't True', *The Week*, 9 February 2008.

116. 'Legal News', *Private Eye*, 13–26 June 2014.

117. M. Horne, 'Sects Tells Sick: Seek God's Aid before GP', *The Times*, 20 June 2018.

118. Z. Donczyk-Hnat, 'How and Why Do the Print Media Frame Religion?', University of Aberdeen, unpublished MA research project report, 2018.

119. The argument is presented in S. Bruce, *Politics and Religion* (Oxford: Polity Press, 2003).

120. 'Terror Plotter Told to Read the Koran in Jail to Learn Peace', *Daily Telegraph*, 1 September 2018.

121. J. Bingham, 'Fear of Muslims Is Tearing British Society Apart, Warns Welby', *Daily Telegraph*, 3 October 2015.

122. Z. Sardar, *Balti Britain: A Journey through the British Asian Experience* (London: Granta, 2008).

123. N. Farndale, 'God's Own Country', *Daily Telegraph*, 7 March 2010.

8

Gods of the Common People

Folk Religion and Superstition

The gleam from the oil lamps in the tall windows of the chapel that dominates the skyline of the Welsh mining village; the church bell tower visible for miles across the flat Fens; the Bible stories told in stained-glass windows; or the robes of the clergyman placing ritual vessels before a crucifix on an altar: official religion is visible. The beliefs that inform its rituals and structures are elaborated in texts that bear the institution's stamp of approval. The Church of England has its Thirty-Nine Articles; the Church of Scotland has its Westminster Confession and Shorter Catechism. As previous chapters have shown, the popularity of official religion can be measured: we can count the number of people who join and attend churches or who use religious ceremonies to sanctify such rites of passage as births, marriages, and deaths.

But religion's presence is not confined to formal institutions. There is a 'rich flora and fauna of religious beliefs and practises...profoundly shaped by an apparently seamless web of religiosity drawing on folk, superstitious and orthodox elements' that exists beyond the world of churches and chapels.[1] We may define popular or folk religion as 'a generally shared understanding of religious meaning including both folk beliefs as well as formal and officially sanctioned practices and ideas, operating within a loosely bounded interpretative community'.[2] Institutional religion causes ripples that carry some good social distance from their original source, and, to pursue the metaphor, on striking obstacles, such ripples are reversed and interfere with the outgoing ones so that the popular appropriation of Christian activities and ideas may be at odds with the intentions of the churches: not just beyond but against institutional religion.[3]

Folk Religion

In general, popular religion can refer to any, or any combination of, the following: survivals from some earlier religious culture, informal appropriations of some element of the official religion, occasional participation in such religion, and superstition.[4] Each of these will be described and explained, and then some attempt will be made to assess just how popular they remain. This is important, because some scholars have used the dual meaning of the word 'popular' to dispute the fact of secularization. The religion they describe is popular in the sense that it is uninstitutional; that is, of the people at large rather than of the churches. Without further evidence, that cannot be taken to mean 'liked by a lot of people'.

Survivals

Innovations imposed from above take time to trickle down, and even the most effective imposition of some new orthodoxy will be incomplete. Once widely accepted practices may continue on the margins of the new order. In many parts of Britain, pagan rituals survived the imposition of Christianity in attenuated forms. Fire festivals, for example, remained common. A 1900 source refers to a Burghhead, Morayshire, 'custom dating back to dim, distant days' of making a large tar-filled wooden vessel, which, having been lit in a ritual manner, is carried around the village by strong lads before being recharged and burned further on a local hilltop. Finally, it is rolled down the hill, and people scramble to collect bits of the remains. Once the memento has been secured, 'the possessor bears it home in triumph, for it is credited with the power of preserving those under the roof tree that shelters it from ill for a year'.[5] The Devon village of Ottery St Mary's still have an annual 'tar barrelling' event.

Serious historians of paganism (such as Ronald Hutton) point out that many such rituals and customs are not so much survivals as recent inventions.[6] Much modern Druidry was the creation of one Edward Williams, who, in the early nineteenth century, sought evidence of druids in early Welsh manuscripts and, finding none, 'he proceeded to forge the missing evidence and pass it off as scholarly discovery'.[7] Although older antecedents are claimed, the first Up Helly Aa festival in Shetland took place only in 1876.[8] Some, like the fireball ceremony held in Stonehaven, Aberdeenshire, at New Year are clearly secular in intent: they are occasions for people to mix with neighbours and strangers. Some are modern pastiches of a supposedly ancient past, devised by middle-class people who wish some of the benefits of religion but who reject Christianity as hierarchical, authoritarian, dogmatic, and doctrinaire. Wicca is a good example. To quote his obituary, Gerald Gardner

(1884–1964), a British civil servant, 'under the craft name Scire, had taken advantage of the 1951 repeal of the Witchcraft Act 1736…to revive the ancient neopagan religion of Wicca, supplementing it with ideas borrowed from Freemasonry, ceremonial magic and the writings of the notorious diabolist Aleister Crowley.'[9] Hutton is too polite to accuse Gardner of pure invention, but he does say 'there is no definite evidence for [Wicca's] existence before his involvement in it'.[10] One follower, Raymond Buckland, took Gardnerian Wicca to the US but gradually came to dislike the hierarchical model and founded 'Seax Wicca'—'ye olde' spellings are a favourite of modern arcanists—'which he claimed was based on more open and democratic Saxon Wicca traditions'.[11]

Informal Appropriations

Second, elements of the dominant religion may be popularized in the sense of being simplified, liberated from their institutional context, and made into superstitions. The spiritual power of the church, for example, can be turned into folk medicine: at various times, rainwater from church roofs, communion wine, moss from churchyards, and lead scraped from church window frames or cut from gutters have been used to cure ailments.[12] When the major institutional religion changes, people may be slow to conform and may well continue with some of their previous practices. Freed from their original context, they survive as tokens of good luck or rituals that ward off ill-fortune. Keith Thomas's magisterial *Religion and the Decline of Magic* documents many examples of people being tried before church courts for such corruption.[13] The kirk sessions of Scottish parishes in the seventeenth century spent a great deal of time and effort examining charges of un-Protestant behaviour such as 'superstitious chapel going'. The Canisbay, Caithness, parish kirk session repeatedly censured women for crawling twice round the ruins of the pre-Reformation St Moddan's chapel on their knees—an informal ritual held to bring curative power.[14] In the same area, 'it was customary for people to visit the Chapel of St Tears on Innocents' Day and leave bread and cheese as an offering to the souls of the children slain by Herod but which the dog-keeper of a neighbouring gentleman used to take and give to the hounds'.[15]

In this case, the Reformation marked an abrupt change and thus created a clear divide between institutional and now-deviant folk religion. For an example of more gradual change creating a category of deviant appropriation, we can consider the ritual 'churching' of mothers. In the early modern period, most Christian churches had some sort of service to mark the new mother's return to her normal social roles and interactions after a short period of postnatal rest and recuperation. To quote from the Church of England's Book of Common Prayer:

> O Almighty God, we give thee humble thanks for that thou hast vouchsafed to deliver this woman thy servant from the great pain and peril of child-birth: Grant, we beseech thee, most merciful Father, that she through thy help may both faithfully live and walk according to thy will, in this life present; and also may be partaker of everlasting glory in the life to come; through Jesus Christ our Lord. Amen.

The formal church reasons and procedures for the churching of women were accompanied by a popular variety of taboos regarding the evil consequences for any new mother of not being churched and, for everyone else, of the dangers of meeting a mother who had not yet been churched. Over the nineteenth century, the service was first reinterpreted to remove the suggestion that there is something unclean about childbirth and then dropped altogether. Yet informal taboos remained in various relatively closed communities. The fishing families of Staithes, North Yorkshire, continued to regard the unchurched mother as unlucky well into the 1970s, but the antidote was simplified: it was enough for the new mother to attend any church service. In the families least well integrated in the village's chapel culture, the requirement was reduced even further.[16] It was enough for a mother to set foot briefly in the empty chapel—a practice that most Protestant Christian bodies would dismiss as superstitious because it attributes sacramental power to the chapel building itself.

A related phenomenon is the continued use—for largely secular purpose—of knowledge and expertise acquired within a formal religious context. In the late 1960s, a traveller found drinkers in a Devon pub singing hymns.

> For no particular reason that I can recall, a man who had been sitting near me, reading the local newspaper, put it down and began to sing a well-known hymn tune...To my surprise, the rest of the company joined in, harmonizing the refrain with mounting volume until the little bar shock with noise....the landlord...told me later that he knew people liked to sing and the tunes they knew best were usually hymn tunes.[17]

Given that the dominant strand of Christianity in Devon was teetotal Methodism, it is unlikely the pub singers were committed Christians. More likely, as the landlord said, they were people who enjoyed communal singing, and, as most had attended Sunday schools as children, the best-known songs were revival hymns. Similarly, rugby crowds in South Wales still sing *Cwm Rhondda* (or 'Bread of Heaven'), despite less than 4 per cent of the people of South Wales now attending the chapels where such hymns were composed.

The same principle—familiarity—explains why religion often featured in children's play and games. In the early twentieth century, the young girls of the Stewart family in Glenlyon, Perthshire, called a large stone they climbed in their garden the 'Pulpit Stone', and they regularly pretended to be ministers preaching from it: 'Gracie and Jesse... would stand on the flat grey stone and... harangue each other and anyone else who happened to listen in something like the sonorous style common in the kirk.' This is no surprise, because there were only two types of adult authority figure they could mock: teachers and clergymen.[18]

The two themes so far discussed—survivals and folk appropriations—are not mutually exclusive. Pagan rituals can be given a Christian gloss and religious innovators (though not the Canisbay kirk session just mentioned) will often ease the introduction of their new religious culture by permitting the most popular parts of the old one to remain in place. One folklorist describes in detail a sea-placating ceremony supposedly common among Scots coast-dwellers (who depended on seaweed for fertilizer) in the eighteenth century. On Hallowmas (1 November) a man walks knee-deep into the sea and pours ale and gruel while saying:

> O God of the sea
> put weed in the drawing wave
> to enrich the ground
> to shower us food.

The ritual began in the local church and afterwards the people returned there: 'where a candle was burned, and at a signal its feeble light was extinguished. Then armed with provisions not wasted on [the sea God], they adjourned to some field, where they ate and drank and sang till dawn.' As the author notes: 'The church... had evidently decided to pander to the god of the sea and allow his worship.'[19]

Occasional Participation

Like ideas and activities, people can have a thin or peripheral connection to the dominant official religion. As a character in a Dorothy Simpson novel put it: 'I'm not saying anything against religion, mind. I go to church regular myself, at Christmas and Easter.'[20] For centuries the Church of England regarded communicating at Easter as the minimum required of a decent Christian: one reason why the parish clergy recorded Easter Day communion and reported the data to their bishops. Obviously, a good Christian attended at all the other 'high days and holy days' and conformed in many other ways, but Easter was the touchstone. In 1676 in the small Kent village of Goodnestone-next-Wingham, 'with only sixteen exceptions every person in the community known by their priest to be qualified for the sacrament had actually taken it at some time during the festival'. All but one of the defaulters (the single self-consciously dissenting family in the village) promised to make amends at Whitsuntide, and most of the absentees had good reason. One man was barred for 'notorious drunkenness'. One woman was excused as 'melancholy'; another because she was 'under a dismal calamity, the unnatural death of her husband'.[21] By the middle of the twentieth century all the indices had declined markedly, but Easter Day still attracted people who never attended at any other time. In 1953, Valdo Pons found that 28 per cent of the people of Little Munden, Hertfordshire, were on the parish's electoral roll (a convenient mark of church membership). At 14 per cent, the average Sunday attendance was only half that of membership, but 18 per cent turned out for Easter.

As one would expect, those church services that were treated either as rites of passage or as communal celebrations of important status changes and events were always more popular than those with no additional social significance. Until the second half of the twentieth century, almost all children were baptized and most weddings and funerals were religious. As we saw in Chapter 2, in the 1950s, almost everyone in the Cumbrian village of Gosforth was 'confirmed', though the vast majority regarded that ritual as the end rather than the start of their church involvement.

Superstition

Which brings us to the general category of superstition, much of which has some connection with Christianity. Even a cursory examination of the subjects of superstitious folklore suggests an ironic recognition of the power of institutional religion. In Catholic Christianity, the clergy are sole possessors of sacramental power, and, even in Protestant churches, denominations, and sects (which reject any abrupt divide between clergy and laity), the clergy are expected to be exemplars of piety or of a 'Christian walk with the Lord'. But folklore treats what is especially good in its proper place as a threat when it is out of place. Thus, in many fishing communities in the nineteenth century, it was held to be unlucky to pass or see a clergyman on the way to launch the boat, and many fishermen prohibited clergy from boarding their vessels. The fishers of Newhaven prohibited any on-board mention of hares. They also treated as taboo any direct reference to clergymen. If a minister had to be mentioned, he was 'a man in the black coat'.[22] Presumably this, like the miner's refusal to work his shift if he passed a nurse on the way to the pithead, was connected to the clergy role in burying the dead: to think of things associated with accidents is inadvertently to encourage them. Important for my theme, the fishermen of Cromarty had weakened the clergy taboo by the 1950s:

> No-one liked to take a minister out in a boat or to meet one on the way to
> sea— the antidote was to step off the road and to stay off it all the way to the
> boat. It is a strange fact that even in deeply religious seafaring communities
> there is an ancient and almost universal dislike of meeting a clergyman on
> the way to the boats or near to them.[23]

How Popular Is Popular Religion?

One weakness of claims for the continued importance of popular religion is that the best evidence for them suffers from being ahistorical. Authors such as Sarah Williams correctly note that at the start of the twentieth century there was a considerable body of non-institutional religion in British culture and then suppose, with no evidence, that such a penumbra still survives and thus refutes the proposition that Britain has become markedly less religious. A second problem is that folklore studies often focus on one small place, which may be atypical. The survival of an attenuated form of the churching of women in Staithes has been mentioned, but 'Staithes is...most unrepresentative...its geographical location and economic function has cocooned it in a time warp'.[24]

To assess the salience of popular religion we need to treat it in the way we treat institutional religion: we need data for long time periods for large areas so we can consider how the trajectories for formal and informal religion move against each other. For popular religion to be used as refutation of secularization, it has to be the case that it remains as popular as ever it was. Assessing the impact of unofficial religion is not easy, but if it is to figure in our assessments of just how religious or secular is modern Britain, then we must make some attempt. I will consider each type in turn.

Survivals

It is very difficult to measure an absence. We can use structured interviews and survey questionnaires to ask about specific events, activities, and ideas, but it is near impossible to ask people about their ignorance of, lack of participation in, or indifference to a general realm. However, though others may not share my confidence, my extensive reading of autobiographies and local histories over some forty years leads me to conclude two things. The sorts of popular religious survivals described in the first few pages of this chapter are now almost entirely absent from contemporary narratives. As with folk music, what remains are modern reinventions devised and promoted largely by middle-class immigrants to some area. Often such migrants are retreating from cosmopolitan urban life in search of community. They are embarrassed by the actual religious culture of their chosen home and thus want to skip back ten centuries to pre-Christian times: the Hebrides and North Wales and Cornwall are beautiful, but who wants to be a puritanical Nonconformist Christian? Such incomers may well work in the tourist industry and thus have a specific reason for wanting to 'revive' some supposedly ancient ritual to give the area some distinction that will attract visitors; it is noticeable that ceremonies such as the fire festivals in Stonehaven and Ottery St Mary's are advertised on tourism websites. They may want to create community events to offset the individualization of modern life. So they set fire to wicker men, ride hobby horses, burn fireballs, and roll cheeses down hills. Especially when we note how few people are involved, it is hard to interpret this as evidence that the modern Britons who lack any connection to institutional religion are nonetheless really religious.

Informal Appropriations

Again we have the same problem as before: how we identify an absence? One subtle sign is the dating of superstitions listed in such collections as that of Iona Opie and Moira Tatum (of whom more later). Many of them involve elements of Christian ritual and belief. For example, in some parts of England it was held to be very bad luck to use holly (the special status of which was enhanced by it being incorporated into Easter myths and Christmas decor) to sweep out chimneys. Almost no superstitions for which the first recorded usage comes after 1900 incorporate Christian themes, while they are common in older examples.

Occasional Participation

The first two expressions of popular religion are difficult to measure, and, though most commentators are sure that they are much less common than they were at the start of the twentieth century, it is difficult to generate the data that would convince the secularization denier. But there is no difficulty at all in demonstrating that occasional church attendance has all but died out and that what little remains is almost entirely secular in motive. A summary of polls from the early 1960s shows about 25 per cent claiming to attend monthly or more often and only 35 per cent saying they never attended.[25] In 2010, half of Britons said they had 'no religion'. For those aged 18–24 the proportion was two-thirds. And 56 per cent said they never attended church.[26] Although the precise figures produced by different polls vary considerably, there is a clear trend within the overall pattern of decline: attending 'less than once a month' falls sharply and attending 'never' grows.[27]

As rites of passage are family and community occasions requiring solidarity, they have always attracted the widest audience, and most Britons will still go to church for baptisms, weddings, and funerals. However, baptisms are declining in popularity, and weddings and funerals are increasingly secular.[28] In 1851, almost all marriages were religious; in 2015, it was only 19 per cent.[29] Well over three-quarters of 'disposals' are now cremations, and, even in the minority where a member of the clergy coordinates the ceremony, religious content is largely absent. Funerals used to commend the dead to God's care and remind the audience of their need to repent of their sins; now they are secular celebrations of the life of the deceased.

The one element of occasional participation that has survived and possibly grown in popularity is attending church at Christmas. From 1900, most Anglican parishes show Christmas catching up with, and then overtaking, Easter. In Bolton in 1937, Christmas attendance was only one-third of normal Sunday turnout.[30] In Little Munden in 1901, thirty-six people communicated at Easter while twenty-five took communion on Christmas Day; as few people would have left the village between those dates, one-third of churchgoers thought Easter more significant than Christmas.[31] By 1921, Easter had lost some of its lead over Christmas: forty-four to thirty-six. By 1981 it had fallen behind: twenty-seven people communicated on a typical Sunday, forty-two communicated at Easter, but ninety-five people took communion at Christmas. Those data conceal a significant innovation. Sometime between 1951 and 1961 the Little Munden incumbent introduced a Christmas Eve service. We know that it was usually at 8pm, because the 1962 Register of Service notes that, because of heavy snows, the service was held an hour early at 7pm and only four people communicated: presumably the priest's family, who were able to walk from the adjacent rectory. Other churches introduced special Christmas Eve services, and towards the end of the century it became common for many to start after 10pm. In 2006, almost three million people attended Church of England Christmas services—twice as many as attended at Easter and three times as many as attended a typical Sunday service.[32]

It may seem paradoxical, but I would describe the change in the relative importance of Easter and Christmas as a symptom of secularization. Easter was primarily a religious festival—a celebration of Christ's resurrection from the dead three days after his crucifixion—and only secondarily a popular holiday. As the country's general stock of religious knowledge has declined, the religious importance of Easter, and hence its social significance, has declined. Celebrating the death of the son of God makes sense to core Christians, who believe in an afterlife and who see Christ's subsequent resurrection and appearance to various followers as vital assurance of his promise to humankind. When a large part of the population was Christian, Christmas had much less significance. Indeed, the Presbyterian Scots and the attenders at the various Protestant chapels in Wales barely marked it at all. To people largely ignorant of the core tenets of the Christian faith, the birth of Christ seems a much easier event to celebrate than his death, and it is around Christmas, rather than Easter, that a great deal of seasonally appropriate but entirely unbiblical flummery has developed. It is worth noting that Charles Dickens, whose accounts in *A Christmas Carol* and *The Pickwick Papers* did so much to shape our modern images of Christmas, makes almost no reference to orthodox Christianity. A Christmas Eve service appeals to non-religious people because, for those within walking distance of an old church, it provides an annual connection with the social history of the area and is a useful way for families to entertain visitors and distract small children excited about Santa's impending visit. Christmas thus becomes the one time of the year when people with little church involvement will attend church.

Superstition

Finally, we can consider the changing popularity of superstition. Opie and Tatem's *A Dictionary of Superstitions* contains almost two thousand entries, most illustrated with more than one example of use.[33] The illustrations are dated, so we can gauge some idea of when the superstition was current. In many cases the date of the illustration is that at which a collection of folklore was published, and many such entries hint at the near-extinction of the custom. For example, a Manx source adds 'it is still occasionally done even in Peel or Douglas', which implies both that the superstition is dying out, and that superstition is generally confined to rural areas outside the Isle of Man's two towns.[34] Other illustrations show the personal source dismissing the superstition as outdated. For example, a 60-year-old woman is recorded as saying in 1988: 'In County Durham we used to say if you dreamed of a baby you would hear of a death.' That few illustrations date pre-1800 does not, of course, mean that earlier people were not superstitious. It only tells us that folklorists rely on published sources, and hence most of what we know about ancient folklore comes from works published more recently. It is also misleading in that many superstitions with a relative modern example also had examples of much older usage. Because the speakers in the illustrations may be referring to their childhood or the views of their parents or even grandparents, my method of counting may disguise a degree of obsolescence, but that is fine, because it means the evidence is slanted against, rather than in favour of, the case here being made.

To illustrate the age of various superstitions, we can create four time periods: pre-1800, the nineteenth century, 1901–1950, and post-1951. Sampling the eighty or so entries under the letters H shows that 38 per cent date from before 1800, a similar proportion date from the nineteenth century, and half the remainder come from the first half of the twentieth century. Most recorded superstitions concern rural life: hares, hay, heather, hemp seed, hens, herons, herrings, holly, hops, horse hooves, and heather, for example. None—not even those first recorded after 1950—concerns any item or activity that is distinctly urban, modern, or industrial. Machines, for example are entirely absent. The items recorded for 'P' show the same pattern: 83 per cent are pre-1900. Only 9 per cent have their first recorded use after 1950, and, of those, only three concern distinctly modern items: there are two about prams and one about paper bags (apparently bursting one will cause a death somewhere). This is a list of the topics under C with the number of entries for each if it is more than one: cabbage stalk; calendar; candle (13); cards (2); cats (24), cat or dog (2); caterpillar (2); cattle (4); caul (2); cave; chain-letter; chair (7); chamber pot; champagne cork; charms in food; Childermas Day; children (2); chime child; chimney; chimney sweep (2); christening (9); Christmas (14); church (13); churching (4); cigarette (2); cinders; clergy (4); clock (11); clothes (6); clover (4); coal (6); cock/hen (4); coffins (4); coin (4); comet; communion (3); confirmation; conversation; cooking; coral; cork; corn dollies; corner house; corpse (19); counting (3); cows (3); cradle (2); cramp (2); cricket (2); cripple; crockery; crooked things (4); cross (5); crossed fingers or legs (3); crown; crows/ravens (2); cuckoo (10); cutlery (2). Only two of these involve objects or actions extant only after 1900: cigarettes and chain letters.

The same point about age can be made by listing those topics that have generated the largest number of entries. Those with five or more entries are candles, chairs, Christenings, Christmas, church, clocks, clothes, coal, corpses, crosses, and cuckoos; all common or important objects in preindustrial societies. We can also clearly see a strong link between superstition and institutional religion. Of the eleven topics with five or more entries, four directly concern Christian rituals or the Church. Holly apart, there are few 'H' entries that link to the Christian faith, but under 'P' we have prayers, palms (because of Palm Sunday, which marks Christ's entry into Jerusalem), and pancakes (because of the association with Shrove Tuesday—the day on which Christians prepared themselves for fasting during Lent).

Beyond counting, clear evidence of the decline of superstition can be seen in the difference in tone between nineteenth- and twentieth-century illustrations. The former tend to be confident statements of fact and practice. The latter tend to be hesitant and to distance the speaker from the superstition being noted. For example, a 1950s entry had a middle-aged London woman saying: 'It's superstition really. It's supposed to be unlucky if you go out before you're churched.' A 1950 illustration of the use of clergy in divination has a women saying: 'If you counted all the ministers you saw up to 100, the next man you spoke to would be your future husband. We used to haunt the Lour Road, where most ministers lived.' The use of 'haunt' in the second sentence's confession of cheating the outcome suggests a lack of faith in that particular oracle. Another speaker cited a superstition only to deny its applicability: 'I know corner houses are supposed to be unlucky but we haven't done too badly in this one.' In 1941, Mass Observation published a report on superstition: the majority of female respondents and half the men apparently practised one or more superstitious act: the most common was throwing spilled salt over the shoulder to ward off bad luck. But most respondents were also at pains to point out that they did not actually believe in the efficacy of such acts.[35]

Most studies of folklore collect illustrations and analyse the content of superstitions with little or no attempt to assess their popularity. But there is a universal recognition in all of the many such collections I have read that what is being described has passed. For example, an elderly Shetland man reported old people in the early decades of the twentieth century (that is, people born in the 1850s) maintaining an apparently ancient custom of burying food in the first furrows ploughed on Bogle Day at the start of the farming year: 'they did it secretly as if they would have been ashamed to be caught doing it.'[36] The author of that volume concludes his chapter on sea lore by noting that 'many of Shetland's old beliefs and customs died out or lessened their hold towards the middle of the nineteenth century'.[37] Paul Thompson's fishermen, studied in the 1970s, contrasted their scepticism with the credulity of previous generations: 'Some of the previous generation were "ridiculous. You couldna mention a mouse or a cat...They would put a knife in a mast if they wanted wind...Terrible—but I didna believe in that at any time at all." '[38] Writing about Whalsay in the early 1980s, Tony Cohen makes no mention of superstition. In his autobiography, Scarborough skipper Fred Normandale, who fished from the early 1980s, describes in great detail the role of heavy drinking and practical joking in the working lives of Yorkshire fishermen but makes only one mention of superstition: a fellow skipper reported on a dreadful maiden voyage on his new boat, which he blamed on the champagne bottle not having broken properly at the launch ceremony.[39]

As well as noting the declining presence of superstition, we can observe three significant things about what does remain, all of which seem like evidence of secularization. First, much superstition is now idiosyncratic. Universal principles—for example, that, without the appropriate ritual action, spilling salt and breaking mirrors brings bad luck—have been replaced by highly personal rituals of reassurance. Many sports people believe that they will perform best if they prepare in some precise and ritualized manner. Many tennis players at Wimbledon have their racquets restrung before every match: 'if they win, they'll come back and say, "Who strung my racquet?' and they'll say "He has to string it again." '[40]

Secondly, we can note that the causal model that informs such rituals has changed. There is an element of continuity with traditional superstition in that rituals of reassurance fill the gap left after all possible rational action has been taken. But the underlying mechanism has changed. Most people who talk about their rituals do not claim that there is some moral order in the universe that will reward or punish them depending on whether they obey or disobey the superstitious rules. Instead they psychologize the explanation. Canadian sprinter Aaron Brown said: 'If I play songs that remind me of a time when I was successful and I realise I've done it before, it calms me down.' Even though the inspirational warm-up music was Christian, the explanation was psychological: 'I've listened to the same six Christian rock songs during my warm-up or on the way to the race since high school...To me, it's familiar and it creates the right attitude in my mind...[it] helps remind me why I run and my purpose.'[41] Harriet Harmon, a leading Labour politician at the end of the twentieth century, had a lucky jacket that she always wore for key speeches. She wore it when she made her first important speech, and, as that went well, it reminds her of previous successes and calms her nerves.[42]

The third apparent change is the pacification of superstition. Just as the Christian churches have abandoned hell but retained heaven and now advertise the therapeutic effects of belief far more often than they warn of the dangers of unbelief, superstition has become largely positive. Modern rituals of reassurance offer improvement but do not have a terrible penalty for getting them wrong. Where ancient astrologers predicted dire consequences as often as they promised benefits, modern horoscopes accentuate the positive. One driver of that change—in religion as much as in divination—is the market power of the consumer. Religious liberty and diversity free people from obedience to any church, and those who choose their religion are less likely to choose ones that excoriate them for their sins and threaten dire punishment; therapy and the promise of only good things is much more attractive. Most astrologers either directly, through one-to-one services, or indirectly, through newspapers, magazines, and TV programmes, serve customers who are unwilling to pay for bad news or warnings of an unpleasant future.[43] Though his explanation was more social obligation than popularity-winning, an astrologer friend told me that his predictions were never more severe than advising due caution, because 'the folk who read these have enough problems. They are wanting reassurance. I like to think I give my readers a wee boost.'

To summarize: if we are going to present folk religion as some sort of counterbalance that refutes the proposition that, as it modernized, Britain became less religious, we would have to claim not just that there was still some of it about but that it had grown as institutional religion has declined. Curiously, none of the scholars who use popular religion to challenge the secularization thesis has made that case.

The Secularization of Popular Religion

The decline of popular religion can be explained in precisely the same way as the decline of its institutional counterpart. Diversity is a threat to shared beliefs because it shows that things can be otherwise. Superstitions can be persuasive if they are widely shared. If everyone believes that bees are special creatures that should never be bought and sold but only bartered, that injunction will remain in force. But if people who take the barter-only view come to interact with those who hold that bees can be sold but only for gold (or, in some places, only for silver), the alternatives weaken the rules by exposing their human origins. They become optional. Popular religion is probably more vulnerable than official religion to the delegitimating effects of diversity because it lacks any accepted authority able to maintain conformity or reconcile competing ideas. When five different views of the nature and significance of re-enactments of the Last Supper confront each other, there are church officials with some influence and standing trying to find some common interpretation that will preserve some authority for the ritual. When five different customs relating to the sale of bees collide, there is no office or institution to perform such rescue work.

Rapid change has a similar effect. For folklore to develop around actions or material object, they need to remain stable. In preindustrial worlds, material objects changed little and only slowly. Once innovation becomes constant, the knowledge and expertise of one generation (which includes both the technical knowledge and the attendant folklore) becomes redundant. The broom or besom (around which a great deal of superstition accumulated) was a common tool for centuries. Since the late nineteenth century, improvements in cleaning technology have given us mechanical sweepers, electric hoovers, bagless and cordless vacuum cleaners, and now cleaning robots. Candles had folklore; personal computers do not.

Closely related to the above two points is the stability of community explored in Chapter 2. Shared beliefs of any sort are most successfully transmitted across generations and reinforced in stable communities with populations that change little and slowly. An excellent study of *Witchcraft, Magic and Culture 1736–1951* offers five causes of decline in belief in witchcraft (and of an accompanying shift from belief in specific witches to general bad luck), and the first is communal instability. Owen Davies notes that the very rare examples of twentieth-century witchcraft accusations 'all occurred in fairly isolated rural communities...where social relations and the pattern of life had not yet been profoundly affected by new external social and economic forces'.[44] The growth of new towns and urban redevelopment were significant: 'In areas...where the mutual reinforcement of kinship and neighbourhood ties had been disrupted, traditional beliefs were not always successfully passed on through the generations'.[45] As the British fishing fleet declined over the late nineteenth and early twentieth centuries, the fisherfolk of coastal villages were replaced by middle-class professionals attracted to clean air and quaint architecture. They bought the fishermen's cottages but not their culture. Technological innovation adds to the fluidity, either by providing better solutions to problems that were managed with superstition and religion (the structure and equipment of modern fishing boats make them far safer than their predecessors) or by changing the material world too rapidly for superstitions to accrete. A comparison of deep-sea fishermen and North Sea oil-rig workers will illustrate the point. Because the oil rigs date only from the 1970s, involved entirely novel machinery and techniques, and recruited an international workforce that dispersed when on leave from the rigs (rather than living side-by-side in small isolated communities), no shared folklore comparable to that of the fishing villages developed.

Any general explanation of the decline of religion must include a reference to declining utility. Religion (especially in its popular appropriations) is never just a matter of abstract propositions about the origins of this life or access to the next. It is also practical. Before the development of secular institutions of education, social welfare, public administration, the Christian churches penetrated the lives of their communities by providing a wide variety of social services. And their rituals were used to solve problems. Farmers sprinkled holy water on their livestock. Ailments were treated with folk remedies, many of which involved religious elements that ranged from the quite formal (for example, the wearing of amulets blessed by a holy person or bought at a shrine) to the informal (intoning customary prayers over a sick person or animal, for example). Just as clergymen ceded their medical role to better trained and more successful secular doctors and surgeons, so the therapeutic use of superstitious rituals and objects declined as science and technology provided patently more effective solutions. In the nineteenth century, the people of Banff cured warts by touching the leg of an unsuspecting virgin. The declining value of virginity has made that particular recourse difficult, but, more importantly, Banff chemists now sell drops that invariably work.

Finally, and most generally, we can note that popular and institutional religion share a common belief in the existence of supernatural power. Anything that encourages a rational this-worldly problem-solving orientation (which is exactly what modern technology does) mitigates against popular religion every bit as much as against formal institutional religion.

The Death of the Host Plant

What is often missed in the claim that folk religion persists despite the decline in formal religion is any appreciation of the extent to which folk religion is parasitic on its institutional counterpart. That reliance may be ideological or practical. Obviously, if there are no Christian institutions promoting Christian beliefs, the children of the north-east of England will not be chanting words associated with Easter as they skip. Without the remains of the pre-Reformation chapels, the women folk of Canisbay could not practise their clergy-offending superstitious chapelgoing. Without a large professional clergy that managed death, fishermen and colliers would not bother to treat religious officials as bad omens.

The belief that new mothers are unlucky until they had been churched could not survive the absence of churches. If people hold that certain commonly understood rituals are essential, they will find the necessary resources, but, when rituals are only half-believed, the absence of the opportunity to act on such beliefs will kill them off. So long as the requirement to be churched could be met simply by stepping into one of the never-locked three chapels in Staithes, the practice continued. But once two of the three closed and the other opened only for Sunday worship, the practice died out. Women could have driven to a number of extant churches in the neighbourhood; they did not bother.[46]

The domino effect can be seen in the sabbath. When most people were committed Christians and the churches powerful, the inviolability of Sunday was maintained by theology, by law, by social pressure, and by superstition. For the committed Christian, anything other than 'works of mercy and necessity' on the sabbath was sinful. Social pressure ensured that such a preference spread well beyond the core of regular churchgoers, and, when the state (often in the form of local councils) began to regulate such matters as the availability of alcohol and shop opening hours, sabbatarianism was buttressed by the law. Most importantly, it was often supported by popular superstitions. In the early twentieth century in Cromarty, 'it was unlucky...to sew buttons on a Sunday and of course to fish on Sunday'.[47]

The churches were also essential in providing common cultural products (such as popular hymns) that could be deployed for secular purposes. The Welsh tradition of male voice choirs grew out of its nineteenth-century chapel culture and flourished in the first part of the twentieth century. By its end they were dying out: 'a lot of the audiences are the same age as us and are dying off as well.'[48] Even more basically, Christian liturgy and teaching provided a very large part of the population with a common language. That has now gone.

This is somewhat speculative, but a more detailed observation about the effects of secularization on formal and informal religion is plausible. Not only do *both* decline with secularization, but the area of overlap shrinks as quasi-institutional religious expressions die out or are drawn back into the institutional orbit. 'Chesting' was a short service, conducted in the home of the deceased by local ministers or church elders, which gave religious significance to the placing of the body in the coffin. In the north of Scotland in the nineteenth century it was universally observed and was attended by even those relatives and friends who were not regular churchgoers. By the 1950s, chesting had all but died out, and the only remaining religious gloss to death was given in the church funeral or in the words spoken by a clergyman during a crematorium service. As interest in, and hence knowledge of, religion declines, it increasingly becomes the preserve of that very small minority of those with a serious commitment to, and deep indoctrination in, religion. Thus, paradoxically, as the range of clergy authority, and the number of people who respect it, shrink, their authority over what little remains is enhanced.

All of this suggests that, far from growing in popularity to compensate for the decline of institutional religion, folk religion is being killed off by secularization. Popular religion's parasitic relationship with the formal variety can be positive or negative. That is, it can borrow or it can reverse. But either way, when formal religion dies, the informal version goes with it.

Conclusion

In a religious society, folk religion is a socially important phenomenon. Except in the smallest and the most authoritarian societies, there will always be considerable variation in knowledge of, and commitment to, shared cultures. Just as understanding of a political party's agenda (and reasons for supporting it) will become ever more varied as one moves outwards from the party's officials and core activists to nominal members to the electorate at large, so understanding of the hegemonic religion will become more diffuse and variable as one moves out from the clergy and the regular church attenders to the general population. That we can distinguish institutional or formal religion from popular or folk religion makes possible the argument that the latter and the former exist in some sort of steady-state balance: that one compensates for the other and that, as secularization erodes Christianity in the West, popular religion will persist or even grow. This would be an important observation because it would imply that the demand for, or receptivity to, religion is independent of indoctrination in official religion creating the needs that such religion then claims to meet. That in turn would make plausible the claim that there is something in the human constitution (for example, our ability to think of the personality as distinct from the body, and thus possibly surviving its death) that predisposes us all to ask the sort of existential questions that religions have traditionally answered. The way in which any society meets such a need varies, but the basic interest in matters religious and spiritual is constant.[49]

However, while that line of reasoning is entirely cogent, it does not seem supported by the evidence. Those who make the theoretical case offer very little evidence, and their argument often rests on accidental exaggeration. Consider the popularity of fortune-telling at the start of the twentieth century. In 1914 *The Times* published a leader vigorously denouncing the then-popular practice of offering palm-reading or crystal-ball-gazing at middle- and upper-class charity fund-raisers. That story can be told in such a way that the audience for divination is added to the realm of churchgoers to increase the total number of believers in the supernatural. But those who engaged in such sports did so at best half-seriously, and almost all of them were conventional churchgoers. That we can treat folk religion and official religion as two analytically separable spheres does not mean they involved two distinct populations.

My case is that secularization erodes popular religion and superstition as much as it erodes the institutional form. Indeed, we could go further and argue that popular religion is *more* vulnerable to secularization than the institutional variety on which it is to a large extent parasitic, because churches, sects, and denominations have the material resources and organizational structures to maintain their beliefs and rituals even as they decline in popularity. Resources garnered in a more religious era can sustain religious organizations for some considerable time after they have peaked in popularity. The current income of Christian churches in the West is falling, but bequests and income from past investment can keep the buildings open and sustain a body of officials. Popular religion has no such institutional base: it relies entirely on current application, and its transmission from one generation to the next is immediately threatened by any decline in popularity. When the legitimacy of a culture rests only on its current popularity and there is no reservoir of cultural capital that can maintain a presence despite decline, its survival is unlikely. Or, as a major study of changes in British Catholic culture put it: 'the beliefs and practices that make up customary religion are the product of formal religious socialization but subject to trivialization, conventionality, apathy, convenience, and self-interest.'[50]

Notes

1. R. Sykes, 'Popular Religion in Decline: A Study from the Black Country', *Journal of Ecclesiastical History*, 56 (2005), 288. See also J. Obelkevich, *Religion and Rural Society in South Lindsey, 1825–1875* (Oxford: Oxford University Press, 1976); J. Cox, *The English Churches in a Secular Society: Lambeth, 1870–1930* (Oxford: Oxford University Press, 1982; and S. Williams, *Religious Belief and Popular Culture* (Oxford: Oxford University Press, 1999).
2. Williams, *Religious Belief*, 11.
3. D. Clark, *Between Pulpit and Pew: Folk Religion in a North Yorkshire Fishing Village* (Cambridge: Cambridge University Press, 1982).
4. Sykes, 'Popular Religion in Decline', 288.
5. E. B. Simpson, *Folk Lore in Lowland Scotland* (Wakefield: EP Publishing, 1976), 125–6.
6. R. Hutton, 'Modern Pagan Festivals: A Study in the Nature of Tradition', *Folklore*, 119 (2008), 255.
7. Hutton, 'Modern Pagan Festivals', 256.
8. For a detailed study of Up Helly Aa, see C. Brown, *Up-Helly-Aa: Custom, Culture and Community in Shetland* (Manchester: Manchester University Press, 1999).
9. 'Obituary: Raymond Buckland: High priest of Wicca and author credited with leading the revival of witchcraft in the United States', *Daily Telegraph*, 21 October 2017.
10. Hutton, 'Modern Pagan Festivals', 257.
11. 'Obituary: Raymond Buckland'.
12. A. W. Smith, 'Popular Religion', *Past and Present*, 40 (1968), 181–6.
13. K. Thomas, *Religion and the Decline of Magic* (London: Allen Lane, 1978).
14. M. Pottinger, *Parish Life in the Pentland Firth* (Thurso: WhiteMaa Books, 1997), 2–3. It was then spelt 'Cannesbay'.
15. C. Thomson, 'Parish of Wick', in *New Statistical Account of Scotland Vol 15: County of Caithness* (Edinburgh: William Blackwood, 1845), 161.
16. Clark, *Between Pulpit and Pew*.
17. J. Bellamy, *Journey through Britain* (London: Folio Society, 1987), 31.
18. A. Stewart, *Daughters of the Glen* (Aberfeldy: Leura Press, 1986), 43.
19. Simpson, *Folk Lore*, 123–5.
20. D. Simpson, *Second Inspector Thanet Omnibus* (London: Warner Books, 1995), 65.
21. P. Laslett, *The World We Have Lost* (London: Methuen, 1983), 74.
22. Simpson, *Folk Lore*, 133.
23. J. Macdonald and A. Gordon, *Down to the Sea: An Account of Life in the Fishing Villages of Hilton, Balintore and Shandwick* (Cromarty: Ross and Cromarty Historical Society, 2000), 133.
24. D. Hempton, 'Popular Religion 1800–1986', in T. Thomas (ed.), *The British: Their Religious Beliefs and Practices* (London: Routledge, 1988), 200.
25. D. Martin, *A Sociology of English Religion* (London: SCM Press, 1967), ch. 2.
26. I must thank my former colleague Tony Glendinning for his analysis of the original British Social Attitudes survey data, which are available from the UK Data Archive. See also L. Lee, 'Religion: Losing Faith?', *BSA Report 28* (London: NatCen, 2010), 173–83.

27. Of eighteen surveys between 1955 and 1982, the figure for attending 'less often than monthly' is greater than that for 'never' in six of ten polls before 1974. For 1974–82, 'never' exceeds 'less often than monthly' in five of eight polls; see C. D. Field, *Secularization in the Long 1960s* (Oxford: Oxford University Press, 2017), 97.

28. S. Bruce, 'Appendix Two', in B. R. Wilson, *Religion in Secular Society: Fifty Years On* (Oxford: Oxford University Press, 2016).

29. P. Brierley, 'Marital Mayhem', *Future First*, 57 (June 2018), 1.

30. C. D. Field, 'Religion in Worktown: Anatomy of a Mass Observation Sub-Project', *Northern History*, 53 (2016), 121.

31. These data come from the respective parish Registers of Services held by Hertfordshire Archives and Local Studies, the staff of which I would like to thank for their assistance.

32. Church of England Press Office, 'Latest Figures Show Changing Trends in Church-Going', 31 January 2008, http://www.cofe.anglican.org/news/pr1008.html (accessed March 2009).

33. I. Opie and M. Tatem, *A Dictionary of Superstition* (Oxford: Oxford University Press, 1989). See also such collections as C. S. Burne (ed.), *The Handbook of Folklore* (London: Sidgwick and Jackson, 1913); W. Henderson, *Notes of the Folklore of the Northern Counties of England and the Borders* (London: Satchell, Peyton and Co., 1879); R. Tongue, *Somerset Folklore* (London: Folk-Lore Society, 1965).

34. Opie and Tatem, *A Dictionary of Superstition*, 76.

35. C. D. Field, 'British Religion and the Second World War: An Audit of Sources in the Mass Observation Archive', https://clivedfield.wordpress.com/presentations (accessed August 2018).

36. J. Nicholson, *Shetland Folklore* (London: Robert Hale, 1981), 109.

37. Nicholson, *Shetland Folklore*, 116. He explains the decline as resulting from improvements in the size and safety of boats.

38. P. Thompson, T. Wailey, and T. Lummis, *Living the Fishing* (London: Routledge and Kegan Paul, 1983), 333.

39. F. Normandale, *Slack Water* (Scarborough: Bottom End Publishing, 2004), 128.

40. M. Fletcher, 'Inside Wimbledon: What Really Goes on behind the Scenes', *Daily Telegraph*, 3 July 2017.

41. R. Marsden, 'Now that's what I Call a Warm up', *Guardian*, section 2, 8 August 2016, 10.

42. S. Bruce, *Secularization* (Oxford: Oxford University Press, 2011), 138.

43. D. Parker, *The Question of Astrology: A Personal Investigation* (London: Eyre and Spottiswoode, 1970).

44. O. Davies, *Witchcraft, Magic and Culture 1736–1951* (Manchester: Manchester University Press, 1999), 277.

45. Sykes, 'Popular Religion in Decline', 301.

46. This observation is based on extensive conservations with residents of the village and with the superintending minister of the Methodist circuit in 2009.

47. Macdonald and Gordon, *Down to the Sea*, 135.

48. C. Crampton, 'Songs of the Valleys', *New Statesman* 4 January 2017, 17.

49. Although such a case is often made from biology, Rodney Stark and William Bainbridge constructed an elaborate social theory for the persistence of religion.

We all have desires that are not met. Hence, we are in the market for 'compensators', which are both explanations for the lack of expected reward and promises of future reward. As religion can invoke the supernatural, the compensators it provides will always be superior to purely secular ones. Hence the underlying demand for religion should be stable, and such differences we see between societies in the popularity of religious activities must be explained by 'supply' features of the religious market. See R. Stark and W. S. Bainbridge, *A Theory of Religion* (New York: Peter Lang, 1987), and S. Bruce, *Choice and Religion: A Critique of Rational Choice* (Oxford: Oxford University Press, 1999).

50. M. P. Hornsby-Smith, R. M. Lee, and P. A. Reilly, 'Common Religion and Customary Religion: A Critique and Proposal', *Review of Religious Research*, 26 (1985), 244.

9

Spiritualism, Spirituality, and Social Class

If there were no patterns in human behaviour, there would be nothing for scientists to explain, and, if those patterns were entirely a product of biology, the natural scientists would have the field. Social science is possible only because people influence each other and are similarly influenced by circumstances so that social characteristics tend to cluster. It is a commonplace that societies are stratified and that beliefs and attitudes tend to have some regular relationship with social class. People differ in their circumstances and material interests, and, though the links are often subtle, those interests affect self-image and shape visions of the next life as much as of this one.

Such interest links are reinforced by the logic of social trust. There are, of course, many reasons why we trust one source more than another and some are context-specific: despite the apparent popularity of such science-deniers as opponents of vaccination and snake-oil merchants of every stripe, on matters of health most of us still trust our doctors before our drinking companions. Beyond specific fields of expertise, a general principle is that trust is created by social bonds: we trust those with whom we have enduring positive relations more than we trust strangers.[1] And social similarity is an important component of such enduring bonds: we become more like those with whom we interact and we choose to interact with those who are like us. This allows an important shortcut in decision-making. When faced with some new circumstance or choice—will this new expression of religious sentiment appeal to me?—we often look at those promoting the innovation and ask 'Are these my kind of people?'. They should be better than us, of course, because they are trying to persuade us that getting right with Jesus, or listening to the Bhagwan Shree Rajneesh, will improve our lives, but the ability of the promoter to say, directly or implicitly, 'I was once like you but now I am happier or healthier or holier because I tried new improved Snibbo' is an important element of persuasive discourse. That logic explains why advertisers now use 'social media influencers' to punt their products to viewers of YouTube. Young women may take dietary advice from their mothers, but they are more attracted to a social media star such as 'Deliciously Ella', who despite her moneyed background presents herself as 'every young woman'. In short, social science is possible because shared material circumstances give people common interests, and social interaction stabilizes ideas, beliefs, preferences, and attitudes into packages that are maintained and transmitted by the logic of social trust.

We see the combination of shared interests and persuasion clearly in patterns of religious change. Methodism in England initially recruited mainly from farmers with security of tenure, skilled craftsmen in town and cities, and the rising middle classes. These were people who had good reason to think well of themselves and hence to prefer more egalitarian styles of religion that gave them important roles to the largely passive and submissive posture allowed to the laity by the hierarchical Church of England. And they had the social and financial independence to defy the preferences of the ruling classes. As Methodism grew, it divided around class between Wesleyan and Primitive strands. And even the regional divisions (the Bible Christians, for example, were popular in the south-west) had something of a class element to them. Class conflict also shaped Scottish Presbyterianism in the nineteenth century, with the middle classes supporting first the Secession churches and then the 1843 formation of the Free Church. The subsistence farmers and fisherfolk of the highlands and western isles were always out of step with the lowlands. When the lowlands became Protestant at the Reformation, they remained Catholic and Episcopalian. When their entire way of life was undermined by the agricultural reforms known collectively as 'the highland clearances', they converted en masse to an evangelical Calvinistic Protestantism at the same time as the industrial lowlands was becoming liberal and moderate. Welsh dissent similarly had a large political component: in this case, class conflict was combined with nationalism so that resentment at the English and the upper classes (and the two were often the same people) expressed itself in defection from the Episcopalian Church of Wales to the chapels.

This chapter will use the social-class background of those involved in two minority strands of British religion—spiritualism and spirituality—to explore one of the major causes both of secularization and of religious change: the decline of fate or, to put it positively, the increasing assertive and selective attitudes of those who remained interested in religion and spirituality.

Spiritualism

Modern Spiritualism is generally credited to the teenage Fox sisters of Hydesville, New York, who, in 1848, claimed to hear a spirit rapping a signal with snaps of her finger. Neighbours were called to witness what gradually became a complex series of communications based on raps that could be yes or no answers to questions or could indicate a letter of the alphabet.[2] Kate and Margaret were sent away to Rochester during the excitement, and the rappings went with them. Their hosts, a leading Quaker couple who were long-standing family friends, became convinced the phenomenon was genuine and helped to spread the word among their radical Quaker friends, who came to form the core of the Spiritualist movement. The Fox girls became famous, and their public séances in New York in 1850 attracted such notable people as James Fennimore Cooper, author of *The Last of the Mohicans*, and William Lloyd Garrison, the leader of the anti-slavery movement. The movement spread to Britain, where it found receptive audiences in both a superstitious working class and a fashionable elite already interested in phrenology, mesmerism, and various other pseudo-science fads.[3]

Spiritualism was always a diverse movement. For some the point was simply to demonstrate the existence of psychic powers and of a supernatural realm. Spirit mediums contacted the dead, and they demonstrated their powers by making objects materialize (flying trumpets were common) and 'psychokinetically' moving tables and chairs. Although the interest could be bloodless scientific curiosity, for many the point was reassuring contact. It was not enough for relatives to believe that the departed lived on in some other realm; they wanted to hear from their loved ones. Much of the US growth of spiritualism was fuelled by the death in the Civil War of an unprecedented number of young men. For the British, the First World War provided a similar stimulus. The mother of Siegfried Sassoon, the celebrated war poet, used a medium to try to contact his younger brother, who had died at Gallipoli. As Geoffrey Nelson puts it: 'Britain became a nation of bereaved. There were thousands of persons who had lost relatives and friends and who were attracted by the promise of a message from the departed.'[4]

A third interest was in healing. The psychological benefits of reassuring contact with the souls of loved ones broadened into the psychic's ability to diagnose and treat, not just such psychological problems as bereavement, but also physical ailments.

Spiritualism also provided a popular form of domestic entertainment. The wealthy hired professional mediums; others engaged family and friends in amateurish efforts with Ouija boards and rappings. But communicating with the dead also became lucrative public entertainment. Like contemporary pop stars, mediums toured provincial towns competing for paying audiences with ever more florid displays of sounds and signs.

Over the twentieth century, spiritualism developed in a variety of directions. Individual practitioners continued to contact spirits on behalf of clients and some also performed in public, though there was no return to the vaudeville of the previous century. The preference for the term 'private sitting' over the Victorian 'séance' suggests a wish to avoid the grand guignol of the past. Many mediums made the transition to the media age: Derek Acorah and Sally Morgan, for example, have had very successful television careers with subsequent spin-offs in newspaper advice columns and touring live shows. Mediumship is sometimes associated with the power of divination, which adds an extra frisson to the typical horoscope. For example, in the 1980s, Joan Charles used runes and tarot in her 'Psychic Postbag' column for the *Sunday Post*. Those seeking advice were asked to 'handwrite your letters, stating your date of birth and whether you're male or female...'. Her replies to readers differed from secular advice columns mainly in claiming to see outcomes rather than listing preferences: 'I do see you buying your house, but I don't think you should rush into anything. April next year looks good.'

And many spiritualist groups evolved into church congregations.

Spiritualist Churches

Although the main Christian churches reject the principles of mediumship and clairvoyance, the culture of British churches and chapels has had a considerable influence on the spiritualist movement. The Spiritualists' National Union (SNU, founded in 1902) is organized like a denomination. Its larger congregations meet in buildings that—apart from the mediums' armchairs on a raised platform and the absence of an altar—look like Baptist chapels. 'The form of the service, though not its content, has been largely taken over from familiar Nonconformist models.'[5] The lay leader begins with a short prayer and introduces the visiting medium. There is then a hymn, prayer, and short address from the medium. Another hymn is followed by the service centrepiece: the medium's display of clairvoyance. One medium wrote: 'The vast majority of those attending spiritualist meetings, week in, week out, do so in the hope of establishing once again contact with family and friends who are no longer here.'[6] In a typical meeting, the medium may receive messages for five or six members of the congregation. The lay leader then reads out notices and introduces the final prayer and hymn. For most of the twentieth century, the hymns were generally taken from the Church of England's *Hymns Ancient and Modern* or the Methodist hymn book. Those that were sufficiently vague could be left unedited; others had specific referents changed. For example, replacing the first two words of 'Jesus Lives! Thy terrors now can, O death, no more appal us' with 'Loved ones live!' creates a perfect Spiritualist hymn.[7]

British spiritualist churches often display the Seven Principles, made suitably sombre by being painted in gold gothic script on a black background: the Fatherhood of God; the Brotherhood of Man; Communion of Spirits and the Ministry of Angels; the Continuous Existence of the Human Soul; Personal Responsibility; Compensation and Retribution Hereafter for All the Good and Evil Deeds Done on Earth; Eternal Progress Open to Every Soul.[8] There is nothing there that would make it specifically Christian, but also nothing that could not, with a little fudging, be acceptable to Christians.

Although spiritualism has no activity similar to the ordination of the clergy of the main Christian churches, the SNU offers training for those who believe they have psychic gifts. Some of its premises and its members are licensed for marriages, offer 'naming ceremonies' for children, and conduct funerals. At a time when other churches are abandoning dress codes that distinguish the clergy from the laity (and discouraging formality of every sort), the SNU in 2009 debated encouraging leaders to wear clerical collars.

Even closer to the Nonconformist Protestant churches than the SNU are the congregations of the Greater World Christian Spiritualist Association (GWCSA; formerly 'League'). These grew out of the mediumship of Winifred Moyes, who in 1921 started to receive messages from an 'entity' called Zodiac. He claimed to be the temple scribe mentioned in the New Testament (Mark 12: 28) who asked Jesus: 'Which is the first commandment of all?' Apparently Zodiac was persuaded by Christ's answer, because he became an early follower, with similar status to the original apostles. Moyesian groups were united around a mission—to spread in all directions the truth of survival after death, of spirit communion, of healing by the power of Holy Spirit, and to disseminate the teachings received from highly evolved messengers—that would have been acceptable to most spiritualists, depending on quite how they interpreted 'Holy Spirit', but the Pledge—'At all times we endeavour to be guided in our thoughts, words and deeds by the teaching and example of Jesus the Christ'—made clear their wish, the rejection of the main churches notwithstanding, to be seen as Christian. Many GWCSA groups have the adjective 'Christian' in their title, and some even use saints' names for the venues.

Patterns of Adherence

Measuring the popularity of spiritualism is not easy. Involvement may not be exclusive. Even those groups organized like traditional Christian congregations are sometimes attended by people who also have a more conventional Christian affiliation. The 2018 website of one of Dagenham's two spiritualist churches says it welcomes 'people of all religions and faiths', and that attitude explains the typical schedule of meetings.[9] The *Signpost 1998–99* directory of spiritualist meetings list 590. Of these, fifty-three are clearly the homes of individual mediums, organizational headquarters, or have no service days and times listed. Some 15 per cent of the rest meet only on weekdays, and only a tiny handful have meetings on a Sunday morning—a structure that would not interfere with mainstream church attendance. Furthermore, at least one quarter meet in rented public accommodation, and a brief listing gives some sense of the culture surrounding spiritualism: Conservative clubs, village halls, halls owned by temperance and mutual insurance associations such the Foresters and the Rechabites, St John's and Red Cross ambulance rooms, drill halls, scout huts, and Masonic halls. We can almost smell the dry rot and dust. Remarkably, the most popular rented venue after the village hall is the Society of Friends meeting house. This might be a continuation of the closeness between Quakers and spiritualists seen in the US at the movement's foundation, but more likely it reflects the almost unlimited toleration (plus the need to raise funds to pay maintenance costs) that now characterizes the Quakers.

A second obstacle to an accurate enumeration is the autonomy of the spiritualist circle. As we can calculate from the column totals in table 9.1, the Spiritualist National Union accounted for only 60 per cent of the groups listed in the *1998–99* directory. Data for the GWCSA in 1998 are not available, but, if we assume it was more popular then than it was in 2018, it might have had fifty affiliated groups. That still leaves almost 100 groups with announced days, times, and places of meeting in 1998 that were not affiliated to either of the main spiritualist bodies.

Such congregational autonomy derives from a characteristic that itself makes enumeration difficult: the reliance on the charisma of individual mediums and psychics. People are usually drawn to meetings by word-of-mouth reports of the psychic skills that are deployed there, and those are often the attributes of the circle's founder. Like Methodist lay preachers, most mediums rotate around a local area, but many circles also have a resident draw. Some enjoy long lives and careers: Phyllis Roberts, for example, presided over a Dagenham church for forty years. But many had much shorter careers, and so, while Methodist or Anglican congregations endure independently of—and sometimes, despite—their clergy, many spiritualist congregations tend to be short-lived.

One estimate for membership of the SNU at the start of the twentieth century guesses some 25,000 spiritualists in Britain. The movement grew during the First World War, and Nelson estimates its 1930s peak as around 2,000 societies: about a quarter were SNU, a similar number were affiliated to the GWCSA, and half were independents. If we extrapolate from what we know of average congregation size, we can guess some 50,000 spiritualists before the Second World War. It is important to note that, although the 1939–45 war saw mass death, wounding, and destruction, it did not produce the fillip seen after 1919. Nelson gives practical reasons. As spiritualist groups usually met in the evenings, they were severely hindered by the reluctance to go out in the 'blackout' that was imposed to make life difficult for German bombers. The publicity surrounding a number of high-profile prosecutions of mediums and psychics under the 1735 Witchcraft Act scared off some interest.[10] And credibility was damaged by a spectacular failure of prophesy. In the autumn of 1939, renowned medium Estelle Roberts's spirit guide Red Cloud announced there would be no war. Maurice Barbanell's Silver Birch confirmed the message.[11]

An Aside on Failure

Getting it wrong does not always hurt religious movements. A number of fringe Christian sects have repeatedly and mistakenly predicted the end of the world and seen their subsequent membership grow rather than fade. The Jehovah's Witnesses and the Seventh Day Adventists have been repeat offenders.[12] There are ways of representing failure as success. Claiming that the predicted event has actually happened in some spiritual sense, and furthermore insisting that it was the actions of the saved that bought humanity more time, worked for those examples, as it did for the founders of the Findhorn New Age Community in Forres, Morayshire. In 1966, Eileen and Peter Caddy and friends assembled on the beach, confident that they were about to be lifted up by a Venusian spacecraft. Nothing happened, although one witness was sure that a bright light had caused one of the circle to disappear briefly. Eileen received a message from her divine source that told her:

'Let none of you have any feeling of disappointment regarding last night...All was in preparation for something far, far greater than any of you contemplated. Raise your thinking and you will raise your living to an entirely new level.'[13] Far from their beliefs being refuted by a failure of prophecy, the actual events, properly understood, just proved what a good job they were doing.

If Nelson is right that the inaccurate 1939 promises of peace cost spiritualism credibility, we might conclude the following about the circumstances in which a positive spin can be put on failed predictions. First, mistakes about future events that are independent of believers are more damaging than those that can be explained by either the actions or the faith of the adherents. Christian millennialists try to have it both ways, with the imminent end times both fixed (in the sense that they are fore-ordained in the Bible) but also somewhat reliant on God's attitude to his people. Hence there is wiggle room to reinterpret things not going according to what was thought to be the plan by the believers having impressed God enough to buy more time. The predictions of spirit mediums are less amenable to reinterpretation, because—like weather forecasts—they are presented as known facts independent of our behaviour in this life. Logically, there is no reason to suppose that the spirits of the dead know any more about the future than do the living, but the socio-logic is different: if they can be wrong about some big things, why trust them at all?

Second, the more obvious-in-this-life are the events predicted, the more difficult it is to put a positive spin on failure. While the end times of Christian millennialism, when they finally occur, will be pretty brutal, there is a lot of scope for claiming that, though the mountains have not yet been laid low by the hand of the Lord, something important has changed in God's plan, because much of the business goes on out of humanity's sight. Leading spiritualists said there would be no war; the war that followed could hardly be spun as peace.

While Nelson's short-run practical explanations for the wartime halt to the growth of British spiritualism are reasonable, they do not seem sufficient to explain fully why the First World War stimulated interest and the Second did not. It is difficult to escape the conclusion that secularization—evidenced most obviously by the declines of the mainstream churches—made the public less susceptible to spiritualist interpretations of their losses.

There was something of a recovery in the 1950s before a slump.[14] The SNU peaked in 1962, with 434 affiliated churches; down 20 per cent from its 1938 high.[15] It was to lose another quarter by the end of the twentieth century, when it had only some 20,000 members, and one estimate put the total number of British spiritualists at 36,000.[16] We can learn something from the religious identity question in the censuses. The 2011 census for England and Wales (the religion questions for Scotland and Northern Ireland were importantly different) offered tick boxes for broad religious labels such as Christian and Muslim but also included a write-in line. There were just over 39,000 write-ins for 'Spiritualist', which placed that label third after the flippant choice of 'Jedi Knight' (176,632) and the more serious 'Pagan' (at 56,620).[17] So, roughly speaking, the number of spiritualists in the UK declined by two-thirds over the twentieth century at a time when the general population grew from forty-one million to fifty-nine million. The pool of people who could have been spiritualist grew by 44 per cent; the number who actually were spiritualist shrank by over 60 per cent.

Interest in the general phenomena of mediumship and psyche powers must, of course, be greater than these numbers imply. Far more people consult a spiritualist once or twice than attend a spiritualist church regularly; multi-channel cable and satellite TV have allowed a number of spiritualists to become well-known performers and entertainers; and the internet offers many ways in which people can privately pursue their interests. It is hard to know just how strongly such audiences or web-surfing individuals believe, and in what, when there is no accompanying public action, but we can be sure that the possibility of contact with the dead is entertained by far more people than identify as spiritualists.

Gender and Social Class in Spiritualism

Like the Christian churches, British spiritualism is overwhelmingly female. A vast array of evidence shows women to be more religious than men in all religious traditions and all sorts of societies. Quite why is complex.[18] Attempts to find a single big explanation (such as Rodney Stark's use of the observation that women are generally more risk-averse than men) have been unpersuasive, and, because of the point made at the start of the chapter, a big gender difference is probably not necessary. A small difference in the appeal to men and women of any activity will soon turn into a large gender gap simply because of the way we use similarity as a shortcut to deciding whether some novelty will suit us. Most men contemplating joining an exercise class are unlikely to join a Pilates or Zumba session once they realize they will be vastly outnumbered by women. But for spiritualism one gender difference is salient: longevity. As any age cohort becomes elderly, the gender gap will grow as the husbands die younger than the wives they accompanied to church and chapel.

Given that one of the purposes of spiritualism is to contact the dead, the fact that there are far more widows than widowers is significant.[19]

While the congregations of spiritualist churches are mostly female, there are higher proportions of men in the ranks of the seriously involved.[20] Nonetheless, spiritualist churches are unusual in that a disproportionate number of mediums and founders of circles are women. In the last decade of the twentieth century, the Church of England's decision to ordain women considerably boosted the number of female religious officials; their previous exclusion from Christian pulpits meant that women leaders were only on the fringes: the founders of Theosophy (Helena Blavatsky), Christian Science (Mary Baker Eddy), and Seventh Day Adventism (Ellen G. White) are examples. But from the start with the Fox sisters, most mediums were women.

There are few decent statistical data, but most social-science writing on spiritualism makes at least passing mention of social class. Such comments as 'visiting a medium has been part of a traditional working class fatalism' are routine.[21] While Nelson says the membership of the spiritualist movement has always been socially mixed, he also notes: 'the majority appear to be members of the lower middle and artisan classes.'[22]

There may be some evidence of class links in the regional distribution of spiritualist churches in England. Nelson notes that 'few societies exist outside large towns except in mining and industrial villages of the Tees–Tyne area and South Wales.'[23] Table 9.1 shows a distinctly skewed spread of SNU churches. There are more than population would predict in the north-west (13 per cent of the population but 16 per cent of SNU churches), in the north-east (5 per cent of the population but 10 per cent of churches), and in Yorkshire and Humberside (10 per cent of population but 14 per cent of churches); fewer than there should be in London, the east, and south-east (43 per cent of population but only 32 per cent of churches). However, the distribution of the churches known to the compilers of The Signpost directory is much more even, because the avowedly-Christian GWCSA churches tend to be in areas where the SNU is weak.[24] The unaffiliated churches are also skewed (below par in the north-west, Yorkshire, and the Midlands; above par in the more prosperous south). We should beware of making too much of such patterns, because the differential appeal of any one form of religion is affected both by the attraction of religion as such and by the relative appeal of alternatives. For example, Nelson correctly notes that British Catholics (who in the early twentieth century were primarily Irish migrants) were unimpressed by spiritualism: in 1969, Manchester had fifteen spiritualist societies but Liverpool, with its concentration of Catholics, had only four. In

Table 9.1. Regional distribution, Spiritualist churches, England, 1999 and 2018

Region	Population, 2001	Spiritualist churches, 1998	SNU, 2018		GWCSA, 2018		Non-SNU churches, 1998		
	%	n	%	n	%	n	%	n	n
North-east	5	36	9	26	10	0	0	10	7
North-west	13	59	14	44	16	7	17	15	10
Yorkshire and Humberside	10	45	11	37	14	4	10	8	5
Midlands	19	78	18	59	22	9	22	19	13
West Country	10	26	6	18	7	4	10	8	5
London, east, and south-east	43	181	42	87	32	17	41	92	61
Total	100	425	100	271	101	41	100	152	101

Note: Percentage totals are not always 100 because of rounding.

Sources: 1998 data are from *The Signpost 1998–99*. SNU and GWCSA are from their respective websites: https://www.snu.org.uk/find-us-near-you; https://www.greaterworld.net/ (accessed June 2018).

addition, age seems to have been a consideration: outside the industrial areas there were strong pockets along the south coast of England, where there was an unusually high proportion of the elderly and retired, widows and widowers.[25]

Despite such cautions, Nelson's suggestion of an association with the industrial working class seems plausible, especially when we look closely at precisely where spiritualist churches are found in large towns and cities. Within London, for example, spiritualist societies and meetings were more common in working-class areas such as Walthamstow and Dagenham than in more prosperous and middle-class suburbs, and, in the east of England region, societies were more common in places that imported large number of poor Londoners in the era of post-Blitz reconstruction.

If the numerical estimates presented here are reasonably accurate, then the twenty-first century has seen one or both of two major changes: an overall decline in popularity of spiritualism and a shift from being a deviant form of Christian Nonconformity to being something closer to the eclectic New Age spirituality that will be discussed shortly. In 2017, the SNU claimed only 11,500 subscription-paying members: little more than half of the total it claimed in 2000.[26] There seems to have been a similar decline in the GSCSA. We could interpret this simply as part of the general secularization of British culture, but a number of small changes in spiritualism suggest something a little more complex. In the 1970s, the Brighton and Hove Spiritualist Church built itself a brutalist concrete structure with a large worship area. In the first decade of the twenty-first century, it gave up holding Sunday services, though it continued to host an increasing number of small groups and individual consultations. Similar changes in many other churches suggest a gradual drift from the sect's congregation model to a more individualistic service-oriented movement characteristic of the New Age spirituality in which many of the themes of Victorian occultism survive and prosper in a more modern psychology of human potential and self-help improvement.[27]

Contemporary Spirituality

The last quarter of the twentieth century saw a discernible growth in interest in the occult. Occult titles were 3.3 per cent of all religious books in 1928 but 17.3 per cent of religious titles in 1990.[28] Some idea of the enormous range of material can be found in the list of one New Age publisher. Element produced a series called 'Elements of...' and the nouns that followed included Alchemy, Astrology, Buddhism, Christian Symbolism, Creation Myth, Dreamwork, Earth Mysteries, Feng Sui, Herbalism, Human Potential, Meditation, Mysticism, Natural Magic, Pendulum Dowsing, Prophecy, Psychosynthesis, Shamanism, Sufism, Taoism, Aborigine Tradition, Chakras, The Goddess, The Grail Tradition, Greek Tradition, Qabalah, Visualization, and Zen. For reasons that will become clear when I describe the structure of the milieu of New Age or contemporary or holistic spirituality, it is difficult to produce a list of the key beliefs that define this world and distinguish it from other forms of religiosity. Nonetheless, there are common themes. This presentation simplifies a great deal and omits much, but it should do enough to convey a sense of what has changed.[29]

Although many New Agers are critical of the materialistic culture of industrial economies and support efforts to reduce humanity's threat to the environment—for example, the Findhorn Foundation has long pioneered sustainability—the general ethos is upbeat because the milieu supposes that people can improve themselves. Some of the techniques for doing this are developments of Freudian psychology, but many borrow from Eastern religions and cultures.

Romanticism is probably eternal and universal. Every major change can be greeted with the grudging acceptance that material life has improved but we have lost our souls. In the early nineteenth century, poets such as William Blake, William Wordsworth, and Samuel Taylor Coleridge held that cities and factories killed the spirit and that humanity, authenticity, and enlightenment were to be found in barren and remote places. Now that Wordsworth's

Lake District is full of tourists, it can no longer serve in the romantic contrast of the unspoiled natural versus the urban and artificial. So wisdom must now be found in Nepal and Tibet, in South America, and in the Australian Outback. The West is good for cars; the East and South are where we find spiritual enlightenment.

However, it is important for understanding the New Age to appreciate that, in borrowing from Hinduism, Buddhism, Taoism, and the like, it has westernized many ideas by giving them a positive and egotistical spin. For example, in its original Asian context, reincarnation was part of a general assumption that the self is unimportant. For the Buddha, the cause of human suffering was the mistaken belief that there was a 'real' self that suffered. Instead, we should accept that we are just fleeting embodiments of a spirit that dissolves into the cosmic consciousness. Because the people who embraced Hinduism and Buddhism typically lived lives that were nasty, brutish, and short, eastern religions stress life's impermanence. In the words of the motto that Beatle George Harrison used for the title of his first solo album: *All Things Must Pass*. The western version of reincarnation starts with the Christian afterlife idea that the self is so precious that it must persist, but, instead of residing in a static heaven, it comes back to earth in a new body. The relationship between self and the cosmos is also flipped: in eastern religions, the former is insignificant compared to the latter. In western New Age thought, the enlightened self is immensely important because it can draw supernatural power from the cosmic consciousness that inheres in all of us, if only we knew it.

New Age spirituality differs from the major theistic religions in the location of the divine. Christianity, Islam, and Judaism suppose a creator God who is external to us. God is the source of all truth. He may speak to us in diverse ways: indirectly through a sacred text such as the Bible or the Quran, or directly, as when mystical Christians or Sufis are filled with the Holy Spirit. But, however he communicates, God is outside us, and our job is to obey and worship him. Contemporary spirituality represents a 'subjective turn' in two senses: the divine power is within us all, and, because of that, each of us is the final arbiter of truth. Sir George Trevelyan, one of the doyens of the British New Age, concluded one of his talks by saying: 'This is what things look like to me. If it doesn't seem like that to you, you don't have to accept what I say. Only accept what rings true to your own Inner Self.'[30] Where the theistic religions posit a clear divide between creator and created, natural and supernatural, humanity and the divine, contemporary spirituality locates supernatural power within each of us and offers rituals, therapies, and beliefs to unlock that power.

The New Age is individualistic in its theory of knowledge or how we distinguish the truth from falsity. We are used to individualism in cultural choice: we may not like country and western music, but we accept that others have a right to sing maudlin ballads and play banjos. We are used to individualism in political choice: everyone has an equal right to contribute to the choice of government. But conventionally we suppose that there is an objective reality and that truth is a matter of expertise, not preference. The New Age rejects the division between obdurate reality and personal preference and replaces an objective notion of truth with endless subjectivism. The individual consumer is the final arbiter of what he or she must believe, and intuition is the final arbiter of truth and falsity. In that sense, tolerance taken into the world of epistemology produces relativism. In place of one world that can be understand through expertise, there is your truth and there is my truth.

Like traditional spiritualists, New Agers believe we can contact the dead, but what is now called 'channelling' differs from the work of mediums described at the start of this chapter in that it takes for granted what such mediums wanted to establish—the persistence of the dead—and so need not take up time with the news that 'Fred says he's fine and so is the dog'. Instead it concentrates on what Helena Blavatsky pioneered with Theosophy in the late nineteenth century: ethical, political, social, and moral guidance.[31]

Divination is popular with New Agers, though its forms have changed from the forms once favoured by working-class holiday-makers of the 1930s. Nella Last, a Cumbrian housewife who kept detailed diaries for Mass Observation, wrote in 1952 of Ulverston Fair: 'Last year two long rows of luxury motor trailers and caravans had palmists' and clairvoyants', crystal gazers' and phrenologists' signs. This year only five fortune tellers and no one in the least interested.'[32] Last herself gave up consulting fortune-tellers because the war and her husband's debilitating illness killed her desire to know the future: 'I firmly refused to have my hand read. It was always my custom before the war to do so when I went to Blackpool. There was a Madame Curl in Olympia who was uncannily good.' The gypsies who could tell you what would happen were replaced by experts who used detailed horoscopes, Tarot cards, and the I Ching to help people understand their personalities. Focus shifted from predictions to self-awareness.

The New Age attitude towards magic suggest a similar drift. Books of spells to achieve by supernatural power what cannot be achieved naturally are still published, but much New Age occult activity is directed more towards self-understanding and psychological well-being than to magical manipulation.

The Structure of the New Age Milieu

Just as the contrasting views of Catholics and Protestants about the role of a hierarchy in preserving and transmitting sacred power produced the very different outcomes of an enduring international organization, on the one hand, and, on the other, a fragmented world of competing denominations and sects, so the key themes of New Age spirituality have important structural consequences.

New Agers are, in rhetoric at least, extremely liberal. When they say that we should be true to our inner selves, they do not expect our inner selves to be racists, Nazis, homophobes, or misogynists. But, beyond those limits, New Agers are remarkably tolerant. I have rarely heard people in New Age circles openly argue. And, of course, they cannot, because they do not accept that there is a single authoritative standpoint from which competing theories and assertions can be judged. As there is no external authority, there is no ground for saying that someone else's truth is nonsense. Instead, they politely sidestep those things that do not 'ring true' on the grounds that 'I am sure there is something in it but it doesn't work for me'.

An alternative is to weave together a plethora of ideas and rituals from very different cultures using the loom of analogy. So we start with the idea borrowed from Hinduism that, in addition to the known-to-science nervous and circulatory systems, we also have invisible psychic energy, concentrated at various chakra points on the body. Now that sounds like the Chinese anatomy that lies behind acupuncture. So we can put together Ayurvedic medicine and Chinese acupuncture and drop the needles in favour of releasing psychic energy by 'tapping' on significant spots on the body where congestion blocks energy flow. And then we read about ley lines (which were originally identified as lost routes across the countryside made by people) and hear a lecture on chakra points and conclude that ley lines are actually channels of spiritual power, and that our meditation or healing ritual will have more powerful effects if conducted close to Glastonbury Tor or near the Pyramids. Instead of the absolutism that forces conventionally religious people, and conventional scientists, to decide which of competing alternatives is correct (or, in the case of natural science, least wrong), the relativism of the New Age allows us to suppose that there may well be 'something' in every rediscovery of ancient wisdom and every new therapy and that it is up to the consumer to freestyle a combination that best suits him or her.

There are some organizations within the cultic milieu that would like to be sects but cannot persuade their customers to become followers—for example,

Transcendental Meditation—but much New Age activity is built on structures that give opportunities for exploring a wide variety of ideas and products. A key event is the annual 'Mind, Body, Spirit' festival that occurs in London over the May bank holiday weekend. The main hall holds stalls promoting Bachian flower remedies, Reiki healing, Shiatsu massage, iris reading, astrology, and the healing power of crystals. Organizations such as the Swedenborgians, the Theosophical Society, and the Baha'i have their stalls. Lecture rooms offer a rich array of forms of enlightenment and therapy: 'Shamanic Journeys to the Spirit World', 'Becoming a Warrioress: A Celebration of Strength and Self in Women', and 'UFOs: Their Plan on Earth' are examples. Instead of punting one spiritual product, New Life Promotions acts like a concert arranger, booking all sorts of acts and taking a percentage of the fees, and it manages national tours for potentially popular speakers. There are a large number of retreat houses that offer weekend or week-long courses in whatever form of enlightenment or spiritual growth might attract customers. Publishers, shops, periodicals, and websites present a raft of ideas, therapies, and rituals and leave it up to the consumers to take what they want.

Beyond such commercial enterprises is a world of self-employed part-time producers. Much of the work of New Age trainers, therapists, healers, and diviners is hardly lucrative and can best be understood as 'subsistence and exchange': people service themselves and their friends, who in turn reciprocate. So a retired couple with a large house holds Tai Chi weekends for which they charge just the costs of board and lodging. One guest organizes days of mindfulness training and invites the Tai Chi people to attend those. Another offers Reiki therapy. As with music-making (where amateurs and semi-professionals vastly outnumber people who live from their music), the New Age milieu is sustained essentially by people doing what interests them as a hobby.

One important consequence of the New Age insistence on each of us being the final arbiter of truth is limited attachment. Most New Agers are not members or followers or disciples, or they are none of these things for long. They sample this and that. You might be into pyramids as a source of mystic power for a while, and then try TM. And then you read about Shree Bhagwan Rajneesh and try his Dynamic Meditation. You might attend evening classes for a while and even holiday at the Rajneesh Centre in India. You might visit Findhorn for the Experience Week course. In all of this it is you who decides what to take from any of the hundreds of available sources of inspiration and revelation.

Any important sign of the consumer's authority is the financial transaction. The major religions have always found ways of extracting money from adherents, but they have condemned the explicit selling of salvation. The New Age milieu has no trouble with charging fees. No one expects Jill Purce to instruct people in Tibetan overtone chanting for free. In part, this is a function of the New Age's cafeteria structure. The Methodists hope to recruit loyal followers who will fund the clergy and building maintenance in perpetuity. New Agers offer products that consumers take away to do with as they wish. As there is no enduring tie between producer and consumer, the service must be sold. But there is a second reason why New Agers are willing to pay: it leaves them in charge. People who join a sect such as the Brethren or Scientology will find themselves pressed by the organization to show appropriate levels of commitment and made to feel guilty if they fall short. Customers who pay for a week-long residential course in Tai Chi can walk away on the third day without feeling guilty. Commercial exchange may seem unspiritual, but it acknowledges the authority of the consumer.

The Popularity of New Age Spirituality

One popular way of denying secularization is to insist that the decline of the mainstream churches has been compensated for by the growth of contemporary spirituality. Paul Heelas and Linda Woodhead—whose ethnographic study of the New Age milieu in Kendal remains one of the best alternatives to the survey—entitled their report *The Spiritual Revolution* and made extravagant claims for the popularity of the ideas and activities just described. In essence, they accept half of the secularization thesis: the social changes that came with industrialization and the rise of liberal democracy weaken traditional Christian beliefs and institutions. But they insist that, because people are enduringly religious, new expressions will arise. We are witnessing, not secularization, but transformation: dogmatic, authoritarian worship of an external God is giving way to a liberal, tolerant exploration of the supernatural for personal therapy.

Unfortunately, their research provides no evidence that contemporary spirituality comes anywhere close to compensating for the decline of conventional religion: only 1.8 per cent of Kendal residents engaged in activities that could broadly be defined as spiritual. That is a very small number, but almost three-quarters of 'acts of participation' involved yoga, T'ai Chi, massage and bodily manipulation, and healing—activities that could easily have been informed by secular motives. Indeed, when asked, only half of those involved gave spiritual development (or anything like it) as their primary motive.[33] So 99 per cent of Kendal residents were not New Agers, and those who were came from a very narrow social band: the modal New Ager was a middle-aged white female graduate in the arts and humanities, who had worked in teaching, social work, or professions allied to medicine.

That class component has a geographical surrogate. The Findhorn Foundation is in Moray because the southern English founders were beached there after losing their jobs in Forres. The Throssel Hole Zen Priory is in Northumberland, the Samye Ling Tibetan Buddhist monastery is in Dumfriesshire, and the Manjusri Institute is in Cumbria, not because the natives of those places founded them but because rural depopulation meant large properties were cheap, and there were few neighbours to complain about the influx of weirdoes.[34]

The social class of New Agers is confirmed by data from a survey that asked about four groups of arguably spiritual activities. The only one in which working-class women showed more interest than their better-educated sisters was divination.[35] This is an exaggerated contrast—after all, in some contexts, knowledge is power—but we can contrast an essentially passive or fatalistic attitude with an assertive approach to life. The former wants to know what is coming down the pike, at best hoping the worst errors can be avoided (as when a horoscope warns that this is not a good month to embark on a new love affair), but otherwise supposes that life is to an extant fore-ordained; it is something that happens to you. The activist supposes that we have within ourselves considerable, even limitless, power to achieve our desires, if we just learn the right rituals, therapies, attitudes, and incantations. We can make the same distinction about healing. In traditional faith healing and in the work of current psychic healers, the healer directs *external* divine power to cure the sufferer. Although some New Agers see themselves as possessing magic powers that can heal even those who do not believe in them—my Reiki therapist, for example, treats horses—most contemporary spirituality healers suppose that they are essentially midwives: they help the sufferer cure herself by releasing her inner power or learning to think positively or visualizing desired outcomes. Hence, in the world of contemporary spiritual-tinged well-being, healing often sits alongside yoga, meditation, mindfulness, careful diet, and other ways in which we can through our own efforts improve our bodies and our lives.

The detailed links between such background characteristics and being attracted to New Age ideas and therapies are teased out elsewhere.[36] Here

I want to make a general observation about personal autonomy and liberation from fate, but, to indicate the point's broad application, I will first consider the class base of the charismatic movement described in Chapter 5.

Class and the Charismatic Movement

This may seem an unusual connection, but one reason for thinking that the class contrast in the appeals of spiritualism and spirituality point to a fundamental, class-shaped, change in social confidence is that we can see something similar in the contrast of 1930s Pentecostalism and the charismatic movement of the house churches and then the New Churches.

The early twentieth-century wave of interest in supernatural powers that produced such denominations as the Elim Pentecostal Church and the Assemblies of God appealed primarily to the working class and hence to industrial towns and cities and to the north of England, South Wales, and the central lowlands of Scotland. The distribution of the New Church suggests a very different base. In 2001, Wales had 5 per cent of the UK population but only 2 per cent of its New Churches; Scotland had 9 per cent of the population but only 3 per cent of New Churches; and Northern Ireland has 3 per cent of the population but only 1 per cent of New Churches.[37] That pattern could, of course, be explained by the very different religious cultures of the UK's peripheral nations, but there are also very strong regional patterns in England.

The first column of Table 9.2 show the regional division of the general population in 1990; this shows what we would expect of the New Churches if they appealed equally across the country. The second columns show the 2005 distribution of congregations; the year gap between the two data sets may affect specific numbers but not the general picture. The third column shows the discrepancy between expected and actual New Churches in each region, and those figures have been used to order the rows. As Peter Brierley noted: 'The movement was very strong in the South East of England.'[38] It was correspondingly unpopular in Northumberland, County Durham, Yorkshire, and Humberside and not for want of trying. The collapse of once-popular Methodism in the Durham coalfields had left a large space in the market. An independent evangelical congregation was founded in the new town of Peterlee in the 1980s, but only fifteen adults attended Peterlee Evangelical Church in 2018 when hundreds had attended the area's chapels in the 1950s.

In brief, the popularity of the charismatic movement could be predicted simply by drawing a line from the Bristol Channel to the Wash. The more prosperous southern part of England liked it a lot more than did the rest of the UK.

Table 9.2. New Church distribution, English regions, 2005 (%)

Region	Share of population, 1990	Share of New Churches, 2005	Divergence as proportion of population share
South-west	11.4	16.5	+45
South-east	26.0	36.6	+39
East Anglia	5.0	6.4	+28
East Midlands	9.8	9.5	−3
West Midlands	12.7	9.6	−24
North-east	7.5	5.4	−28
North-west	15.6	9.2	−41
Yorkshire and Humberside	12.1	6.9	−48
Total	100.1	100.1	

Note: Percentage totals are not always 100 because of rounding.

Source: P. Brierley (ed.), *UK Christian Handbook Religious Trends*, vi (London: Christian Research Association, 2005).

Class, Culture, and Control

The absence of racial and ethnic minorities, recent immigrants, and poor people from the New Age milieu is often explained by the cost of New Age therapies and activities, but this is unconvincing. A yoga holiday in the Seychelles might be pricey, but a hen party weekend in Amsterdam or a Saturday of drinking, football match, more drinking, and a late-night curry will cost as much as a T'ai Chi weekend.

More important than a direct link with income is the roundabout connection between social class, income, sense of personal autonomy, and culture. Contemporary spirituality is literate. The workshops, lectures, seminars, DVDs, and books are familiar to the professional middle classes because they are an extension of high school, college, and university. And contemporary spirituality assumes that the individual is an autonomous agent capable of self-driven improvement. A working-class friend who accompanied me to a Mindfulness seminar said afterwards: 'Bunch of middle class tossers who like the sound of their own voices. Well up themselves. Not a scooby about the real world. They should catch themselves on.' What he meant was that they were self-absorbed and they were comfortable talking about themselves; his contrast was the working men's club, where self-importance would be squashed by mockery and where getting 'above yourself' would invite a deflating and scornful response.

That contrast neatly expresses a basic social division. Max Weber made an important point when he qualified Karl Marx's great divide of capitalist and worker, or bourgeoisie and proletarian: not all people who live only by selling their labour power are in the same boat. Because each is readily replaceable, unskilled workers can improve their circumstances only by collective bargaining: strikes and other forms of common action force employers to pay all their workers more. Labourers rise or fall as a class. Middle-class professional workers are in a very different position. They invest in long periods of education and gradually move up in a career that rewards the individual's experience and credentials. Scarce and valued skills command generous rewards and a considerable degree of self-direction. That basic structural difference is reflected in cultural differences: middle-class people are much more likely than the working class to imagine that they are in control of their lives.[39] We could add a book's worth of detailed elaboration here, but we need only accept a basic class difference in self-confidence to provide a plausible explanation for the subtle pattern of association that sees early twentieth-century spiritualism appealing most in rust-belt towns with a large working class, and New Age spirituality appealing most to the prosperous south. The limited appeal of the charismatic movement may well have a similar explanation. Although New Churches are superficially old-fashioned in promoting supernatural 'gifts of the spirit', their adherents are similar to New Agers and liberal Christians in putting personal experience above dogma and in having a selective rather than a deferential attitude to their faith.

Conclusion

In one sense, Heelas is correct to identify a spiritual revolution. In conservative Protestantism, there has been a shift from dogmatic, hierarchical, authoritarian, and puritanical sectarianism to a more fluid, therapeutic, and experiential religion of the charismatic movement. In spiritualism, there has been a small but noticeable shift from the initial clear divide of us and the spirit world towards a more holistic spirituality. The cultic milieu of the New Age is very much based on the role of intuition and the individual's right to decide what to believe. Even in the Catholic Church—often the exemplar of institutional rigidity—there has been a discernible weakening of authority.

What is wrong with Heelas and Woodhead's optimistic assessments of the growth potential of these trends is their failure to appreciate that the spiritual revolution has been confined to the ever-smaller part of the population that is at all interested in religion. To say that New Age spirituality and the charismatic movement are accommodations with the prevailing secular climate of consumerist individualism is to say that, if modern people want to be religious, these forms are more likely to appeal than the traditional religions of Catholicism, the Brethren, or the Spiritualist National Union. The mistake is to suppose that most modern people want to be religious or anything close. The religiously indifferent are no more likely to be attracted to a faith that has capitulated to modern consumerism than to one that rejects it. On the contrary, that so much of Britain's religious culture is now trying hard to pretend it is not religious (or at least not in that old offputting way) is likely—if they notice it at all—to reinforce the view of the religiously indifferent that secular is better than religious.

Modernizing innovations appeal, not to those who are doing just fine without religion, but to young people in conservatively religious circles who wish to break out of the straitjacket in which they were raised. Moving from the Brethren to a charismatic fellowship, or from a Baptist church to a self-defined holistic spirituality, is like moving from a high-security prison to an open prison: the change is liberating. But people who are at liberty will not be volunteering to enter a relaxed open prison just because it is not as oppressive as Alcatraz or a bleak fortress on Dartmoor.

Notes

1. P. Sztompka, *Trust: A Sociological Theory* (Cambridge: Cambridge University Press, 1999).
2. R. Pearsall, *Table Rappers: Victorians and the Occult* (London: Michael Joseph, 1972). Forty years after the first rappings, one of the sisters confessed that they had been a hoax, but most spiritualists refused to believe her.
3. For the British background, see O. Davies, *Witchcraft, Magic and Culture 1738–1951* (Manchester: Manchester University Press, 1999) and G. Nelson, *Spiritualism and Society* (London: Routledge and Kegan Paul, 1969).
4. Nelson, *Spiritualism and Society*, 155.
5. B. Martin, 'The Spiritualist Meeting', in D. Martin and M. Hill (eds), *A Sociological Yearbook of Religion in Britain*, iii (London: SCM Press, 1970), 147. See also Nelson, *Spiritualism and Society*, ch. 12.
6. D. Wilson, 'Protestant Shamans? Spiritualism and Spirituality in 21st Century Scotland', lecture, New College, University of Edinburgh, 21 November 2007.
7. Martin, 'The Spiritualist Meeting', 149
8. Martin, 'The Spiritualist meeting', 151.
9. www.candleoflightspiritualchurch.co.uk (accessed June 2018).
10. Nelson, *Spiritualism and Society*, 162–4. For details of one high-profile prosecution for witchcraft, see M. Gaskill, *Hellish Nell: The Last of Britain's Witches* (London: Fourth Estate, 2001).

11. R. Skemman, *One Hundred Years of Spiritualism: The Story of the Spiritualist Association of Great Britain 1872–1972* (London: Spiritualist Association of Great Britain, 1972), 37.

12. J. Beckford, *The Trumpet of Prophecy: A Sociological Study of Jehovah's Witnesses* (Oxford: Basil Blackwell, 1975); R. Wallis, *Salvation and Protest* (London: St Martin's, 1979). 44–50.

13. P. Caddy, *In Perfect Timing* (Forres: Findhorn Press, 1996), 262. Findhorn is discussed at length in S. Bruce, *Secular Beats Spiritual: The Westernization of the Easternization of the West* (Oxford: Oxford University Press, 2017).

14. A 1954 estimate gives 41,000 spiritualists in England and Wales and 4,000 in Scotland; A. K. Cairncross (ed.), *The Scottish Economy: A Statistical Account of Scottish Life* (London: Allen and Unwin, 1954), table 141.

15. Nelson, *Spiritualism and Society*, 166.

16. P. Brierley, *UK Christian Handbook: Religious Trends 2007/2008* (Swindon: Christian Research Association, 2007), table 10.3. There is always a danger of confusing 'UK' and 'British' in religion data, but in this case they are much the same: the strongly conservative Christian climate of Northern Ireland has ensured there have never been more than a few hundred spiritualists there.

17. The difference between the 2011 census figure and Brierley's estimates may well be explained by the fact that the census figures include children.

18. M. Trezbiatowska and S. Bruce, *Why Are Women More Religious Than Men?* (Oxford: Oxford University Press, 2012).

19. G. Nelson, 'Membership of a Cult', *Review of Religious Research*, 13 (1972), 170–7, notes that there were three times as many widowed people in his sample of spiritualists as in the population at large. In 1980, there was a seven-year gender gap in life expectancy.

20. Nelson, 'Membership', 174.

21. T. Walter, 'Mediums and Mourners', *Theology*, 110 (2007), 97. Nelson's survey of spiritualists, which did ask about class, is of limited value, because it sampled only heavily involved and committed spiritualists, mostly group leaders, who tended to be of a higher social class than attenders; Nelson, 'Membership'. Spiritualists are too thin on the ground to show up in national surveys in sufficient numbers for analysis, and the very many women who did not work outside the home would not, until the very end of the twentieth century, have an 'occupational class' to be analysed.

22. Nelson, *Spiritualism and Society*, 264.

23. Nelson, *Spiritualism and Society*, 189.

24. These figures were calculated from the 2011 census population data and from the 2018 listing of churches on the SNU website. The Spiritualist Association of Great Britain has been ignored; in the 1960s, it claimed 7,000 members, but they were not organized in anything like churches and were often more concerned with a 'scientific' research approach to the subject. Also overlooked are the numerous clients of spiritualist healers; see Nelson, *Spiritualism and Society*, 200–1.

25. It is possible that this was not an independent effect of bereavement but simply part of the general relationship between age and religiosity. The aged might have been more interested in spiritualism than the young because they were generally more religious than the young: a function, not of ageing per se but of the decline of Christianity

following a cohort pattern with each generation being only half as religious as the proceeding one.

26. Spiritualist National Union, https://www.snu.org.uk./find-us-near-you (accessed January 2018).

27. I am grateful to two members of the Brighton and Hove group for this information. I found similar observations in conversations with other spiritualists in the south, but not the north, of England.

28. P. Brierley, *A Century of British Christianity: Historical Statistics 1990–1985 with Projections to 2000* (London: MARC Europe, 1989).

29. For a detailed study of the New Age, see Bruce, *Secular Beats Spiritual*.

30. L. Revell, 'The Return of the Sacred', in S. Wolton (ed.), *Marxism, Mysticism and Modern History* (London: Macmillan, 1999), 123.

31. B. F. Campbell, *Ancient Wisdom Revived: A History of the Theosophical Movement* (Berkeley and Los Angeles: University of California Press, 1980); J. J. Franklin, *Spirit Matters: Occult Beliefs, Alternative Religions, and the Crisis of Faith in Victorian Britain* (Ithaca, NY: Cornell University Press, 2018).

32. P. Malcolmson and R. Malcolmson (eds), *Nella Last in the 1950s* (London: Profile, 2010), 249.

33. For a detailed evaluation of the Kendal data, see Bruce, *Secular Beats Spiritual*, ch. 6.

34. This observation is based on my extensive but casual acquaintance with many New Agers, on published biographies, and on the histories of these establishments. It is confirmed by detailed analysis of census data for the relevant areas. See S. Bruce, *Scottish Gods: Religion in Modern Scotland, 1900–2012* (Edinburgh: Edinburgh University Press, 2014), 171.

35. T. Glendinning and S. Bruce, 'New Ways of Believing or Belonging: Is Religion Giving Way to Spirituality?', *British Journal of Sociology*, 57 (2006), 399–41.

36. Bruce, *Secular Beats Spiritual*, 139.

37. Population is from 2001 census; the distribution of New Churches is from P. Brierley (ed.), *UK Christian Handbook Religious Trends*, iv (London: Christian Research Association, 2003), table 9.9.1.

38. P. Brierley, *'Christian' England: What the English Church Census Reveals* (London: MARC Europe, 1991), 68.

39. My impressions of many New Age practitioners and enthusiasts suggests a more specific connection. Many have taken early retirement from white-collar work in education and the health service because of their frustration with increasing bureaucratization and loss of autonomy. What they most value about their work as healers, diviners, and the like is that it restores a freedom that they either expected in their work or actually enjoyed when younger.

10

Religion and Politics

Since Henry's 1534 break with Rome, the Church of England has been the legally established state church of England. It was also the state church of Ireland until 1869, and of Wales until 1914. Although the theological justification was somewhat different, a similar arrangement obtained in Scotland. The Presbyterian Church expected the state to make people support it, and in return it was expected to support the state. That privileged position invariably meant that religion was political: those who refused to conform (and, more importantly, refused to pay their church taxes) were punished. For example, the Five Mile Act of 1665 prohibited any priest who rejected the new regime in the Church of England from living within 5 miles of a corporate town or any place where he had formerly served. The Test Act of 1673 barred Catholics from civil and military offices. Property was seized from those who refused to pay their tithes.[1]

Gradually such disabilities were relaxed from the late eighteenth century onwards as grudging toleration gave way to religious liberty. That change was made possible by the weakness of the state churches and the strength of the state. Repression failed to discourage dissent. The more moderate movements of the English Civil War period—the Independents and the Baptists—thrived despite periodic persecution, as did the Quakers. The appreciation that punishment was not working coincided with the realization that, contrary to contemporary political theory, a shared religion was not necessary for political stability. The French Revolution did not inspire a comparable British upheaval. Those who lived through the English Civil War, the periodic unrest in Ireland, the Jacobite rebellions of 1715 and 1745, or the Gordon Riots of 1780 (well described by Charles Dickens in *Barnaby Rudge*) would not have seen it like this, but the evolution of Britain's absolute monarchy into parliamentary democracy was relatively smooth and peaceful.

The Gordon Riots were a militant Protestant reaction to the Papists Act of 1778, which aimed to extend to Catholics the toleration previously granted to Protestant dissenters. That hostility was fuelled by a not-entirely-erroneous belief that Protestantism was more conducive to democracy than Catholicism.[2] The Vatican was vocally opposed to representative democracy well into the twentieth century—a stance that fitted well with its view that ordinary people could not be trusted to find God. It took the disaster of 1930s European fascism and the resulting Second World War to bring the Church round to the notion that people had a right to be wrong.

Underlying values aside, another crucial difference linked the competing tendencies in Christianity with political agendas. For obvious reasons, any dominant church (even if not formally supported by the state) will be conservative. If it were not, the ruling classes would not allow it to remain dominant. That applies as much to Protestant churches (such as the Church of England or the Lutheran Churches of Scandinavia) as to the Catholic Church. But, because it is based on the idea that all people have an equal ability (and hence right) to discern the will of God, and that a hierarchical priesthood is a hindrance rather than a help to piety, Protestantism permits factionalism and schism, and we see the consequences of that in the endless fragmentation into competing sects and denominations that occurred in Britain and in the United States.[3] In contrast, the Catholic claim that sacramental power was controlled by the Church's hierarchy forced an abrupt choice: either accept the Church's direction or abandon religion altogether. Hence the pattern of Catholic countries such as France, Italy, Spain, and Portugal splitting into conservative Catholic and radical secular blocks. The quotation is attributed to a number of supporters of the French Revolution, but the sentiment that 'the Revolution will not be complete until the last aristocrat has been strangled with the guts of the last priest' contained an important truth. Although the supportive church–state model of the UK acted as something of a brake on the fissile tendencies of Protestantism, it could not prevent the growth of religious diversity, and the Union of Scotland and England created a patent absurdity: the church imposed on England, Ireland, and Wales was Episcopalian but Scotland's was Presbyterian, and the monarch was required abruptly to change faith at the border. The UK's increasing diversity had the happy consequence, once the stability of the state was appreciated, of allowing people who objected to the conservative politics of the state churches to create their own more liberal and democratic sects and denominations. The British could argue about the specific privileges of the state churches, but, unlike the French, they could do so from within Christianity rather than from without.

The avowedly reactionary Tory Jacob Rees-Mogg said in 2017 that, on matters such as gay rights and abortion, 'I'm a Roman Catholic and have made it clear…that in this sort of matter I will take my whip from the hierarchy of the Catholic Church.'[4] Although even that sounds strange in a parliamentary democracy, it is a much more circumscribed allegiance than that feared for much of the eighteenth and nineteenth centuries when Protestants argued that Catholics could not be loyal to the state while they owed a superior loyalty to the Bishop of Rome. Such suspicions were not groundless. The Gunpowder Plot of 1605 had been a Catholic project. The Jacobite Rebellions of 1715 and 1745 had been led by Catholics. And the religion of the people on either side of mainland Britain gave an international dimension to the tension. Despite the formal imposition of the Anglican Church, Ireland remained largely Catholic and hence was always suspect, because Britain's traditional enemies—France and Spain—were Catholic states that could mobilize their Irish co-religionists. So, while the disabilities imposed on Protestant dissenters could be relaxed safely, extending religious liberty to Catholics was always more problematic, and it was not until the 1820s that Catholics were permitted the vote and allowed to hold a variety of public offices. That move ended the relative alienation of English Catholics from the state, but it did not kill off Irish demands for degrees of autonomy and then independence. The status of Ireland shaped British party politics for most of the twentieth century.

The Liberal Party split over William Gladstone's plans to grant Ireland a degree of autonomy or 'Home Rule', and the 'Unionists' who opposed him gradually drifted into the Conservative Party, which in Scotland retained the Unionist title until the 1980s, when Margaret Thatcher insisted that it conform to English usage. The close association between progressive politics and the Nonconformity of the chapels strengthened as the franchise was expanded and led to the most unusual feature of British trade unionism and worker representation. A number of people are credited with the observation that the British labour movement owed far more to Methodism than to Marx. I have on my wall a photograph of the Winsford, Somerset, Wesleyan Methodist Sunday school of 1877. One of the young (and formally attired; it must have been the annual picnic) pupils was Ernest Bevin, who became a Baptist lay preacher, co-founded the Transport and General Workers Union, joined the Labour Party at its inception, and served in Winston Churchill's wartime cabinet.[5] Conflict over the relative autonomy of the UK's peripheral nationalities reinforced that alignment, with the wholesale defection around the end of the nineteenth century from the Church of Wales to the Methodist, Baptist, and Presbyterian chapels often being at least partly motivated by a wish to reject 'English' imposition. Fifty years later, the Labour–Chapel links were still strong: Garfield Davies, the general secretary of the Union of Shop, Distributive, and Allied Workers in the 1990s, 'was a Labour loyalist in every respect, except on issues that conflicted with the social conservatism of his Christian beliefs and the influences of those Methodist roots'.[6]

Migrant Politics

For the second half of the twentieth century the line-up of religion and politics in England was what Margaret Stacey found in Banbury: the local Conservative Party was the preserve of Church of England members and identifiers, while Nonconformists (Protestant and Catholic) dominated the Liberal and Labour parties. In part that reflected the long struggles against the privileges of the established church: as the Tories were in favour of the status quo, those who wished radical change were drawn to the opposition. But there was also a underlying class dimension to both religious and political preferences: the upper middle classes, and the gentry and the servants they could influence, were Anglicans and Tories, while the lower middle and the workers were Liberal or Labour.

In that context, the political alignment of ethnic minorities is paradoxical. Though the Irish Catholics, Caribbeans, and Asians who migrated to Britain in the twentieth century were, on socio-moral issues, more conservative than the natives, they supported parties of the left. Across Europe in the interwar years, majority Catholic politics were conservative.[7] For example, the Irish constitution prohibited divorce, contraception, and abortion and made the gendered division of labour a keystone of its domestic policy. Clause 41.2 of the 1937 constitution said: 'by her life within the home, woman gives to the State support without which the common good cannot be achieved' and said that mothers 'not be obliged by economic necessity to engage in labour to the neglect of their duties in the home'.[8] But where they were a migrant minority—in Britain, Australia, New Zealand, and North America—Catholics supported the most progressive parties.

That reflected the priority given to social-class issues. As noted in Chapter 6, the Irish immigrants were escaping poverty; lacking capital or technical skills, they entered the labour market at the bottom and so supported movements for trade-union rights, for the vote, and for public expenditure on housing, mass education, health-service provision, and the like. Initially they continued to support Irish parties, but, once two-thirds of Ireland was granted autonomy in 1921 as the Free State, they shifted en masse to the Labour Party. That laid the foundations for an internal division that did not erode until the end of the twentieth century: in areas with large Catholic populations such as Liverpool and Glasgow, Labour MPs tended to be working-class trade unionists and social conservatives; in London and the south-east, they were more likely to be middle-class professionals who supported gender equality, gay rights, abortion, and a host of other progressive measures.

There was a similar tension in post-1960s West Indian support for the Labour Party. The origins of the 'Windrush generation' (so-called after the *Empire Windrush*, a boat that brought the first significant party of people to Britain from the Caribbean) lay in the 1948 British Nationality Act, which gave British citizenship to citizens of the colonies. Hostile reaction to black immigration led a Conservative government to constrain that right in 1962 and again in 1968 and 1971.

Both major parties were formally more moderate than their members. The Conservatives expelled Enoch Powell for the speech in which he quoted Virgil's *Aeneid*: 'as I look ahead, I am filled with foreboding; like the Roman, I seem to see the River Tiber foaming with much blood.' But many grassroots Conservatives supported Powell's sentiments. The Labour Party was officially opposed to Tory racism, but many of its working-class members were unhappy about immigrants competing for jobs and housing. Nonetheless, the power of the party (to which I will return shortly) was such that its illiberal grass roots could largely be ignored, and black Britons enthusiastically supported the Labour Party, even though most did not share its progressive social values.

The same reasoning can be seen in the political allegiances of the third wave of twentieth-century migrants: Asians, the majority of whom were Muslims. As many of the first generation were self-employed and socially conservatives, Muslims should have been Tory voters, but the Conservative Party's general xenophobia and its fondness for nostalgic harking 'back to basics' (which meant an at-least-nominally Christian society) pushed Muslims in the direction of Labour, and the Labour Party was happy to encourage Muslim 'community leaders' who claimed to speak for (and more importantly could deliver the votes of) their people. In particular, the 1980s Labour activists (the generation of Ken Livingstone and Jeremy Corbyn) solicited Muslim support by promoting multiculturalism. The French response to immigrants was to insist that all citizens had an equal right, or obligation, to embrace a homogenous French culture and identity. The US model was to permit considerable nominal attachment to previous ethnic identities provided they were confined to the leisure sphere of Irish pubs and Italian delis. The Labour councils of the big British cities promoted a very different approach. Partly because economic changes were eroding Labour's traditional class base, councils pioneered 'identity' politics, funding women's and ethnic minority groups in the hope of building a mosaic of disparate interests. Instead of insisting that Muslims accept liberal and secular values, Labour argued that such values had to accommodate those who wished to maintain the relationships and mores they had brought from Pakistan and Bangladesh.

Pervaiz Khan tells the story of his uncle, who came to Britain in the 1950s and by the 1960s was a shop steward for the Transport and General Workers' Union. He developed strong ties to the Labour Party leadership in Birmingham.

> He was never an elected councillor but he was treated as if he was. He had his own office in the council building, a pass and a parking space. He effectively acted as a 'whip', making sure that other Asian councillors voted the 'right way'. In return he got council grants for the Asian community, for community centres and other projects.[9]

The Labour Party courted community elders who could instruct their people how to vote. Such a system was encouraged by the relative isolation of some migrant communities, low levels of education, poor English-language skills, and the subordination of women. Brokers mediated between minority communities and government agencies. Such brokers lost their influence as immigrants, and their children became effective representatives of their own interests, but in both legal and illegal forms clannishness remains a political force. In June 2004, six leading Birmingham Muslims (including Muhammad Afzal, a city councillor for 23 years) used forged postal ballots to steal an election for Labour.[10] In 2009, six Pakistani men in Slough received prison sentences for vote-rigging: this time in the Conservative interest.[11] The same year, five Muslim Tories in Bradford were found guilty of forging postal ballots in the Bradford West Westminster seat. In 2015, Luthur Rahman was stripped of his post as mayor of Tower Hamlets for vote-rigging, bribery, fraud, and using 'undue spiritual influence'.[12]

Between 1981, when Labour gained control of the Greater London Council, and 1986, when the Tories abolished it, 'the GLC pioneered a new strategy of making minority communities feel part of British society. It arranged consultations with them, drew up equal opportunities policies, established race relations units, and dispensed millions of pounds in grants to minority groups.' The GLC redefined racism so that it meant not the denial of equal rights but the denial of the right to be different... Black people, so the argument went, should not be forced to accept British values or adopt a British identity. Rather, different peoples should have a right to express their own identities, explore their own histories, formulate their own values, pursue their own lifestyles.

Hence anti-racism meant 'preserving the "traditions and cultures" of the different ethnic minorities'.[13]

The GLC model was influential. Birmingham City Council created nine groups to act as channels of representation between it and the city's minorities: the African and Caribbean People's Movement, the Bangladeshi Islamic Projects Consultative Committee, the Birmingham Chinese Society, the Council of Black-Led Churches, the Hindu Council, the Irish Forum, the Vietnamese Association, the Pakistani Forum, and the Sikh Council of Gurdwaras. By funnelling money and influence through these organizations, it encouraged people to identify with one of these interest groups, and it encouraged them to compete. As Malik puts it: 'In applying multicultural snake oil to the problems of Birmingham, the council created rifts between communities where none had previously existed and exacerbated divisions that had previously been managed.'[14] The same story could be told for Bradford and for Sheffield, and, once Labour won the country in 1997, the multicultural approach was applied by central government. The focus on religio-ethnic identity was, of course, not simply a consequence of Labour Party policy. The tendency of migrants to settle alongside their kin and co-religionists had already laid the foundation for what Amartya Sen has called 'plural monoculturalism', but, as Sen argues, the British enthusiasm for 'recognizing' cultural differences exaggerated the problem it was designed to solve.[15] The threat from Islamic terrorism exacerbated the problem, because successive governments tried to isolate the killers from the simply reactionary by rewarding the latter for not being the former.[16]

There is evidence for Sen's critique of plural monoculturalism. A major 2006 international survey of Muslim attitudes showed that Muslims in Britain were more critical than those in France, Spain, and Germany, despite those countries doing far less to accommodate minority sensibilities. When asked 'Is there a conflict between being a devout Muslim and living in a modern society?', 47 per cent of British Muslims but only 36, 28, and 25 per cent of Muslims in Germany, France, and Spain agreed.[17] When asked to say whether relations between Muslims and Westerners were generally good or bad, 'bad' was chosen by 62 per cent of British Muslims, 60 per cent of German Muslims,

58 per cent of French Muslims, and only 23 per cent of Muslims in Spain. There are, of course, so many other differences between the Muslims of these four countries that we cannot directly ascribe British Muslim views to government policy, but we can minimally say that the policy has not been an obvious success. Nor did the Blair government endear itself to Muslims with its wars in Iraq and Afghanistan. Two-thirds of white British respondents but 83 per cent of British Muslims disapproved of involvement in Iraq; the figures for Afghanistan were 58 and 88 per cent, and, for Sunni Muslims, the more seriously respondents took their faith, the more hostile they were to Blair's 'war on terror'.[18]

Jews and Anti-Semitism

Muslim attitudes exacerbated an old problem for the Labour Party: anti-Semitism.[19]

The position of British Jews has always been precarious. They were initially invited to England in the eleventh century by William the Conqueror, who hoped their commercial skills would enrich his new domain. Two centuries later, they were driven out by violence (the York community was massacred in 1190) and by legal restrictions imposed by Edward I. Jews were not banned from Scotland, which was still an independent kingdom.

In part because he wanted to protect Protestant opponents of the Church of England, Oliver Cromwell was more tolerant, and the Jewish population grew slowly but steadily. In the nineteenth century, legal restrictions on Jews were repealed, and they became sufficiently accepted that Benjamin Disraeli's Jewish heritage did not prevent him leading the Tory party and twice serving as prime minister. That numbers were swollen by waves of migrants fleeing persecution in Europe did not mean Britain was free from anti-Semitism.[20] There is ample evidence of casual disparagement in popular literature. Dornford Yates, whose lightweight romantic and humorous novels and short stories were immensely popular from 1910 to the late 1940s, frequently used stock Jews as villains: in his fiction, 'all Jews, without exception, are sly, odious, and frequently quite dishonest'.[21]

In the 2011 census, about a quarter of a million Britons identified as Jewish, though the high non-response rate from ultra-orthodox Haredi Jews probably means the actual figure is higher. The previous fifty years show two opposing trends. Mainstream Jewish numbers declined, as large numbers—20 per cent in the case of Liverpool's Jews in the 1970s—married out: 'with the increased prosperity and social emancipation of the community, a steady decline in membership and commitment to its institutions and to religious practice has become more evident, increasingly since the late 1950s.'[22] But Orthodox numbers grew, partly from migration but mostly from fertility: Haredi women have an average of more than six children.[23]

In Britain, as in the rest of Europe, there has been a rise in anti-Semitism coincident with growing hostility to Muslims. In 2005, there were 532 anti-Semitic incidents—many desecration of Jewish cemeteries—known to the police.[24] In 2006, there were proportionately more attacks on Jews than on Muslims in London, and the number of incidents grew over the next decade.[25] The causes are complex. It is partly an expression of the general xenophobia encouraged by populist right-wing movements such as UKIP, the BNP, and the English Defence League. Some of it comes directly from Muslim hostility to Jews. The Egyptian paper al-Akhbar, which unashamedly advocates their murder, is on open sale in newsagents serving Muslim areas.[26] And the growth of the isolated and highly distinctive ultra-orthodox community has increased fears of a disconnected minority while making its members easier to identify for those who want to vent their spleen on 'aliens'.

This is the background to the Labour Party's problems with anti-Semitism. As noted in Chapter 7, although British Muslims are mostly from south-east Asia rather than the Middle East, and hence not personally close to the Palestinian issue, many are happy to embrace the anti-Semitism common in the Arab world. Leaving aside the fact that Holocaust denial and the scape-goating of Jews as the authors of the world's financial problems are in them-selves discreditable, anti-Semitism divides the Labour Party in a way it does not the Conservatives, because, like the Irish, British Jews were a considerable presence in the party. Although under-represented among the working class from which Labour initially drew its votes, Jews, ever the underdog, have tended to support the progressive side in British politics.

That connection came under threat when Jeremy Corbyn was elected leader, and the hard left, which has long been pro-Palestinian and anti-Zionist (largely because the hated US supports Israel), began to increase its influence in the party. Although the British banking system was built on Quaker family firms, many unthoughtful leftists buy the line that greedy Jews (personified by the Rothschilds) are the masters of global capitalism and so that being anti-capitalist justifies being anti-Jewish. From 2016 on, there was a series of embarrassing incidents of Labour activists expressing rabidly anti-Semitic attitudes on social media. Ken Livingstone, former leader of the Greater London Council, Labour MP, and then Mayor of London, offended by likening an irritating journalist to a concentration camp guard, repeating the slut that Hitler was a Zionist, and refusing to accept that there was anything undiplomatic, let alone immoral, in such similes. In 2017, a member of Labour's ruling National Executive was recorded saying that 'Jewish Trump fanatics' were behind the row.[27] It took the party two years to discipline him. Yet, when Dame Margaret Hodge, who had established herself as a leading parliamentarian skilled at chairing the Public Accounts Committee, criticized Corbyn for failing to act effectively against anti-Semites in the party, she was immediately threatened with disciplinary action. In 2019, the Equality and Human Rights Commission began an investigation into anti-Jewish discrimination in the Labour Party.

To summarize, few of the connections between religion and politics in Britain just described concern religion as such. Very few people seriously made the case that this or that party was especially pleasing to God. Rather, the links derive from such shared social bases as age, gender, ethnicity, and social class. As we will see in the next section, what in the US is often called 'values politics' or 'culture wars' had little impact.

Conservative Christian Parties

In the late 1970s and 1980s, there were a few signs of fringe right-wing Christian political activity, most concerning race and involving the same handful of activists. A good example is Dowager Lady Jane Birdwood. An avowed racist—she famously declared that, if a service provider (such as her electricity company) sent her a black worker, she would turn him away—she was a leading figure in the Anti-Immigration Standing Committee (which became Self-Help) and the World Anti-Communist League. Like the better-known Mary Whitehouse, she regularly demanded the banning of 'filth' from the stage and TV screens. She stood for election to Westminster as a British National Party candidate in Dewsbury in 1992 (where she secured 1.1 per cent of the vote). Two years later she was convicted of distributing anti-Semitic literature.

Insofar as this demi-monde had any popular causes (and 'popular' is nearly ironic), they were racism, anti-Semitism, and anti-communism, and they attracted the support of a few conservative Christians at a time when the British churches were overwhelmingly opposed to such principles and were associated with bodies such as the World Council of Churches, which, in the 1960s, supported Third World liberation movements. So the conservative fringe supported the Portuguese colonial regimes in Angola and Mozambique, the apartheid regime in South Africa, minority white rule in Rhodesia, and military dictatorships in Latin America—all on the grounds that these supposedly Christian regimes were a bulwark against godless communism.

One fringe conservative Christian claim was correct: the officials of the main British denominations were more left wing than most of their members. Hence the paradox of Margaret Thatcher winning elections while the main churches campaigned against her policies.[28] But, while the people in the pews and the people in the pulpit might have divided, with the former leaning to the right while the latter leaned to the left, there was almost no appetite in mainstream Christian circles for Lady Birdwood and her ilk. Over the 1980s, the issues that excited right-wing Christians were resolved, though with no help from them. Portugal relinquished its southern African empire; Rhodesia became Zimbabwe; and the apartheid regime in South Africa negotiated its own disappearance with Nelson Mandela. The Latin American dictatorships were eventually replaced by democratically elected civilian governments. And, outside of North Korea, China and Cuba, godless communism collapsed in the early 1990s.

What replaced those issues were socio-moral concerns such as abortion and gay rights and arguments over the rights and privileges of Islam.

Post-1990 Conservative Christian Political Activity

Post-1990, the British Christian Right worked on a number of fronts. It persuaded right-wing papers to run a stream of stories based on the claim that Christians were being unfairly marginalized by governments intent on placating secular or Muslim interests. Between 2008 and 2013, the *Daily Mail* and the *Mail on Sunday* ran at least forty-five stories quoting the spokeswoman for the tiny Christian Concern, while the *Daily Telegraph* and *Sunday Telegraph* ran at least thirty similar stories. In contrast, the director of the much larger and more influential Evangelical Alliance was mentioned in only fifteen stories in all four titles and the director the Christian NGO Tearfund was cited only twice.[29] It was not just the right-wing press that inflated the fringe conservative Christian lobby. The supposed need to provide balance in coverage meant that those people who opposed popular changes, such as Stephen Green, the CEO of Christian Voice (membership a few hundred), got as much BBC air time as those who spoke for the majority view.

Fringe Christian organizations were active in funding and supporting landmark court cases. In 2013, the European Court of Human Rights passed judgment on four cases concerning the right of Christians to ignore or defy legislation or workplace regulations that they believed offended their Christian principles.[30] Three of the cases—a registrar who refused to record civil partnerships, a nurse who insisted on wearing a crucifix despite her hospital's no jewellery policy, and a Relate (formerly Marriage Guidance) counsellor who refused to counsel gay couples—were lost. The one that was won concerned an airline worker who wore a crucifix in defiance of her employer's dress code.

Little more successful were attempts to mobilize voters. In imitation of its US parent organization, Christian Voice awarded a socio-moral score to each Westminster MP. Despite their ineffectiveness, the Catholic Church in Scotland has long issued pastoral letters of voting guidance. Such campaigns were routinely exaggerated by journalists keen to find anything to enliven otherwise often predictable elections. The *Scottish Daily Express* puffed Scotland for Marriage, which in 2013 published a list of sixteen liberal members of the Scottish parliament with small majorities and asked voters to oust them in 2016: 'MSPs need to pay heed to what we are saying and our supporters will not be frightened to demonstrate their feelings at the next election.'[31] Actually, MSPs needed to pay no heed at all. The 2016 Holyrood election, like the Westminster election the previous year, was dominated by the backwash from the 2014 independence referendum. The Labour Party was again punished for its failure to support independence, and the Conservatives managed to present themselves as the most effective opposition to the Scottish Nationalists and mobilized a large part of the anti-independence vote.

Christian Party Formation

The US Christian Right very successfully used the primary election process to foist its preferred candidates on the Republican Party and to turn out its supporters, who make up in commitment what they lack in numbers. British parties have been impervious to such entrism, and so conservative Christians have been forced into direct electoral intervention.[32]

In 1997, Josephine Quintavalle and her son Bruno founded the Pro-Life Alliance (PLA), which contested 56 seats in that year's general election and attracted an average of 345 votes per constituency contested. Two years later, the PLA contested the first elections to the Scottish Parliament. Scotland had proportionately more Catholics than England, and it was made further attractive by the 'additional member' form of proportional representation used in its election.[33] Voters could split the ticket and choose, say, Labour for their constituency vote and Liberal Democrat for the regional top-up. Parties that had little or no chance of winning a first-part-the-post constituency election (the Greens, for example) could stand only on the regional list and hope to gain one or two representatives from the aggregation of support that otherwise was so thinly spread that no constituency seats would be won. But, instead of going up, the PLA vote went down. It fielded no candidates in three regions with few Catholics. In Lothians it won 0.3 per cent and in Mid-Scotland and Fife 0.2 per cent of the vote. In the three regions with the highest Catholic concentration (Central, West of Scotland, and Glasgow), it scored respectively 0.8, 1.0, and 0.8 per cent of the vote.[34] At the 2001 general election, the PLA fielded thirty-seven candidates, this time averaging only three-quarters of its 1997 votes-per-seat figure. It did not contest the next general election and disbanded in December 2004.

As an aside, it is worth noting that many anti-abortionists opposed direct electoral involvement. Edward Leigh, a former Tory minister, explained: 'This has been tried time and time again. You get a derisory number of votes, 400 to 500, and you hand a weapon to your opponents.'[35] When few of even those who object to abortion will make it the prime reason for their voting preference, using elections to publicize a cause must backfire by showing its relative unpopularity.

A more significant electoral intervention came from two parties that initially presented themselves, not as single-issue movements, but as part of the European tradition of 'full spectrum' Christian Democracy. The Christian People's Alliance (CPA) claimed to embody the principles of active compassion, respect for life, social justice, wise stewardship, empowerment, and reconciliation. It also said: 'The CPA is a party rooted in the historic Christian faith that seeks to demonstrate the love of God through political service. Our faith and principles are drawn from the Bible, especially the life and teaching of Jesus Christ, as well as from Christian political insights through the centuries.'[36] Initially, the CPA had a surprisingly liberal agenda, or, perhaps more accurately, its agenda was so broad and vague that it was difficult to place politically. For example, under the leadership of Ram Gidoomal, an Indian multimillionaire businessman, one of the CPA's main items on its 'build reconciliation and seek justice' agenda was action to regularize the status of refugees and make it easier for them to find work legally.[37]

In May 2002, the CPA fielded sixty-nine candidates in local-government elections (mostly in London) and won one seat in the East London district of Newham. Gidoomal ran for mayor of London twice. In 2000, he gained 2.4 per cent of the vote, coming behind the three main parties but ahead of the Green Party candidate. Four years later, his percentage vote was the same, but he now came behind the United Kingdom Independence Party (UKIP),

Respect (a party led by former Labour MP George Galloway and supported largely by Asian voters), the Greens, and the British National Party (BNP). In between, the CPA had gained two further local council seats in Newham. The CPA also fielded candidates in the Scottish parliamentary elections, where they competed with the Scottish Christian Party (SCP).

This second intervention was the work of George Hargreaves—a black British Londoner who worked as a pop-song writer before becoming a Pentecostal clergyman. Although a founder member of the CPA, Hargreaves left to mount his own election campaigns, initially under the title of Operation Christian Voice (OCV) and later the Christian Party, with its Scottish and Welsh variants (hereafter CP, SCP, and WP respectively). Unlike those of the early CPA, Hargreaves's interventions were based on the most controversial and newsworthy parts of a conservative Christian agenda: abortion, gay rights, and Islam.

In their formal statements, candidates were cautious. One complained that 'minority groups are privileged and preferred before the majority'.[38] Another said:

> some of our cities will become predominantly Muslim in a relatively short time, and they will be naturally seeking political representation for their faith in some form or other, as Islam is more of a political ideology than a faith....Islam will assert its values and expectations...Already, it has been estimated that there are some 90+ Sharia courts operating in the UK, in a parallel legal system, which has been given the force of law by the UK government, where it does not contravene parliamentary laws....this will eventually open the door to a fuller implementation of Sharia laws in the UK, by Sharia courts, possibly leading to punitive justice (a somewhat worrying prospect!).

In less-guarded moments, the xenophobia was more pungently expressed. At a Vale of Glamorgan meeting during the 2010 general election, the CP candidate said: 'I have heard that there are more white British people leaving this country to live elsewhere and more people coming in who do not actually want to integrate themselves—especially the Pakistani community. Shouldn't these people just go home?'[39]

Opposition to gay rights was adopted in a particularly opportunistic manner for the Scottish elections of 2007. In 2000, the Scottish Parliament moved to repeal Conservative legislation that had made it an offence to promote homosexuality as an acceptable lifestyle in schools. Wealthy businessman and conservative Christian Brian Soutar funded a pressure group 'Keep the

Clause' (a reference to a section of the Local Government Act of 1988), and there was much heated talk about targeting MSPs, but it came to nothing. Four years later, gay rights again became an issue when a bed-and-breakfast provider in Wester Ross refused a booking from two gay men and provoked a long-running debate in the media over the government's equality agenda. Seeing the opportunity for a great deal of press coverage, Hargreaves stood in the Glasgow region so that he could confront Patrick Harvie, the openly bisexual leader of the Green Party in Scotland.

Many candidates preferred old-fashioned evangelism to electioneering. In Clwyd West, one said: 'In my speech after the count I appealed to the heart of all parties that this election was not about politicians, not about parties but about our nation, a nation that had turned away from Jesus Christ. It was about HIS LORDSHIP.' Another told the people of Bolton South East: 'It is time for the people to turn to the Great Healer Jesus. It is time for us to wake up and realise that with Jesus there is a hope and a future and there is real healing.' The candidate for Maidstone and the Weald gushed: 'My name is Heidi, I'm 23 years young, and I love God with all my heart. He really is my Everything.'

In the 2010 UK general election, the CPA/CP alliance took 0.1 per cent of the vote; its 71 candidates averaging 262 votes. And it lost its only elected representatives in England. As part of a concerted response to the BNP, Labour made strenuous efforts to mobilize its London vote and succeeded to the extent that, in the local elections that accompanied the general election, the CPA lost its council seats in Newham.

With a larger churchgoing population, the two-votes system of proportional representation, and a weak Conservative Party, Scotland offered Christians as fertile an environment as they were going to find, but the CP and CPA failed to make anything of it: the total CP/CPA vote in 2011 was less than half of its 2007 level. A small part of the decline might be explained by demography: older voters were more likely than the young both to be Christian and to support conservative moral positions, and some of them would have died between the two elections. But that still would have left many who once voted Christian but did not repeat the experience.

Paper Money and Paper Candidates

What became apparent in the 2015 elections is that the CP and CPA had been a baseless hype: the social-movement equivalent of 'build it and they will come'. Only they did not. There were a very small number of highly ambitious activists and a very large amount of cash donated by four financiers. There was no popular movement.

The Electoral Commission's reports of party funding show the following pattern of growth and then decline. From 2002 to 2005, the CPA averaged donations of around £8,000 per annum. From 2006 to 2010, donations averaged around £18,000—most of this coming from the Newham councillors donating their office expenses to the party. In 2010, the CPA was given £190,000. The two main donors were William Richards, a hedge-fund manager, and Frank Timis, a Romanian-born entrepreneur with a colourful history and interests in mining.[40] After the loss of all deposits in 2010, donations slumped, with the Newham councillors losing their seats and expenses and wealthy backers declining to fund further failure.

The Christian Party finance record is similar: very little, a lot, and then nothing. The first donations recorded by the Electoral Commission were in 2004: a sum of £10,000 from Hargreaves (which may well have been a collection of smaller donations). There is no record for 2005, while 2006 records only £12,000 from a clergyman and his wife. The figure for 2007 was £171,000. There is a blank for 2008. The figure for 2009 was £426,000 and for 2010 £160,000. As with the CPA, that boost came from a small number of very wealthy financiers. Richards and Timis, who were also funding the CPA, gave £360,000 and £100,000 respectively. Chris Siepman gave £55,000. Crispin Odey gave the CP £25,000 in 2009. After the 2010 election losses, donations dried up.

The unpopularity of Christian politics is clear from the difficulty the CPA and CP had in recruiting candidates. At least half of those who stood in elections in 2008, 2009, and 2010 did not campaign or even bother to fill in the online forms helpfully provided by local newspapers. Very many had no connection with the areas in which they stood. Candidates were not only scarce; they were also unusual. A disproportionate number were either clergy (usually West African Pentecostalists) or lay people active in church-related work. The parties were also regionally unrepresentative. In 2015, two-thirds of seats contested by the CP were in London. A further four were in constituencies close to London (two in Essex, one in Kent, and one in Surrey). Nothing is known of the candidate for Suffolk South, but the Cambridgeshire candidate worked in central London. Some London concentration is to be expected when the capital is around 18 per cent of the total population of England, but this is a notably short reach, and the only two English contests not connected to London were in Dewsbury in West Yorkshire and

Birmingham Edgbaston in the West Midlands. Both constituencies had very large Muslim populations.

One sign that the CP and CPA had all but given up by 2015 is that neither party produced a manifesto: they had learnt that there was no point gifting their critics a contentious agenda when they had no chance of power. Instead they issued a 'Declaration of British Values', which had four principles: Christian Conscience (or we claim religious exemptions from laws we do not like); British Constitutional Law (we do not like the European Union's liberalism); Traditional Marriage (we do not like gays); and Sanctity of Life (we oppose abortion).

The CP fielded only two candidates in Scotland in 2015, and they stood in the seats with the highest proportion of churchgoing Protestants: the Western Isles, and Inverness, Lochaber, and Strathspey. It took 6.6 per cent of the Western Isles vote and 0.7 per cent of the Inverness etc. vote. Neither candidate made much of the party's agenda. When the Western Isles candidates were given an opportunity to say their piece by the *Stornoway Gazette*, the CP's John Cormack spent most of his word limit on energy policy and the unfair price of electricity. Only at the very end did he add: 'The Christian faith is about making people's lives better and I shall work extremely hard to do just that.'[41] In Wales, the focus was on gay rights. The party leader in Wales was a bed-and-breakfast provider who strongly objected to the requirement to provide his services to all applicants irrespective of marital status or sexual orientation and who had advertised for married couples only.[42]

Rats leaving may signal that a ship is in danger; the captain deserting is a sure sign of doom. In the aftermath of the poor 2010 results, both George Hargreaves and Alan Craig sought a new home where they could advance the most popular parts of their agenda—dislike for foreigners, Muslims, and homosexuals—without the unpopular religious baggage: they joined UKIP and tried to be selected to contest seats for the 2015 general election. In Coventry North the local candidate was told to stand down to make way for Hargreaves, but local dissension (the UKIP candidate for a neighbouring seat tweeted that Hargreaves was 'bonkers') led to the decision being reversed. Alan Craig was inserted in place of the existing candidate for Brent North and then withdrawn when his views on homosexuality (apparently it could be cured by the Christian gospel) were publicized. In shifting from religious to secular politics, Hargreaves and Craig were following the route taken by at least one of their four main funders: by 2014, Crispin Odey was a UKIP donor.

Christian Party Failure

It is not difficult to explain the failure of fringe Christian electioneering. The power of parties in British politics has already been mentioned. Although local branches select their candidates, they are centrally vetted, and in many circumstances (such as a seat becoming vacant shortly before an election) party officials may impose their preferred candidate. Westminster's governing party is both administrator and main instigator of legislation. Both it and the largest opposition party control a large number of well-paid positions as ministers or opposition spokespersons. Hence British parties enjoy considerable power to select and control elected representatives and to manage the political agenda. This is recognized by the electorate, which generally votes for a party, not for individuals. In such a system any pressure group has little chance of infiltrating a major party, and those with an unpopular agenda have even less chance of influencing one. Hence fringe conservative Christians form their own parties. But their record of recruiting candidates and of garnering votes shows that their previous lack of influence was not, as they hoped, a consequence of a political structure that was stacked against them; rather it was an accurate reflection of the general unpopularity of their agenda.

There are two obvious causes of that unpopularity. First, Britain has far fewer Christians of any political persuasion than does the US, and, of those, evangelical and fundamentalist Protestant form a much smaller part. The mainstream Church of England, Church of Scotland, and Catholic Church together account for 80 per cent of British Christians, and, on a generous estimate, they would be only 10 per cent of the electorate.[43]

But there is a further difference. Even the charismatic and independent evangelical churches in Britain, which are theologically and structurally the closest approximation of fundamentalist churches in the US, are not generally and particularly right wing.[44] Indeed, the financial crisis of 2008 and the subsequent climate of austerity caused many charismatic and evangelical congregations to support the poor through food banks, soup kitchens, and debt-counselling services. One might describe this as an individualistic (and hence 'right-wing') response to structural problems, but it is nonetheless engagement with the problems of the poor rather than a disdainful (or even condemnatory) indifference to such problems.[45]

Furthermore, detailed surveys suggest that British Christians have become accustomed to their political impotence and hence do not share the US

Christian Right's vision of regaining cultural domination. Most are hardly more keen on religious leaders enjoying more public influence than are non-religious Britons. That may, of course, be because the circumstance imagined by a respondent who is asked if religion should have greater public prominence is now not a bishop supporting world peace but Muslims demanding exemptions from British laws and social norms. But, whatever its source, the absence among British Christians of any great ambition for power is obvious.

The Secularization of Politics

If specifically religious political interventions have been a bust, what of general religious orientations? Table 10.1 shows party voting patterns for the UK Westminster elections of 2015 arrayed by nominal religious identity (which is, of course, very different from religious commitment).[46]

Traces of the late-twentieth-century links are still visible. Church of England identifiers are more likely to vote Tory than Labour. Other Protestants (the Welsh chapels, Scottish Presbyterians, English Nonconformists), Catholics, and Muslims—the largest presence in the 'Other religion' column—tend to vote to the left. However, the differences are not great. Nearly 40 per cent of Anglicans were Conservative, but an almost equal number supported Labour and the Liberal Democrats. Most interesting is the religious spread of UKIP support. The leaders of both the CP and CPA joined UKIP, but its politics were not widely shared by the constituency that provided most of their election candidates. Pentecostalists, charismatics, and independent evangelicals

Table 10.1. Party voting and religion, UK, Westminster Elections, 2015 (%)

Party	Anglican	Catholic	Other Christian	Other religion	No religion
Conservative	39.3	27.6	26.2	19.5	23.0
Labour	30.8	40.2	29.4	33.9	28.4
Liberal Democrat	7.8	6.4	11.5	9.7	10.3
UKIP	4.8	3.9	3.5	3.6	3.6
Other	1.3	5.9	11.5	7.5	7.9
None	12.4	12.0	14.6	18.5	21.8
Don't know	3.5	4.0	3.4	7.3	4.9
Total	99.9	100.0	100.1	100.0	99.9

Note: Percentage totals are not always 100 because of rounding.

Source: Clements, 'Religion and Political Attitudes'.

would be coded as 'Other Christian'. UKIP support from that category was much the same as from people with no religious identification, and it was less than that from nominal Anglicans. That suggests that UKIP's xenophobia appeals more to people who identify as Church of England as a heritage category than it does to people who are committed, informed Anglicans.[47] A women who was briefly an official in Nigel Farage's Brexit Party inadvertently exemplified the point. She tweeted: 'I want my country back. I want seaside donkeys on the beach and little village churches, not acid attacks, mobs and mosques.'[48] Churches versus mosques is, like seaside donkeys versus acid attacks, an expression of national rather than religious identity. Such people cite a Church of England identity, not because they are personally religious, but because the presence of Muslims is a convenient shorthand for many features of the modern world they dislike and because Christian practice was much more common in the past they would like to re-create than it is now.

Conclusion

For most of the twentieth century, British religion was politically anomalous. It benefited from inertia in being given a degree of respect that reflected its nineteenth-century popularity. Despite most pupils not being at all religiously observant, the Catholic Church and the Church of England are still funded by the taxpayer to run schools, and recent governments have extended that privilege to other faith groups. Despite the paucity of followers, religious officials are still routinely invited by governments and by the mass media to opine on socio-moral questions. Religion remains one of the best grounds for claiming exemption from standards imposed generally. On the other hand, on every argument where they have taken distinctive positions—the sanctity of the sabbath, the use and availability of beverage alcohol, gambling, divorce, abortion, the status of women, and gay rights—the churches have been comprehensively defeated. In 2012, Catholic Archbishop Vincent Nichols threatened the Conservative Party with a significant loss of support if it backed gay marriage. The following year more than 1,000 Catholic priests signed a letter opposing gay marriage.[49] Westminster legislated for same-sex marriage for England and Wales in July 2013; six months later the Scottish parliament did likewise.

Ironically, it took the interventions of British Muslims (detailed in Chapter 7) to align the status of religion with its current unpopularity. The example of blasphemy can represent many other contests. The criminal offence of insulting

Christianity stayed on the statute books long after the state gave up prosecuting it because an administrative instruction neutered an unpopular position without the fuss of arguing against the churches. The last Scottish conviction for blasphemy was in 1843. There were only a handful of prosecutions in England after that date, and the last one was in 1921. Mary Whitehouse mounted a private case against *Gay News* in 1977 because the state refused to prosecute. Then Muslims demanded that Islam be given similar protection. The government dragged its feet but eventually levelled the playing field in the other direction by repealing the blasphemy laws and leaving all religions equally unprotected.

So long as the religious consensus that was given undue influence was what their grandparents took for granted, most British people seemed content to leave well alone. When a faith from outside the Christian consensus drew attention to the residual privileges of the country's once-dominant religion, the only viable resolution was to bring laws and norms into line with contemporary religious indifference. This can be seen very clearly in the 2010 Equality Act, which, while it made religious identity one of the stated characteristics given especial protection (along with gender, sexual orientation, age, disability, race, and ethnicity), also severely constrained the circumstances in which religious exemptions could be claimed.

Some conservative British Christians are fond of complaining that they have been marginalized by aggressive secularists. This is nonsense. Far from driving God out of the public square, the non-religious majority of British people have, until the twenty-first century, been remarkably tolerant in allowing Christians a voice and a respect quite out of proportion to their numbers. What has marginalized religion is its unpopularity. The causes of secularization are complex, but, if one is looking for a proximate lever, it is not to be found in the campaigns of rationalists and secularists; it lies in the failure of religious parents to pass on their faith to their children in sufficient numbers to replace the saints as they die. The churches have become politically impotent because they have become numerically insignificant.

Notes

1. The material in this chapter is presented at greater length in S. Bruce, *Politics and Religion in the United Kingdom* (London: Routledge, 2012).
2. The case is complex, and the most plausible connections between the Reformation and the rise of democracy were long run and inadvertent; see Bruce, *Politics and Religion*, Chs 4 and 5.

3. S. Bruce, *A House Divided: Protestantism, Schism and Secularization* (London: Routledge, 1990).

4. *Private Eye*, 1456, 3–16 November 2017.

5. For a good summary of such links, see R. W. Smith, 'Religious Influences in the Background of the British Labour Party', *Southwestern Social Science Quarterly*, 37 (1957), 355–69, and R. F. Wearmouth, *Methodism and the Trade Unions* (London: Epworth Press, 1959).

6. J. Langdon, 'Obituary: Lord Davies of Coity', *Guardian*, 23 March 2019.

7. J. H. Whyte, *Catholics in Western Democracies: A Study in Political Behaviour* (Dublin: Gill and Macmillan, 1981).

8. Wikipedia, *Constitution of Ireland (Original Text)*, https://en.wikisource.org/wiki/Constitution_of_Ireland_(original_text) (accessed January 2019).

9. K. Malik, *From Fatwa to Jihad: The Rushdie Affair and its Aftermath* (London: Granta Books, 2009), 69.

10. N. Britten and G. Jones, 'Judge Lambasts Postal Ballot Rules as Labour 6 Convicted of Poll Fraud', *Daily Telegraph*, 5 April 2005.

11. D. Kennedy, 'Six Jailed for Postal Vote Fraud over Rigged Election in Slough', *The Times*, 2 May 2009.

12. *The Week*, 1 May 2015.

13. Malik, *From Fatwa to Jihad*, 59–61.

14. Malik, *From Fatwa to Jihad*, 70.

15. A. Sen, 'The Uses and Abuses of Multiculturalism', *New Republic*, 2 July 2006.

16. On the Prevent strategy, see S. Warsi, *The Enemy within: A Tale of Muslim Britain* (London: Allen Lane, 2017); K. Nabulsi. 'Don't Go to the Doctor', *London Review of Books*, 39 (2017), 27–8; P. Thomas, 'Failed and Friendless: The UK's "Preventing Violent Extremism" Programme', *British Journal of Politics and International Relations*, 12 (2010), 442–58.

17. Pew Global Attitudes Project, *The Great Divide: How Westerners and Muslims View Each Other* (Washington: Pew Forum, 2006), 3. British Muslim alienation was not an effect of political marginality; relative to population, there were far more Muslim elected representatives in the UK than in France and Germany; see E. Tatari, 'Muslim Councillors on the Rise in London', *Muslim News*, 25 June 2010.

18. B. Clements, 'Religion and Ethnic Minority Attitudes in Britain toward the War in Afghanistan', *Politics and Religion*, 6 (2013), 25–49.

19. On Muslim anti-Semitism, see R. Koopmans, 'Religious Fundamentalism and Hostility against Out-Groups: A Comparison of Muslims and Christians In Western Europe', *Journal of Ethnic and Migration Studies*, 41 (2015), 33–57.

20. For general histories of British Jewry, see V. D. Lipman, *A History of the Jews in Britain since 1958* (Leicester: Leicester University Press, 1990), and S. Brook, *The Club: The Jews of Modern Britain* (London: Constable, 1989).

21. O. F. Snelling, 'The Disagreeable Dornford Yates', *Wesley Britton's Spywise.net*, http://www.spywise.net/dornfordYates.html (accessed October 2018). With far less justification, John Buchan's work is often described as anti-Semitic, but he was Zionist enough to be listed in the Golden Book of the Jewish National Fund; see G. Himmelfarb, *Victorian Minds* (New York: Knopf, 1968).

22. N. Kokosolakis, *Religion, Identity and Community* (Liverpool: University of Liverpool Sociology Department Paper, 1976), 7.
23. R. Butt, 'British Jewish Population on the Rise', *Guardian*, 21 May 2008.
24. *Independent*, 16 June 2005.
25. T. Harper and B. Leapman, 'Jews Are More Likely to Be Victims of Faith Hatred than Muslims', *Observer*, 17 December 2006; 'The History of Jews in Britain', *The Week*, 28 February 2015.
26. A. Judd, 'The Paper on Sale in London that Wants All Jews Killed', *Guardian*, 9 May 2002.
27. H. Zeffwan, 'Corbyn Has Led Labour into a Mess of his own Making, *The Times*, 4 August 2018.
28. H. Clark, *The Church Under Thatcher*. London: SPCK, 1993.
29. A. Walton, A. Hatcher and N. Spencer. *Is There a 'Religious Right' Emerging in Britain?* London: Theos, 2013, 54–5.
30. J. Taylor, 'A Loss for the Christian Lobby: The ECHR Ruling Reinforces the Crucial Point that Religious Rights Don't Automatically Trump the Rights of Others', *Independent*, 15 January 2013.
31. P. Gilbride, 'Plot to Oust MSPs who Support Gay Marriage', *Scottish Daily Express*, 17 December 2013.
32. In the 1980s, Militant Tendency had some success in taking control of a few local councils, but it was effectively crushed by the Labour leadership.
33. The seventy-three single-member constituencies are grouped into eight regions. Each voter has two votes: one for a candidate in the first-past-the-post constituency part of the election and the other for a party from the regional list. After the constituency elections have been completed, the regional party vote is counted and additional seats allocated so as to compensate parties that have polled well across the pooled constituencies but failed to win an appropriate proportion of seats.
34. Scottish Parliament. *Election Results 1999*, http://www.parliament.scot/msps/19172.aspx (accessed January 2016).
35. M. White, 'New Row over "Evil" Abortion', *Guardian*, 30 December 1996.
36. Christian People's Alliance, *Manifesto* (London: Christian People's Alliance, 2001).
37. Christian People's Alliance, *Mayflower Declaration* (London: Christian People's Alliance, 2002), http://www.cpaparty.org.uk/resources/Mayflowerbooklet.pdf (accessed November 2009).
38. This and subsequent quotations come from CP and CPA candidate profiles on websites that died when the parties folded. The reader will have to trust I have reproduced them accurately.
39. *Guardian*, 27 April 2010.
40. C. Blackhurst, 'Ex-Regal Boss Frank Timis Set for Another Rich Seam', *London Evening Standard*, 13 January 2010.
41. *Stornoway Gazette*, 9 April 2015.
42. A. Wightwick, 'Head of Christian Party UK Plans to Stand as Parliamentary Prospective Candidate in Cardiff North', http/walesonline.co.uk/wales-news/general-election-2015-head-Christian-8945895 (accessed May 2015).

43. P. Brierley, *UK Church Statistics 2005–2015* (Tonbridge, Kent: ABCD Publishers, 2011), table 1.

44. For an evangelical critique of the CP and CPA, see 'Why I'm not Voting for the Christian Party', *Ekklesia*, http://www.ekklesia.co.uk/node/12072 (accessed May 2012).

45. A small but significant theological observation: UK conservative Christians are far less likely than their US counterparts to accept the 'dispensationalist millennialism' of the Scofield Bible (which divides world history into epochs controlled by a particular God-given dispensation and predicts the fairly imminent end of the world).

46. B. Clements, 'Religion and Political Attitudes: The British Election Study 2015', *British Religion in Numbers*, http://www.brin.ac.uk/news/2015/religion-and-political-attitudes-the-British-election-study-2015-wave-4/ (accessed May 2015). See also his *Religion and Public Opinion in Britain: Continuity and Change* (London: Palgrave Macmillan, 2015).

47. Smith and Woodhead note an association between nominal Anglican identity and support for Brexit in 2016, but they also note that evangelical Christians were more likely to be pro-EU; G. Smith and L. Woodhead, 'Religion and Brexit: Populism and the Church of England', *Religion, State and Society*, 46 (2018), 206–33. The analysis of the 2018 BSA data that David Voas kindly performed for me shows very clearly that the religion–populism link is weak (in that much of both are explained by age) and that, while non-churchgoing Anglicans had voted 30% remain and 51% leave, churchgoers had voted 43% remain and 41% leave.

48. P. Walker, 'Leader of Nigel Farage's Party Resigns over Anti-Islam Messages', *Guardian*, 20 March 2019.

49. A. Bond, 'Gay Marriage RC Rejection', *Daily Mail*, 12 January 2013.

11

Can the Decline be Reversed?

Previous chapters have amply justified the assertion made at the book's start: Christianity was once powerful, persuasive, and popular and now it is none of those things. Identifying with a religion, active involvement in religious institutions, assent to supernatural beliefs, use of religious offices for rites of passage such as weddings and funerals—all measures of religious sentiment show a similar decline trend over the twentieth century.[1] What at first sight seemed like counter-trends (the charismatic movement, for example) turned out to represent, not net growth, but churning within the shrinking body of Christians. Irish, West Indian, Asian, West African, and Polish migrants added numbers but came nowhere near compensating for mainstream losses. The 'New Age' cultic milieu, in which human potential psychology and physical therapies mix with idiosyncratic notions of supernatural power and snake-oil medicine, has expanded a little, but even enthusiasts for the movement find less than 2 per cent of the population involved.[2] Furthermore, what remains of Britain's Christianity has seen a significant shift in a secular direction: increasingly concerned, not with pleasing God, but with therapeutic improvement in the lives of believers, who have become more assertive in deciding what they will believe and how much they will commit. And, as the New Age has imported spiritual insights and practices from the Orient, it has 'westernized' them so that Buddhism becomes mindfulness and Hinduism becomes yoga and meditation. The migration of Hindus, Buddhists, Sikhs, and Muslims from traditionally religious countries has offset only a fraction of the Christian decline, and those faiths have attracted very few native converts. Their main effects have been to give some xenophobes reason to claim a nominal religious identity and the rest of the population reason to question their previous toleration of religion in general.

Whenever I present data on the secularization of Britain, at least one person in the audience will assert that there is no reason to assume that current trends will continue: there may well be a religious revival. It is true that we are often surprised by social change. In the 1960s, the communist bloc in Eastern Europe seemed as solid as its favoured concrete bunker architectural style. Yet, barely twenty years after the tanks of the Warsaw Pact crushed the 1968

Prague Spring, communism, like an elderly budgie, coughed twice and fell over dead. The unexpected is always possible.

But that does not mean it is likely. One riposte to the 'things always change' rebuttal of the secularization thesis is the longevity and universality of the decline trend. Churchgoing in the UK peaked in the middle of the nineteenth century, church membership around the start of the twentieth century, and the best efforts of church officials and activists to reverse those trends have patently failed. So the decline trend is no small thing.[3] Nor is it confined to just a few religious organizations or to a few countries. Although the date when decline begins varies, secularization is common to all industrial liberal democracies, including the US.[4]

My second riposte is that admitting that the future need not continue the past does not justify expecting any particular alternative. Most believers naturally hope for positive divine intervention, but they must allow the possibility that God may punish us further. He may send, not showers of reviving rain, but another great flood.

However, there is one good reason for considering the possibility of religious revival: by identifying likely constraints, we can clarify the present and recap the past. This chapter will consider the social requirements for revival and current obstacles to it. In brief, I will argue that features of our current situation—a combination of a formally secular society and an active-involvement-in-organized-religion rate of less than 10 per cent—make revival markedly less likely in the future than at any time since the nineteenth century.

Declining Stock of Religious Knowledge

The reversal of secularization is made difficult by ignorance. Few people under 60 (that is, those who were not taught its basic ideas at school or Sunday school) have any knowledge of Christianity or indeed of such foundational aspects of religion as 'worshipping God' and 'forgiveness of sins'. The absence of religious knowledge is no small matter. The people of the Hebrides were not genetically programmed to speak Gaelic. They learned it in their homes, from their parents and friends and neighbours. As we see in the fate of Cornish, when the stock of knowledge becomes seriously depleted, the language dies.

Those who see the green shoots of religious revival often rest their case on the notion that, unlike other elements of culture, religion does rest on biology: the human condition causes us all to need or desire religion. We can readily rebut that idea by noting that many parts of the UK and Europe have been secular for at least two generations. If so many people can get by with little or no religion (think 'Denmark'), then being religious is clearly not a fixed part of the human constitution.

But, even if there is something about being human (such as our ability imaginatively to separate body and person or to anticipate and fear death) that encourages us to ask the sorts of questions traditionally answered by religion, the absence of shared religious knowledge is still crucial because, without a common culture to shape the answers, people are unlikely to agree, and agreement is essential to building the momentum that will draw others into the movement. As the fragmentation of Protestantism after the Reformation shows, consensus is not automatic.

State Neutrality and the Loss of Ambient Religion

Furthermore, such consensus must now arise without a key feature of previous major religious changes: the active support of the ruling class or the state. Most religions first spread by force. The elite converts and imposes its new faith on the populace. Schools, colleges, mass media, and every other social institution, both directly and implicitly, support the dominant religion and provide the backcloth against which shared ideas are reinforced by frequent interaction.

As previous chapters have shown, the British government is no longer in the business of supporting any particular faith and that severely reduces the amount of ambient religion. Girl Guides used to pledge to 'love my God, to serve my Queen and my country'; now they 'promise that I will do my best; to be true to myself and develop my beliefs'.[5] That change may seem trivial, especially when we recognize that many who swore the theistic version were not particularly loyal to deity, monarch, or nation. But such secularization has been repeated across every institution, voluntary association, and social gathering. Church work and religiously inspired philanthropy have been replaced by secular institutions in the provision of basic welfare. The vast majority of state schools no longer promote any religion. Few public meetings now open or close with prayer.

Add here an important consequence of science and technology. Our ever-increasing ability to understand and manipulate the material world need not make us atheists. Like many early scientists, we could become more impressed by divine creation as we better understood it. But what matters for most people is not knowledge but usage and familiarity. Whether farmers understood its chemistry, an effective cure for fly-strike in sheep removed one occasion on which they resorted to prayer and holy water. Ditto plague. Ditto many illnesses. Religious problem-solving has been displaced by better secular solutions. Those who wished to retain some spiritual component could have praised the Lord for effective sheep dip, but, because that was patently unnecessary, such embellishment became ever less common.

Religion in the West has not been marginalized by malevolent secularists; it has been sidelined by its redundancy: it no longer provides the only or the best solution to most of our day-to-day problems. Nor, I might add, does it offer plausible solutions to the problems (such as environmental depletion) caused by technology. No amount of prayer or fasting will reduce global warming, and, to their credit, very few religious organizations suggest otherwise.

The Public Reputation of Religion

An important consideration for the likelihood of mass conversion is the public standing of religion. Because the elements of reputation are extremely complicated, this is not easy to demonstrate, but the following seems to depict reasonably accurately the attitudes of the British to religion. Many of the 1950s area studies discussed in previous chapters mention anticlericalism. It was common for people to claim that priests and pastors were self-interested busybodies and hypocrites. The clergy's gradual loss of wealth and status, and most people's loss of contact with the clergy, blunted resentment, and by the end of the twentieth century most Britons regarded religion benignly. Most of us did not have any religion, but religion in the abstract was probably a good thing because it promoted morality and was a consolation to people in troubled times.

Such general approval can be seen in the way that religion was accepted as reason for exempting people from general obligations. For example, 'conscientious objectors' were often allowed to substitute other good works (such as ambulance-driving) for military service. British political parties, which expect members of parliament to vote the party line, have long allowed free votes on topics with a clear religious component. In Northern Ireland in the 1970s, terrorist organizations demanded the enduring loyalty of members. But even the thuggish enforcers of the Ulster Volunteer Force and the Ulster Defence Association permitted prisoners to leave the segregated wings of the prisons to serve their time with the common lags if they 'got God'.[6]

A marked change in attitude has been clear since the start of this century. A man who organized 'faith literacy' sessions with government workers asked his classes to write down three words they associated with Christianity: the most common ones were 'homophobic', 'misogynist', 'Bible basher', 'bigot', and 'intolerant'.[7] Such negative responses are amply confirmed by opinion polls. A 2007 survey offered respondents the description of religion as generally beneficial or generally harmful; 17 per cent chose the former while 42 per cent chose the latter.[8] A similar question a decade later showed that twice as many Britons felt the world has been damaged by religion as said it has benefited from it: 'Respondents were shown a list of eight social, cultural, and economic trends and asked to rate their impact on a scale running from minus 100 (denoting severe damage) to plus 100 (great benefit), religion receiving the lowest mean score of all (even worse than immigration).'[9]

Chapter 7 introduced the 'feelings towards' temperature question used in recent surveys. A 2008 version added the 'deeply religious' and the 'non-religious' to the standard list of religions and found that the deeply religious were the second least popular group.[10] Because the survey also asked about the respondent's religious beliefs and activities, we can be precise about who did not like whom. Committed believers liked the deeply religious, scoring them at 57 (out of 100). Committed unbelievers disliked them: they scored them at 41. The key observation concerns the middling mass of the population: they also disliked the deeply religious and scored them at a below-par 46. Recurrent surveys of the confidence that people express in various social institutions show the same change: between 1981 and 2008, the proportion of Britons having confidence in the churches fell by 14 per cent while the proportion who were critical grew by 10 per cent.[11] Faith schools are now deeply unpopular—disliked by two-thirds of survey respondents.[12]

A more subtle sign of the general disdain for religion is the way it is now judged by secular principles. As noted in Chapter 10, the churches lost the power to dominate society in the first half of the twentieth century. In the last quarter, they also lost many of their previous exemptions from general norms. Outsiders now regard gender equality, for example, as more important than theological propriety and so find it ridiculous that the Church of England refused to ordain women and, when it did ordain them, spent a decade arguing over how high they could be promoted. The lack of sympathy for religion now goes so far to challenge the right of religious organizations and officials to define, maintain, and promote their ideological interests. One of the consequences of growing ignorance of religion is that Christianity (indeed all religion) is reduced to a parody of the Golden Rule. Christianity is about being nice. People who are not nice are not real Christians. Self-interest is not nice. What could be seen as a proper wish to safeguard and promote sincerely held beliefs is instead read as mean-spirited sectarianism. Clergy who point out that the flummery that now surrounds Christ's birth is unbiblical are attacked for ruining Christmas. When the Catholic Church defends faith schools on the grounds that it should teach Catholic beliefs to the children of Catholics, it is criticized for being self-interested. When the Calvinistic Free Presbyterian Church expelled a member for attending a Catholic requiem mass, it was accused of bigotry. In these cases, religious people were not condemned for having the wrong religion. They were condemned by the religiously indifferent for misunderstanding the proper nature of religion, which is to be tolerant, inclusive, generous, and kind.

One obvious threat to the public reputation of religion is its contemporary association with violence and terrorism. We need not argue about exactly what role faith plays in conflicts around the world to appreciate that, for those with no interest in becoming well-educated in foreign politics or the causes of terrorism, the general impression of war in Syria, Yemen, Iraq, and Afghanistan, of European hostility towards migrants, and of jihadi hostility to Europe, is that religion taken too seriously is dangerous.[13]

When it is not a threat to life, it is a nuisance. As noted in Chapter 7, many British Muslims want to maintain a distinctive sub-society to support their culture: an implicit and an explicit challenge to the mores of the majority. The implicit challenge is the disdain for liberal values. The explicit challenge is a demand for exemptions. Ritual animal slaughter, face coverings, unusual work schedules, the right to ignore equality legislation; with good will on all sides, many minority preferences can to a degree be accommodated. The problem is that there is sufficient ill will to create the impression that very small religious minorities want everyone else to change to suit them.

Those small minorities include conservative Christians. The Muslim taxi-driver who refused to take a passenger carrying alcohol has his parallel in the Christian who refused to drive his bus because it had an advert for atheism on its side.[14] Conservative Christians complain that successive governments have bent over backwards to accommodate British Muslims while ignoring the much larger Christian interest. As a letter from six Anglican bishops put it: 'We are deeply concerned at the apparent discrimination shown against Christians and we call on the government to remedy this.... Christian beliefs on marriage, conscience and worship are simply not being upheld.'[15] Quite what 'upheld' means in this context is obscure, but I suspect they mean that their preferences are no longer accorded social honour. The Dean of

Westminster preposterously claimed that 'Christians are being forced to pray in secret for fear of offending others'.[16] He was responding to a nurse being disciplined for offering to pray for a patient.[17] We may reasonably guess his position would have been different if the nurse had been a Scientologist rather than a Christian.

The game of competitive victimhood is hardly attractive, but the standing of the churches has been further damaged by two topics that have dominated new stories about British churches in the twenty-first century: equality legislation and sexual abuse.

The Church of England's difficulties with women clergy have been mentioned. We can add to that its opposition to gay rights. As with gender, the churches have gradually changed, but always behind public attitudes and bitterly contesting every metre. While the current Anglican position on gay clergy (they can live together but not have sex) may make sense to Christians, to most people it looks hypocritical or mean. I make special mention of these two themes because for young people (who will have to be converted for a religious revival) gender equality is taken for granted and homosexuals are unremarkable.

The charge of hypocrisy is encouraged by the sex scandals that have engulfed the Catholic and Anglican churches. We now know that very many priests have sexually abused young and vulnerable people and that church officials have engaged in a systematic cover-up. Christians can see such crimes as proof that we are all sinners and we all need to be saved, but, to the religiously indifferent majority, sex abuse destroys any claim to moral superiority. Why take lessons from the Catholic Church when Cardinal Keith O'Brien (who repeatedly opposed every advance in gay rights) sexually abused young priests whom he was training? A 2018 survey asked a sample of Scots (divided by stated religious identity) if the sex scandals had made them more or less likely to attend church. For each group the most common response was that they made no difference, but almost no one said they were more likely to attend, and 25 per cent of Church of Scotland, 33 per cent of Catholics, and 16 per cent of 'Other Christians' said they were less likely to go to church.[18]

To appreciate the impact of specific points of conflict, we need to go back to the lack of religious knowledge. Religious people distinguish between good and bad religion. Theirs is good; that of others is bad. But the religiously indifferent do not make such distinctions. Instead they divide 'odd and demanding' from 'normal and nice'. When, as described in Chapter 4, a quality daily newspaper confuses distinctive Catholic and Protestant beliefs in a story about the marriage of the grandson of the Queen, who is the titular head of the state—and Protestant—Church of England, we are well past a popular understanding of religious differences. Hence opprobrium attached to one faith gets generalized. To put it starkly, in a largely secular society, trouble created by people claiming religious justification is blamed, not just on their specific religion, but also on religion in general.

Social Influence in Religious Conversion

In the nineteenth century, when the core of committed Christians probably contained about 20 per cent of the population, it was surrounded by a much larger penumbra of people who had experienced some religious socialization, were vaguely familiar with Christian culture, and were periodically involved in religious rituals. Now we have a core of less than 10 per cent, a very thin layer of the occasionally involved, and, among the rest, ever-firmer hostility to religion.[19] Any revival now will require people to change a great deal. So we can now move on to what is known about religious conversion.[20]

Conversion is rare in modern liberal democracies. Surveys that ask about people's current religious affiliation and about their childhood upbringing suggest that, over the twentieth century, only some 5 per cent of adults who say they were raised with no religion later acquired one.[21]

When it does occur, conversion owes much to positive links between believer and convert. Even when the expected change in behaviour involves an entirely technical matter that can be rationally assessed, personal influence is a major force in the spread of innovation.[22] Many farmers were initially sceptical about the superiority of new varieties of seed corn when presented with the innovation by academics or seed-company reps; they looked to people they knew and trusted for a lead. Once people of influence in the local farming community adopted the new varieties, the rest fell into line behind them.

Positive social bonds are even more important in religious conversion, because the demeanour and character of the person presenting the new revelation are crucial to the pre-convert's evaluation of the innovation. When the Korean Unification Church first tried to recruit members in California in the early 1960s, it was remarkably unsuccessful. Its Korean missionaries could not get a hearing, and recruitment was very slow until they had converted enough locals so that the evangelists were white, university-educated, middle class, Americans. Then they recruited people like themselves.[23] Despite promoters of the Alpha programme spending very large sums on mass-media advertising, two-thirds of participants were recruited through their churches, and, for the rest, the most common answer to the question 'How did you get to know about Alpha?' was 'Friends'.[24]

There are many context-specific bases to trust.[25] The growth of sceptical movements such as the Anti-Vaxxers notwithstanding, most of us trust that our doctors know more about anatomy and illness than do our friends. But, beyond specific realms of expertise, trust, because it is cumulative, often relies on pre-existing friendship and kinship ties. Here social similarity matters for two reasons. The short one is that people are more likely to trust others who seem like them.[26] The longer one is that friendship and kinship both build on social likeness and reinforce it. Of course, close ties can develop between people of very different backgrounds, but more often liking comes from being alike.

What research on the diffusion of innovation and on religious conversion shows is that people are more likely to entertain some new idea or practical innovation when it is presented to them by friends or by people who are sufficiently similar to become friends. This is not casual prejudice. It is simply one instance of a general practice we use to simplify choice. Life is too full of opportunities for us to consider each and every one afresh.[27] Habit-forming is one way of simplifying decision-making. Another is relying on simple cues based on familiarity. I walk into a bar in a strange town, see young men wearing hair product, and immediately know that these are not my people and this is not my place. A few of us are thrill-seekers frequently attracted to the exotic, and most of us occasionally break out of the familiar with holidays and other brief diversions.[28] But for most of our lives, most of us judge novelties by how well they fit our existing identities. We ask: 'Are the people presenting this new idea like me but happier, more content or more successful?' This is especially important for innovations—such as a new religion—that require personality change. We want some evidence that it will work; that getting right with Jesus will indeed improve our lives. The best evidence is that it has worked for people who are sufficiently similar that we can see them as models for emulation.

Religion Is Now Alien

Shortly before her resignation, a perceptive political scientist said of Prime Minister Theresa May's churchgoing: 'Steady Anglicanism would once have helped connect May with her public. Now it is just another of the things that stand between her and them. It makes her, weirdly, more like the Queen, who is also photographed most Sundays heading to or from a church service.'[29] In the coal-mining villages of County Durham in 1900, Anglicans, Catholics, Methodists, the religiously indifferent, and avowed atheists lived side by side in the same terraces, and they worked together in the pits. Most Methodists would not drink in the club, but otherwise, religious and irreligious colliers mixed socially. The religiously indifferent might resent the smugly pious, or envy their children being a little better dressed and their houses slightly better furnished, but they did not see them as foreign or avoid them. Indeed, they often voted for them. As we saw in Chapter 10, many of the early miners' union officials were Primitive Methodists—chosen for their self-discipline, integrity, and skill in public speaking. In short, in the early stages of secularization, religious people were pretty much like everyone else except in being religious.

That is no longer the case. The social causes of secularization strike different social groups at different times and with differing degrees of intensity, and as all cultural consumption tends to be socially patterned, being religious has become largely the preserve of a few distinct carriers: hence a major social divide between the religious and non-religious and the regal oddity of May's churchgoing. In the UK that gulf is reinforced by immigrants being markedly more religious than the natives. With not much exaggeration we can say that the religious are now disproportionately recruited from five sections of the British population.

First, as is well-established from surveys, from official church data, and from independent censuses of churchgoing, most churchgoers are elderly women.[30] Second, there are the native inhabitants of the rural peripheries. Church attendance in the Scottish Hebrides and western highlands is now falling rapidly towards the British norm, but, until the 1980s, the Gaelic-speaking areas of the north and west were an exception to the general decline in churchgoing; likewise for Welsh-speaking North Wales. Third, there are migrant Christians. After Poland joined the European Union, the movement of a large number of Poles to Britain retarded (but did not reverse) Catholic decline: in major cities Polish priests now conduct masses in Polish. British Christianity has also been boosted by West African Pentecostalists, who now form some 40 per cent of English evangelicals.[31] Finally we have non-Christian migrants—of whom the Muslims are the most numerous and visible—and their offspring.

In 1800, the characteristic of being religious was spread thickly across the population. In 1900, it was spread thinly but evenly across the population. In

2000, it was primarily associated with people who were demographically, ethnically, and culturally unusual. For most twenty-first century Britons, religion is what other people do.

That impression is compounded by the extent to which the religious are socially isolated. The reasons vary for our various carriers. For the elderly: circumscribed lives with few contacts outside their families and similarly situated friends. For the regional peripheries: geographical isolation compounded by language barriers. For West Africans and Muslims: residential concentration reinforced by important differences in social mores and cultural preferences. That alcohol plays such a large part in British social life is a major barrier to informal mixing between Muslim and non-Muslims, as are major differences in how they expect men and women to behave.

If the depiction of the primary carriers of religion as distinctive seems extreme, consider language. All but one of the five carrier groups—elderly women—uses a language other than English. Welsh and Gaelic figure high in the identities of the churchgoers of the peripheries. Polish and Lithuanian Catholics attend services in their native tongues. West African Pentecostalists are likely to speak Yoruba or some other Nigerian or Ghanaian language. One London church planning a move to Peckham was 'looking at doing three or four services...in different languages such as Twi, Yoruba, and French'.[32] British Muslims are often linguistically twice-removed: the core religious business is conducted in Arabic, while the enveloping social interaction is often in Urdu.

An Aside on Othering

It is worth repeating a point made at several places in this text: the distinctiveness of the religious is not a false impression created by malevolent observers. They really are different. 'Othering' is the regarding of some minority group as markedly different and usually, though not always, of less value. The notion is probably best known from Edward Said's argument that the West created and sustained elaborate fantasies about Islam, which allowed us to treat Muslim people and Muslim countries in a way we would not treat Christian people and Christian countries.[33] That is, othering often justifies bad politics.

No one can object to the proposition that analysts should not exaggerate differences nor treat them as if they were set in stone. However, in this context the charge of othering is misplaced for two reasons.

First, even erroneous perceptions matter, because people act on the basis of what they believe to be the case. Even if the current carriers of religion were

Table 11.1. Proportion 'definitely accepting' a relative marrying someone of a different religion, BSA 2018 (%)

Religion	Age	
	18–49	50+
No religion	51	38
Roman Catholic	47	37
Church of England/Anglican	45	29
Other Christian	30	33
Non-Christian	25	37

Source: As ever, I owe these data to David Voas.

exactly like the rest of the population, if enough people believe them to be importantly different, such misapprehensions will have the effects I will shortly describe.

Second, the primary carriers of religion in modern Britain are objectively alien. Our religious minorities are mostly distinctive because they do their best to remain so. For example, as we see in Table 11.1, they are unusually determined to prevent their children marrying out.[34] Attitudes to religious intermarriage are largely determined by age: the elderly of all religions are similarly hostile, but, among the under-50s, there is a considerable difference between the non-religious and the mainstream Christians, who are generally accepting, and the conservative Christians and the non-Christians, who are strongly opposed.

When religious minority spokespeople appear in public, it is usually to criticize everyone else and claim moral superiority. They fight court cases to claim exemption from laws and social norms. Many wear clothes that publicly identify them and advertise their religion. The moral worth of such distinctions and demands is irrelevant. My point is not about good and bad; it is about majority and minority, about nondescript and distinctive, familiar and unusual. One cannot, as liberals do, argue that religious and ethnic minorities should be encouraged to maintain the distinctive features of their sub-societies and subcultures, and then accuse those who note such differences of 'othering'.

The Odds of Meeting a Believer

That the carriers of religion are markedly unlike the majority of the religiously indifferent has consequences for conversion. If it is the case that the trust created by enduring rewarding social ties is a common condition for conversion, the fact that the religious are distinctive (and not in a manner that is admired) is a major obstacle to revival.

In that sentence I used the phrase 'enduring rewarding social ties'. The current context for religious conversion is far worse than that suggests, because, far from befriending them, the religiously indifferent are unlikely knowingly to interact with a committed believer. Consider the odds. Around 5 per cent of the population regularly attends church and less than 1 per cent is seriously interested in contemporary spirituality. Adding non-Christians might just take the religious and spiritual to 10 per cent of the population. Were such people evenly distributed, the odds on an unbeliever meeting one of them are only 1 in 10. Now recognize that people tend to socialize with family and friends and with people like themselves, and my chances of meeting a true believer are perhaps 1 in 20. Add in residential concentration, and distinct leisure and work patterns, and those outside one of our carrier populations probably have a less than 1 in 40 chance of any interaction with a religious person more enduring than a shop purchase or a task-oriented phone call. When 97 per cent of people aged 16–34 do not attend church, the chances of them developing a relationship with any committed believer are pretty small.

Possible Game-Changers

To summarize thus far, what we know about the importance of social relationships in conversion combines with what we know about the scarcity of religious people and their seclusion to suggest that, if there was not a religious revival in the twentieth century, when believers were more numerous and the general population more familiar with Christianity, then one in the twenty-first century is remarkably unlikely.

However, there are reasons for thinking that some of the current obstacles to religious revival might be overcome, and I will now consider these.

Reactions to Conflict

One argument, popular with conservative Christians, is that the threat of militant Islam (and that could be terrorist violence or just changes to British customs and norms) will provoke a return to Christianity. People who are offended by, for example, the insistence of some Muslims on gender segregation will react by remembering the virtues of the once-hegemonic alternative: the antidote to bad religion is the right religion. That hope is encouraged by some xenophobes, as we noted in Chapter 7, claiming a Christian identity. However, those identities are shallow. Although post-2016 surveys show an apparent connection between self-description as Church of England and hostility to immigrants and voting to leave the EU, the link is weak once we control for age (the old are more likely than the young to be both xenophobic and religious), and it holds only for those Anglicans who do not attend church. That is, the religious identity of the English nationalist is very largely nominal. There is no sign that such nominalists are becoming more religious, and, were they so to do, they would find the Christian congregations they joined generally unsupportive.[35] As noted in Chapter 10, the seriously religious tend to be more welcoming of immigrants and more liberal than the nominals.

The positive reason for this is that the seriously religious natives admire the religiosity of those aliens who offend the xenophobes. The negative reason is that the thoughtfully religious find it harder than the nominally religious to suppose that God approves of one ethnie or nation more than another. Outside of the ethnic religions of Judaism and Hinduism, the idea of an entire people enjoying divine approval is not easily compatible with the personal piety that the deeply religious demand of themselves or with the obvious impiety of much of their nation. And even Jews and Hindus suppose their religion requires more than an identity tag.

A further reason why dislike for non-Christian religions is unlikely to provoke a Christian revival is that the religiously indifferent have readily available secular grounds for criticizing the troublesome features of religion. A young woman who thinks Muslim women are being coerced by male relatives into drastically circumscribed lives can root her objections in secular feminism; she does not have to become a Catholic or a Baptist to justify disliking veiling. Furthermore, the enemy's enemy is my friend principle is unlikely to operate when the Christian churches share many of the unpopular features of Islam: homophobia, anti-Semitism, racism, and sexism, for example. Hence it seems improbable that conflict over the rights and privileges of Islam will prompt a Christian revival.[36] Far more likely is the reaction we see in current survey data: all religion taken too seriously is dangerous.

Reactions to Disaster

Another reason for hoping that the future of religion will not be a continuation of its recent past is the belief that some catastrophe will shake the religiously indifferent into earnest contemplation of their post-mortem fate. This is the social version of the old adage that fear of death makes people religious. That gains some support from a misunderstanding of the link between age and religiosity. Churchgoing is more common among the elderly than the young because each age cohort is less religious than its predecessor but those who do not understand the underlying demographics can easily assume that ageing makes people mindful of their souls.

No doubt many people who hardly entertain the possibility of a God pray when this-worldly options have been exhausted. However, we come back to the problem with which this chapter started. As people's life experiences differ greatly, it is unlikely that, even if they all ask the sort of questions that religions have traditionally answered, they will give similar answers. That is, even if social crises trigger a common fear or anxiety among a large number of people, there is no certainty they will respond with similar changes in beliefs.

We can actually test the proposition that disaster makes people more religious. The many technical difficulties in agreeing on what counts as a social crisis are discussed at length elsewhere. Here I observe only that none of four possible catastrophes of the twentieth century—the First World War, the Great Depression, the Second World War, and the post-2008 banking collapse—was followed by a measurable increase in any index of religious interest.[37]

Religion and Demography

Migrants are more likely than the natives to be religious. A large sample of people were asked 'Which of the following things would say something important about you, if you were describing yourself'. Of the fifteen options, the most popular—family—was chosen by 75 per cent, while only 7 per cent chose sexuality. Religion was in ninth place; picked by 20 per cent. However, for black people it came third after family and ethnicity. For Asians it came second after family but before ethnicity.[38] One way in which Britain could become a markedly more religious country is by the more religious immigrants out-breeding the non-religious natives. Much hostility to migrants and to religious minorities comes from an exaggeration of their numbers—popular estimates are often twice the actual figures—and from an assumption that British Muslims will continue to have more children than non-Muslims.[39]

There is also a serious and more generalized social-science version of the same logic. To abbreviate the case made by Eric Kaufmann, religious families have more children than secular families and, among the religious, conservatives have larger families than liberals. Therefore, the religious will multiply more quickly than the secular, and the climate of the country will slowly change. In a nutshell, 'religious fundamentalists are on course to take over the world through demography'.[40]

That case may be persuasive for relatively underdeveloped parts of the world, but it works for affluent countries such as Britain only if it is not too closely examined. It forgets that every generation of believers needs to raise its own replacement if that particular subculture is not to die out: Christianity has declined, and is declining still, because same-religion parents have only a 50 per cent chance of keeping children in the faith. Even if conservatives are twice as good at family transmission, if they have only two children, they would only stand still. Kaufmann's expectation of growth requires that the conservatively religious remain more fertile than everybody else and remain markedly better at recruiting their own children for the faith.

Both are possible, but since the 1960s conservative Christians have not proved particularly adept at retention. Of Scots surveyed in 2001 who said they had been raised in a conservative Protestant denomination (mostly Baptists or minority Presbyterians), one-third said they were still conservative Protestants, one-third described themselves as Church of Scotland (but for most this was a largely nominal attachment), and one-third said they had no religion.[41] Such figures remind us that Muslims (the usual suspects in population growth fears) are not pandas. All panda cubs become pandas, but not all Muslim children become Muslims. If religion was biologically transmitted, Britain would be every bit as Christian now as it was in 1851 or 1901. Societies change, and the reasons for those changes, which Kaufmann does not represent well, are more pressing now than they were in the nineteenth century when Christianity's decline began.

We can also doubt that religious conservatives will continue to have unusually large families. There are sound reasons why families shrink as societies prosper. Having children is expensive, in direct costs and in opportunities forgone. Modern low levels of infant mortality reduce the need to have large number of children to ensure that some survive. Once paid work can produce more than mere subsistence, aspirations for comfort and pleasure grow. Once reliable and easy-to-use contraception frees women to pursue careers and interests other than motherhood, they see advantages in delaying marriage and childbirth. Modern societies expect parents to invest time and effort in their children; much easier with two than with six. Of course, the pious can make sacrifices for their faith, but, despite the Church's very clear rejection of artificial contraception, the average Catholic family size has declined to be exactly the same size as that of socially similar non-Catholics. Why suppose that other religious minorities that currently have larger than average families will indefinitely resist the opportunities that low-mortality societies provide?

What Kaufmann does not consider is the effect of fundamentalist growth (if there is any) on the majority's views of, and contact with, religion. If the presence of religion increases just because the religious people have big families, then religion will seem all the more alien: strange beliefs *and* weird lifestyles. Paradoxically, such growth (if it occurs) will not increase the odds on any non-religious person developing a rewarding relationship with a true believer, because the larger the religious family, the more the time and energy of members is taken up with each other. A Muslim or Mormon woman with only two children will have far more child-free years to spend working outside the home (and thus meeting and possibly influencing people who are not Muslim or Mormon) than will one with four children. Add in the social isolation that most fundamentalists encourage, and it becomes obvious that growth in their number makes the conversion of the religiously indifferent less rather than more likely.

Increasing Persuasiveness of Mass Media

Arguably the weakest element of my argument is the assertion that personal bonds are vital to conversion. The research on the two-step flow of communication pioneered by Robert Merton, Paul Lazarsfeld, and Elihu Katz, and work on the diffusion of innovation led by Everett Rogers, were done in an era when television was still novel, when talking pictures and the radio were not much more than a generation old, and when mass-media products were patently impersonal. Future generations will have been immersed in electronic media, and the new social media will do an ever-better job of pretending to be personal. Twitter, Instagram, and Facebook allow millions to feel they know people my generation have regarded as strangers. In 1950, closeness to a celebrity meant reading an autobiography and cutting a few staged photographs out of a magazine. Now we can have apparently intimate knowledge of the lives of the Kardashians. Someone can talk direct to a camera on a laptop and post the resultant video so that strangers on the other side of the world can receive what feels very much like authentic person-to-person communication. People continents apart can play video games together.

If it is the case that impersonal and personal communication are now harder to distinguish, it may be that my children will find it easier to trust mass-media sources than I do. This in turn may reduce the salience of the point that, to date, religious conversion has rested on social similarity and friendship. The two-step flow approach to persuasive communication would say, for example, that a 1950s young women might be impressed by a photograph of a star in a certain dress, but imitation is more likely if her friends 'mediate' the communication and endorse her choice. Arguably new media social influencers are bridging the gap by being both admirable celebrities and quasi-friends: the initiators of persuasive communication can also act as endorsers. We frequently see suggestions of that shift in repeated claims that terrorists have been radicalized by their internet viewing.[42] YouTube videos not only transmit information and ideas; because they are semi-personal, they are more influential than the old mass media.

However, even if future generations are more likely to trust, and thus be directly persuaded by, impersonal sources, this may not invalidate my argument, because all religions are more or less communal. The convert still has to meet and interact with co-religionists 'IRL' (which is apparently internet speak for 'in real life') and that brings us back to the issue of social oddity. Modern media may prove better at attracting some interest for religious ideas because they can better pretend to be intimate, but they cannot entirely solve the problem of the increasingly unusual nature of the religious people in a largely secular society.

Conclusion

Pre-industrial Britain was a largely religious society. That most people were to some degree Christian was more a feature of the society, and hence its culture, being religious than a consequence of the aggregation of individual preferences. Every major social institution supported and reinforced an essentially Christian worldview, and, as a consequence, large parts of everyday life were also Christian. Levels of ambient religion were very high, and behind the specifically Christian, and filling the gaps, was a mass of supernaturalist folklore and superstition. Industrialization brought a raft of unintended consequences for religion. Advances in science and technology sidelined religious solutions to practical problems with more effective alternatives. Increasing human self-confidence made implausible the attitude of prostration and subordination that was at the heart of historic Christianity: as people gave up worshipping their masters, they also gave up worshipping God. Rapid social changes allowed the individualism inherent in the Protestant Reformation to shift the focus of religion from the society to the individual. In many western countries, increasing religious diversity divided the population into competing churches, denominations, and sects and forced the state to reduce the support it gave, first to any particular Christian tradition and then to religion per se. The religious liberty that was necessary for social harmony in religiously diverse countries then became a principle that was adopted widely, even in states where religious dissent was rare. In the short run and in particular places, competition improved religious knowledge and deepened religious commitment, but it also allowed large numbers of dis-affiliate. Hence in Victorian Britain we had people who were better informed and more personally committed than their ancestors, and people who were entirely adrift from the churches in a way that was impossible in rural preindustrial societies.

The contemporary situation is importantly different in that the number of people who are avowedly religious has declined below a level where they impinge on or influence others around them. As we see in the rapid decline of the sabbath in Lewis or North Wales, most people no longer feel the need to avoid offending the religious minority. They no longer bother to mislead survey administrators by making inflated or false claims to church attendance. They no longer celebrate major life events by reciting religious vows they have no intention of keeping. They have almost no contact with religious officials, institutions, and practices.

Since the 1851 Census of Religious Worship, the typical Briton has gone from churchgoing Christian, to nominal Christian, to non-Christian who nonetheless thinks religion (in the abstract at least) is a good thing, to being someone who supposes that religion does more harm than good. Whether Christianity and Islam are necessarily antagonistic, or whether Islam can shift from authoritarian dogmatism to tolerant liberalism, are irrelevant to understanding public responses to the violence of Al Qaeda, Islamic State, Boko Haram, and the like. Those who have no interest in untangling the complex links between secular and religious causes of conflicts around the globe simply see acts of war and terrorism that the protagonists justify as required by God. We could compile a long list of the many practical and emotional ways that people benefit from their faith. We could list all the quiet good works performed by churches, chapels, mosques, temples, and gurdwaras. But such enumeration will never be as dramatic or arresting as a jihadi bomb killing young girls at a concert in Manchester or another Catholic priest being convicted for sexual abuse.

None of this means that religion will die out any time soon, but it does make it highly probable that the 50 per cent reproduction rate shown by

Christians over the twentieth century—two same-religion parents keeping only one of their two children in the faith—is very unlikely to improve.

There will always be people who speculate about life after death or the possibility of supernatural sources of power. Logic alone allows us to insert the words 'does not' into such propositions as 'the personality dies with the body'. The loss of a shared religious culture does not preclude religious questing; it just makes it unlikely. And there is a world of difference between a community united around shared religious beliefs and some anxious people freestyling their idiosyncratic responses to the questions such religions have traditionally answered.

For the final word we should return to the trends in the data with which this study began. Religion in the UK has been steadily declining in power, popularity, and plausibility for 150 years. The social conditions for a reversal of that decline were more promising in every year than in the subsequent year. If those who were on the fringes of the churches in 1900 or 1920 or 1950 could not be persuaded into a more active commitment, why suppose that those who now have no familiarity with religion and little admiration for it are likely to become believers? That something did not happen in circumstances that were considerably more conducive is very good reason to suppose it is unlikely to happen now.

Notes

1. For the most comprehensive review of the evidence, see C. D. Field, *Secularization in the Long 1960s: Numerating Religion in Britain* (Oxford: Oxford University Press, 2017).
2. P. Heelas and L. Woodhead, *The Spiritual Revolution* (Oxford: Blackwell, 2005).
3. Callum Brown has argued for an early 1960s onset for secularization, but even he sees the collapse as a working-out of earlier debilitating changes; see C. Brown, *The Death of Christian Britain* (London: Routledge, 2001). Hugh McLeod and Clive Field favour the longer trajectory; H. McLeod, *The Religious Crisis of the 1960s* (Oxford: Oxford University Press, 2007); C. D. Field, *Britain's Last Religious Revival: Quantifying Belonging, Behaving and Believing in the Long 1950s* (London: Palgrave, 2015).
4. D. Voas, 'The Rise and Fall of Fuzzy Fidelity in Europe', *European Sociological Review*, 25 (2009), 155–68.
5. S. Morrison, 'After 103 Years, Organisation Changes Oath to Welcome All Girls', *Independent*, 19 June 2013.
6. My research on loyalist terrorists is reported in S. Bruce, *The Red Hand: Protestant Paramilitaries in Northern Ireland* (Oxford: Oxford University Press, 1992), and *The Edge of the Union: The Ulster Loyalist Political Vision* (Oxford: Oxford University Press, 1994).

7. K. Kandiah, 'Our Society Condones Discrimination against Christians', *The Times*, 21 July 2018.
8. YouGov, *John Humphrys Religion Survey* (February 2007), http://iis.yougov.co.uk/extranets/ygarchives/content/pdf/Humphrys%20Religion%20Questions.pdf (accessed January 2008).
9. C. D. Field, 'Counting Religion in Britain 2017', *British Religion in Numbers* (September 2017), http://www.brin.ac.uk/2017/counting-religion-in-britain-september-2017/ (accessed July 2018).
10. B. Clements, 'The Sources of Public Feelings towards Religious Groups in Britain', *Journal of Contemporary Religion*, 27 (2012), 419–3. On church attendance, see B. Clements, 'Changes in Attendance at Religious Services in Britain', *British Religion in Numbers* (June 2014), http://www.brin.ac.uk/news/2014/changes-in-attendance-at-religious-services-in-britain/ (accessed 24 June 2014).
11. B. Clements, *Religion and Public Opinion in Britain: Continuity and Change* (London: Palgrave, 2015), 19.
12. ICM Research, 'Poll Prepared for the Guardian', 12–14 August 2005, table 19.
13. For a review of survey data on attitudes towards Muslims, see C. D. Field, 'Islamophobia in Contemporary Britain: The Evidence of the Opinion Polls, 1988–2006', *Islam and Christian–Muslim Relations*, 18 (2007), 447–77.
14. M. Beckford, 'Christian Driver Boycotts Atheist Poster Bus', *Daily Telegraph*, 17 January 2009.
15. G. Carey et al., 'Letter to the Editor', *Sunday Telegraph*, 28 March 2010. For a compendium of such complaints, see Christian Institute, *Marginalising Christians: Instances of Christians Being Sidelined in Modern Britain* (Newcastle: Christian Institute, 2009). Parts of the press have provoked conservative Christians by exaggerated and misleading reporting. For example, every Christmas there are stories of the Post Office 'banning' religious imagery from commemorative stamps. In fact, since the 1960s, secular and religious images have alternated; J. Moran, 'Stamp of Disapproval', *New Statesman*, 18 December 2006–4 January 2007, 19. Another annually aired trope is the local-councils-ban-Christmas story, which invariably manages to find one school somewhere that is not mounting a nativity play.
16. G. Paton, 'Worried Christians Worship in Secret', *Daily Telegraph*, 15 May 2009.
17. C. Gammell, 'If I'm Nursing I'll Continue to Offer Prayer', *Daily Telegraph*, 7 February 2009.
18. Panelbase, 'Online Survey for *Sunday Times*', 23–8 March 2018.
19. Comparison of survey questions asked in 1998, 2008, and 2018 show a steady hardening of attitudes and a growing gulf between the religious and the non-religious; D. Voas and S. Bruce, 'Religion', in J. Curtice, E. Clery, J. Perry, M. Phillips, and N. Rahim (eds), *British Social Attitudes: The 36th report* (London: NatCen Social Research).
20. For a summary of the sociology of conversion, see S. Bruce, *Researching Religion: Why We Need Social Science* (Oxford: Oxford University Press, 2018), ch. 7.
21. S. Bruce and T. Glendinning, 'Religious Beliefs and Differences', in C. Bromley, J. Curtice, K. Hinds, and A. Park (eds), *Devolution—Scottish Answers to Scottish Questions* (Edinburgh: Edinburgh University Press, 2003), 86–115. The 2018 BSA survey shows that only 4% of those who say they were raised with no religion later acquired one; Voas and Bruce, 'Religion'.

22. E. Katz, 'Communication Research and the Image of Society: On the Convergence of Two Traditions', *American Journal of Sociology*, 65 (1960), 435–40; E. Katz and P. Lazarsfeld, *Personal Influence: The Part Played by People in the Flow of Mass Communications* (New Brunswick, NJ: Transaction, 1964); E. Katz, M. L. Levin, and H. Hamilton, 'Traditions of Research on the Diffusion of Innovation', *American Sociological Review*, 28 (1963), 237–52; J. S. Coleman, E. Katz, and H. Menzel, *Medical Innovation: A Diffusion Study* (Indianapolis, IN: Bobbs-Merrill, 1966).

23. J. Lofland, *Doomsday Cult: A Study of Conversion, Proselytization, and Maintenance of Faith* (Englewood Cliffs, NJ: Prentice Hall, 1966).

24. S. Hunt, *The Alpha Enterprise* (Aldershot: Ashgate, 2004), 182.

25. P. Sztompka, *Trust: A Sociological Theory* (Cambridge: Cambridge University Press, 1999).

26. Katz and Lazarsfeld, *Personal Influence*, 238.

27. The consequences of this are articulated in A. Gehlen, *Man in the Age of Technology* (New York: Columbia University Press, 1980).

28. As Stan Cohen and Laurie Taylor demonstrate, such 'escape attempts' are often as programmed and familiar as the mundane routines from which we are trying to escape; S. Cohen and L. Taylor, *Escape Attempts: The Theory and Practice of Resistance in Everyday Life* (London: Routledge, 1992).

29. D. Runciman, 'A Change is Coming', *London Review of Books*, 21 February 2019.

30. P. Brierley, 'The Ageing of English Churchgoers', *Future First*, 32 (2014), 4. For example, in 2017 only 19% of the Scots population but 35% of the churchgoers were 65 and over; P. Brierley, *Fourth Scottish Church Census* (Tonbridge, Kent: ABCD Publishers, 2017).

31. P. Brierley, 'Black and Minority Ethnic Groups', *Future First*, 51 (June 2017), 2.

32. A. Duffuor, 'Moving up and Moving out? The Expansion of a London-Based "African Pentecostal" Church', in D. Goodhew (ed.), *Church Growth in Britain: 1980 to the Present* (Aldershot: Ashgate, 2012), 151.

33. E. Said, *Orientalism: Western Concepts of the Orient* (Harmondsworth: Penguin, 1995). Given Said's popularity with social scientists, it is worth noting that he was, by training and career, an art historian.

34. The numbers are small, but some confidence in these data is provided by the fact that Tony Glendinning and I found precisely the same pattern in the 2001 Scottish Social Attitudes survey data. Total levels of acceptance were then lower, but the relativities were the same.

35. See the discussion of xenophobia and nominalism in Chapter 10.

36. Detailed research in Germany found no links between being seriously religious and feeling threatened by alien cultures; D. Pollak and G. Rosta, *Religion and Modernity* (Oxford: Oxford University Press, 2017), 135.

37. S. Bruce and D. Voas, 'Do Social Crises Cause Religious Revivals?', *Journal of Religion in Europe*, 9 (2016), 26–43.

38. M. O'Beirne, *Religion in England and Wales: Findings from the 2001 Home Office Citizenship Survey* (London: Home Office, Research, Development and Statistics Directorate, 2004).

39. The French right-wing intellectual Renaud Camus claims that Muslims are displacing European Christians in 'the great replacement'. He was cited as an authority by

Brenton Tarrant, the Australian who murdered fifty Muslims in a Christchurch mosque in April 2019.

40. E. Kaufmann, *Shall the Religious Inherit the Earth? Demography and Politics in the Twenty-First Century* (London: Profile Books, 2010).

41. 2018 BSA data comparing religion in which respondents were raised with what they are now show that identity was most successfully transmitted intergenerationally for the non-religious (94% unchanged). Of those raised as Anglicans, not quite half retained that identity. Other specific Protestant denominations fared worse; Voas and Bruce 'Religion'.

42. Closer examination usually shows that, while terrorists may have found their interest sparked by something viewed on the internet and may have cited internet sources as justificatory authorities, they have usually developed their jihadi personas in collaboration with close friends. While the 'lone wolf' is a popular media trope, most are not that lone.

Index